Nature Works

Nature Works
Activating Regenerative Leadership Consciousness

GILES HUTCHINS

FOREWORDS BY
GALAHAD CLARK, CAROLYN EDDLESTON,
PAUL HARGREAVES, VERONIQUE LETELLIER

Copyright © 2024 by Giles Hutchins

All rights reserved. No part of this book may be reproduced or used in any manner without written permission of the copyright owners except for the use of quotations in a book review.

ISBN: 978-1-78324-311-2 (paperback)
ISBN: 978-1-78324-312-9 (ebook)

Author: Giles Hutchins
www.gileshutchins.com

Editor: Janna Hockenjos
www.jannahockenjos.com

Publisher and Illustrator: Wordzworth
www.wordzworth.com

We have chosen print-on-demand for this book as that is the most regenerative way of getting physical books out into the world. Traditional offset printing usually requires large orders and any books that go unsold are destroyed. This results in wasted paper, wasted energy, added greenhouse emissions, pulping, and landfill overflows. Print-on-demand reduces supply chain waste, greenhouse emissions and conserves valuable natural resources.

**All paper for the publication of this book
is sourced from SFI and/or FSC certified mills.**

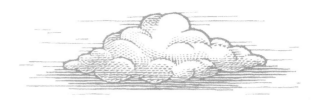

Nature Works is essentially about the love of life. It's therefore befitting to me that this book is dedicated to my mother, Diana, who has nurtured and loved my own life through pregnancy, birth, childhood, youth, and into adulthood. From the bottom of my heart, Thank you! And this mark of respect goes out to all mothers—including my own wife (Star) and sister (Pippa)—who so tirelessly serve life through their nurturing love. Thank you, Mother Earth, for all you endure and provide, and for your loving patience in our waking-up to all you are.

Foreword

By Galahad Clark, CEO & Co-Founder, Vivobarefoot

This is an ode to the impact Giles Hutchins has had on myself, and my business Vivobarefoot (Vivo).

Vivo BG ('Before Giles') had an organizational structure that was disconnected from its company mission of reconnecting people to nature. Thanks to Giles, we are realigning with natural systems and starting to become the people, leaders and business we naturally aspire to be. A timely metamorphosis.

I first 'met' Giles on a beautiful sunset beach in South Devon in September 2020. He wasn't physically there (as Giles himself, it seems, seldom actually leaves the beautiful Springwood where he is based in life and in work) but he had given our feisty Regeneration Lead some guidance on how to steer an introductory workshop on regenerative leadership. With the rest of the Vivo senior team, I used marker pens to draw network maps of relationships – arrows between stakeholders with different colors, sizes and densities to convey the different relational complexities of our personal and professional 'ecosystems.' I recently re-drew my map to help me write this Foreword and the change in four years has been profound.

Around the same time, one of Giles' earlier books *Regenerative Leadership*, co-authored with Laura Storm, was spreading through the Vivo team like scandalous gossip. It was all too apparent Vivo was stuck in mechanistic thinking, and it made perfect sense for us to adopt the book's mantras: to organize using natural systems. So, soon after our warm-up on the beach in Devon, we headed to Springwood in Sussex to find the hermit prophet himself!

Since first walking into Springwood's magnificent hexagon shaped Arrival Hall, Vivo has grown from about 50 people to over 150! Every Vivonista has spent meaningful time with Giles 'in the woods', and those experiences have contributed to Vivo's transformation at every level: individual, team, organization, stakeholder group and wider community. It has been wonderful to witness colleagues grow and blossom among those trees. Particularly given the new remote-working order of the day, which has made this ride even more adventurous!

In fact, it's hard to think about Vivo without Giles' impact. Our culture is simply unrecognizable from four years ago. It's akin to the journey I went on as a cobbler getting to know barefoot shoes. Once you understand the anatomy of the foot and biomechanics of the body (as surprisingly few people in the shoe industry do), as well as 'feel' the earth beneath your feet every day, you can't un-know it or un-feel it. Once you reorientate to natural systems in business thinking, going back to old mechanistic ways is unthinkable.

This is all captured in the 'Vivo Way', which brings together our values and our way of working, connecting the principles behind natural movement to the way we want to operate as a business and culture. The Vivo Way came to us in the woods and embeds nature connection into the heart of our organization.

The 'way' into Springwood is a well-trodden path. The Arrival Hall is a gateway from the outside world into the sanctum. With the small talk and preparations complete, we set intentions and walk down a gentle slope through a paddock into the woods. Usually either in pairs or in silence we go 'into the woods.' Letting go of the normal strictures of the mechanized world, we are met by vibrant ferns and young saplings. We arrive in a clearing and gather our energies as a group and within ourselves, connecting to the resonant frequencies of the land.

Across the lake, the 'Elephant Tree' (a big red Victorian implant with a second 'trunk') already knows we're coming. We reorganize ourselves to walk there. Soaring over 100 feet high, this magnificent tree holds a vast array of Vivo secrets. I hope she looks forward to our earnest shares into her generous bows. We walk on in silence across the 'Bridge of Intention', and on again to find a magnificent fire waiting for us in the 'Womb.' We are ready to do the work.

We talk by the fire late into the night, we walk across stepping stones and we leap into the lake (oftentimes literally breaking ice). We commune with an amazing array of trees – from native yews, oaks and beeches to a variety of Victorian trophy species brought back from the 'new world.' And gradually, naturally, we have worked our way to a re-organization: turning the Vivo-system into a flatter structure with autonomous business units bringing decision-making closer to the customer, building a wider offering of services, and evolving the business from a shoe company to a natural health brand.

It's been a wild ride through the seasons since we first found our way to Springwood in the late autumn of 2020. Though Vivo has more than doubled in size and is becoming far more resilient, the initial re-org didn't immediately pan out. Much like many of those transitioning from cushioned shoes to barefoot footwear, we went too fast. We tried to run before we could walk and nature slapped our ankles; fast growth and sudden change rarely bodes well in nature. But we learnt through our missteps and the often-painful sensory feedback. We built our muscle memory, corrected our structures, took smaller more nimble steps, and built up our capacity to sense-respond. We are now building an inner and outer culture that is aligned to our barefoot rhythms.

Living ecosystems are always in a state of flux, just as the seasons and the climate are ever-changing. External 'normal' pressures are no help: we are surrounded by unnatural systems both in the way we move, sit around, think, organize and how we bring in new people to the organization. The Vivo Way helps us meet the challenge of guiding new-joiners and old-timers to a healthy transition back to natural movement.

Giles has been a strong rudder and regular sounding board over the last four years of Vivo's evolution, and for my own development as a human and a leader. For example, through meditating with trees in Springwood I have encountered the different energies of the wise oak, the mystical yew, the bristling beech, the upstart ash, the alchemic redwood and the fragrant pine. Giles is deeply connected to Source and to share his 'field' is to energize any nature aligned mission. He's always been careful not to give answers, but rather, in his inimitable way, he gently stimulates and coaches to uncover the insights, tools and skills for us to find the way ourselves.

Over the years, Springwood has hosted Vivo board meetings, strategy days, woodland feasts, field circles, coaching clinics, B Corp gatherings, book launches, sales meetings (with shoes displayed in branches) and seminars, as well as countless epiphanies, team buildings and personal transitions. My favorite overnight solo spot is amongst a bunch of young oaks in a formally planted 'Yew Square' – symbolic of being born into an old power structure but forging a wilder response that will ultimately bring old and new together.

There is no under-estimating the influence that Giles has had on all of us and Vivo itself. We are a bolder and more connected organization wrestling with uncomfortable truths that will make us a better business and more resilient ecosystem for many years to come.

Ultimately, we share a mission with Giles to help people reconnect to natural ways. Giles has connected with his land on a level that not many people in the West ever manage to do. He is truly sensitive to her energies and interconnections on a level that our indigenous ancestors would have known. Vivo is earlier on that journey, but we're happy to be helping more and more people on their path back to nature. Thanks to Giles, we are more effective in achieving our mission.

Springwood has evolved remarkably in the last four years. It's been a privilege to be part of Giles' sensitive development of this magical space, which has in turn inspired us to build our own nature home. We are readying for life at Vivo AG ('After Giles'). We know he will always be there, and we hope to do him proud by becoming a living embodiment of how people, cultures and companies can put nature back at the top of the hierarchy. If we don't urgently move in this direction our Earth will expel us anyway, but we'll have a lot longer if more of us start to follow the wisdom of ~~Giles~~ nature!

#MakeDecisionsInNature

Galahad Clark

CEO & CO-FOUNDER, VIVOBAREFOOT

Foreword

By Dr. Carolyn Eddleston,
Traditional Chinese Medicine Doctor &
Founder of Cycles of Change Acupuncture

In my fifty-five cycles of seasons, there have only been a handful of individuals who have not only inspired me but supported a vital shift in my life's trajectory. Giles is one of those people.

When a name pops up several times, I have learned to take note. I watched about twenty minutes of a YouTube video, where Giles was presenting his work on regenerative leadership, and I was curious enough to email him. We arranged a brief phone call and then I signed up to work with Giles for the next six months, not really knowing what I was up for, but trusting a familiar 'calling/knowing' from a place far from my logical thinking mind. I am still working with him, as our dance deepens, and I now celebrate the unseen, the not knowing that has become familiar in this new way of being, and leading by nature with its infinite wisdom and resourcefulness.

This journey feels different. It's slow at the linear time level, yet rapid at the level of spirit, emotions, and our inner environment, our individual garden. It demands commitment to a full expression of self, brutal self-honesty, visiting the dark and the light parts of ourselves, and trust in the facilitator, the holder of a sacred space, and in the great mystery of the divine mother, the natural world, both seen, and unseen. It demands quiet, undistracted, still time in nature.

My personal journey of questioning and healing officially began in 1996, when I decided that the predictable, medical, social, and professional life as a general practitioner was looking terrifying and contracted, if safe and sensible! I had qualified as a GP in 1994, having studied for eight years, and I couldn't look ahead and feel free and excited. I had never fit the box. I talked my way in apparently, and was known as the re-take Queen until I got into the wards where my love of people and what made some people thrive kicked in. It all started to make sense. I take pride in knowing that I was a good traditional family doctor who had the privilege of witnessing thousands of phenomenal life and illness stories. What fascinates me most is what makes some people thrive.

In 1996, I decided to get a job in a small A&E (urgent care) in New Zealand and was doing shift work, so I had time in the day to reflect and explore. I started to try complementary therapies, as I was aware that I hadn't had the time to heal or even really get to know myself. I met some inspirational older female practitioners. One of whom arrived synchronously as a flyer in a café, advertising a short course in the philosophy behind Traditional Chinese Medicine. I went, and light bulb flashes of recognition of the interconnectedness of the organ systems that I saw as a GP but had no reference for activated within me, and there was no turning back. My curiosity had been ignited, and this ancient, complete system of medicine that honored our unique connection with the cycles of the natural world had woken me up to something magical that I already somehow knew.

I ended up writing, getting accredited, and teaching the Western medical component of a three-year diploma in Acupuncture. After eighteen months, I threw down my teaching hat and went to sit with the class, taking three years out to re-train in Acupuncture. Taoism, the philosophy underpinning Traditional Chinese Medicine, continues to shape my world in a beautiful way.

It will be no surprise to you, that when Giles appeared on the scene, inviting corporate leaders to think again about the familiar top-down approach, I was already converted to living with, not against, the natural world. I like his down to earth, accessible approach that he has gathered from his own transitioning and questioning of his previous corporate positions. He too took a huge, intuitive leap of faith when he and his family felt called to the large native woodland that he knows intimately as Springwood, which has become his home and the playground for many transformative immersions, including my own.

My twenty hours in Springwood, a few of which were with Giles, and fourteen of which were alone, in the rain, being held in the boughs of a giant Redwood, with my trusty little tent, were beyond words. I had no torch, no phone, no book, and nothing to write with. No distractions, and no way out. It took a while to settle, and then the magic happened. We all talk to ourselves either internally or externally, don't we? Or is it just me? My voice told me to "Take off your glasses so you can see!" OK. I looked up at the blurred canopy above me and saw a cellophane-like sparkling dome just below the canopy. "An illusion created by the blur," I hear you say. All our visual interpretations filtered by our visual cortex are illusions! So how exciting to 'see' something different. The canopy had huge holes in it, and yet I was dry. This kind of settling of the nervous system, devoid of the chronic stress and sensory overload of other people, traffic, Wi-Fi signals, screens, and music, reminded me of the unseen magic of everything. I used to know this place as a child. The place where magic was the norm. Time slowed down. I am so rarely still in nature. I walk, run, cycle, picnic, camp, but to be still… My imagination was waking from a dormant slumber. I realized I was alone, and yet I felt the most held I had ever felt. I had a cry, a shout, and a dance with all the trees around the circle that the Redwood had commanded. Every tree expressed a different personality if I let my mind open and unravel from its contracted state.

When Giles collected me at 8:00 a.m., I was quiet and reflective. It was hard to convert the experience to words, as if the words took away the mystery of my experience.

What I didn't tell you was that in three weeks after my time in Springwood, I was moving my entire clinic to a brand-new commercial building that was a white, dead box, and I felt no inspiration or idea as to how to bring it alive. The space prior to this was a Grade 2 listed building built in 1690. Quite a contrast. In my debrief with Giles, he suggested that I was to breathe life into this new space using the wisdom of the trees that I had rediscovered, and that the 'how' would be revealed.

I decided to have another night and day in an Airbnb close by, to digest this immersion before returning to 'the real world'. I kept my phone off, put all devices away, and stayed quiet, and sure enough a huge stream of ideas began to come in. Everything started to fall into place, and three weeks later, we were at home in a living, breathing space that felt and still feels incredible.

Giles is a practitioner, a healer, an intuitive. He does not assume the role of teacher or guru. He is willing to shapeshift and go to the unseen liminal places where all the magic happens. The space he holds for me is unique, sacred, and incredibly safe. With his support, I feel more seen than ever before. I am expressing my gifts to the world in celebration, rather than service. There is an ease and lightness to my work with Giles that is a joy, and so much more liberating than being told what to do. My work is changing subtly as is the way I lead my team. I am the Mother Tree, and I get to witness and hold my team as they flower into the full expression of their gifts to the world.

There is an urgency to the regenerative approach that Giles is promoting and facilitating, and what a joy to ride the waves of this rebirth into remembering the great mystery of nature's wisdom. *Nature Works* is another vital piece in the jigsaw of how to align heart, mind, gut, and soul with nature's wisdom, walking with Mother Earth, not against her.

Dr. Carolyn Eddleston
TRADITIONAL CHINESE MEDICINE DOCTOR &
FOUNDER OF CYCLES OF CHANGE ACUPUNCTURE

Foreword

By Paul Hargreaves, CEO & Founder, Cotswold Fayre, and Flourish

During the coronavirus pandemic many of us felt awakened to nature and this was certainly true for me. After spending the first half of my life living in cities (Manchester and London), even a move to a Cotswold market town in my late thirties didn't really change my outlook on life and business too much. I ran my business, Cotswold Fayre, in a modern, mechanistic way, despite the company being founded to make a positive difference in the world and being one of the first cohort of B Corps in the UK in 2015.

Could nature help me run my businesses in a way more fit for the VUCA (volatile, uncertain, complex, and ambiguous) world we now live in? My work in the woods with Giles has answered this question with a resounding 'Yes!' Giles has not only helped me become a better future-fit leader but also a more fulfilled, connected human being.

One of the first questions Giles ever asked me once we started our coaching relationship was, "What do you need to let go of?" It is an important question and one that isn't asked enough in today's world but used to be a critical part of the initiation ceremonies for boys becoming men across the world. Becoming a man consisted of letting go of childhood and embracing the new, and, of course, nature was the place where these initiations took place. We need a new initiation. The vastness of trees and the landscapes emphasize our smallness and, I believe, help us let go of those things that no longer serve us. Knowing our smallness is a vital part of becoming an authentic human and we often miss this when surrounded by man-made buildings. The vastness and age of trees, which were there long before our grandparents, help us contextualize our lives against the backdrop of past and future generations.

For several years as a leader of a growing business I have endeavored to encourage my people to work and make decisions from the heart and soul rather than simply the mind. All three are important, and being in the woods with Giles has helped my own personal shift toward a more holistic way of being, which has impacted the way I see and lead our two businesses (Cotswold Fayre and its more recent sister company Flourish). A truly human organization is full of people who are in flow at work and operating from all parts of their being. Too often businesses have operated only from a head-strategy level, which no longer works, if it ever did!

Our ancestors lived on the land and were surrounded by nature. In fact, they wouldn't have seen nature as something outside of themselves. They saw themselves as intimately wrapped up within the natural world. How far we have fallen from this! This explains how we have managed to mess up the planet so badly—we have lost that connection with nature over the past centuries.

Connecting with nature is perhaps the most significant lesson learned at Giles's leadership immersion center in Springwood. There is something innate within us that craves to 'come home' and nestle into the arms of the natural world. The trees, plants, and animals are not separate to us but form part of our integrated lives, and to truly know our interdependence and create more life-giving businesses we must reconnect. I spent a night sleeping under the trees at Springwood and was incredibly aware of this connection–I even woke up to see a deer looking at me in my warm sleeping bag!

Nature spoke to me that night at Springwood, giving me the sense that I was a wounded healer, as indeed we all are. I spent several hours looking up into the branches of an old, gnarled tree. Several of its 'limbs' had broken off over the years, leaving scars, but it had continued to grow into a magnificent tree giving a home to millions of other creatures. This reminded me of a tremendous sense I'd had in India a few years previously; that it is through our own unique experiences of life that makes us unique individuals. We are all broken and scarred, yet it is coming through these experiences that enables us to give our unique gift to others. The Japanese art of Kintsugi is when broken ceramics are joined back together with gold or precious metals, filling the gaps, leaving the pot more beautiful than before. So, it is with us—our unique purpose comes out of our unique past experiences and pain.

I remember when I first moved to the countryside from the city becoming aware of the seasons for the first time. I hadn't even realized that the sun rose in a different place in the winter than summer! Being in the woods at Springwood, it is impossible to ignore the seasons, yet that is what many of us do in our lives. I have probably spent much of my life striving for perpetual summer, when that is simply not how life works.

I remember the first time I met Giles, and he had put a rope on the ground in a figure-of-eight and indicated where on the eight, spring, summer, autumn, and winter were. He asked me and others to walk around the rope and feel what season we were in our personal lives and where our businesses were. Our bodies can sometimes detect these things better than our minds. This sense of seasonality is something that has stayed with me. Since then, we have been through more difficult times in our main business but knowing that spring always follows winter gives encouragement. Indeed, winter is essential for spring to come round again. Some things and ways of doing need to die off for new ways to emerge in the spring. So, rather than seeing difficult winters as a hindrance to growth, I now see them as an essential part of our regeneration.

In the same way, for a beautiful butterfly to emerge from the caterpillar, it must go into a cocoon, where seemingly there is no life, just a period of nothingness, a waiting. The ancient mystics often went into the wilderness to reflect and spend time on their own before emerging with new wisdom to bring back to their communities. How much more business leaders would benefit in learning from this—not only to connect with nature but also to connect with themselves, to have space away from their people and devices. We have much to learn from modern-day gurus, and I would describe Giles as one of them.

Someone said to me recently, "There are no straight lines in nature." We often try to run our businesses as if there were. Everything in boxes with neat lines connecting the boxes. Cogs in a machine synchronized with other cogs to make the flywheel of productivity turn faster. Yet humans are not like this; they are not machines. They have emotions, heart, and soul, and go through different seasons themselves, and it is that which makes them beautiful individuals. Still, we run our companies as if they were machines with the people as straight lines and cogs. If we learned from nature, we would do it better. If we, and previous generations, hadn't disconnected from nature, we wouldn't have tried doing it like this. *Nature Works* and the wisdom within the woods will transform and regenerate our organizations.

I have started using the word 'spirituality' in my talks and discussions with other business leaders. No doubt some think of me as 'woo-woo' but I define spirituality as simply connecting with ourselves, connecting with others, and connecting with nature. Most people would agree that we desperately need more connection in our lives and work, and Giles's work has helped me and others do just that.

The etymology of the word 'company' is 'com pane', 'with bread', and the several times spent with Giles at Springwood usually involves simple but nutritious food. It is through food that true relationship and humanity connect with each other and nature. Read this book, but then also come to eat and drink at Springwood. Many are discovering the old ways, the ways inherent within our world are the new ways we must embrace again, before it is too late.

Paul Hargreaves

CEO & FOUNDER OF COTSWOLD FAYRE, AND FLOURISH

Foreword

By Veronique Letellier, CEO & Co-Founder, Butterfly, and Head of Regenerative Business & Culture, AXA Climate

Throughout my life, the desire to do good, help others, and embody kindness has been a guiding force, shaping my actions both personally and as a leader. This intrinsic motivation has driven me to seek out ways to make a positive impact on those around me, striving to leave the world a little better than I found it. However, it was through embracing a regenerative mindset that I experienced a profound epiphany that fundamentally altered my understanding of my place in the world.

Regenerative consciousness introduced me to the concept that I am not the central figure in the narrative of life but rather a part of an intricate web of interconnected living systems. This realization was both humbling and enlightening. It shifted my perspective from a human-centric viewpoint to a more holistic understanding of existence. I recognized that our lives are deeply intertwined with the lives of other beings and the natural world itself.

This epiphany has been transformative, influencing not only my personal beliefs but also how I lead and engage with others. In recognizing that we are all part of a larger, living system, I understood that true benevolence extends beyond human-to-human interactions. It encompasses all living systems, necessitating a respect for and a commitment to the health and wellbeing of all life forms.

Adopting this regenerative approach has changed how I view success, leadership, and progress. It's no longer solely about achieving goals or advancing personal and organizational agendas. Instead, it's about ensuring that our actions contribute to the vitality and resilience of the broader systems we are a part of. This means making decisions that not only benefit the present generation but also safeguard the ability of future generations to thrive.

This journey has been one of awakening to the beauty of our interconnectedness and to the power we have to contribute to a more regenerative, sustainable, and compassionate world. My epiphany fueled my determination to establish a school, the Butterfly School, with the mission to universalize regenerative business practices. This institution, having already educated over a 1,000 pioneers, also plays a pivotal role in AXA Climate's own transformative journey. It was along this regenerative path that I encountered Giles, who has been a guiding companion on this voyage for me over the past couple of years.

Giles stands as a beacon in the realm of regenerative business. He draws deep from the well of nature's inherent wisdom. His mission transcends mere knowledge-sharing; it's about catalyzing a profound transformation within the very core of our being. By tapping into the ancient insights of the natural world, Giles seeks, through his work at Springwood and through online coaching, to unlock our minds and souls, guiding us toward a more profound, intentional existence.

Being enveloped by the verdant embrace of Springwood serves as a gateway to the profound teachings of nature's wisdom. This tranquil haven, with its ancient trees standing as silent sentinels, offers a unique sanctuary, allowing for a genuine communion with the natural world.

As one ventures into the core of Springwood, the sensory journey unfolds. Winding paths meander through ferns, ancient trees stand guard over the landscape, and small clearings invite moments of pause. A quaint lake, bordered by magnificent rhododendrons, adds a touch of serenity, while a large clearing features a central fire circle, further enhancing the forest's allure. Another unique spot is nestled beneath a parachute canopy, creating a sheltered haven within the woods. This immersive, sensory experience marks the initial step toward unlocking the mind and soul to the profound insights offered by nature's wisdom.

Springwood, with its vibrant ecosystem, serves as a living classroom. Each element, from the smallest fern to the tallest oak, contributes to an intricate web of life that exemplifies resilience, interdependence, and harmony. Observing the natural cycles of growth, decay, and rebirth within the forest instills a deeper understanding of life's ebbs and flows, teaching valuable lessons on adaptability, patience, and the beauty of impermanence.

The forest's innate ability to thrive without human intervention offers powerful insights into the essence of being. It invites introspection on our place within the natural world, encouraging a shift from a human-centric view to a more holistic, interconnected perspective. This realignment fosters a sense of belonging and stewardship, inspiring a profound respect for nature and all its inhabitants.

Engaging with Springwood is not merely a physical experience but a spiritual journey that nurtures the soul and expands the mind. It teaches that wisdom doesn't always come from books or discourse but often from the silent, profound interactions with the natural world. By opening ourselves to the lessons offered by places like Springwood, we not only gain insights into nature's wisdom but also discover pathways to our own inner peace and enlightenment.

The wisdom imparted by Giles has been a beam of enlightenment on my own journey. In an era where our schedules overflow and our minds are besieged by a relentless onslaught of tasks and decisions, Giles champions the counterintuitive virtue of stillness. It's in the tranquil moments, in the sacred pause between our thoughts, that we touch the boundless creativity of the cosmos. This quietude, often obscured by the shadows of fear and the whispers of ego, is where true innovation and clarity emerge. Giles taught me that it's in surrendering to stillness that we unearth our most profound insights and solutions.

Giles introduced me to a transformative perspective on leadership as well, where the confluence of self-awareness and systemic understanding ignites the spark of emergence. My personal epiphanies and decision-making processes have always danced at the crossroads of introspection and a holistic grasp of my surroundings. Giving voice to this intuitive practice has refined my ability to navigate complex situations with agility and insight. This approach to leadership, rooted in a grounded, intuitive understanding, transcends conventional analytical methods and offers a swift, more nuanced way of engaging with the world.

Giles illuminates the often-misunderstood path of creativity, revealing how chaos is not merely an obstacle but a vital precursor to creation. The journey from disarray to order, from turbulence to tranquility, mirrors the natural cycles of transformation and growth. Recognizing the inevitability and necessity of chaos provides solace and strength, allowing us to persevere through the storm with the knowledge that periods of upheaval pave the way for innovation and renewal. Before the harmony of synergy is realized, there must first be a dance with dinergy.

Through Giles's teachings, the principles of regenerative business and the profound wisdom of nature are woven into a tapestry of transformative insights. These lessons invite us to reflect, to pause, and to embrace the dynamic interplay between stillness and action in our quest for a deeper, more meaningful way of living and leading.

A journey with Giles reshapes our leadership paradigms and enriches our daily lives with depth and purpose. His mentorship has not only guided me through the practical aspects of integrating regenerative practices into my work and leadership style but has also strengthened my spiritual connection to the world around me. This profound journey of transformation, guided by Giles's wisdom and the serene teachings of Springwood, has opened a path not just to personal and professional growth, but to contributing to a more regenerative, sustainable, and interconnected world.

This journey of regenerative transformation, both personally and through the establishment of the Butterfly School and the evolution of AXA Climate as a business, underlines the immense potential of regenerative principles to redefine success, leadership, and our collective future. Giles's mentorship and the experience of Springwood have been instrumental in this journey, offering a blueprint for living and leading in harmony with the natural world.

It's a testament to the power of reimagining our role in the ecosystem, not as dominators but as stewards, fostering a world that thrives on interconnectedness and mutual respect. This path, though challenging, is rich with the promise of a regenerative legacy for generations to come, embodying the true essence of making a difference.

Veronique Letellier

CEO & CO-FOUNDER, BUTTERFLY,
AND HEAD OF REGENERATIVE BUSINESS & CULTURE, AXA CLIMATE

Words – Giles Hutchins; Art – Jodie Harburt *www.jodieharburt.com*

Table of Contents

Introduction		1
PART 1	**EXPLORING (THE WORLDVIEW SHIFT)**	**21**
Chapter 1	Setting the Scene	23
Chapter 2	Journeying toward Regeneration	61
Chapter 3	Returning to the Root of Regeneration	79
Chapter 4	Human Nature & Awakening our Minds	103
PART 2	**UNDERSTANDING (HOW NATURE WORKS)**	**139**
Chapter 5	The Nature of Living Systems	141
Chapter 6	The Three Levels of Living Systems Awareness	171
Chapter 7	Nature's Wisdom	201
PART 3	**JOURNEYING (INTO RIGHT RELATION)**	**243**
Chapter 8	The Journey	245
Chapter 9	The 4 D Foundational Pillars for Regenerative Living and Leading	285
Chapter 10	The 5 E Dynamics of the Process of Becoming	301
Chapter 11	The Four Soul Virtues of Regenerative Leadership	313

Chapter 12	Cultivating Soil Conditions	331
Epilogue		347
Appendix	Compendium of Practices and Further Notes	357
References		427
Other Books by Giles Hutchins		439
About the Author		445

Introduction

We are living through a once-in-a-civilization moment. We are at an inflection point with profound consequences for the future of humanity and the very fabric of life on Earth. Time is not on our side. Tipping points that risk unravelling our life support systems are looming large on the horizon. Every aspect of the dominant socioeconomic model that we operate by—how we live, how we engage in our enterprises, how we create and deliver value, and why we do these things—is in need of a radical review. We need a revolution, no less.

This revolution isn't 'out there', and it isn't something to outwardly achieve, fix, or fight for. This revolution is 'in here'. Right here, in our own hearts and minds. It's a revolution in consciousness.

From Separation to Right Relation

This book in your hands speaks to the revolution. And while *Nature Works* has a wide scope, it's purposefully focused on the exploration and the transformation of the Western mindset. At the very least because the Western mindset has an enormous influence worldwide, but more so because I, the author, have experienced the modus operandi of this dominant worldview first-hand for over thirty years as a professional business adviser and leader, and feel able to authentically challenge it.

My work is characterized by what I refer to as 'regenerative leadership consciousness' or the developmental cultivation of a quality of awareness that overcomes the root problem at the heart of our myriad crises. This root problem is our sense of separation from nature, a sense of separation that is the very hallmark of the Western mindset that dominates business, politics, and society throughout much of the world today.

> "The story of mind exiled from nature is the story of Western Man."
>
> —Ted Hughes

I have no axe to grind against the West, nor is this book about labelling or polarizing East verses West. *Nature Works* addresses this dominant worldview that is ripe for revolution regardless of geography, which I refer to as 'Western' because I wish to acknowledge how various cultures today, and throughout history, have not succumbed to this sense of separation from nature in the same totalizing way as the modern Western mindset has. I would also like to acknowledge that the Western mindset has brought with it monumental accomplishments in science, medicine, manufacturing, transportation, digitization, social life, and material betterment from which many people across the world benefit. Yet, due to its built-in sense of separateness, it is a mechanistic mindset with an insidious and malignant quality that undermines our very existence. Its historic tendency has been to colonize new lands and 'markets' using methods that are fundamentally destructive to its host. It's like a cancer, causing a rapid demise of life on Earth, which extends well beyond the hot topic of climate change.

Take our planet's biodiversity, for instance. Biodiversity loss is now assumed to be happening at a rate of 100-1000 times faster than normal. I invite you to pause for a moment. Reflect on *that*. A mass extinction of life on Earth is happening right now. Not in 2050 or 2030, but today. The last time such an exceptional rate of species death occurred on Earth was 66 million years ago. At that time, it was likely due to an asteroid hitting the planet around what is now the state of New Mexico. This time, life on Earth is rapidly declining as a result of human activity—this dominant mindset running amok.

And the destruction doesn't stop at climate change or biodiversity loss. We have accelerated soil degradation, ocean acidification, deforestation, and the widespread destruction of natural landscapes and rainforests. We live with country-sized plastic islands coalescing in our oceans, the exploitation of our children in factories, rampant pollution coursing through our waters, and countless natural disasters taking lives, homes, and communities. In fact, Earth's unique atmosphere, cultivated through billions of years to protect us, is saturated not only with fumes and pollutants but with Wi-Fi, 5G, and other artificial and disruptive frequencies.

Today, thousands upon thousands of satellites orbit, track, and apparently serve our consumerist desire by pulling our attention out of real life and into internet realities. From our eyes glued to our TV screens and smart phones, to the semi-permanent mobile headphones found in our ears, to the always open smart apps tracking our everyday habits, we are spellbound in a virtual world. Multi-billion investments are siphoned into augmented reality, to create biologically integrated computer systems with wearable devices (including chips to embed into the body) that link us to always-on smart devices, smart meters, smart grids, smart cities, and even a smart planet electrifying the very atmosphere we live in.

We have entered the era of transhuman materialism and surveillance capitalism, offering counterfeit connection through commercialism. We're sleepwalking into technospheric totalitarianism. Just look around at people sitting in cafés, having meals, walking dogs, out and about, during meetings, and driving cars to witness the widespread addiction to the devices that take us out of touch with reality. Scientific studies show that we've never been more distracted, stressed out, disenfranchised, and psychologically sick as a collective than we are today.

Instead of cultivating the inner potentiality of our humanity, our dominant worldview conditions us to manufacture superficial outer appearances to fulfill material advancements that are achieved by climbing the slippery corporate ladder. Lacking any sense of connection to our true nature, our individual identity becomes little more than an ego-projection we validate externally by what people think of us. It doesn't matter whether our in-crowd is obsessed with mainstream consumer fashion and celebrity culture or a trending counter-culture meme, too much attention is drawn into managing others' impressions of ourselves. Pretense and artifice abound. Our Western worldview is destroying life 'out there' and it's destroying life 'in here.' This widespread degenerative tendency begs the question.

Do we have what it takes to change our ways to ones that work with, rather than against, life?

In the pages that follow, we explore how the Western mind was exiled from nature and how we can revolutionize it. We dive into the coming age of regenerative consciousness that enables us to solve these 'wicked' systemic challenges amid increased volatility and uncertainty. We expand our meaning-making and strengthen our deeper nature to gain increased resilience and productivity while becoming more purposeful, centered, and authentic.

Welcome to the Regeneration Revolution. It's time for humanity's upgrade— enhanced creativity, embodied empathy, increased resilience, and improved agility. We have at the ready all we need to shift our mindset to one which is more future-fit for ourselves, for those around us, and for the organizations we serve.

Why Regenerative?

There's a lot of hot air around 'regenerative' these days. The term is applied to many things, like regenerative agriculture, regenerative economics, or regenerative leadership which is my own area of specialism. The term 'regenerative' signifies 'working the way nature works.' We're regenerative when we're in tune with inner-outer nature. When we're in tune, we flow as life flows, and we co-create with the evolutionary potential of life on Earth. When we are regenerative, we are in right relation. Regeneration involves a never-ending and ever-evolving journey of deepening into inner-outer nature by becoming more of who we truly are, individually, organizationally, and societally.

Regeneration is a journey toward wholeness and authenticity for both the leader and the organization. For an organization to be on this regenerative journey, it must actively work toward enriching all stakeholder relations, including employees, customers, suppliers, investors, the wider society, and the environment to enable all life to flourish. It necessitates an understanding of today's disparity between the way life on Earth works and the way our value-creating ventures work and an understanding of what it means to close that gap by activating a shift in leadership consciousness.

> "The major problems in the world are the result of the difference between how nature works and the way people think."
>
> –Gregory Bateson

While mainstream sustainable business aids the identification and reduction of an organization's negative social and environmental impacts, it does not rectify the gap between how nature works and the way people think. Measuring and reducing one impact over here may have unintended negative consequences over there, all the while the underlying mindset that is at odds with life is left largely unchecked.

MINDSET SHIFT FROM MACHINE TO LIVING SYSTEMS

	THE SHIFT	
Worldview:	Mechanistic Materialism	Quantum Complexity
Self-orientation:	Self-as-separate	Self-as-participatory
Metaphor:	Organization-as-machine	Organization-as-living-system
Leadership dynamic:	Control-manage	Sense-respond

Through regenerative leadership consciousness, we can open into the powers and laws innate within life to help us live, lead, operate, design, and construct our enterprising futures in ways that work with the grain of nature and not against it. Until we find this attunement with nature's ways and wisdom, our solutions, no matter how well-funded, will only exacerbate the growing crises facing humanity. Hence the urgency of this task at hand, which is not some lightweight philosophical musing, but—when embodied into our daily consciousness—curtails the rampant waste of human energy that is increasingly devoted to distraction, escapism, titillation, commercialization, short-lived highs, techno-fixes, and control fetishes. All of which are often portrayed as helping humanity while busily corrupting the harmonies of life on Earth and selling our souls downstream toward more anti-life carnage.

Contrary to popular opinion, the complex, interconnected, and wicked problems facing humanity today are fairly simple to solve. As Oliver Wendall Holmes knew, on the other side of all this complexity is a beautiful simplicity, and it's this beautiful simplicity that the pages ahead reveal. However, should we remain beholden to the current dominant mindset, which is singularly at odds with nature, we may as well kiss humanity goodbye.

Science shows us that the world we live in is a living system interwoven in both the here-and-now and a realm beyond space-time, and each of us make up a unique thread of this rich tapestry. Both our inner and outer worlds are part and parcel of this living system. Act in ways that are at odds with the way nature works, and we unravel life on Earth and corrupt our own psyches. Learn to attune with the way nature works, and we become regenerative, resilient, coherent, and conscious beings that flow how life flows. We—ourselves and our organizations—become life-affirming.

Humanity's future relies on our capacity to revolutionize our consciousness. And for any revolution in consciousness to endure, it needs to be dressed of our time *and* timeless, and it must contain the perennial capacity to continually renew, which is the very essence of regeneration.

The Mindset Shift

ORGANIZATION-AS-MACHINE TO ORGANIZATION-AS-LIVING-SYSTEM

On this regenerative journey we begin to see the organization differently. It's no longer a machine used to manage and control in top-down, power-based hierarchic ways. It becomes a complex adaptive system, a living system with its own essence, life-force, sense of purpose, inner-nature (the culture, values, and behaviors), and outer-nature (the value propositions and external stakeholder relationships).

Traditionally, the branding of a business has focused on the outer-nature of the organization—how it shows up in the world through PR, external communications, advertising, social messaging, product packaging, and such like—but as we journey toward regenerative business, branding shifts. As the inner-nature and outer-nature of the organization start to cohere as an integrated whole, the brand is less an outward presentation (with the inevitable tendency for embellishment, perhaps even greenwashing) but now emanates from an inner way of being that pervades the inner workings of the organization. The culture and atmosphere of how people show up each day for work is as much a part of the brand as how the organization shows up to suppliers, customers, investors, and the wider world. Regenerative brands radiate a coherence of inner-outer nature, and this authenticity and wholeness informs their regenerative right relation.

It's heartening to come across more and more organizations shifting. Many are integrating People & Culture functions with ESG & Sustainability functions, which is a sure sign of an increasing understanding of how these inner and outer aspects work together to inform the authenticity and purposefulness of the organization. In fact, sustainability measures are a step in the right direction toward regeneration and right relation. Yet, regenerative business differs from sustainable business. I find the following illustration a helpful tool for my clients that shows the continuum of an organization's evolution—from conventional to sustainable to restorative to regenerative.

BUSINESS MINDSET CURVE

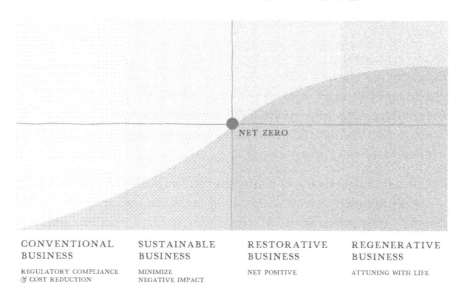

CONVENTIONAL BUSINESS	SUSTAINABLE BUSINESS	RESTORATIVE BUSINESS	REGENERATIVE BUSINESS
REGULATORY COMPLIANCE & COST REDUCTION	MINIMIZE NEGATIVE IMPACT	NET POSITIVE	ATTUNING WITH LIFE

While this is indeed helpful in conveying a progression, it can indicate that the progression is incremental without any shift in consciousness taking

8 \ NATURE WORKS

place. In reality, there is a threshold-crossing from the dominant Western mechanistic mindset into a living systems mindset that is endured during the journey of becoming a regenerative business.

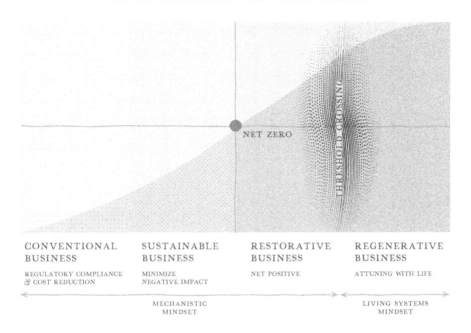

As we transition through the mindset shift from machine to living systems, we experience a breakdown of the old ways of working and a breakthrough in how we can work organizationally. This threshold crossing affects both leadership and organizational development (L&OD). It's a metamorphosis, no less. It's a profound death-rebirth revolution in our own selves as leaders, reorientating our self-other-world relation, and shifting how the people within our organizations relate, work together, and engage with stakeholders.

To further convey the interrelating aspects of this Regenerative L&OD threshold-crossing at both the leader-self level and organization-system level, I use four overlapping domains or circles. The two 'self' circles relate to the individual leader, one to personal consciousness and self-care (labelled 'Living') and the other to leadership development (labelled 'Leading'). The two 'system' circles relate to the organization, one to people and culture (labelled 'Culture') and the other to the sustainability domain (labelled 'Impact').

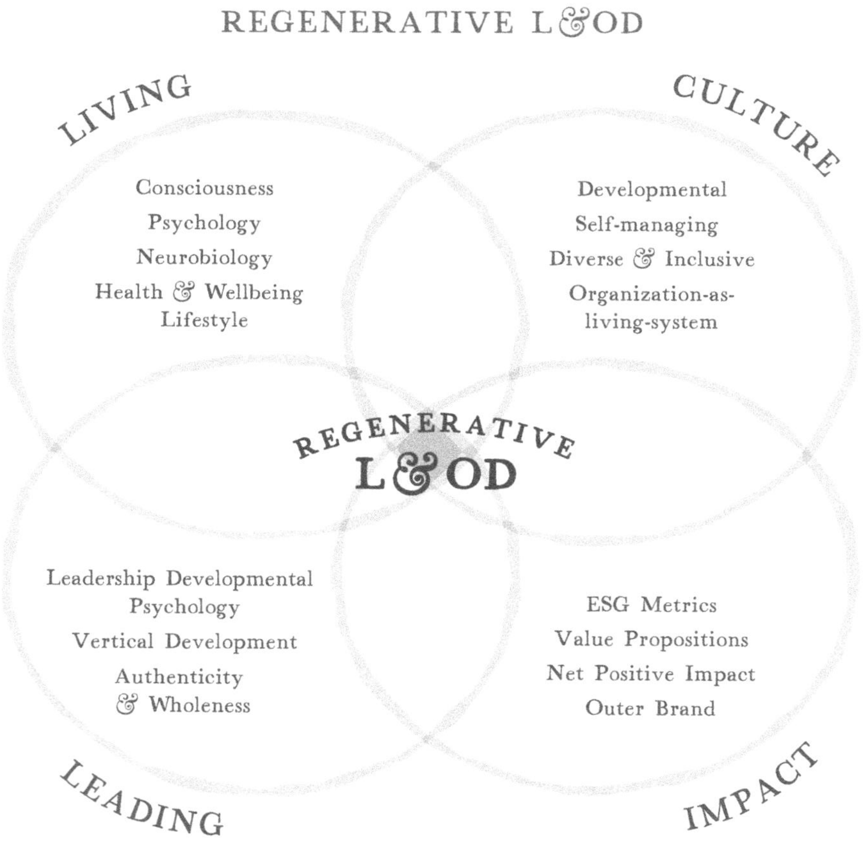

REGENERATIVE L&OD

LIVING

Consciousness
Psychology
Neurobiology
Health & Wellbeing
Lifestyle

CULTURE

Developmental
Self-managing
Diverse & Inclusive
Organization-as-living-system

REGENERATIVE L&OD

LEADING

Leadership Developmental Psychology
Vertical Development
Authenticity & Wholeness

IMPACT

ESG Metrics
Value Propositions
Net Positive Impact
Outer Brand

The Regenerative L&OD threshold-crossing from mechanistic to living systems involves all four circles undergoing a significant metamorphic death-rebirth process of letting go of old ways and opening into a deeper state of meaning-making that comes with a shift in our orientation of self and system from separateness to connectedness.

It's this metamorphic shift in consciousness that we explore here in *Nature Works*.

The Substance and Structure of this Book

You will find that insights from non-Western and Western ways of attending to life play significant roles in formulating what unfolds on the regenerative journey in this book, as both have enriched my own life and leadership development work in innumerable ways. I also hope to convey the great respect I have for contemporary science, the findings of modern-day practitioners, and the sages of antiquity regardless of whether they are Western or non-Western in theory or practice. Lastly, within the pages ahead, may you sense the deep reverence and respect I have for nature, Earth, and cosmos.

> "Nature is a totally efficient, self-regenerating system. If we discover the laws that govern this system and live synergistically within them, sustainability will follow and humankind will be a success."
>
> —Buckminster Fuller

The Book has Three Objectives

1. *To open into a regenerative worldview rooted in right relation of self-other-world*

The first objective is to catalyze a regenerative worldview where humanity, nature, and spirit come together as a unified whole. Being regenerative not only involves understanding how nature works, but it also involves finding right relation within our own selves, with others around us (humans and nonhumans), and with the world (both inner and outer worlds). This is a never-ending developmental journey of becoming more of who we truly are in our lives, individually and collectively. I refer to this right relation as 'self-other-world', where 'self' is rooted in an integrated ego, heart, and soul-consciousness and we find authentic connection with the 'other' through empathic relationality and with the 'world' through an embodied attunement of inner-outer nature.

2. To rekindle our capacity to sense the inner dimension of nature

Nature is not limited to what we see 'out there' but contains an invisible realm that is ever-present. This inner realm interpenetrates the outer world that we see and sense with our normal, waking consciousness. As we learn to expand our consciousness, we gain access to this inner dimension of nature, and with it we awaken the psyche and soul with the source of life. This inner dimension of nature has been ignored to such an extent that it has become desperately impoverished and almost completely overlooked with devastating consequences for humanity. By remembering 'inner-nature', we remember our true sense of place and purpose in this world. This grounds us and roots us, allowing for a more holistic view of reality to inform our way of leading and living.

3. To explore processes and practices for the psychospiritual maturation journey

The third objective of this book is to highlight the importance of the mid-life psychological development of the adult and to provide frames, processes, tools, and practices that aid this personal transformation toward right relation of self-other-world. For regenerative leadership consciousness to endure beyond short-lived one-off epiphanies, a profound life-changing psychospiritual death-rebirth journey is to be undertaken, and along this journey we have specific frames, tools, and practices to aid the reconciliation of modern human consciousness with the way nature works.

The Book is Laid Out into Three Parts

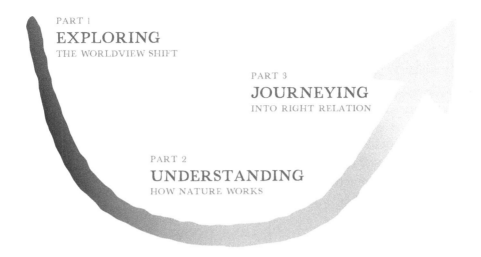

Part 1: Exploring (the Worldview Shift)

In Chapter 1, we take a canter through Western history and what led to our minds' exile from nature and then on to a new and emerging worldview that integrates the necessary understanding of inner-outer nature. In Chapter 2, we challenge and transcend the old mindset and discover what a threshold-crossing into a newly emerging living systems worldview would entail for the organization, and in Chapter 3, what it would entail for the individual. We wrap up Part 1 with Chapter 4, where I couple the latest scientific findings in neurobiology with ancient wisdom tradition insights.

Part 2: Understanding (how Nature Works)

Chapter 5 describes the nature of living systems and what this means for a Regenerative L&OD approach to the living-organization. In Chapter 6, we dive into different ways of sensing and working with living systems, and in Chapter 7 we enter the vast and vibrant realms of Nature's Wisdom.

Part 3: Journeying (into Right Relation)

Chapter 8 unpacks the three-phase nine-stage personal journey of becoming regenerative, and Chapter 9, 10, 11, and 12 each explains and exemplifies the various and valuable qualities that aid this regenerative journey for both the individual and the organization.

The Epilogue, *Mastering the Art of Regenerative Living & Leading,* is as much a conclusion as is it a reflection.

At the back of the book, you will find a wealth of information in the Appendix, such as tools and techniques that aid specific parts of the journey. In addition, numerous practices can be downloaded from my website here *https://gileshutchins.com/content/*.

Key Terminology Used Throughout the Book

Outer-nature: the outer dimension of nature that includes all the forms and processes involved in the physical manifestation of living systems, including the ensemble of organic and inorganic creations and creatures, from molecules to mountains, from water droplets to the Milky-way, from crystals to civilizations. Think of outer-nature as everything that's tangible, explicit, or measurable that can be sensed by our normal five senses. Outer-nature is physical and material, as opposed to psychological, energetic, or spiritual.

Inner-nature: the invisible, intangible metaphysical dimension underpinning and infusing the outer dimension of physical form and matter. This inner dimension of life may be comprehended through quantum complexity science, depth psychology, contemplative and embodied human experience, sixth-sense intuition, non-ordinary states of consciousness, and wisdom tradition practices. One of the features of regenerative leadership consciousness is the awakened capacity to sense the psychospiritual inner-nature dynamics that work with the creative manifestation and emergence of outer-nature.

Inner-outer nature: Conscious attunement of 'inner-outer nature' is an important goal of regenerative leadership consciousness—to live and lead in ways that harmonize inner and outer nature. All too often, amid today's mechanistic mindset, we focus primarily on outer-nature. Even in many of today's regenerative endeavors, outer-nature is prioritized, and inner-nature overlooked, unwittingly compounding the problems of today's imbalanced psyche and mindset. The rekindling of the capacity to sense and work with the inner dimension of nature is therefore a vital aspect of Regenerative L&OD. It's in this inner dimension that we find our capacity to work with the essence and life-force of the living organization.

The organization-as-living-system ('living-organization' for short) has two dimensions: 'outer-nature' and 'inner-nature.'

Outer-nature of the living-organization: the value propositions, products and services, impact, outward-facing brand and PR, external relations, supply chain, and value web. Unlike current sustainable business models, the outer-nature of regenerative business is not limited to net positive impact, but rather is rooted in an understanding of how inner-outer nature works. It involves a serious and committed quest toward healing and revitalizing the living systems the organization engages with. In this regard, regenerative business tends toward right relation with the essence and evolutionary potential of these living systems, which may likely involve the application of sustainability metrics, but not without an awareness of and respect for the inner-outer nature of the living systems it interrelates with.

Inner-nature of the living-organization: the culture, embodied values, individual and collective consciousness, organizational essence and sense of purpose, individual and team purposefulness, and the life-force running through organizational relationality, creativity, decision-making protocols, and power-control dynamics. In terms of the 'inner-nature' of a regenerative business, it is a developmental journey toward wholeness. This journey is as fresh as it is ancient, and it opens us up to living with more presence, purposefulness, coherence, and connectedness. This happens in the activation of regenerative leadership consciousness through deepening self-awareness and systemic-awareness (or 'self-and-systemic awareness' for short).

Activating our super-nature: Over the last fifteen years, I've explored powerful ways of activating this regenerative leadership consciousness that blend the shamanic and spiritual with the scientific and sensorial, so all of our natural intelligences (rational, emotional, intuitive, and somatic) are enlivened. I refer to this process as 'activating our super-nature', which aids the unlocking of human potential and the attunement with inner-outer nature.

As Mahatma Gandhi said, "As one changes one's own nature, so does the attitude of the world change toward oneself." It's this changing nature of our revolutionized and metamorphosed inner being in the world that informs our self-other-world right relation.

Are you Ready for the Revolution?

"So, is it going to be the Grail Quest or the Wasteland?" the great mythologist Joseph Campbell asked. "Are you going to endure the creative soul's quest or are you going to pursue the life that only gives you security?" (Campbell, 1990, p10)

Exploring the nature of human consciousness calls upon subjectivity and experience rather than a reliance solely on objectified facts and figures, and for this exploration I have found mythology to be hugely resourceful. Mythology speaks to the psyche in a timeless way that transcends different worldviews and mindsets and touches the soul in profound and partly unconscious ways.

Take the myth of the wounded Fisher King, whose injury affects not only the king's fertility but the fertility of the entire kingdom. This tale has been used as a basis for various questing stories, including the Western one of the Holy Grail. The myth in these legendary quests speaks directly to how one revitalizes the regenerative potential within one's self for the wider benefit of society and the world, unlocking innate regenerative powers in nature to transform the wasteland—today's soulless technospheric consumerism—into a world of regeneration and wisdom.

Inside each of us is an authentic voice asking for the Grail Quest, which involves both agony and rapture. The agony is the questing through perilous trials and tribulations while trying to slough-off old habits and personas, and the rapture is the insights and revelations where we experience 'Aha!' moments as we learn to live into our true nature. It's this simultaneous agony and rapture which sacralizes our experience of living intentionally, purposefully, and regeneratively in right relation. In enduring such a quest, we find a sure-footedness in the ground of our own being and learn to detect subtle signs and ques in others who have also embarked upon the quest, our soul brothers and sisters who, like us, are embracing this never-ending ever-enduring process of becoming regenerative.

Life no longer becomes an outer set of activities to achieve or set of problems to solve. It becomes a mystery to be lived by finding accord with inner-outer nature, whereupon we find sanctity with life on Earth.

Amid today's hype and doomsaying about possible biblical apocalyptic events looming ahead, it's perhaps intriguing to know that the ancient mythic motif of the 'second coming' was not in regard to an outer historic apocalyptic event but an inner 'born twice', a dying before you die in order to be reborn with a shifted consciousness.

Essentially, *Nature Works* is about our consciousness—how a shift in consciousness is now needed, and what this shift in consciousness entails for the individual.

The invitation for you, the reader, is not to accept any of what is written here with blind faith. Instead, test it out in your own laboratory of life. In fact, the main thrust of this book is an encouragement of a continual contemplation of one's experience of life in order to find an embodied sense of right relation, a felt sense of when one's life experience feels in tune with, rather than out-of-synch with, inner-outer nature. This is the way into regenerative leadership consciousness.

The regenerative leadership journey is not for the faint hearted, and it requires immense courage. We are unpicking, unlearning, and letting go of the habits and patterns inured in the dominant mechanistic mindset. At the same time, we are reawakening, remembering, and renewing ancient, almost forgotten, ways of being in right relation as we apply findings from contemporary scientific studies.

Research shows that organizations that mimic life consistently outperform their mechanistic counterparts. (Bragdon) Yet, there is a fundamental difference between seeking to become regenerative because it makes us more agile, purposeful, and profitable amid an uncertain marketplace and seeking to become regenerative because serving life feels like the right thing to do and aids the authenticity of our enterprising endeavors while also helping the organization become more agile, purposeful, and future-fit. The former puts the cart before the horse. The latter is in good order.

Regenerative leadership consciousness weaves us back into real life, into who we truly are and into how life truly is. The primary reason for embarking on this quest is because we know deep inside that right relation with life is our birthright. Quite frankly, why would we wish to be anything other than regenerative? It's a no-brainer and a heart-opener. It's the founding mission that binds our humanity, and it's our only way out of our present predicaments.

This book is for the leaders, practitioners, change agents, consultants, and edge-walkers who are serious about regenerative change, who recognize the importance of engaging in the inner work when activating outer transformations. If, while reading this book, you wish to reach out, contact me via my website, because I am here to offer my support to you, you the leaders, practitioners, change agents, consultants, and edge-walkers who are serious about a revolution.

Now, let's embark on this life changing journey!

"Without a global revolution in the sphere of human consciousness the catastrophe toward which the world is headed will be unavoidable."

—Vaclav Havel

"As we let go of the machine model of work, we begin to step back and see ourselves in new ways, to appreciate wholeness, and to design organizations that honor and make use of the totality of who we are."

—Margaret Wheatley

"Understanding the illusion only comes after the understanding of reality, not before…Until we have the experience of reality, in all its stillness, we are still lost."

—Peter Kingsley

PART 1

EXPLORING
(THE WORLDVIEW SHIFT)

Setting the Scene

Any real and lasting transformation in business and the wider socio-economic system is predicated upon a transformation in mindset. As the much admired, award-winning former Chairman and CEO of Interface, Ray Anderson, explains it:

> "We have been, and still are, in the grips of a flawed view of reality—a flawed paradigm, a flawed worldview—and it pervades our culture putting us on a biological collision course with collapse."

Our worldview affects how we perceive life and our sense of place and purpose within it. Without a new understanding of reality and the shift in consciousness this demands, we will continue on a collision course with collapse. The time has come to get radical and deal with the root problem—a flawed view of reality.

But this brings up so many questions. *How and why is our current worldview flawed? What does this mean in practice? What might a new understanding of reality mean for us as leaders and practitioners? And how might we go about engaging in the shift in consciousness that is now needed?*

In this first chapter, we explore the major worldview shifts that have transpired throughout Western civilization over the last couple of thousand years. In particular, we home in on the most recent shifts and what they signify for how we lead and operate in business and beyond.

A Canter Through Western Worldview Shifts

Spanning from around 100,000 to 10,000 years ago (8,000 BC), evidence points to *Homo sapiens* living in deep communion with nature. The norm in these aboriginal cultures was to uphold a sense of reverence for all life. Nature was perceived as sentient and sacred, with every living being forming part of a greater whole. Humans worked in harmony with the rhythms innate within nature. Let's call this worldview **Animism**.

For the animist, the spiritual energies encountered in the depths of the psyche were also working in the depths of nature. The 'outer' world of nature was an opening into the 'inner' world of energy, psyche, and soul. The boundary between 'inner' and 'outer' was more permeable than what we experience now, and there was an essential unity between humanity and nature. The human soul participated in a psychospiritual world common to all. By bringing one's consciousness into a harmonious relationship with archetypal patterns and forces innate within nature and the psyche, one achieved a sense of self-integration and wholeness.

Life is full of subtle energies active behind the scenes in an animistic world. Everything is perceived as made up of energy (or spirit). This energy is conscious, and therefore everything is conscious; everything is part of a living, interconnected web of energy. Right relation is found through practices that bring an earnest empathy with, and reverence for, all things. Shamanic rituals like dancing, drumming, journeying and vision questing, keep the psyche open and permeable with these subtle energies for right livelihood. Nature is experienced as not simply 'out there,' perceptible only to the senses, but instead contains an inner soul life that enacts eternal myths and archetypal narratives through natural processes and events amid everyday life experiences.

As far as we can tell from historic records, all ancient cultures have animist roots. Ancient cultures held the belief that nature was sacred, full of spirit flowing with divinity. Nothing was perceived as inert matter, not even mountains or rocks, for instance, which flow with their own spirit and aliveness. When speaking of the animism of the Etruscans of ancient Italy, the writer D.H. Lawrence wrote, "To the Etruscan all was alive, the whole universe lived… and had a great soul, or anima: and in spite of one great soul, there were myriad roving, lesser souls; every man, every creature and tree and lake and mountain and stream, was animate, and had its own peculiar consciousness." (Lawrence, p17)

These animist cultures are essentially shamanic. Shamanism is keen attunement with inner-outer nature—the belief system or practice of animism. In studying different shamanic cultures, the anthropologist Michael Harner, author of *The Way of The Shaman*, realized that there was a remarkable consistency of thought, beliefs, and practices between animist cultures worldwide. He coined the phrase 'core shamanism' for these common practices. (Harner) Our ancestors used to shape these core shamanic practices to the times and environment in which they lived, instilling a sense of empathy for other human and nonhuman beings and the environment as an ensemble.

Here are some basic principles of core shamanism:

1. Everything is made of energy (spirit).
2. This energy is alive and conscious.
3. Everything is therefore alive and conscious.
4. Everything and all human beings are included in a living flow of energy.
5. Everything is conscious and within communicative reach (through what is known as 'shamanic journeying' using concentrated awareness and intention).
6. When we communicate with things, we understand them and feel empathy with them.

7   Shamanic practices bring a heart-felt empathy with, and reverence for, all things.
8   Shamanic practices help us live in harmony and right relation with each other as people and the environment and engage in right action.
9   Human beings have the (seemingly unique) ability to unplug themselves from the flow.
10 When humans unplug from the flow, they unplug from this sense of empathy and right relation and no longer act with right action.
11 Separation makes us physically, mentally, emotionally, and spiritually ill, as individuals, as organizations, and as societies and leads to us harming others and the environment.
12 In unplugging and separating, we lose something profound. This is known as 'soul loss.'
13 Healthy human beings (and so, healthy human organizations and societies) feel included within nature, not separate from it or superior to it. (Hutchins, 2012, p66-67)

Far from living brutish lives, ancient animist cultures tended to live quite peacefully, enjoying excellent mental health, and functioning cooperatively and sustainably. In fact, no evidence has been found that the Paleolithic people of Europe fought each other. In the words of scientist Stephan Harding: "[We] are beginning to realize that animistic peoples, far from being 'primitive', have been living a reality which holds many important insights for our own relationships with each other and with the Earth." (Harding, p27)

Mythologists Anne Baring and Jules Cashford have extensively explored the Western psyche and how its mythology changed through prehistoric Paleolithic and Neolithic Europe. They note that our ancestors had two fundamental kinds of vision: the myth of meaning, which is rooted in connectedness, wholeness, and an understanding of the eternal within the temporal; and the myth of survival, which is rooted in hunting and gathering resources for utility. Both myths are essential to human experience. Baring and Cashford found, "When the myth of survival is contained within the myth of meaning, all life is experienced as sacred. But when the myth of survival gets split off from the myth of wholeness and eternity, we suffer the loss of meaning and lose our sense of the sacred." (Baring & Cashford, p38)

From what we can puzzle together from pieces of archaeological evidence, it seems that the myth of survival and the myth of meaning coexisted together until around 10,000 years ago. At that time, there occurred both a shift in climate and a shift in society, beginning what anthropologist Steve Taylor refers to as the Ego Explosion. (Taylor) Our sense of self-identity shifted from seeing ourselves as part of nature to a sense of separateness rising in the human psyche. This rise of ego-consciousness brought increasing self-agency and self-empowerment, along with a significant shift in how we operated and organized. With it, Animism in Europe gave way to the Neolithic and Agricultural Revolution, rising patriarchy, increased aggression and social stratification, and the rise of Hellenistic Greece, the Roman Empire, Christendom, and the Middle Ages of Medieval Europe. The myth of survival began to take precedence over the myth of meaning. This heightening ego-consciousness and increasing prioritization of rational intellect over intuitive empathic connection witnessed a departure from shamanic principles and a deep empathy with nature, and a new worldview formed. Let's call this worldview **Greco-Medieval**.

Western civilization is viewed as commencing with the ancient Greeks. This ancient Greek mindset was born out of a rich infusion of Neolithic European shamanic death-rebirth rites, ancient wisdom from Mesopotamia and Egypt, and influences from the Indus in the East, Hyperborea in the North, and further afield from the Far East. What's common to these diverse influences is an understanding of celestial and terrestrial rhythms, resonances and energies, and the understanding of wisdom found through attuning with these energies of inner-outer nature.

Recent findings have shed light on how influential the nearby neighboring civilizations of Mesopotamia and Egypt were to the early Greek mind. (Kingsley, Naydler) It's worth reflecting on the fact that Mesopotamia and Egypt were already as old to the ancient Greeks as the ancient Greeks are to us today. Both Mesopotamian and Egyptian civilizations worked with texts, technologies, and practices that express a distinctively shamanic wisdom and an intricate understanding of awakening human potential by attuning with rhythms, resonances, and subtle energies throughout inner-outer nature, Earth, and cosmos. (Naydler, 2018) This ancient shamanic wisdom informed the entire Mediterranean world for centuries, from the Greek mystery cults to the Pythagorean, Platonic, Neoplatonic, Alchemic, Hermetic, and Gnostic traditions throughout the West. Though, as we explore, this wisdom was driven underground during the Middle Ages.

Two of the key formative minds of the Greco-Medieval worldview were Plato and his student Aristotle. Plato is reputed to have spent thirteen years studying with Egyptian priests. (Naydler, 2005, p51) For Plato, the goal of philosophy—the love of wisdom—can't be attained through normal, daily consciousness but is accessible only through the soul which is awakened through death-rebirth experiences that reorientate the human psyche into a deeper soul-consciousness. His student, Aristotle, explains how ancient Greek mystery rites were not aimed at providing the initiate with intellectual understanding but rather a transformative experience of touching the transcendent realm to reorientate the sense of self into right relation with life and to realize the divine and immortal aspect of one's soul. (Naydler, 2005, p54)

Aristotle's 'eudaimonia'—wellbeing, happiness, and good spirit—is cultivated by connecting with one's soul. Soul virtues such as 'synesis' (right understanding, inner conscience, insight), 'Sophia' (intuitive spirit-wisdom), and 'phronesis' (practical wisdom, mindfulness, prudence) help cultivate our way into inner-nature to find harmony with outer-nature. The human soul is a portal into the World Soul pervading all life. Aligning inner-outer nature provides for right livelihood, a morality found not through ethical codes of conduct, religious commandments, or shamanic rituals, but through an inner-sense of rightness. No longer was the human having to consult the gods or oracles for decision-making. Instead, the human becomes an autonomous decision-maker, which results in a drawing away from the archetypal forces in nature and a focusing in on the human soul as a moral compass.

Aristotle's 'eudaimonia' recognizes the human soul as a portal into the spirit-realm innate within nature—the World Soul—yet puts the human soul at the center of things. So, let's call this Greco-Medieval mindset 'humanist-animist' as it acknowledges the importance of attuning inner-outer nature for wellbeing and right livelihood (animism), yet prioritizes human agency (humanism).

We start to see an increasing intensification of head-based logical reasoning happening in Greek thought around the time of Plato and Aristotle, while both saw the need to shepherd this logical reasoning with the more profound, intuitive, and embodied knowing they called 'contemplative thinking'. This is a soul-centered way of knowing which taps into the psychospiritual dimension of inner-nature. For Plato and Aristotle, this contemplative dwelling within soul and World Soul was key to the right relation that illuminates our lives with eudemonia, wholeness, and happiness.

This contemplative dwelling within inner-outer nature is present through Roman and Medieval times. Yet, over the next few centuries in the West, emphasis was placed more on logical reasoning than intuitive embodied knowing. Add to this the rising dominance of Christendom in the Middle Ages, and we see further separation of the human psyche from nature. The last vestiges of animism were suppressed and pushed underground within the Western worldview during this time.

To be clear, this is not because the Christian teachings of Jesus encourage a sense of separation from nature, as his original teachings clearly emphasize the sacredness of all life. It is also not because Christianity as a belief system is anthropocentric, as many Christians throughout the ages regard the sacredness innate in nature (John the Scot and Francis of Assisi being two well-known medieval examples) and many practicing Christians today resonate with Aristotle's 'humanist-animist' approach. The suppression of animism was a result of a form of Christian fanaticism that rose during the Middle Ages.

As with many organized belief systems at scale, power-control tendencies started to dominate the Church infrastructure. A quest for supreme control rather than living the values of Jesus's original teachings took hold. Inner connection to the divine soul within us was deprioritized by the Church in favor of worshipping a transcendent God separate from nature and humanity. In this quest for total power, the few remaining vestiges of animism practiced amongst European communities were viewed as heretical and violently stamped out or driven underground. Mythologist Joseph Campbell notes, "the Christian separation of matter and spirit, of the dynamism of life and the realm of the spirit, of natural grace and supernatural grace, has really castrated nature. And the European mind, the European life, has been, as it were, emasculated by this separation." (Campbell, 1988, p197)

During the High Middle Ages (1000-1300 AD), what has been called the '12th Century Renaissance' occurred. The word 'renaissance' means 'to be reborn', and this period bore witness to an upsurge of interest in the sacred dimension of life. This upsurge influenced social, political, and economic change which paved the way for the later Italian Renaissance (1460-1530 AD). The 12th Century Renaissance saw the craftmanship of Gothic cathedrals and churches apply ancient wisdom principles of attuning with the subtle energies of nature, Earth, and cosmos. This was the time of the Troubadours, the alchemists, and the legend of the Holy Grail—all celebrating the vitality of the sacredness within nature. During this time, we find the mystical Jewish text the Zohar and Arabic alchemic texts translated into Latin, making their first recorded appearances in Europe. Along with a reigniting of earlier Neolithic shamanism (with its indigenous, oriental, and Near East influences), Hermetic-Alchemic and Neoplatonic traditions, Presocratic Greek mysticism (Orphic, Dionysian, Eleusinian), and a revitalization of the Homeric rhapsodies and Pagan nature-orientated practices. All of which aided an increasing recognition of the importance of directly connecting to the divine through the immanence of nature and through a direct 'gnosis', an intuitive embodied experience of the transcendent spirit realm pervading nature.

This gnostic upswelling invited people—regardless of background, education, or status—to cultivate their own direct experience of the divine. An act that was seen by the Church as heretical, invoking the urgent need to suppress this upswelling. Hence the Crusades, Inquisitions, and Witch Hunts and the burning and torturing of thousands upon thousands. A previously compatible relationship between Muslim, Christian, and Jew was ruptured. The prioritization of worshipping a patriarchal transcendent God separate from nature and accessible only through the Church reigned from the late Middle Ages onward, coupled by a more mechanistic consciousness that was coming to the fore.

A key aspect of the evolving mechanistic consciousness was the advent of the mechanical clock, an instrument which quantized time. The widespread social uptick of placing the clock at the center of life, in the town hall, the church, living room, and soon the pocket, changed the Western worldview's relationship to the passage of time. It also changed the conception of the cosmos itself to that of a machine.

The Greco-Medieval humanist-animist consciousness was threatened. Philosopher Jeremy Naydler notes, "As the clock became ever more pervasive, so did the intuition of the organic wholeness of the cosmos begin to seem less credible. The human being's instinctive sense of belonging within this greater organic whole begun to flounder. A new malaise began to creep into the soul, an indefinable sense of being an outsider to, and an alien observer of, the natural world." (Naydler, 2018, p87)

Amid this time of change came the Italian Renaissance, a cultural era that commenced in Italy in the 14th century and spread throughout Europe till the early 17th century. It spawned revolutionary and innovative philosophical views that challenged the dominant Christian orthodoxy. Great minds like Leonardo Da Vinci, Nicolaus Copernicus, Francesco Patrizi, Giordano Bruno, and Tommaso Campanella revisited ancient animist, mystical, and Presocratic perspectives, as well as Platonic, Aristotelian, Neo-Platonic, Alchemic, Pagan and Christian perspectives.

Bruno viewed all forms as animated by a World Soul. He felt that the imagination, if trained through visualization and contemplative exercises, could assist personal transformation toward inner harmony and greater outer coherence with the world, enabling a cosmic connection with the rhythms of the universe. (Yates) The emphasis on a transformative path to achieve divine connection through meditative and imaginative expressions (such as dancing or chanting) had origins in the ancient Greek mysticism of Orpheus, which itself was influenced by mystic alchemic practices from further afield as well as the earlier shamanic practices of Neolithic Europe. Unfortunately for Bruno, his visionary views were seen as heretical by the Church, which burned him alive.

Campanella, who combined both the experiential with the conceptual to form a comprehensive philosophical system, considered all matter to be sensory and all living beings sentient. All things participate in reality with love and are part of God. He said, "If animals are sentient... the elements whereby they and everything else are brought into being must be said to be sentient." (Bonansea, p156) While Campanella joined the Church's Dominican Order at the age of fifteen, his views on the divinity of animist nature led to him being cited before the Church, confined to a convent for a number of years, and then later tortured and imprisoned whereupon he feigned madness to avoid death.

The affluent and influential Italian Medici family aided in the translation of ancient texts, such as the Greco-Egyptian 'Corpus Hermeticus' and Plato's works. The interest in Egyptian and Platonic texts came with a renewed interest in initiatory death-rebirth rites aimed at reorientating the human psyche into a deeper soul-consciousness. This, along with a rising interest in ancient Sufi, Alchemic, Kaballic, Pythagorean, Neoplatonic, and mystic-shamanic teachings, started to blend with the humanist focus of late Medieval times. Again, the individual soul finding harmony with the World Soul of nature was seen as a way to realize wholeness and right livelihood. Across Europe a wide range of thinkers, philosophers, scientists, and artists were affected by a revival of nature philosophy, such as the English playwright and poet, Shakespeare.

Despite the acts of rebirth, Europe entered a time of great upheaval. Plagues and famines as well as the Thirty Years' War (1618-48), the breakup of the Church through the Reformation, and a 'mini-Ice-Age' (approx. 1645-1715) kept much of society in perpetual conflict. Enter another cultural shift hand-in-hand with a shift in climate. Around 400 years ago, in Europe, the Middle Ages, with its cultural norms and mindsets, gave way to a new worldview, which we shall call here **Mechanistic Materialism**.

The great minds of the period—Francis Bacon, Galileo Galilei, Johannes Kepler, Thomas Hobbes, René Descartes, and many others—built upon the transformative and revolutionary climate of the Renaissance to form the Age of Enlightenment, which witnessed the Scientific Revolution. The Scientific Revolution was then followed by the Industrial Revolution with its profound effects on the Western world, greatly accelerating our ability to transform the environment for better or worse. Of particular relevance for us here, is the rise of scientific positivism and the de-sacralizing effect it had on the Western way of attending.

Scientific positivism drew upon an increasingly reductive and mechanistic perspective of life that coincided with the heightening of ego-consciousness and separateness. Any archetypal immeasurable inner-realm in nature was ignored as irrelevant or non-existent. A fissure occurs between mind (inner-nature) and matter (outer-nature), and the dynamism of life, along with its emergent and evolutionary potential, is drained of sacredness. Nature is now viewed as a collection of objects to be managed and controlled for human betterment. The evolution of life on Earth is seen as a process of selfish ascendency where separate species struggle for survival in a dog-eat-dog world devoid of meaning or purpose.

Mechanistic Materialism takes over the dying Greco-Medieval worldview, thus liberating us from the superstitious religious dogma of Medieval times, however substituting religious dogma for materialistic dogma. Scientific positivism states that only verifiable facts attained through rational deductive reasoning and empirical measurements can be understood as truths. "What gets measured gets done" becomes the new maxim, and reductive objectified science becomes the new religion. In other words, objectified scientific knowledge is the only truth. 'Inner' intangible experience becomes unscientific and de-emphasized, and 'outer' measurable forms and physicality of nature become prioritized. So, the Enlightenment's fissure of mind (inner-nature) split from matter (outer-nature) creates a prioritization of outer objectification over inner subjectivity and left-brain hemisphere rational-analysis over right-brain hemisphere intuitive embodiment. This rising prioritization starts to encourage, in the Western mind, a mechanistic and materialistic domination of outer over inner and rational over intuitive.

René Descartes, who is widely regarded as the most influential philosopher of the Enlightenment, was a first-rate mathematician and applied mechanistic concepts to humanity. He wrote, "All of these functions unfold naturally in this machine (the body) by virtue of the arrangement of its organs, just like clockwork." (Van Lysebeth, p26) Descartes along with other Enlightenment thinkers like Mersenne, Bacon, and Gassendi, felt compelled to repudiate the notion of nature as living, psychic, and sentient. In 1630, Descartes wrote to Mersenne saying, "God sets up mathematical laws in nature, as a king sets up laws in his kingdom." (Berman, p111) Descartes famously set about excluding any mind-like consciousness from nature, leaving it inert with his 'mind-body' dualism belief where the mind is separate from matter.

Separating mind from matter was the necessary precondition for the objectivity of modern scientific positivism. Rather than imbued with divine sentience, nature is perceived as chunks of matter; building blocks that collide and coalesce through deterministic push-pull forces definable through the abstract rationality of mathematical propositions. Other great minds of the Enlightenment, such as Thomas Hobbes and Francis Bacon, contributed to the rise of scientific positivism by focusing on empirical observation and rational mathematical logic as the only way to ascertain truth. Notably, Hobbes's basic assumption was that humanity and nature consist of atomized, competitive units embroiled in a "war of all against all." (Berman, p148) The political philosophy of Hobbes profoundly influenced many great minds to follow, including Charles Darwin.

By the 1650s, key figures in the Royal Society of London, the Montmor Academy in France, and later the re-organized French Academy of Science championed the notion of a 'value-free' science, which is based solely on proven fact through empirical experiment and rational deductive logic. Modern science was founded upon the materialistic notion of a de-spirited mechanistic worldview, and the Hermetic, Neoplatonic, and Pagan notions of God's immanence within nature came to be perceived as 'evil magic' to be dispelled. The surviving remnants of sacred nature that had co-existed within Christianity in the form of accepted Paganism were banished from the dominant worldview. (Hutchins, 2014)

Humanity's participation within nature through its divine immanence was withdrawn as science heralded the dogmatic belief in dualism. Man as the son of God was perceived as apart from nature and nature was no longer imbued with divinity. Nature became viewed as 'impure'. The way to God was 'upwards' through the transcendent realm, not tainted by the impurity of a de-spirited nature. Nature was seen as nothing more than a material collection of objects, a mere utility to be managed and manipulated for human betterment.

By the second half of the 18th century, the majority of Europe's leading establishments had fallen in line with this modern and alluring scientific outlook. It was assumed that everything in the world and the cosmos beyond could be understood, defined, measured, and so eventually manipulated by humanity. God's grand design was there to be understood by humanity for humanity, who—as the chosen species—had dominion over all aspects of His creation. (Hutchins, 2014)

The major innovation of the Enlightenment was Mechanistic Materialism's theory-based rationalistic explanation verified by repeatable, systematic empiricism. This innovation was profound, in that it enabled the great feats of techno-science that triggered the Industrial Revolution and the subsequent transformation this has had on our Western world and now across the globe.

Mechanistic Materialism banishes any perspective of an animate 'inner' consciousness or spirit-realm within nature. Along with this banishment so too comes de-prioritization of receptive, intuitive, and soulful ways of knowing. The 'humanist-animist' approach of Greco-Medieval times morphs into a 'humanist-materialist' mindset and the rational-analytic mind reigns supreme. It's here that the human being is not only set apart from nature but from its own soul. It's in the rational thinking mind that we find happiness 'out there.' This happiness is attained through the material 'good life', with its ethics and morality bound to rational-analytic moral codes mapped out by reason and science.

This mindset has come with all sorts of advancements that we all enjoy today—from the morality of human rights and liberalism to the technological improvements in modern medicine, transportation, and digitization. There is nothing inherently wrong with Mechanistic Materialism, and yet it has had the effect of separating the human psyche from the sacredness of life and the insights of the soul. By denying the inner dimension of nature, we strangle the ability to integrate our own psyche and soul with our outer social and business conduct. We cut ourselves off from at least half of life creating an immense imbalance in the psyche. All too easily we are consumed by the ego's fickle wants and needs. Rather than a quest for harmony with life, or for wellbeing through right livelihood, the purpose of life orientates around satisfying material needs. Enter the rise of capitalist consumerism, egotism, and individualism. As Frankie Goes to Hollywood infamously notes, "Sex and horror become the new gods."

It's this ego-mind ungrounded from soul and nature that lies at the heart of our manifold social and environmental crises today. Trying to deal with today's crises with the same level of consciousness that created them (Mechanistic Materialism) is futile and wastes precious time, energy, and resources. By entering into the Age of Regeneration, with its emerging worldview of **Quantum Complexity** we allow for a new mindset rooted in soul and nature to be born.

The foundations of Quantum Complexity have already been painstakingly laid by pioneers for us to build upon. This newly emerging worldview sees a return to the themes of ancient insights that informed Animism and aspects of the Greco-Medieval humanist-animist worldview, all while working with, but not constrained by, the scientific paradigm of Mechanistic Materialism. Some of the key themes of Quantum Complexity that are worth exploring here are: the scientific discoveries of an all-pervasive Field of background energy; how this 'inner' formless Field of energy relates with the 'outer' world of form; and the nature of our own mind in relation to this Field.

Arriving at Quantum Complexity

At the beginning of the 20th century, breakthrough scientific discoveries in physics were made by great minds such as Albert Einstein, Erwin Schrödinger, Max Planck, and Walther Nernst, which helped determine our understanding of how the universe works. With these discoveries Quantum Physics was born along with a scientific understanding of the innate interconnectedness of life and the presence of an invisible realm—the Quantum Vacuum or Field.

> "Let there be light."
>
> —Book of Genesis

The Field exhibits a background hiss of electromagnetic (EM) energy—a form of light—that pervades the entire space-time dimension. This invisible Field is everywhere. Intangible and unseen, it underpins and pervades the here-and-now immanence of life. Transcendent, it lies beyond normal space-time.

In fact, this Field is now viewed by some quantum scientists as being an infinite source of energy that can be accessed at any point within our universe. Meaning, if we had the capability, we could tune into all the energy we need and more, right here, right now. This all-pervasive infinite light energy is *imperceptible* to us, because it exists beyond the range of frequency that our senses can detect. We cannot notice it. It's perhaps a good job we can't notice it, as it could easily overwhelm us if we were able to tune into it. A useful analogy to imagine this quantum reality is this: We are living deep underwater with the sea all around, the all-pervading ocean of energy in our midst. We are like fish who are not mindful of the water they live in. But the water is always here, and we are never separate from it.

Particle physicist and Nobel laureate Steven Weinberg found that arising out of this Field are fields of energy constellating and concretizing in ways that appear to our senses as solid matter. More recently, astrophysicist Bernard Haisch and others explored the relationship of matter and inertia within the Field. In Haisch's words, the "underlying sea of quantum light" is what gives matter its solidity. (Haisch, p93) According to Haisch, all matter is a form of EM vibrational energy originating from the Field. Matter is vibrating energy that appears as solid matter to us yet is actually projections of energy from the Field. This seemingly solid world of objects which we interrelate with are now regarded as charged vibrating waves of energy projecting as particle-like from the uncharged background Field. Intangible inner-nature informs tangible outer-nature. Haisch explains: (Haisch, p115)

> "Picture a snowflake with its fine crystalline pattern; picture an igloo with its solidity; picture an ice sculpture with its form. Snowflakes, igloos, and ice sculptures are all made from water, which, in its normal state, has no form at all."

Some scientists have been exploring the notion that our universe is holographic and that the interference patterns of the ripples upon the surface of the Field we call reality have stored information. Within a hologram, the image of the whole can be reproduced from a fragment of it—the whole is contained within the parts as each part contains information of the whole. Some physicists view the universe as a big hologram with each Field ripple (making up matter) containing the image of the universe. Physicist David Bohm, for example, called this 'holomovement' in which the Field's sea of light flows into matter and back into light again and where any part of the universe is a partial realization of the relationships within the whole universe. In this regard, the universe can be viewed as a rich sea of consciousness, a holographic web of information. (Bohm, 1980)

> "The true ground-of-all-being is the infinite, intangible, spirit that infuses all living beings."
>
> —David Bohm

Cosmologist Brian Swimme describes this Field as an all-nourishing abyss, the hidden heart of the cosmos, nature, and humanity. (Swimme) Everything is vibrating expressions of the interconnecting Field, each vibration imbued with a unique frequency. As Haisch alluded to, each snowflake is unique, yet all are of water. We are all continuously interrelating with the waves, eddies, and vortices in our midst in a manner that is both unique and connected.

The concept of an all-pervading Field may have entered Western science at the turn of the 20th century through the discoveries of Quantum Physics, but it's not new to humanity. Ancient cultures have long recognized the existence of an all-pervading presence. For instance, around 3,000 BC, the Neolithic Celtic-Druidic traditions of Western Europe knew of nature and cosmos flowing with a life-force called 'nwyfre' that gave all life its consciousness, joining mind with matter. Later, in the West around 600 BC, when the ancient Greek Presocratic philosopher Thales spoke of water as everything, he was not speaking of the water that flows in rivers but a psychospiritual substratum that informs all life, the inner-nature dimension flowing through the entire physical world, as in today's Field. Similarly, in India around 800 BC, Hindu philosophical religious texts known as the

Upanishads, refer to the Source of life as the all-pervading 'Akasha', with 'prana' the life-force that emanates from within Akasha. Akasha underlies all of creation and contains memory of the self-creating universe through the 'Akashic Records', much like an ocean retains memory of what happens upon its surface through the ripples and waves formed. Also, around 600 BC, in the Far East, the ancient Chinese philosopher Lao Tzu spoke of the Source of life as an all-pervading presence permeating throughout nature and universe called the 'Tao' out of which arises yin-yang life-force energy called 'chi' (or 'qi' in Japanese).

This is what the death-rebirth rituals inherent in our Western history aimed to achieve, a thinning of the veil between outer and inner nature, so our human awareness can 'walk between two worlds', which is what the mythic phrase 'Heaven on Earth' meant for the mystic-philosopher. This not only allowed for a flow of vitalizing life-force energy from inner-nature into one's psyche and soul, but also into one's relationship with others and the world at large. As a result of the death-rebirth threshold-crossing, our new way of being regenerates our experience of life. We act as conduits for right relation and regeneration by bringing the fructifying energies of the inner spirit realm into everyday outer life. This ancient approach of living in right relation is being reawakened with the findings of Quantum Physics.

Contemplate this for a moment: Our individual minds, psyches, and souls are immersed within a Field where ripples, resonances, and memories lie beyond normal space-time. Learning to tap into and attune with the Field provides for a receptive openness which has been known to sensitives through the ages. Shamans, seers, and mystics enter the Field (or the Akashic Records) by tuning into levels of consciousness beyond our normal realm. They use their individual mind and psyche to enter inner-nature and then bring insights and visions into outer-nature. These individuals act as conscious conduits between an invisible inner realm and the outer world of our daily interactions.

No longer is empty space viewed as nothingness, but a buzzing field through which all activities originate, and seemingly unconnected particles interrelate in non-local ways. String theorist Michio Kaku proclaims that the mind of God is "music resonating through hyperspace." (Kaku, p48) This begs the question posed by scientist Manjir Samanta-Laughton, "Is every note of that music imbued with an inherent sentience?" (Manjir, p138) Imagine for one moment, each wave and particle of vibration within every aspect of reality is sentient.

Everything is a dance of energy continuously vibrating, infinitely humming away. Each aspect of nature, and every particle making up each aspect, whether living or not, is humming away. Each with a unique tune immersed in a Field connecting all life and universe.

The more we delve into the nature of reality, the more we find that vibrations, harmonics, music, and dance are everywhere.

Dancing with the Cosmic Rhythm

In the 1950's and 60's Hans Kayser founded the modern scientific study of harmonics in nature. He studied how harmonics—rhythmic vibrations—are literally everywhere in nature, from sub-atomic particles to our own bodies through to galaxies and supernovas. His work has influenced many scientific studies since. But again, this insight is not new, not even to the Western mind. Legend has it that the ancient Greek philosopher Pythagoras, some 2,500 years ago, was the first to discover the nature of harmony in the West upon hearing the sound of different anvils hammering in a smithy. He then explored vibrating strings and found the importance of whole number propositions for not just music but for nature, human relationships, and the cosmos, in his 'Music of the Spheres.' Then, thanks to the 17th century German astronomer Johann Kepler, the harmonic nature of the planets entered Western science and is still informing astronomy today.

Yet it was Kayser, whilst drawing upon a timeless wisdom found across the world, who brought the study of harmonics into the domain of contemporary Western science, further aiding the quantum vibrational understanding of reality. Kayser notes, "The concept of the harmony of the spheres is as old as the first awakening of mankind to consciousness. First in myth, then in astral symbolism, and as the integrating constituent of nearly the whole of mankind's poetry, this concept became the presupposition for astrology and the first astronomical inquiries of all ancient peoples." (Berendt, p65)

The more we explore harmonics today, the more scientists are beginning to realize that this is primary to the inner and outer workings of nature. The more we look, the more we see that the nature of nature is rhythmic vibration, and the basic unifying principle of life is the rhythm created through the harmonious sharing of diversity.

Rather than noise, harmonics have a pleasing fullness, vitality, and beauty which appear quite organically in nature. Think of a leaf or flower as emanating harmonics both through their unfolding process of becoming (their growth patterns) and in their structure and form. The 'architecture' of the leaf is based on harmonic relationships, as is its dynamic unfurling process of becoming into more of itself. This is the same for everything in nature. Hence the ancient notion of 'As above so below, as within so without' conveying that what's true at the quantum vibrational level also plays out in the planetary Music of the Spheres.

This harmonic unfolding is found in our own human nature; our process of becoming more of who we truly are depends on inner-outer harmonic right relation within ourselves, with others, and the world. Finding right relation of self-other-world is central to the Age of Regeneration supported by the science of Quantum Complexity, which draws upon, but is not limited by, the earlier worldviews of Mechanistic Materialism, Greco-Medieval, and Animism.

A vital aspect of our regenerative journey is learning to find harmony with nature. This involves a remembering of how to tap into and attune with the harmonic nature of life. At the foundations of Western philosophy, Pythagoras affirmed the paramount importance of finding accord with the harmonics of nature, and the whole 'Pythagorean way of life' revolves around living in harmony with life by working with the inherent grammar innate within nature. One must engage in life as a sacred art, learn to work with the intangible forces permeating existence, and bring these energies and our own life-force into alignment through a conscious way of living. It's this inner-outer 'accordance' which enables right relation and a sense of relatedness with everything around and within us, and through this right relation we find our sense of place and purpose in the world. Animism is regenerated through Quantum Complexity yet in a contemporary way that can transcend-and-include learnings gleaned from Mechanistic Materialism and Greco-Medieval worldviews. The myth of meaning and the myth of survival are once again working together.

An example of this contemporary examination of right relation is architect Gyorgy Doczi's work in the early 1990's, which explores how harmonics are found throughout nature and also in our humanity through not only our physiology but also our art and architecture the world over. He notes, "The essence of all vibration and rhythm is a sharing of diversities—weak and strong, in and out, up and down, back and forth—at recurrent time intervals. This holds as true for the tides of the ocean as for our heartbeat; for light, weight, and sound as for patterns of plant growth." (Doczi, p51) We might define harmony as a joining of diversities which in themselves may harbor contrasts; a unifying harmony found through the tension of diversity.

The Western Presocratic philosopher Heraclitus is credited with having developed the concept of diversity-in-unity. Yet again, we find this concept as old as humanity, where earlier shamanic cultures understood the harmonic rhythmic nature of life, as evidenced in early cave art and archaeological findings. Archaeologists researching the sites of the Caral peoples of ancient Peru found no weapons, only hundreds of musical instruments such as tone flutes. It would seem that their over-arching cultural goal was one of nourishing life through music—the ancient art of elevating vibrations to enhance the resonance reverberating throughout nature. Seeing themselves as caretakers of this world, the Caral peoples connected with the sacred rhythm of the cosmos and sought to help nourish it. (Fisher, p96) A descendant of these Peruvian people is Arkan Lushwala who, in his beautiful book *The Time of The Jaguar*, warns us, "If we do not listen to the cosmic rhythm, we trip and fall." (Lushwala, p21)

Mechanistic Materialism has tuned us out from the cosmic rhythm. We have turned a blind eye, a deaf ear, and a closed heart to the divine dance and music of inner-outer nature. And with it we have lost our capacity for right relation. We can regenerate ourselves and our worldview by learning to open our eyes, ears, hearts, and souls once again to this dance of life.

As Sufi Master Hazrat Inayat Khan notes, "Every person is music, perpetual music, continually going on day and night; and your intuitive faculty can hear that music." (Berendt, p161)

Throughout the mid-20th century, ground-breaking scientific discoveries started to unfold across the fields of biology, chemistry, cybernetics, and social science made by modern minds such as Gregory Bateson, Ilya Prigogine, Donella Meadows, and Fritjof Capra. Through them, we gained a new perception of how nature works, and Complexity Science was born, along with a scientific understanding of the emergent and evolutionary nature of life. Acknowledging living systems as self-organizing, inter-relational, and ever-changing helped dispel the reductive and mechanistic myths of Mechanistic Materialism. Add into the mix the pioneering findings in developmental psychology, analytical psychology, depth psychology, transpersonal psychology, ecological psychology, integral psychology, and spiritual psychology made by the likes of Carl Jung, Marie-Louise von Franz, Clare Graves, Susan Cook-Reuter, Robert Sardello, and Ken Wilber, and soon the modern Western mind started to understand the human psyche and soul as immersed in an invisible inner-outer relational realm. Now it was Mechanistic Materialism's view of mind as separate from matter that was threatened. More and more scientific studies began to point to something underneath not just the outer forms of everyday experience but also underneath the inner expressions of mind and body—a deeper inner-nature.

Early on in the 20th century, Jan Christian Smuts illustrates how the individual mind attunes and reverberates with the Mind of Nature in his pioneering work on *Holism & Evolution*, a concept that resonates with the Greco-Medieval notion of our individual souls embedded within the World Soul. This World Soul or Mind of Nature forms the basis of the systemic, social, ecological, planetary, and cosmic relationality from which our individuality springs. The individual mind learns to open into the Mind of Nature and cultivates the capacity for psychical sensing or intuition.

According to Smuts, this is "a holistic sense of relating." (Smuts) Psychoanalyst Carl Jung shared a similar perspective with his Pleroma or 'collective unconscious' within which our individual soul is immersed, never separate from.

Through a process of 'individuation' the individual can develop the capacity to become a truer version of oneself in finding accord with the World Soul. Systems scientist Gregory Bateson too explored the Mind of Nature and the importance of inner-outer coherence, along with many other notable pioneers (such as Alfred North Whitehead, William James, and Henri Bergeson) who acknowledged the importance of attuning with an animating force innate within life.

More recently, in the 1980s groundbreaking scientific explorations into how inner-nature and outer-nature interrelate were made by scientist Rupert Sheldrake. Sheldrake developed and tested a concept of forcefields, containing memory and information much like the ancient Hindu Akashic Records. His research suggests that all self-organizing systems (be they living organisms, societies of organisms, or crystals, for instance) exhibit these subtle energy forcefields, which Sheldrake calls 'morphic fields'. These morphic fields guide, inform, and animate the development of self-organizing systems through resonance, or what Sheldrake calls 'morphic resonance'. The organism picks up on inherited habits from others through morphic resonance instantaneously, regardless of distance. And so collective memory of both an organism's past habits and present behaviors can affect current and future behaviors and thus contribute to evolution. (Sheldrake, 2012)

Sheldrake's morphic resonance theory appreciates the importance of DNA and other proteins in organisms, but also recognizes the role of influences from outside, deep inside, and from other organisms, all of which are transmitting information with resonance. From this point of view, living beings inherit not only genes but also morphic fields, and they interrelate through these fields with past, present, and future behavioral implications. Clearly, there are similarities here to how animist peoples have long perceived the world, hence why Sheldrake refers to his theory as 'new animism.'

Individuals and the collective have a reverberate effect on each other as the dialogue of sensing and responding happens both individually and collectively. It seems, from scientific research, that as animals learn new things, a new 'behavior field' is reinforced by morphic resonance that affects not only the animal's learning, but also other animals picking up on the same resonance, i.e. the same morphogenetic type of animal. For instance, when a certain bluebottle fly learns something novel, other bluebottle flies can pick up on this learning in their morphic field due to morphic resonance. The 'collective learning' becomes instilled within communities of similarly attuned organisms in ways that transcend known epigenetic modification.

To help explain his morphic resonance theory, Sheldrake uses a TV set. The TV can be affected by component faults (analogous to genetic defects or physical ailments), but the TV set's components cannot explain the images broadcasted for the evening news. These images are not produced by the TV set's components but are produced by energy being broadcast by a specific evening news transmission which is then picked up by the frequency channel the TV set is tuned into (analogous to the organism's specific morphic field). Likewise, genetic defects, mutations and ailments can affect an organism's form and behavior, but its overall form and behavior is no more purely genetic than the evening news being governed by the components inside the TV.

For Sheldrake, it is the morphic resonance that provides the broadcast transmission (the news). As organisms, we have our components (such as DNA), and we are tuned in to certain transmission frequencies (that of a human or that of a fly, for instance). Further, we have the agency to attune ourselves to a more conscious and open frequency with inner-outer nature through the quality of our attention and intention—rather like tuning into different news broadcasts. This further attunement is what can enhance our ability to sense and respond to subtle changes within and all around us.

Intuitively tuning in to the systemic dynamics of the team, sensing stuckness in a team meeting, deeply connecting with the life-force of the organization, and practicing super-sensory capacities like intuition, gut knowing, and clairsentience (the extrasensory ability to pick up on psychic energies, for instance, telepathy, remote-viewing, or distance healing) are all examples of expanding our capacity for resonance with subtle changes within and all around us. As we learn to become more receptive to inner-outer nature, we can cultivate these natural abilities that strengthen our self-awareness and systemic-awareness thus helping advance our regenerative leadership consciousness.

Ancient traditions have long understood each psyche as exhibiting a subtle energy system that transcends space-time and filters consciousness. This energy or life-force is both immanent (here-and-now, in the body) and transcendent (beyond the here-and-now, in the morphic field with the capacity to tap into the wider Field). Our limited senses and ego-consciousness might conceal a deeper cosmic connectivity but that does not mean this deeper cosmic connectivity does not exist. The more we find out about inner-outer nature, the more we are scientifically recognizing that each distinct and collective psyche has its own field effects of memory and resonance; the individual and also the living-organization. As we open up, or rather tune in (like Sheldrake's TV set) we allow this transcendent nature of reality into our conscious awareness.

Whilst Mechanistic Materialism views mind as an epiphenomenon of the brain, these days the scientific frontiers of consciousness see mind pervading matter and space—it's everywhere in the Field. Our individual minds are like TV sets tuning into specific channels, discerning each from a sea of frequencies. The brain, rather than being the producer of consciousness, becomes a limiter, honing specific signals from a sea of consciousness in order to make sense of this otherwise fluid and connective reality we are immersed within. We can learn to open up this limiting function of the brain, and our overall 'bodymind' (the whole TV set) to bring in more information and sensitivity to what is going on in outer-nature, whether it be in the systems and fields of interrelation in the living-organization, our local community, neighborhood, or more-than-human world.

We have likely been taught to think of the body and the mind as two separate entities. In the 1980's research started to reveal otherwise—the body and mind are inextricably linked. Neuroscientist and pharmacologist Candice Pert coined the term 'bodymind' when her research found that the mind pervades the entire body (and beyond). Every cell and sinew in our body is imbued with mind. Our bodymind is enlivened when we cultivate coherence of the three major neurological centers in our body—the head, the heart, and the gut. The coherence of these centers encourages coherence across other networks in our body, such as the nervous, lymphatic, and hormonal systems.

Rather than thinking of our mind as encapsulated in the thinking-head, we begin to see that this bodymind permeates our entire body. Rather than physiology (matter) viewed as separate from psychology (mind) they interpenetrate as one bodymind, which continuously senses and responds to changes within and all around us. Through practices that align the head, heart, and gut, we enhance our 'bodymind coherence'. This allows us to become more sensitized to perturbations, energy shifts, and insights within the bodymind that might be picking up on outer systemic dynamics, relational shifts, and energy fluctuations during everyday exchanges such as meetings, conversations, emails, and online messaging. At all times our bodymind is sensing and responding to ripples, reverberations, vibrations, and repercussions within the Field and its morphic resonances. We contribute regenerative or degenerative ripples to the Field depending upon the state of our bodymind. Are we fearful, judgmental, and defensive or are we open, receptive, and compassionate?

As mentioned earlier, Jung found that each of us, by means of the process of individuation, can learn to open up our daily awareness to become more conscious of our bodymind's deeper nature. In doing so, we become more aware of the shadow aspects, suppressed feelings, and biases influencing our lives—anything from personality traits to family habits to cultural assumptions to ancestral imprints to archetypal forces. For Jung, this process of becoming conscious of the unconscious aspects within our deeper nature and the wider Field, is how we psychologically develop or individuate. It's this process of individuation that enables a shift in our meaning-making from one stage of leadership consciousness into a more expanded state that invites an increased capacity to embrace complexity, unlock creative potential, cultivate imagination and insight, and live into our truer nature or 'dharma.'

The scientific explorations mentioned here are a mere sample of the multitude that have occurred through the 20th and into the early 21st centuries, each contributing to an emerging worldview of Quantum Complexity. This new worldview echoes our animist past yet is inclusive of the experiences and wounds endured through the departure from the connectedness of Animism and the rising ego-consciousness and sense of separateness of Greco-Medieval and Mechanistic Materialism.

The self-agency, autonomous decision-making, and freedom from earlier superstition and religious dogma is not lost, nor are the immense technological advances in medicine, automation, and digitization we enjoy today. Quantum Complexity is a 'return', a remembering (a literal re-membering) and embodying process of becoming more of who we are. It's a fulfilment of our natural potential, a realization of Aristotle's 'eudaimonia' by connecting with one's soul, and a re-animation of nature. It's a new understanding of and relationship with the subtle energies active behind the scenes of everyday life and a recollection of the ancient death-rebirth practices vital for psychospiritual maturation and being of service in right relation with self-other-world. Quantum Complexity is a worldview that welcomes a deepening relationship with inner-outer reality to find accord once again with the way life works—for our own wellbeing and for the wellbeing of all life on Earth.

Remembering of the Soul within World Soul

The mechanistic attempt to separate humanity from nature and prioritize outer-nature over inner-nature is at the heart of our problems today. Mechanistic Materialism assumes that human beings have minds that are totally separate from nature. This creates an artificial separation of inner and outer-nature, which impoverishes the science and socioeconomic logic still dominant today.

Quantum Complexity research into consciousness shows that mind pervades the entire human body *and* nature. The more we examine how nature works, the more we find that the inner depths of nature interpenetrate with the outer forms of nature. Just as our human bodies work with an 'inner' intangible mind, so too does nature. Each living being—and even, as some scientists suggest, non-living systems like water and crystals—is interpenetrated with inner-mind and outer-matter. There is no separation of anything in nature from this all-pervasive field of consciousness. We are all immersed in 'it'.

> "The greatest illusion in this world is the illusion of separation."
>
> –Albert Einstein

Even if we choose to ignore the presence of this Field, whether we like it or not, the reality is we humans are immersed in nature both physiologically and psychologically. Physiologically, over ninety-percent of the cells in our bodies are not human, and without the help of these non-human cells we would utterly fail at life. Without nature's air we breathe, food we eat, and ingredients we use for clothing, housing, medicine, and transportation, we'd be nothing. Psychologically, over ninety-percent of our human history has seen us spiritually connected within nature, and this long history affects our humanity today. Mounting scientific evidence shows how our psychological sense of separateness from nature is undermining our capacity to become more fully human. In reestablishing a deeper sense of connection within nature, evidence shows that humans not only enhance their creativity, compassion, concentration, and collaborative capacity, they more readily tap into a more profound sense of meaning, purpose, and wisdom. As the inner psyche and outer activity of our being-in-the-world harmonizes, we overcome egotism, hyper-competition, fear, anxiety, and 'othering' (projecting a sense of in-crowd/out-crowd on to an 'other').

The ego is a human tool that enables us to gain perspective, focus, or pull ourselves out of the flow of life. Our individual, self-reflexive minds have the means to create a sense of separateness through the ego, which is an important aspect of the psyche that enables us to function as autonomous individuals. It's a useful tool, but when we get too caught up in our own egos (what we call 'ego-consciousness') and start to believe the separation is reality, we forget who we truly are. Beliefs that we are isolated psyches, apart from nature, pour in. As Einstein knew, this mentality creates a devastating delusion that cripples our humanity and starves our soul. It's this sense of separateness, the hallmark of Mechanistic Materialism, that causes us to act in ways that are out-of-kilter with life on Earth.

> "A human being is a part of the whole called by us universe, a part limited in time and space. He experiences himself, his thoughts and feeling as something separated from the rest, a kind of optical delusion of his consciousness. This delusion is a kind of prison for us, restricting us to our personal desires and to affection for a few persons nearest to us. Our task must be to free ourselves from this prison by widening our circle of compassion to embrace all living creatures and the whole of nature in its beauty."
>
> –Albert Einstein

This task to free ourselves from our own delusion is what *Nature Works* is essentially all about. It's a task to shift our consciousness, to embrace all life, and to lead from this deeper center of being.

As Iranian philosopher Seyyed Hossein Nasr notes, "The ecological crisis is only an externalization of an inner malaise and cannot be solved without a spiritual rebirth of Western man." (Nasr, p17) Mechanistic Materialism creates this inner malaise, and as a worldview it will not solve our crises it will only make them worse. Having leaders and practitioners shift their worldview into Quantum Complexity is vital not only for the future-fitness of organizations and communities but also for the evolution of humanity.

An important step into Quantum Complexity is the recognition that we are not separate psyches bouncing around in a world of separateness. Rather, we have egos to aid our self-agency and self-reflexivity so that we can learn and evolve in order to work with the richer rhythms and song-lines innate within the human soul, which is immersed within the World Soul. This is an important, immersive step into inner-outer nature as it enables us to not only comprehend but also embody the soul within ourselves connected into the World Soul that pervades all life. The interiority of human nature and the interiority of nature arise from the same ground of being, the World Soul, and this World Soul resides in the Field beyond space-time influencing our own being within space-time through the individual soul within our innermost being.

When we treat nature as a utilitarian resource to exploit, we damage our own root, and we become carcinogenic, a danger to our home planet Earth and to our own humanity. The only way out of this predicament is to reconnect with the root and find inner-outer right relation.

We have here in the West a spiritual heritage to draw from, one which reveres the perennial wisdom of inner-outer nature, and we can take inspiration from wisdom traditions and shamanic cultures the world over that convey this reverence and respect for the sacredness of nature, Earth, and cosmos.

Working with Nature's Wisdom for the Metamorphosis of our Time

Adult developmental psychology studies indicate that leaders able to sense and work with the emergent and evolutionary dynamics of life are better equipped to lead 21st century future-fit organizations. Take developmental psychologist Clare Graves, who painstakingly researched levels of consciousness across thousands of adults. What he called Tier Two consciousness (the next stage of consciousness he witnessed emerging in adults across business and society) is marked by the capacity to sense the systemic relational nature of emergence in both natural and human systems.

> "Know how nature functions and you know how to behave [in Tier Two]"
>
> —Clare Graves

This gives way to the rising trend to learn from nature. Yet, even when seeking to learn from nature, we all too often get caught up in Mechanistic Materialism, which seeks to compartmentalize, categorize, and rationalize, and we risk bringing the same mechanistic lens to our biological explorations that desensitized us to nature's relationality in the first place. While a reductive scientific understanding of nature along with a systematic set of nature's principles is indeed useful (and certainly something we can draw upon to inform Regenerative L&OD), the challenge and the opportunity lie in shifting our consciousness to a more holistic attentiveness to the nature of life all around and within us. This endeavor is as fresh as it is ancient.

Chinese sages perceived the manifest phenomena of nature as conveying subtle insights about how change unfolds in life. It is not the forms, functions, and designs of nature but the underlying rhythms of transformation which precede the forms that provide insightful wisdom. My own nature-inspired coaching work draws upon the numerous wisdom traditions that acknowledge the importance of the underlying wisdom innate in life—Ayurveda, Buddhism, Shintoism, Daoism, Confucianism, and Sufism from the East, Alchemy and Hermeticism from the West, and Tantric and Shamanic traditions found the world-over. This underlying wisdom of life is what I refer to as 'Nature's Wisdom', which we shall explore in detail over the coming chapters, including how we can work with Nature's Wisdom to find our sense of place and purpose in the world and cultivate our soul craft as regenerative leaders.

As we have explored in this chapter, the journey out of Animism through Greco-Medieval and into Mechanistic Materialism worldviews bears witness to a rising separation of inner and outer, mind from matter, and human from nature. In terms of leadership consciousness, this affects us in two ways—within ourselves (self-awareness) and outside ourselves in how we attend to life's living systems (systemic-awareness). The inner soul dimension of nature and the inner soul dimension of the human psyche became deprioritized with the rise of reductive science's objectivizing focus on outer measurables and tangibility. Outer doing trumps inner being.

This affects not just our leadership consciousness but also how we perceive and attend to the organization. Rather than attending to the organization as a complex system full of human processes of relating, we compartmentalize and silo it into utilitarian functions and apply a machine mentality to maximize efficiency and effectiveness through outer doing. The organization is seen as a machine to be controlled and managed from above in an objectified mechanistic way.

There is nothing wrong with this focus on the outer, and we need it to get-the-job-done, sure as we need a focus on efficiencies and effectiveness. Yet the de-prioritization of the inner aspect of life impoverishes both the individual (self-awareness) and the living-organization (systemic-awareness) catalyzing a plethora of problems in our organizations today that end up in the very ineffectiveness the machine-mindset is trying to avoid. We have unproductive talking-head back-to-back meetings, people bringing only fragments of themselves to work, cultures of mistrust and fear, sapping of creativity and meaning, inauthentic brands, unsustainable behaviors, mental health and wellbeing issues, loss of talent, and the list goes on. Enter the Great Resignation.

As our leadership consciousness expands its meaning-making and opens to a new perspective of how life works—one grounded in Quantum Complexity—we start to see the organization as a living system participating within an ever-changing, inter-relational systemic context. The living-organization is full of what Organizational Development (OD) specialist Ralph Stacey calls 'complex responsive processes of human relating.' (Stacey, 2012, p16) The individual leader, team, organization, and stakeholder ecosystem are all inter-relating and interdependent, meaning they are not separate from or in competition with each other. Yes, there are competitive edges (which can positively impel entrepreneurialism and creativity, as well as undermine it); however, everything participates, exchanges, and connects through energetic emergent relationships that are nonlinear, complex, responsive, and unpredictable.

ORGANIZATION-AS-MACHINE TO ORGANIZATION-AS-LIVING-SYSTEM

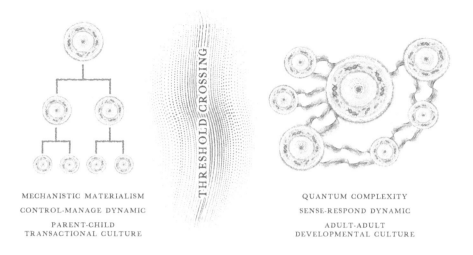

MECHANISTIC MATERIALISM
CONTROL-MANAGE DYNAMIC
PARENT-CHILD
TRANSACTIONAL CULTURE

THRESHOLD CROSSING

QUANTUM COMPLEXITY
SENSE-RESPOND DYNAMIC
ADULT-ADULT
DEVELOPMENTAL CULTURE

Now we take an important step on the regenerative leadership journey; to become aware of the organization-as-living-system with inner dynamics, such as soul essence, emergent tensions, evolutionary purposefulness, and developmental growth challenges. The leader senses and responds with the living system dynamics of the living-organization and seeks to cultivate a Regenerative L&OD culture. I define this culture as a 'DEE Culture' (Developmental, Emergent, Evolutionary) which is explored at length in my previous book *Leading by Nature* and will be revisited in the context of the upcoming regenerative leadership journey in this book. This shift in awareness also entails a recognition that the 'outer' nature of the organization (its value propositions, stakeholder relationships, and brand) is fully enlivened and authentic when in accord with the 'inner' nature of the organization (its culture, values, essence, and ways of relating). (Hutchins, 2022)

One of the products of Mechanistic Materialism is the organization-as-machine sweating assets for short-term returns, often because of pressure from investors, lenders, and shareholders for consistent upward quarterly returns regardless of the growth stages and contextual changes the organization experiences as it matures. In nature, growth is about learning and cultivating new ways and that does not always mean growing bigger and bigger in an outward, obvious way.

Overlooking the inner-nature of life, and the organization-as-living-system, Mechanistic Materialism encourages the leader to hyper-focus on outer-nature and to maximize outer growth irrespective of how that may align with the living system's inner development, learning, and culture. In this situation, the favorable way for the leader to achieve the promised outer growth is to manage and control in what is perceived as the most 'efficient' way possible with little regard for the relational and interconnected nature of the living-organization.

This warped outward focus is a natural by-product of the mechanistic mindset, and it still dominates business leadership and management thinking today. Authenticity and alignment between inner and outer nature is not seen as a business priority within this narrowed machine view. Yet authenticity undoubtedly aids the future-fitness of the organization for a whole host of reasons—attracting and retaining talent, agile decision-making, unlocking brilliance and creativity across the business, improving customer retention, enhancing brand, and the list goes on. As well as a split between the inner (culture) and outer (brand) of the organization, Mechanistic Materialism has encouraged a split within the inner and outer nature of the individual. Inner being is starving at the expense of a relentless outer doing.

The task for Regenerative L&OD is to attune the inner-outer nature of the organization and the inner-outer nature of the leader. It's this integration that allows for regenerative business to find accord through Nature's Wisdom and to authentically thrive amid the volatile times ahead while delivering life-affirming offerings that encourage humanity toward regeneration.

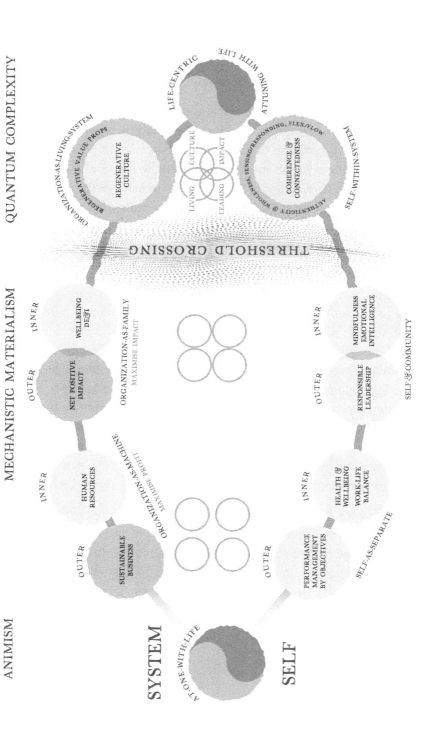

NATURE WORKS

To orientate ourselves within any living system, ecosystem, neighborhood, or society, we must open into the inner dimension of the system that informs its outer forms. Without this orientation we are but lost in Mechanistic Materialism.

Unfortunately, many well-intended endeavors in the sustainable business, climate change, and Corporate Social Responsibility (CSR) movements today are machinations of Mechanistic Materialism, further estranging inner and outer nature, while distracting essential energy from where it's most needed. Without attention being given to a regenerative mindset for leaders and organizations, we shall continue to imprison ourselves in the devastating delusion of separation Einstein speaks of.

Inner-nature and outer-nature are inextricably entwined. There is no separation. Everything evolves through continuous sensing-responding and energetic exchanges within the relational environment of everyday life. We now know this, and science has proven it, in both quantum and cosmological research and amid the complex systems of our organizations and neighborhoods. (Currivan)

Adult developmental psychology research shows us that as we move through deeper stages of meaning-making in our lives, the ego simultaneously maturates and permeates. This is what I refer to as a shift from 'self-as-separate-and-in-competition-with-the-world' ('self-as-separate' for short) to 'self-as-participating-within-the-world' ('self-as-participatory' for short). It's this shift in the sense of self that is at the heart of the shift in leadership consciousness, from 'achiever' to 'regenerator', that we explore in the next chapter.

SELF-AS-SEPARATE TO
SELF-AS-PARTICIPATORY

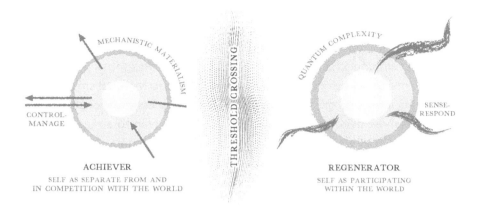

ACHIEVER
SELF AS SEPARATE FROM AND
IN COMPETITION WITH THE WORLD

REGENERATOR
SELF AS PARTICIPATING
WITHIN THE WORLD

We do not need to dissolve our sense of self but rather deepen our sense of who we truly are, and in doing so our ego becomes more receptive and open to life, and our way of experiencing life becomes less defended, judgmental, fearful, and change-averse. We become more able to adapt to adversity, relate to different people and different situations with ease, and tap into the wisdom that the unfolding experiences of life afford us.

This ego maturation and permeation does not subsume us in a grey miasma of uniformity, conformity, and collectivism. It allows us to work with the grand symphony of existence while staying true to our unique tune. We celebrate individuation within harmonization. As we reconnect back into real life, we're invited on an inner journey, a death-rebirth metamorphosis inside ourselves, whereupon psychic fragmentation and reintegration strengthens our communion with the spiritual source of the individual soul and collective World Soul. Only by undertaking this journey, will we shift our consciousness from Mechanistic Materialism into Quantum Complexity.

This process of psychological death, dismemberment, reconstitution, remembering, and rebirth is central to all the initiatory myths throughout the ages. Society is going through this death-rebirth process right now, and it's bringing to bear all the uncertainty, frustration, anxiety, fragmentation, polarization, and fear it can invoke. The more conscious we become of this process, as leader and as practitioner, the more we can work with the archetypal forces innate in inner-outer nature, and the more regenerative we become. Afterall, 'to regenerate' is to die and be reborn while finding deeper accord with inner-outer nature. Regeneration is the task of our time.

As the French writer Antoine Saint de'Expury once noted,

> "If you want to build a ship, don't drum up people to collect wood and don't assign them tasks and work, but rather teach them to long for the immensity of the sea."

The immensity of the sea is all around and within us—Nature's Wisdom—a real and potent presence in our lives. In attending to the inner-dimension within and all around us, we begin to see with new eyes a world that has always been and always will be sacred, sentient, and sensitive to our true nature. What we need now more than anything is to reconnect with the rapture of reality and remind ourselves of the magnificence of this existence. Then, the building of the ship becomes a labor of love filled with passion and enthusiasm. Then, we cocreate futures that cultivate our true nature. We allow our consciousness to become regenerative and we heal the separateness within the human psyche and its division with nature.

Journeying toward Regeneration

There is a near total disequilibrium between modern civilization and nature. This disequilibrium is rooted in a lack of harmony—right relation—between humanity and nature. This impoverished relationship affects us in profound and partly unconscious ways. When life revolves around the surface of things 'out-there' and the surface of our own ego's whims, we lose sight of a reality that feeds the soul and provides our authentic sense of meaning, place, and purpose in the world. Too much outer, and we become rudderless, tossed this way and that by superficial needs and consumeristic mores. We exploit the world out there and exploit others in answering to this imbalanced ego-consciousness that grasps at things in fear due to an existential anxiety created by nothing more than our sense of separation.

Consumerism gives the illusion of self-determination. It plays up to and satisfies our fickle desires that derive from the egotistic self-as-separate. Using the hollow whims taken from focus group research, desires are then magnified through sophisticated public relations, advertising campaigns, and marketing media. Purchasing products we don't really 'need' is 'good' for the economy; the more consumers spend the better. This perpetuation of egotism over authenticity ensures the insatiable desires of the consumer are never truly satisfied. Our consumerist, socioeconomic paradigm is therefore rooted in illusion, and perpetuating the illusion allows us to remain fragmented from sources of real happiness. As the psychoanalyst and social theorist Joel Kovel notes, "Were people either happy or clear about what they wanted, then capital's ceaseless expansion would be endangered." (Kovel, p135)

Amid Mechanistic Materialism's ego-grip, it's increasingly challenging for people to follow any authentic calling in their work as priority is given to jobs that pay well enough to support a lifestyle that fits within our consumerist culture. Psychologist Andy Fisher explains, "We are born into a social world in which our need for personal viability or security gets 'met' by being twisted down along narrow economic pathways which then become difficult to leave, for both emotional and structural reasons. We are just too existentially vulnerable for it to be otherwise, at least for most of us. These pathways, however, fail to bring us the release from fear we desire." (Fisher, p87) In the West, the use of anti-depressants has increased fivefold in the last two decades, and today at least one in ten Western teenage girls suffer from anorexia. We find ourselves living within a socioeconomic system that starves our greatness for creativity, community, and love while exploiting our weaknesses through judgement, jealousy, and fear.

There is no reason for it to be this way. In fact, our current socioeconomic consumerist reality is a quite recent insanity. For the vast portion of our history, humans have lived in communion with nature, attuned to the way nature works. Now though, due to the dominance of Mechanistic Materialism, our capacity to tune in to this metaphysical dimension is all but lost. So pervasive as this illusion of separation has become, you would not find any sort of metaphysical dimension or communion with nature being taught to our children in mainstream schools today, not throughout Europe, America, or likely any mainstream schools the world-over. However, an understanding of the metaphysical dimension of nature is central to moving beyond Mechanistic Materialism into Quantum Complexity's Age of Regeneration.

On the edge of a new epoch, we find ourselves needing a new kind of anchorage that speaks to the depths of our souls, one which includes the death-rebirth mysteries, non-ordinary states of consciousness, and intuitive insights and embodied experiences of inner-nature found in our Western past. Some are animated today through the vestiges of shamanic cultures and esoteric traditions across the globe and others are uncovered through contemporary scientific studies in neurobiology, depth psychology and consciousness. To anchor into our true nature, we must come to terms with inner-nature and learn to think, sense, and know in ways that reach beyond the objectifying tendency of ego-consciousness and its self-made illusion of separation.

Returning to Inner-Nature

For many centuries, science in the West and East drew from a metaphysical cosmology that understood a depth of dimensionality to nature. Humans were seen as innately part of nature's ensemble and possessed the seemingly unique self-reflectivity to either fall out of rhythm or learn to consciously attune with the wisdom of nature. Harmony was the guiding principle defined by a metaphysical comprehension of nature. There was Daoism, Confucianism, Shintoism, Vedanta, Zen, Buddhism, Sufism, Tantra, and such like in the East and Alchemy, Hermeticism, Kabbalism, Pythagorean-Platonic, Druidic and such like in the West, not to mention traditions further afield like the Caral of Peru mentioned in the previous chapter. All variety of traditions are animist-shamanic in origin and center around the practice of attuning with nature and cosmos to be in right relation with life, no different than the core shamanism found throughout indigenous peoples all over the world today.

Ancient wisdom traditions and present-day shamanic practices of indigenous peoples are rooted in a worldview of Animism, where nature is seen as sacred, where all life is informed by an animating spirit or primordial 'tune' that is both transcendent and immanent.

Cultivating our consciousness to become more receptive to this immanent and transcendent wisdom in nature brings harmony for self-other-world. Nature is experienced not only as 'out there' but also as 'in here'.

It is both perceptible to the senses through its physical dimension and metaphysical through a connection to its interiority, inviting us to attune with a wisdom that enacts eternal myths and archetypal narratives amid everyday life experiences. To no longer sense the sacred metaphysical dimension of nature is to fall out of tune with nature, and in turn corrupt our humanity, lose our way, become individually and societally sick, and forget who we are.

This 'losing our way' has come to define the Western mindset over recent centuries. The separation of spirit from nature, of inner from outer, corrupts the mechanistic science that flows from it because this mechanistic science is divorced completely from any ontological aspect other than pure quantity. In fact, the metaphysical aspect of nature is all but overlooked, or even mocked as mere superstition. Modernity's worshipping of supposed science is more an ascendency of technology and the machine that narrows the faculties of knowing into quantized objectification to the detriment of true science, suffocating the soul and degenerating the love of life. Humanity loses its orientation, becoming ungrounded from its psychospiritual root.
(Nasr, p23)

Science today is utilitarian, a tool to support human utilization of a de-animated nature for human material needs. Whether it's dressed up in ethical reasoning (lifting people out of poverty, for instance) or economic motive (giving people employment), what lies beneath the materialistic narrative is an exploitation of self against other against nature. Recall Hobbes' 'war of all against all' philosophic perspective. This perspective is still running rampant in our minds today. Nature is dominated for humanity, and humanity dominates and stratifies itself through power-control urges spawned from a dislocated ego, self-as-separate mentality. There can be no metamorphosis into regeneration without a recognition of nature in all its fullness, along with a reigniting of the sense of the sacred in our scientific understanding of reality, as each will aid our own personal and societal psychological shifts from self-as-separate to self-as-participatory.

Even our present-day Theory of Evolution, which most of us have taken for granted as set-in-stone fact, passing it on to our own children without a second thought to question its truth, is a theory based on this flawed science of Mechanistic Materialism. It ignores the essence of things and condones all manners of exploitation in the name of progress. As we expand our worldview and begin once again to open our minds and hearts more to communion with nature, we begin to see and sense the gaping holes that today's mainstream Neo-Darwinian Theory of Evolution is littered with. While the onset of the 20th century witnessed the breakdown of the classical physics so foundational to Mechanistic Materialism, the spiritual force within the Western psyche was not potent enough to integrate the new quantum science into a more universal and organic perspective—until now, at this epochal precipice.

Throughout the 20th century and into this 21st century, discovery after discovery has prepared the cultural soil for crossing a worldview threshold.

Let's look at the amendments. We have had breakthroughs in psychology (developmental, integral, transpersonal, depth, ecological) and biology (facilitation ecology, Gaia theory, biomimicry, biophilia). We have seen pioneering progress in systems science (general systems theory, complexity theory, complex adaptive systems theory, living systems theory, holistic science) and systems design (systemic design thinking, ecosystemic innovation, regenerative design). Not to mention the sea change within L&OD (teal-evolutionary, deliberately developmental organizations, conscious capitalism, ESG, regenerative business, responsible leadership, regenerative leadership) and across so many other domains like health & wellbeing, economics, agriculture, urban planning, and social sciences. Countless breakthroughs are gathering pace.

Yet when sifting through these shifts, it can become all too easy to get absorbed by the facts, figures, frames, models, and methods. Busying ourselves with new principles and processes, we overlook the metaphysical shift required in our consciousness; an ontological shift in our very being from self-as-separate into self-as-participatory within life.

Is the spiritual potency within the human psyche mature enough to integrate all these breakthroughs into an ontological metamorphosis grounded in a holistic and regenerative way of being-in-the-world? I believe so. The time has come. I believe the decade ahead, from 2025-2035, will bear witness to a wholesale reconfiguration of how we lead and operate in business and beyond, not solely because of our increased understanding of Earth's planetary limits (which is clearly an important part of this) but primarily because the metaphysical dimension of nature is becoming available to us once again. We are living through a psychospiritual 'return' to or 'remembering' of the sacredness of life that will tip the scales of this critical (r)evolution in human consciousness.

Transcending-and-Including the Mechanistic Mind

In reawakening our capacity to connect with the metaphysical animating force within nature, we are 'transcending-and-including' the mechanistic mind. The tools and capabilities we have gained through Mechanistic Materialism are not thrown away but evolved and integrated into a new worldview context, one which is more life-centric than anthropocentric, more humanist-animist than humanist-materialist. The reductive mechanistic tools we have honed over the last couple of centuries (along with all the technological advancements in digitization, medicine, transportation, and so forth) that we benefit from today are still available to us, but as tools that we can pick up and put down rather than totalizing our way of being.

We can transcend this allure of mechanistic dominance by reconnecting to the rapture of reality. As we open our perceptual horizon to inner-nature, we gain perspective on a narrowed outer reductionism as a useful tool that can serve life, rather than life serving it. The reductive ego-lens is still available to us, but as one of many tools that aid our regeneration rather than continually distracting us toward fragmentation and separation.

For illustrative purposes, here is an example of utilizing a tool versus totalizing. The rising interest in blue-green nature economics is based on quantizing nature's ecosystem services into a value-based model that attracts impact investment. If this is applied solely by leaders and practitioners still inured in Mechanistic Materialism, then this quantization of nature ignores the intrinsic sacred quality of nature. 'Ecosystems' and 'bioregions' are mechanized into 'services' that serve human utility. When this rational-analytic undertaking ignores a holistic understanding of the Field, of energy, of systemic and quantum inter-relationality, of the metaphysical dimension of nature with sentient sacredness pervading all ecosystems regardless of their mechanistic utility to humanity, then we are still caught up in Mechanistic Materialism. Regardless of our ecosystem measurements, we are self-as-separate, othering, and projecting the illusion of separation. While the above is trapped in Mechanistic Materialism, the quantization of ecosystem services is not inherently wrong or degenerative. It can be an important tool that serves regeneration by valuing ecosystem services in a way that honors and compliments their innate sacred quality.

To banish, polarize, and judge the mechanistic in this way would be no better than the Scientific Revolution's banishment of the relational and metaphysical dimension of nature. What the metamorphosis into regeneration holds space for is a transcending-and-including of what came before it. Not to be confused with a swinging of the pendulum against history in a purely reactive 'revolutionary' dynamic, this is a responsive, '(r)evolutionary' dynamic that shapeshifts our worldview and our sense of selves. It is metamorphic in that we are integrating earlier phases of the caterpillar into the butterfly. We have a mechanistic left-brain hemisphere for a reason. It ought to serve the more relational and nature-attuned insights of the right-brain hemisphere which is tapped into heart awareness and bodymind coherence.

Back to our blue-green nature economics example. If the rise of impact investment in ecosystem services is a tool that serves the quest for life-affirming futures, then it is a useful tool for the regenerative journey ahead. As long as it finds itself operating within a consciousness that respects life as inherently sacred and intrinsically qualitative (not just quantized/mechanized). The nature economics tool ensures ecosystems are *not* valued at zero and thus plundered without any mechanism of value-based economics to save them from exploitation. Though to merely expand mechanistic domination for impact investment, to mine the last great frontier of capitalism's exploitation of life, is not a regenerative tool.

Discerning the difference between tool and total comes from an inner-knowing of what feels true to our being—an ontological undertaking. If we lack capacity to sense into the subtleties of our own psyches and souls, and the harmonic layers of nature's metaphysical dimension, then this ontological undertaking has not yet happened in us. We are at best gathering at the threshold rather than crossing the threshold into regeneration.

Now, we can see how this metamorphic movement is not a neat and tidy linear transition from mechanistic to regenerative. No, it's more a spiraling inward-outward, transcending-and-including integrative process of reawakening an inner-outer awareness of nature's animating metaphysical quality. A process that invites the modern mechanistic tools to serve our evolving consciousness from ego-centric to life-centric. I refer to this metamorphic movement from Mechanistic Materialism self-as-separate into Quantum Complexity self-as-participatory as a U process of becoming. The U illustrates an inner journey which shifts our ontology (way of being) and epistemology (way of knowing), which we explore further in the next chapter.

This U process applies to mainstream 'Western' society and psyche. 'Western', as it came from the West and yet due to imperialism and globalization it's now dominant throughout the world, although the U process is not necessarily the same for other non-Western cultures. Take Islamic history, where science has never been divorced from spiritual meaning, or the present-day indigenous shamanic cultures, where nature is church and temple. These cultures are engaging with life as an act of worship and reverence with a strong sense of spirit flowing through inner-nature and outer-nature. Hence the ontological clash with Western 'white man' and his diametrically opposed view of nature as profane, a mere utility, for conquest, ownership, and exploitation.

> "The Lakota could despise no creature, for all were of one blood, made by the same hand, and filled with the essence of the Great Mystery. In spirit, the Lakota were humble and meek. 'Blessed are the meek, for they shall inherit the earth'- this was true for the Lakota, and from the earth they inherited secrets long since forgotten. Their religion was sane, natural, and human. The old Lakota was wise. He knew that a man's heart away from nature becomes hard; he knew that lack of respect for growing, living things soon lead to a lack of respect for humans too. The old people came literally to love the soil and they sat or reclined on the ground with a feeling of being close to a mothering power."
>
> –Luther Standing Bear

As we endure an inner U journey and cross the threshold from Mechanistic Materialism into Quantum Complexity, we undertake a return, a remembering within ourselves. We remember the sacred that Luther Standing Bear gives voice to. We sense how inner-outer nature are aspects of a deeper reality we are participating within, never separate from. Dr Iain McGilchrist, neuroscientist, psychiatrist, and polymath, aptly captures this return now starting to form within the Western psyche: (McGilchrist, 2022, Vol 2, p1325)

> "Nature – not some abstract, eviscerated, bureaucratic entity known as 'the environment', which exists to be managed and exploited; not some technical set of mechanisms called an ecosystem; but nature, whose meaning is that-which-is-about-to-be-born, and is feminine – and what's more a goddess. Nature, that, like Kali, is wild, and gives life and destroys – or rather does not destroy, but transforms one being into another; Nature, that is our mother and our healer and our home, as well as our ultimate fate; Nature, that we are reviling and doing our best to devastate – is the great whole to which we belong."

It is clear to me that while the regenerative movement is gaining traction across myriad disciplines, more attention needs to be given to the metaphysical aspect of this necessary (r)evolution. Otherwise, the pull of the mechanistic mind will be too strong for our weak unanchored egos to resist. Only an emerging worldview that is anchored in the psychospiritual depth of nature will contain the power needed to bring forth the regenerative wisdom into humanity's evolution of consciousness. Regenerative leaders and practitioners active during these tumultuous times are being invited to open their hearts and up-stretch their bodyminds to attune with the inherent wisdom in nature and embody the regeneration beyond separation.

This is at once a profoundly personal and embodied experience and a relational and communal affair. Through the inward connection to the metaphysical essence of nature within and all around us, Nature's Wisdom is a simultaneous felt-sense immanence and super-sensory transcendence that engages us with quality beyond quantity and a force without form that informs all form. This multi-layer integration of nature is vital as we journey back home to our true selves.

Today, connecting to nature—whether that be inner-nature or outer-nature—can sound a bit hippy-dippy or a nice-to-have respite from our everyday busyness. Even the word 'spiritual' can invoke an eye roll. But for the vast portion of our human history, we lived at one with nature, and we have a longing, buried deep inside, to be reconnected with the rapture of reality.

Let's still our minds for a moment. Let's reflect on how we modern humans, as a collective across the world, are showing up right now on the streets, in the news, in offices and cafés, along motorways, in airport lounges, in shopping malls, and throughout the various holiday destinations that are encroaching on the most remote corners of the world. We humans are increasingly disconnected and dis-eased. The separation between our inner selves and outer reality is growing at a rapid pace. Walk down the street these days or sit on public transport, and you will no doubt come across people with their eyes locked to their screens or with headphones plugged into their ears, or both.

Continue to pause for a few more moments to contemplate modern humanity. We have mental health issues reaching epidemic proportions, burgeoning new-on-the-scene autoimmune diseases and neurobiological disorders, rising rates of eating disorders, self-harm, and suicide while we busy ourselves sending hundreds of satellites into space to monitor and control our lives, under the guise that we gain more convenience and self-agency. We are always-on, ever-tracked and traced, and at the ready to click purchase, post, take a photo, answer an email, or send a WhatsApp. But to what purpose?

Within each of us lurks a sense of disconnection, which is fueling an insatiable desire to keep busy, buy everything, do more, achieve endlessly, gain a sense of worthiness, feel secure, and try to assert some control over our disconnected experience of life. In our incessant want to quell this insecurity we trample over presence, interrupting each moment with the urge to overcome our own sense of lack. Yet the presence we assault with our lacking expectations is what contains the stillness and connection we desperately seek. The route out of our myriad crises must involve a way inward into this reconciliation with reality.

> "One lives in the midst of a silent sermon all the time."
>
> –Joseph Campbell

Embodying the Shift in Consciousness

In his profound book, *Saving the Appearances*, philosopher Owen Barfield explores the unfolding pattern of consciousness in Western history as a journey from what he calls 'original participation' (Animism), through 'alpha and beta thinking' (Greco-Medieval and Mechanistic Materialism), and into 'final participation' (Quantum Complexity).

BARFIELD'S SHIFT FROM ORIGINAL TO FINAL PARTICIPATION

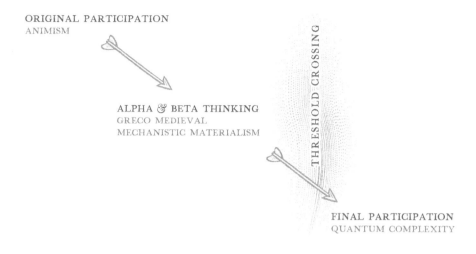

Original participation is an immersive and primal sensory and embodied experience of phenomena. Alpha thinking is where we rationalize, objectify, and define what we experience with phenomena and so abstract it from its lived-in context, and beta thinking is when we reflect on our alpha understanding by bringing in memory of past experiences along with future expectations and conjecture. Final participation is when, after engaging in alpha and beta extrapolations of our original participation, we recontextualize our conscious understanding within its lived-in participatory dynamic of reality. (Barfield)

Barfield's explanation reminds me of McGilchrist's findings on how the left hemisphere and right hemisphere of the brain interact and affect our quality of attention. The right hemisphere sees the world as it is, presencing its dynamic inter-relationality, and the left hemisphere breaks down this wholeness into discrete chunks, mechanizing. When the left hemisphere becomes dominant, we extract ourselves from the lived experience of life. We rationalize and categorize. We sense self-as-separate. (McGilchrist, 2009)

Whereas, with a healthy attentiveness to life, we perceive the world as it is with the right hemisphere (Barfield's original participation) then abstract, rationalize, and reflect with the left hemisphere (Barfield's alpha and beta thinking) and finally put this rational analysis of our lived experience back into its lived-in, embodied context of the right hemisphere (Barfield's final participation). This right-left-right hemispheric rhythm ensures our right relation for regeneration. However, when we get stuck in our own abstraction of the left hemisphere and do not ease its ego-grasp on our sensory experience, we get stuck in separateness, trapped by alpha-beta thinking, and we fail to return into final participation.

Both McGilchrist and Barfield share the view that the rise of left hemispheric dominance (or systemic alpha thinking) began in the West with the advent of the Greco-Medieval worldview. Likewise, both McGilchrist and Barfield view the Scientific Revolution's advent of Mechanistic Materialism as a crucial stage in the Western evolution of consciousness. For Barfield, the Scientific Revolution marked the transformation into what he calls 'modern consciousness', where alpha-beta thinking reigned supreme and original participation, which remained through the Greco-Medieval period, was largely suppressed into the unconscious myth. According to Barfield, "Space, as a mindless, wisdomless, lifeless void, was not a common notion at any time before the Scientific Revolution." (Barfield, p157) Modern consciousness no longer required the inner soul or World Soul because all could be explained through the mechanism of science. Our way of perceiving shifted from immersive, participatory, and integrated to linear, atomized, and materialistic. It's as if the razor-sharp gaze of our 'rational eye' drained the lifeblood from the World Soul, leaving a collection of things to be manipulated for soulless, material betterment.

For a 'return' into Barfield's final participation and McGilchrist's healthy right-left-right hemispheric attention, we must awaken to the transcendent immanence of the sacredness flowing through all of life. In final participation, the objectified method (alpha-beta thinking) of focusing on phenomena 'out there' is enhanced by the perspective of the unfolding 'becoming' of phenomena, a way of perceiving that reveals the integrated inner-outer unfolding of life.

We will soon learn how the many Western phenomenologist philosophers and scientists of the early 20th century paved the way for this (r)evolution toward Barfield's final participation, but for now it's important to recognize that the 'return' from the separateness of alpha-beta thinking to the connectedness of final participation involves not only a shift in how we perceive life, but also a ubiquitous psychospiritual reorientation of how we connect—inwardly with our inner-nature (our own soul and the World Soul) and outwardly when relating with others and the world. This self-other-world healing process expands our connection with life as we learn to grow beyond the psychological dis-ease and find meaning and purpose in nature within and all around us. In doing so, we become more connected, coherent, and wise. We embark on a developmental and evolutionary process in which we learn to flow as life flows, continually trusting and working with Nature's Wisdom.

Our healing from separateness to interconnectedness is at the crux of becoming a regenerative leader. Without this psychospiritual shift, we might be gathering at the threshold, perhaps gesturing toward regeneration through outer activities like net-positive initiatives or self-managing adult-adult ways of working, but we will not actually cross the threshold until we endure this personal yet collective psychospiritual shift. In fact, we cannot cross the threshold without embarking on this metamorphic healing journey. Staying on the surface of things, sticking with outer-nature while ignoring the metaphysical dimension of Nature's Wisdom, is not regenerative. It's a mere continuance of our current Mechanistic Materialistic trajectory, no matter how much it may appropriate biomimetic learnings from nature and apply them to human design for sustainable development goals. To know nature from the inside, involves a reorientation in our being-in-the-world—an ontological shift—which ignites a shift in our way of knowing—an epistemological shift. We can then move from an overly rational-analytic knowledge acquisition to an inner-outer connection through right relation of self-other-world that is both intuitive and rational. This return to wisdom in right relation still involves the ego but now includes the soul of our inner being and the World Soul of inner-nature.

> "As long we are not conscious of the fissure within our own nature, and our catastrophic disconnection from our instinctual soul, we will be driven to seek out and attack an object on which to project our darkness."
>
> —Anne Baring

Finding our True Nature

Adult developmental research shows that as we mature in life, we may reach a point of significant reorientation in how we make sense of our life experiences. This shift affects how we perceive ourselves in relation to others, how we lead and work with the organization we belong to or work for, and our sense of meaning and purpose in the world. The shift can feel like a mid-life crisis and can be quite disorientating as what we thought we knew about leading and operating starts to crumble to allow for new insights to form within us about how the world works and our place within it. It's this life-changing shift that I coach leaders through as they journey toward regenerative leadership. I refer to it as the 'achiever to regenerator' shift. In terms of leadership dynamic, it can be summarized as a shift from a control-manage parent-child dynamic to a sense-respond adult-adult dynamic.

ACHIEVER TO REGENERATOR

ACHIEVER	REGENERATOR
Mechanistic Materialism	Quantum Complexity
Self-as-separate	Self-as-participatory
Control-manage	Sense-respond
Parent-child	Adult-adult
Organization-as-machine	Organization-as-living-system

In my previous book *Leading by Nature* I explore the leadership qualities and capacities invoked during this achiever to regenerator shift, along with the tools and techniques that help aid it. Here I provide an essential overview of the seven main levels of leadership consciousness, which draws upon decades of advanced adult developmental research applied to leadership development. For a fuller exploration of these seven levels and the regenerative leadership capacities of the later stages, see *Leading by Nature* and for some supporting notes to this section about the sensitivity of applying levels of consciousness developmental models to leadership, see the Appendix. (Hutchins, 2022)

THE SEVEN LEVELS OF LEADERSHIP CONSCIOUSNESS

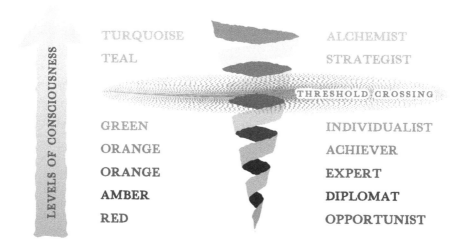

Red-Opportunist – Impulsive, short-termist, narcissistic; leads through dominance and fear. The organization is perceived as a clan exploiting the hostile world around it for self-maximization.

Amber-Diplomat – Order, discipline, conformity; leads through security and sense of belonging. The organization is perceived as a castle, a safe-haven bringing order into the chaos of the world.

Orange-Expert – Technical expertise, efficiency, excellence; leads through data and a quest for perfection. The organization is perceived as a machine to be optimized amid a competitive challenging world.

Orange-Achiever – Entrepreneurial, results-driven, strategic; leads through objectives, team-working, and exploiting market opportunities. The organization is perceived as a machine amid an ever-changing competitive world full of opportunity.

Green-Individualist – Egalitarian, inclusive, stakeholder awareness; leads through emotional intelligence, trust, and empowerment. The organization is perceived as a family amid an ethically-challenged world that needs business to become a force for good.

Teal-Strategist – Systemic, emergent, life-centric; leads through participative multi-stakeholder sensing and responding. The organization is perceived as a living system continuously emerging and adapting amid an interconnected world evolving toward life-affirming futures.

Turquoise-Alchemist – Wisdom, evolution of consciousness, synchronicity; leads through the life-force of the organization and its ecosystem. The organization is perceived as a living system that consciously contributes to the evolution of consciousness.

While it's important to have a sense of all seven stages of leadership consciousness, most of today's senior business leaders are Orange Expert-Achievers and Green Individualists, with an increasing number of leaders embarking on the transition into Teal Strategist. This transition—from Orange Expert-Achiever and Green Individualist to Teal Strategist—is where the important shift in worldview from Mechanistic Materialism to Quantum Complexity takes place. Crossing this threshold is where you will experience a deepening into inner-outer nature together with a shift in organizational perspective (from organization-as-machine to organization-as-living-system) and a shift in leadership dynamic (from control-manage to sense-respond). The transition from Orange-Green into Teal is the achiever to regenerator shift.

It's highly likely, given the fact you are reading this book, that the achiever to regenerator shift is happening in your life. Whether you are conscious of it or not, there may be a metamorphic process of death-rebirth unfolding in you.

This metamorphic process is a journey of self-discovery, of finding our unique destiny and true nature (our dharma) and bringing forth our unique gift of service into the world (cultivating of our soul craft). An inward journey into our own being is also a journey into inner-nature. It's a journey of reorientation that helps us make sense of and read the sacred text hidden within life.

But what does this trip entail? Let's turn to the phenomenologists and philosophers we find in the next chapter.

Returning to the Root of Regeneration

We've already discussed the Field, we are familiar with the notion of the ego, and we are beginning to grasp the soul and World Soul, yet nature's metaphysical inner-nature might be quite uncharted territory. What exactly do we mean by nature's inner-nature? And how does this inner-nature inform how we lead and live regeneratively? To explore these questions, we need to explore how we attend to life itself. We need to explore consciousness.

The topic of consciousness travels well beyond neat and tidy definitions, breaks concrete facts and figures regularly, and defies the ability for words to adequately convey what it is or how it works. What we do know, and many can agree on, is that everyday life is pervaded by some kind of inner dimension. We sense something beyond, before, behind, above, and through ourselves, and that something is a vitality, a life-force, that speaks to us through our super-sensory intuition and imagination. It does not use the language of facts and figures but rather a symbolic numinous synchronistic language. This sense of the sacred calls forth a response in us, a respectful receptivity that flows with a sense of reverence and gratitude, one which gives us meaning and begins our own journey of deepening into inner-nature. For it is there where our true sense of place and purpose in the world can be found.

We'll refer to this dimension as 'inner-nature'.

"Matter and life and consciousness have their 'roots' in a world beyond space and time," notes astronomer Gustaf Strauberg. "In this non-physical realm lies the ultimate origin of all things, of energy, matter, organization of life and even consciousness itself." (Kovacs, p176) We can learn to tap into and work with this ultimate origin of all things and in doing so, we'll get to the root of regeneration.

Not only are the organizing principles of nature found in this inner realm, but so are the organizing principles of the human psyche, as Jung learnt through depth psychology, albeit through a symbolic language which informs the psyche and soul in deep and partially unconscious ways. It's through our own inward U journey that we too can learn to make sense of this sacred text hidden within life. Again, the ancients were aware.

> "As above so below; as within so without."
>
> —Hermes Trismegistus

Jung used the acorn as a symbol of the psyche and soul, unfolding in its psychological potential through its process of becoming an oak tree. "Individual consciousness is only the flower and fruit of a season, sprung from the perennial rhizome beneath the earth; and it would find itself in better accord with the truth if it took the existence of the rhizome into its calculations. For the root matter is the mother of all things." (Jung, 1973)

This rhizome soul-scape is here in our midst, an inner depth to life. The acorn rooted in the rhizome in the soil is destined to return back to the soil at the end of life, like the soul returning into the World Soul ready for reincarnation. Jung called this rhizome 'creative substratum.' We'll call it inner-nature.

We are ever immersed in this substratum, yet modern humanity has severed our conscious contact with it. We need to reconnect with our own root, our inner-nature. "To live fully," said Jung. "We have to reach down and bring back to life the deepest levels of the psyche from which our present consciousness has evolved." (Jung, 1973) This bringing forth from the depths is a psychospiritual maturation journey which Jung calls a process of individuation, a journey which has been symbolized for millennia as a labyrinth. The labyrinth depicts an inward spiraling journey and an outward spiraling journey, illustrating how inner and outer nature work together and in accord with the soul inside us which opens into the World Soul and pervades nature, Earth, and cosmos.

THE LABYRINTH

This inward journey of descent into our own dimensions to bring forth what is within us is the mythological journey that the world myths convey. Mythologist Joseph Campbell researched different myths found throughout the world and arrived at a core myth, a timeless psycho-spiritual kernel common to humanity. The 'monomyth' is a primal pattern of departure ('call to adventure' or *Wintering*), initiation (journeying inward through a death-rebirth process of 'dismemberment' and 'remembering' or *Disintegrating-Reintegrating*), and return (a 'bringing forth' of our true nature, honing our soul craft and then *Serving*).

The monomyth conveys the inner journey of becoming who we truly are by going within in order to bring forth our unique essence and soul craft into the world.

> "If you bring forth what is within you, what is within you will save you. If you do not bring forth what is within you, what is within you will destroy you."
>
> —Jesus Christ

THE MONOMYTH INNER U JOURNEY

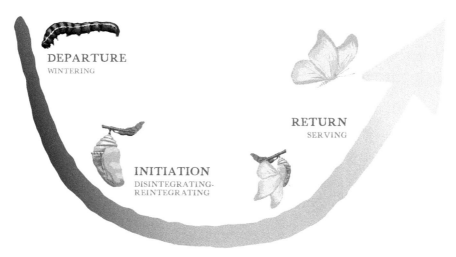

As the pathology of the imbalanced Western psyche becomes increasingly obvious, and the outer-nature of our world becomes increasingly volatile and disruptive, the dissonance this creates inside our psyches beckons a 'call to adventure'. A call to journey inward, to separate from the normalized achiever mode of fixing things 'out there'. This departure from the status quo achiever mode involves entering a 'wintering' inner-journey that is accompanied by all sorts of challenges, treasures, tests, gifts, healers, and helpers.

As we descend into the rhizome, tap into our own soul, integrate the masculine and feminine psychic energies within us, we become more whole. We sense the Source of all things, and in doing so find our own center, the center of the labyrinth, and right relation inside our own selves. When it's time to journey back upward into outer-nature, we are anchored by this sense of center and arrive with newfound insights gleaned from the inner journey. Emerging out from the bottom and traveling up the right-hand side of the U, we not only find right relation within but also without (with others and the world at large). By traversing our own monomyth journey, we act as a living conduit for right relation between inner and outer and live in service to Nature's Wisdom that flows through inner-outer nature. We the achiever have become the regenerator.

The conscious, evolutionary dynamic of life itself is enriched by our own process of becoming who we essentially are through this inner journey. The very act of our becoming a regenerator has a regenerative effect on the consciousness of humanity, the World Soul of nature, and our home the Earth.

Integrating to Individuate

Jung studied in detail the workings of the ego-self in relation to what he called the 'Self' or the soul, essence, or true nature of our being. Jung's 'Self' transcends the ego and is a human manifestation of the World Soul. As Campbell puts it, "The ego is you as you think of yourself. You in relation to all the commitments of your life, as you understand them... The Self is a whole field of potentialities to come through." (Campbell, 1990, p263) The journey of self-realization is a developmental process of unfolding within oneself through a relaxation of our ego's defenses as we open into the world. This is Jung's 'individuation' – the germinating process of breaking through our 'I' ego encapsulation to penetrate the inner soil of our soul rooted in the rhizome of the World Soul. Only then can we enter the field of our natural gifts and potentialities, as we are no longer imprisoned by the delusion of separation or haunted by existential anxiety.

Individuation echoes Aristotle's and Plato's (as well as many other great philosophers') goal of discovering one's truth. It's the inward process of becoming our destiny or dharma. For Jung, the goal of life is the realization of one's own true nature through individuation. This process only comes with the integration of all aspects of our psyche. Even and especially the dark and shadowy suppressed aspects of our unconscious must be allowed to surface and become conscious, which can be a lifelong journey and often begins with a mid-life crisis, a departure from the outer-achiever, and a calling to journeying inward. Without the inner understanding and wisdom that individuation brings, Jung believed that humans are uncentred, uprooted, and adrift in a volatile, windswept world left to cling to material possessions for illusory meaning and fickle happiness. He saw consumerist society as indicative of a lack of authentic meaning, aimlessness at the collective and individual level.

He recognized that these repressed aspects of our psyche (our 'shadow') are frequently projected onto others. We think the problem is out there, but the problem is often in here. As we consciously integrate aspects of our shadowy inner depths by acknowledging and integrating these aspects into our conscious awareness, we embrace a fuller truer Self. In other words, by embarking on a journey to 'Know Thy Self' we individuate.

Jungian analyst, and author of the book *Jung*, Anthony Stevens notes, "To individuate is to realize one's personal existence as a unique expression of humanity and, within the frail vessel of one's little psychic world, to distil the essence of creation. In this microcosmic experiment the great cosmos becomes conscious of itself." (Stevens, p84)

This U journey—this process of individuation—addresses the root of regeneration. The conscious mind is reliant upon the unconscious psyche for its fuller expression, and so too is our everyday ego-consciousness reliant on the eco-psycho-spiritual consciousness of nature for its fuller expression. Going inward comes with a rarefying of the ego. The ego becomes more permeable, gifting us with freer accessibility to our inner-nature of soul within World Soul. How we perceive outer-nature subtly shifts from the objectified focus hallmarked by Mechanistic Materialism to a relationally engaged inner-outer receptivity, and we return to our roots within the rhizome where our inward connection to inner-nature affects our outward attention to outer-nature. The human psychological engagement with animals, plants, and natural surroundings, as well as other humans, transforms as we shift from self-as-separate to self-as-participatory. A self-other-world attunement has taken place.

Becoming Intimate with the Immanence of Life

Ecological psychology (ecopsychology for short) studies the benefits of dissolving the sense of separation from nature that is inherent within the Western mindset. In the words of ecopsychologist Andy Fisher, "Ecopsychologists argue that genuine sanity is grounded in the reality of the natural world; that the ecological crisis signifies a pathological break from this reality, and that the route out of our crisis must therefore involve, among other things, a psychological reconciliation with the living Earth." (Fisher, pXIII)

Research shows that people gain emotional nourishment and enhanced wellbeing, as well as increased levels of concentration, intuition, empathy, and creativity through a healthier engagement with nature. For instance, studies at the University of Wisconsin show that gall bladder patients overlooking nature recovered significantly faster than those with no view of nature, and the Chicago metropolitan district regeneration program evidenced that neighborhoods with easy access to nature recorded significant reduction in dysfunctional behaviors and depression. While this area of study might sound akin to environmental psychology, ecopsychology is quite different. Environmental psychology seeks to understand and value the benefits of nature on the human psyche (such as enhanced health and wellbeing) yet often by perceiving nature as a type of 'resource' for human betterment. Meaning that nature needs to be objectified, measured, and conserved for its anthropocentric value, a viewpoint that leaves the separation between humans and nature largely unchallenged. As for ecopsychology, human-nature integration is its main calling.

By altering our awareness from a left hemispheric, transactional observation of nature into a more balanced right-left-right hemispheric relational felt-sense of nature, the ego sense of separateness from nature will ease. From this new perspective, we will feel an intimacy with nature. We can allow this more expansive state of consciousness and a more porous sense of self to occur through 'presencing'. To presence is to become consciously aware of a heartfelt commingling of felt phenomena—to experience the reciprocal interplay of perceiver and perceived. This intimate embodiment is an ongoing and participatory emergence occurring as each moment unfolds. The ego is permeated, and more of reality comes into our perceptual horizon, which brings with it the potential of a transcendent, other-worldly perspective, like a window of awareness opening beyond our normal space-time existence. Through presencing, we awaken a sense of the sacred, while very much here in-the-now.

The true nature of existence is found not through an objectified analytical analysis of outer-nature but in what arises from inner-nature. Rather than observing nature in a utilitarian or detached abstract way that sees only the objects, names, and outer forms, as we presence we begin to perceive the subtle energies, patterns, relationalities, and rhythms of nature. This intimacy with the immanence of life is a way into Nature's Wisdom.

Attaining such a state of awareness is the beginnings of what shamanic people experience when attuning with consciousness beyond the realm of the human-self and into the realms of other animals, plants, and beyond. This state of eco-psycho-spiritual consciousness comes with an increased sense of reverence for all of life and a reduced sense of separation. It involves a subtle drawing away from the habitual achiever gesture of 'dealing' with the world with a transactional tendency and a moving toward a receptive quality of consciousness that 'senses and responds' to the unfurling flow of life. It's this receptive attentiveness to the flow of life that the school of 'phenomenology' explores.

Phenomenology

As the 19th century ended, German philosopher Edmund Husserl (often thought of as the founding father of 'phenomenology') sought to transcend the objectification of Western science, which prioritized a rational-analytic way of observing nature, by emphasizing the role of empathy, embodied experience, and intuitive feeling. Through an inward and experiential perception, Husserl felt the world could be more truthfully understood, and so he formulated 'phenomenology' as a philosophy. The Greek word *phainomenon* means 'that which shows itself', not the mere appearance of something and its rational analysis of forms, functions, facts, figures, and characteristics but the revealing *experience* as a felt-sense.

In phenomenology, 'experience' is not limited to the sensory qualities of our experience (seeing, hearing, and so on) but includes the significance and meaning our senses arouse such as empathy, imagination, intuition, bodily awareness, and embodied action. These forms of inner-outer experience are what Husserl referred to as 'intentionality' which occurs *through* a given experience and the makeup of its meaning. His philosophy was greatly influenced by Goethe's way of seeing, Stumpf's work on sensory experience, and Hegel's conceptual thinking on the phenomenology of consciousness; however, it was Husserl's assistant, German phenomenologist Martin Heidegger, who further developed this work.

Heidegger felt that Western philosophy had misunderstood what it meant 'to be', to genuinely experience something as opposed to rationally abstracting an understanding of it. For him, a return to practical engagement with reality through lived experience invited an 'un-concealing' of reality. Heidegger viewed the objectified focus on outer-nature as an 'unworlding' of the world, a denaturing which presumes a sense of something lacking, a sense of wanting in us, caused by our fractured perception. This fractured perception isolates us. It uproots us from the intimacy of life, which is what feeds the soul. Unworlding, and Jung's rhizome root is lost.

Heidegger's student Hans-Georg Gadamer and the French phenomenologist Maurice Merleau-Ponty further enriched phenomenology with their own insights, as have many others since. Merleau-Ponty considered phenomenological experience a direct and primitive contact with the world whereupon we experience a 'being-in-the-world', a synergy or communion with reality as our existence continually unfolds. He understood perception as a 'mutual embrace', a conversation between the bodymind and world that reignites our vital embodiment of inner-outer nature. For Merleau-Ponty there is no experience, perception, or self-knowledge without a world to interact with. He viewed the intimacy of our body-world relation like the inhaling and exhaling of air, restricted only by the reflexive abstraction of our ego-consciousness. (Merleau-Ponty)

Through this phenomenology, we can perceive the bodymind as a semi-permeable organ of perception that is in uninterrupted dialogue with the environment reverberating with inner insights and intuitions and with outer changes and events. We are always one with the world we perceive, both inwardly and outwardly. Our bodyminds are not in any way separate from nature but reverberating with and through our sensory and super-sensory perception. It is what contemporary phenomenologist David Abram, refers to as "the reciprocity of the sensuous", as if "the world is perceiving itself through us." (Abram, p66)

For both Heidegger and Merleau-Ponty to 'presence' is to immerse within the 'now', the primordial dimension beyond normal space-time, where the space and time of a moment is transcended into a sacred presence of fully embodied inner-outer awareness. The present expands into a presence, an immersion within a vibrant awareness that is simultaneously immanent and transcendent. Heidegger used the word 'worlding' to express an energetic aliveness as a dynamic presence of the world—presencing as a process. (Watts, p66) Heidegger's philosophy recovers the very natural capacity we have as human beings (which we lost through Mechanistic Materialism) to have a feeling of awe and wonder when presencing life. The radical astonishment of being alive in this immensity of existence.

> "On the top of all the hills, there is silence. In the tops of trees, you feel hardly a breath. The little birds fall silent in the trees. Simply wait. Soon, you too will be silent."
>
> —Johann Wolfgang Goethe

Presencing is the empathic unfolding of a phenomenon or experience. Yet how does one do that? We must move our focus and attention from 'what' is being experienced to the experiencing of the experience, or a certain receiving of the experience. Or what the earlier German philosopher

Goethe referred to as 'active seeing', which is when our perception develops into an active beholding of the unfolding experience within its lived-in ever-changing context. For Goethe, to observe outer-nature one requires a certain purity of inner-nature, a stillness within, free from preoccupation, judgements, or concerns about the past or future, fully receptive to what is unfolding in the moment. Goethe's active seeing goes beyond the normal five senses and into the realm of intuition where the unfurling or becoming of the inner-nature of the phenomenon is perceived. (Bortoft, p17)

We may have experienced this receptivity when, for instance, watching a beautiful sunset, or reaching the top of a mountain and seeing the view, or floating in the ocean, or listening to the owl hoot at dusk. Yet, such a sense of inner-outer connectedness does not have to be limited to brief moments of awe. We can cultivate our consciousness through practice, and in time our inner imagination will participate within the external world more readily and regularly. Our own inner being will develop a stronger connection with outer-nature and allow a full-bodied 'super-nature' experience to occur. As sensuous experiencers—sensate and super-sensate—we can activate an intuitive, heart-and-soul consciousness that lies beyond normal space-time while very much here in-the-now, the eternal shining through into the temporal. This is what I call 'becoming intimate with the immanent and transparent to the transcendent' nature of life.

Becoming Transparent to the Transcendence of Inner-Nature

As we've explored, there is the 'outer' world of form and everyday reality that is sensorial, which we experience through our five senses. In learning to presence through a phenomenological sensorial and embodied deepening into life, our receptivity opens not only to the immanence of life all around us, but also to our inward attentiveness through insight, intuition, and imagination. This is Plato's infamous 'inner turn' where we bend our beam of awareness from outer achieving toward the inner dimension of psyche, soul, and spirit.

We each have a soul, unique to us, which is an aperture—a portal—into the transcendent spirit realm which is not unique to us but common to all. The way we engage with the spirit realm is through the soul, and so opening into the soul (a process referred to as 'opening the Eye of the Heart') helps us become transparent to the transcendent. As the old expression goes 'we switch out the light to see the stars.' This darkness inside is also a place of not-knowing or unknowing.

English poet John Keats spoke of 'negative capability' as we empty ourselves of knowing, or what Zen calls the 'beginner's mind' and what Indian Buddhism, Jainism, and Hinduism calls 'sunyata'. Intuition flourishes only with enough space granted by not knowing. It's through this unknowing that we open into the depths of the soul, a fertile womb-like space. This requires a relaxation of the ego, a surrendering and letting go into the self. Meanwhile, we remain alert to a true source beyond thinking, a ground of all being within and throughout. This transcendent realm beyond all thinking is where we can gain insights to bring back into the thinking realm, all the while being mindful of our ego's right relation with this soulful depth.

Surrendering down into the dark depths of our own soul to access Nature's Wisdom is quite different from the presencing aliveness of our intimacy with the immanence of life, yet both intimacy with the immanent and transparency to the transcendent work together to enable the root of regeneration to grow strong within us.

There are two ways into Nature's Wisdom, that correspond with two aspects of 'gnosis', meaning 'to know' which is not simply a head-based knowing but a knowing in the heart and soul, a 'psychospiritual knowing'. There's 'positive gnosis' and 'negative gnosis.' Positive gnosis refers to the insight we glean from becoming intimate with the immanent, and negative gnosis to the insight we glean from turning inward toward the transcendent dimension. Swiss alchemist Paracelsus defined these two ways into gnosis as 'the light of nature' (positive gnosis), and 'the light of revelation' (negative gnosis). (Bamford, p218) Here we work with both these ways into gnosis, by dwelling deep within outer *and* inner-nature, both intimacy with the immanent *and* transparency to the transcendent. Here, Goethe's active seeing aids us with an intuitive and imaginative yet also rational and empirical observation to alter our normal perception and allow for an embodied engagement with the phenomenon's outer and inner-nature. Hence why Goethe referred to this way of attending as "gentle empiricism" which calls for a "heightening of the spiritual powers." (Bamford, p239)

The ability to blend the positive gnosis of phenomenological presencing with the negative gnosis of imaginal insight—the light of nature *and* the light of revelation—is not dissimilar to Aristotle's and Plato's 'contemplative thinking' explored at the dawn of Western civilization as formative in *eudemonia*. This infusion of immanence and transcendence lies at the root of regeneration and involves the 'activating of our super-nature', which we shall delve into shortly. First, let's spend a moment on the imaginal insight gleaned from becoming transparent to the transcendent.

Thanks to the work of the 20th century French philosopher Henri Corbin, the West had its eyes opened to the existence of an intermediary realm between the immanent realm of everyday awareness and the transcendent realm of spirit. Corbin studied the spiritual science of Shiite philosophy, which had developed in the Eastern Muslim world, and brought the concept of the Imaginal Realm and Creative Imagination (as developed by the Sufi Master Ibn Arabi) to the West.

The Imaginal Realm stands between the two worlds—our sensory immanence and the super-sensory transcendent Field. In cultivating the inner capacity for Creative Imagination, we can work with this intermediary Imaginal Realm and so draw out insights from the transcendent dimension and bring these insights into the immanence of everyday life through our thoughts, words, and deeds, and so work with the deep rhythms innate within inner-nature *and* find accord with Nature's Wisdom.

We explore working with this Creative Imagination in Chapter 7. For now, suffice it to say that there is an intermediary twilight zone between our everyday waking consciousness and the deeper transcendent Field which we can learn to access through our own inner awareness. One way into this twilight zone is through activating our super-nature.

Activating Our Super-Nature

The German philosopher, Rudolf Steiner, studied Goethe's work and brought aspects of it into his own philosophy and metaphysical approach to nature and human nature, which he called 'anthroposophy' or 'the wisdom of the human being'. Steiner's anthroposophic approach is a psychospiritual path of development that involves opening our receptivity to inner-outer nature through both a phenomenological sensorial and embodied presencing, plus a psychospiritual deepening that awakens our super-sensory intuition. This awakening in awareness is what I call activating our super-nature, whereupon we learn to work with sensorial and super-sensory faculties that enable us to receive Nature's Wisdom.

As we activate our super-nature, we begin to sense how the bodymind is an exquisite sensing-responding instrument that detects and cocreates within a sea of self and systemic rhythms, ripples, and repercussions infused by the Field of consciousness that we are always immersed within. Through this inward and outward sensitivity to life, we can discern between the sensations that are helpful and informative to our own growth and development and the growth and development of others (regenerative) and those sensations that are distracting, polluting, and unbeneficial for one's own evolution and the evolution of others (degenerative).

> "The seat of the soul is there where the inner and the outer worlds meet."
>
> —Novalis

There are many depths to human awareness, and no matter how good the book about consciousness is, the book can never beat the reality of becoming more intimate with our own everyday life experiences. If life is teaching us one thing, it's to experience life more fully as it is and learn from the experience to bring forth more of who we truly are.

Seeing Through the Three Lenses

Over many years of coaching senior leaders through their own unique inner journeys, I have found a model that I call 'the three lenses' to be useful. The three lenses are dimensions of awareness that filter our experience of life. The self-inquiry practice of noticing these three lenses aids the inner journey.

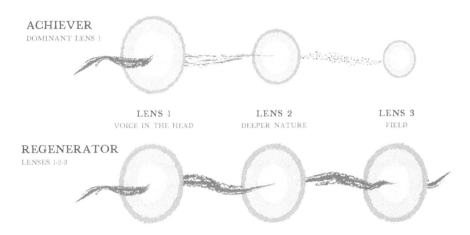

The Three Lenses

Lens 1 – Voice in the Head

Lens 1 is the ego or the 'voice in the head,' which filters much of our experience of life, and it likes to judge, critique, and chat inside the head pretty much all the time.

As we become more intimate with our own awareness, we can start to notice how much we are caught up in Lens 1. The voice in the head provides a running commentary about our experiences, emotions, and the things people say that trigger us. This affects our experience of life as it pulls our awareness out of the present moment. To presence—or to be present—is to free oneself from the voice in the head, if but for brief moments.

When the bodymind is no longer constrained by the voice in the head, it is freer, more vulnerable, and undefended in its relational flow of energy and information and with what is arising within and all around it, and therefore more able to sense-respond. This can be aided by mindful meditation, contemplation, and self-reflection practices which help us notice, tame, and train the voice in the head.

As we learn to ease the voice in the head and to presence life more, we open our way into Lens 2.

Lens 2   Deeper Nature

The more we notice and quieten the voice in the head, the larger the non-judgmental space of observation within us grows. This expansive, present moment awareness provides for increased sensitivity to systemic dynamics within and all around us, allowing Lens 2 to open us up to inner constrictions, shadow projections, trauma, psychological wounds, our inner child, inner purposefulness, and dharma. Once we attend to this inner 'stuff' through our deeper nature we have embarked on Jung's process of individuation, and we begin to Know Thy Self.

This journey inward is not at all straightforward, nor is it a plain sail. It's where we must face up to much of what we have shied away from or suppressed earlier in life. But as we come to terms with our own selves, we release psychic energy and integrate aspects of our selves that enable us to become more whole, purposeful, and authentic as a regenerative leader.

Looking through the lens of our deeper nature, we notice a profound spaciousness underpinning all our thoughts, feelings, constrictions, and perturbations. We start to feel less 'in the head' and more embodied, grounded and centered. Practices like bodymind coherence (discussed in the next chapter) and phenomenological presencing (mentioned earlier) aid this spacious yet grounded sensation. Enter Lens 3.

Lens 3 – The Field

Lens 3 opens us into the Field, where we find a vast, numinous depth that feels like bliss yet is quite beyond words. Lens 3 is also where Nature's Wisdom can be sensed. While advanced meditation practices can help us arrive here – as can the practices of active seeing, Heart Entrainment and the Creative Imagination Process – short-lived moments of this expansive transcendent feeling (like epiphanies) can happen at any time in our lives. The journey inward, when supplemented with practices that regularly activate our super-nature, opens our entire life experience to a transparency with the transcendent dimension through Lens 3. While we are still very much in the here-and-now, we start to sense a numinous eternal dimension shining through. This immanent-transcendent experience is no longer a short-lived epiphany but begins to infuse our whole way of being, knowing, and experiencing life. We realize that an epiphany is woven into the immanent-transcendent fabric of our everyday experience, brought in through a receptive Lens 3, which pours into Lenses 2 and 1. This enriches the sense of meaning in our lives from the inside out and, if sustained through dedicated practice, fuels the up-stretch in our ego stage development from achiever to regenerator.

It's in this conscious state of opening to and integrating Lenses 1-2-3 that we activate our super-nature and can readily call upon our different ways of knowing with ease—intuitive, rational, emotional, and somatic—and flow with the more subtle currents of the Field. This is the ego permeation and ego maturation we mentioned in Chapter 2. Here we attune to the universal life-force that is flowing through us all the time, immanent to all living beings yet transcending space-time.

The potency of this life-force for purposeful living has been recognized throughout the ages. In the Far East this life-force is referred to as 'chi', in India 'prana', in Polynesia 'mana', in Europe courtesy of the French philosopher Henri Burgeson it's often called 'elan vital.' It's through this life-force that Nature's Wisdom flows. Think of a vibrating guitar string being the life-force current which contains the potential for different harmonics, overtones, and undertones. The vibratory life-force emanating from the string contains harmonic wisdom—Nature's Wisdom—which we can learn to make melody and meaning with.

To bring this analogy into practical daily life, imagine we have a brief epiphany, a light-bulb moment. This experience of the moment is simultaneously other-worldly, numinous, and spacious as well as intensely vivid, as if our senses are briefly enlivened. Amid this moment, we are dwelling deeper within the immanent-transcendent nature of life than normal, and knowingness comes into us, whether it be a sensate feeling, a depth of emotion, or a flash of clarity. Everything makes sense, and we gain meaning. This meaning-making moment might be practically bound to a specific task we are focused on, like a project or design challenge, a commercial deal, or a relational tension. We gain a realization, a knowing, about how to move forward, and any impatience or frustration releases. We trust in life, and from oppositional dichotomy and knotted stuckness comes flow. The knowingness may just as likely arise through a less practical and more philosophic insight which is no less meaningful though provides a more generalized awakening in how we perceive the project, deal, or relational pathway in relation to our authenticity and soul-path unfolding through the activity.

Hidden connections become apparent along with a sense of synchronistic right timing, of rhythm and resonance, and an intuition on what is a right or wrong way ahead. The ego 'I' listens and works in right relation with heart and soul-consciousness, and this right relationality of Lenses 1-2-3 infuses our inter-relationality with others. We become sensitized to the synchronistic immanent-transcendent rhythms and resonances of Nature's Wisdom. Using our guitar string analogy, we hear the trueness of the melody and find our inner coherence to play in tune with life.

The Lenses 1-2-3 integration process is a threshold-crossing that is both personal and transpersonal in nature; a simultaneous ego maturation (intimacy) that deepens our personal presence and intimacy within the immanence of life and ego permeation (transparency) that opens us into the transpersonal dimension of Nature's Wisdom within and all around us. Our personal psyche opens into a receptivity of inner-outer when Lens 1's ego-consciousness opens into our deeper nature of Lens 2's embodied heart-consciousness, and then reverberates with Lens 3's soul-consciousness opening into the World Soul and Field.

Inner-outer receptive presencing in this way is a rich, profound experience, quite beyond words. We also find that this occurs during our transition from achiever to regenerator and profoundly shifts our self-and-systemic awareness. In learning how to open our self-awareness beyond Lens 1 and into 2 & 3, we broaden our perceptual horizon and intensify our sensitivity to systemic and quantum field dynamics. Ultimately, we develop and improve our ability to embrace tensions and complexity, work with hidden ordering forces, and sense synchronicities all around us in everyday life.

> "The greatest voyage of our lifetimes is not in the seeing of new landscapes but in the seeing with new eyes."
>
> —Marcel Proust

As French philosopher Proust knew, this is the greatest voyage of our lifetimes. With it comes emancipation—a free flow of psychic energy that cleanses our psychology from constrictions as we learn to flow as life flows. The further we immerse ourselves in this aliveness, the further our awareness reaches. We attune and fall into the flow of inner-outer nature, inwardly attentive to the psychospiritual energies within nature and outwardly sensitive to presencing everything around us.

Assisted by this phenomenological and psychospiritual 'super-nature' way of perceiving, each moment can be viewed as an opportunity for presencing, giving us a camera with a deeper aperture for sensing reality. Interestingly, when we seek to control, analyze, and manipulate this unfolding participation the state of presence is lost, and we close down the co-creative flow with our narrow-mindedness. It's as if this way into the sacredness of life is foolproof from mechanistic ego-machinations.

Rather than the narrow or mechanized mind that sees only an object or subject, presencing allows us to relate to the experience with empathic 'betweenness'. With an empathic sharing, a relating with 'other', a healing of any sense of separation from 'other' can occur. We can then perceive a receptive *and* responsive, spatial *and* energetic, right hemisphere *and* left hemisphere, heart *and* head relationship with reality. We become expressions within, rather than separate from, nature.

Heidegger referred to this reciprocity with the world as 'authenticity', where one becomes authentically engaged within the world by fully engaging 'through' inner-outer nature. We start to perceive the world as it really is—spatially and dynamically continuous, inwardly and outwardly related. Authenticity helps us cross the threshold from achiever, who is outer-oriented and often has a hurried, self-centered, competitive, manipulative engagement with our world, to regenerator, who is inner-outer oriented and has an empathic, embodied, collaborative, reciprocal engagement with the world.

> "When we tie in with the life-force it rights us from our distractions and reconnects us to the rapture of life."
>
> —Richard Strozzi-Heckler

Recall how the myth of survival became a dominant assumption during Mechanistic Materialism. As we return, we reawaken the myth of meaning to cohabit with the myth of survival. We start to see that we—and other living beings—are not mere 'adapters' to life, like Darwin's fitting into the environment for survival assumes. We begin to see that with Nature's Wisdom flowing through us, we are co-creative participants in a profoundly sentient and sacred experience full of meaning.

Life is seen for what it is—an awesome learning experience of meaning-making and potentializing, revealing in us new levels of freedom, expression, novelty, and diversity while increasing our awareness of Source itself as the impulse of consciousness coming into being. From limitless potential this life-force works with the power of limits, and our bodymind vehicle is an exquisite instrument for consciousness to see itself and evolve through greater levels of freedom and order.

> "What is within us is within everything. Once we understand this truth, we step outside of the parameters of our individual self and come to realize the power that is within us. This shift in awareness is a very simple step that has profound consequences."
>
> –Llewellyn Vaughan-Lee

Embarking on the Sacred Journey of Life

The shifting of our consciousness in becoming more intimate with the immanent and more transparent to the transcendent is central to the achiever to regenerator shift. It's quite a subtle, embodied felt-sense shift that can happen for brief moments in our lives (mini epiphanies and peak experiences). By enduring an inward metamorphic journey and engaging in advanced practices, we can allow this consciousness to become more available to us, so it's no longer a brief moment but always accessible throughout day-to-day busyness. This is the hard-won learning journey of embodying regenerative leadership consciousness. It's a never-ending journey, where the point of the journey is not to arrive but to embrace the journey itself.

I symbolize this sacred journey that we undergo with the ancient symbol of the labyrinth, which has been found throughout the world and throughout different cultures and civilizations, from East and West, North and South. The earliest known finding is dated to around 26,000 years ago, a labyrinth symbol found on a Woolly Mammoth's tooth.

The labyrinth represents a twisting, turning, journey of going within, a journey of descent from the outer visible world into the invisible realm found within. Through this journey of descent, we find challenge, tension, learning, healing, and integration. At the center of the labyrinth is the central point of our own true nature—the soul— and also the center point of life as a sacred experience, where the eternal moment meets the temporal, where our sense of life opens to a dimension beyond normal space-time. From this center, the meaning of life, and our sense of place and purpose in the world comes through from the World Soul into the soul to provide illumination into our bodymind. By integrating the masculine and feminine energies within our soul and psyche, inner-outer nature cohere and the central point of the labyrinth brings forth from the World Soul what is within us, through us, all around us—Nature's Wisdom. This is a deep act of love with life and with our own selves.

We are guided through the labyrinth by 'opening the Eye of the Heart' an activating of the spiritual organ of the bodymind centralized in the heart yet emanating throughout the subtle energy system of the entire bodymind, linking with the third eye and the gut or 'hara' as it's known in the East. This opening of the Eye of the Heart increases our capacity to sense the deeper powers and resonances at play in inner-outer nature. We gain the inner gifts of seeing with new eyes and of embodying a deep sense of knowingness—immanent-transcendent gnosis. On our way back out of the labyrinth we return into the normal realm of everyday business, honing our soul craft in service of life, whereupon we can work with integrated Lenses 1-2-3 ego-heart-soul consciousness. We live into the epiphany.

OPENING THE EYE OF THE HEART

INTEGRATED LENSES 1-2-3

EGO-HEART-SOUL
CONSCIOUSNESS

IMMANENT-TRANSCENDENT

This journey into the inner-nature of life not only sacralizes our everyday experience, but it also enriches our way of relating to those around us. Our self-other-world relation up-stretches from achiever to regenerator. We learn to work with Nature's Wisdom through this deep act of love.

In Part 3 we explore Foundations and Soil Conditions aimed at cultivating the capacity to bring in this quality of inner-outer awareness into everyday living and leading, but in this next chapter we continue with consciousness, as we turn to recent neuroscientific findings about the human brain with respect to the shift from achiever to regenerator.

Human Nature & Awakening our Minds

A core premise of Mechanistic Materialism is that human beings have minds that are separate from nature. True, our human minds have the capacity to create a sense of separateness through the ego, but that they are separate is an illusion, a mere figment of our own minds. What Quantum Complexity research into consciousness shows, and corroborates with what the ancients long knew, is that consciousness pervades nature, and our individual minds reverberate within the field of consciousness. (Laszlo, E., Currivan) Separation is not really how life is.

The self-reflexive capacity of the ego remains an important tool for us as human beings, but as we have seen already, it is only a tool. A vital step on the journey toward regeneration is when we recognize that we are not isolated psyches bouncing around in a world of separateness, but rather we have egos as tools to aid our self-agency and self-reflexivity so that we can learn. Our primary learning now—individually and collectively—is to learn how to attune with the deeper rhythms and song lines innate within nature. In doing so, we find right relation and realize our destiny.

Let's take a closer look at the human brain, as its functions can provide insight on how we might help our human consciousness ease out of separateness and into right relation.

Attending to the Tensions in the Human Brain

Much like the ancient yin-yang symbol, we find a tension in the brain between two opposing attention networks that either work together in harmony or struggle with imbalance.

DORSAL-VENTRAL

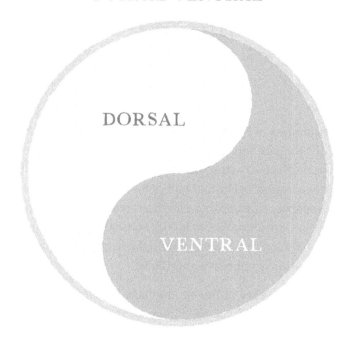

The two attention networks in the brain are the dorsal attention network and the ventral attention network. And for the achiever leader, the tension between the two is frequently out of balance. There's too much dorsal and not enough ventral.

ACHIEVER IMBALANCE OF DORSAL-VENTRAL

Before we explore the dorsal and ventral networks in more detail, let's first explain a little about how the brain relies on 'attention'. As mentioned earlier, the brain has a limiting function to filter out a whole sea of sensory, energetic, and informational stimuli from outside in the physical world and a whole sea of inner stimuli that includes somatic and emotional sensations, rational expectations and goal planning, and intuition, insight, and imagination, not to mention the ruminating voice in the head's incessant chatter. How the brain gives 'attention' to the variety of outer and inner stimuli available has been categorized in neuroscience as 'bottom-up' attention, referring to attentional guidance purely by externally driven factors, and 'top-down' attention, referring to internal guidance of attention based on prior knowledge, willful plans, current goals, and expectations. (Katsuki) Recent brain imagining studies show that this categorization of bottom-up and top-down attention doesn't neatly align with how the dorsal and ventral attention networks in the brain light up. We can't say, for instance, that the dorsal attends only to top-down planning and goal-orientation, because both networks and their neural circuits are used in both top-down goals and bottom-up sensory stimulation. (Vossel) What's important for our exploration is less about the networks' relation to the categories of top-down or bottom-up but more so how they influence our consciousness, and therefore affect our psychospiritual sensitivity.

The dorsal network has a narrowing effect on our consciousness (similar to how the left-brain hemisphere displays a narrowing tendency) and the ventral network has an opening effect on our consciousness (similar to how the right-brain hemisphere expands). Just as we need the left and right hemispheres working together, we need both the dorsal and ventral networks working together. Think of two hands on the piano playing music together, each doing separate activities and attending in different ways, yet making music together. The challenge comes when one hand of the piano—one attention network or brain hemisphere—tries to dominate the other, as then we find a lopsided, imbalanced presence in the music. It's this imbalance, alas, that occurs all too easily in the dorsal and ventral attention networks of the achiever leader.

The Dorsal System

Studies using FMRI (functional magnetic resonance imaging) show that the insula of the neocortex, along with the subcortical striatum region, both of which are located in the top, front part of the brain, are activated when the dorsal attention network is active. Dorsal provides for a sense of striving, a focus on getting the job done, narrowing down on the goal, and achieving it. Essentially, dorsal is an intensified ego-consciousness that encourages left hemisphere domination and high beta brainwave frequencies. While all of this taken together helps us get the job done, home in on, and achieve, the dorsal attention system also takes us out of the natural flow of life. Its hyper focus distracts us and pulls us away from the inner depth of nature. Rather than presencing the moment, through this attention system we are analyzing, separating, and compartmentalizing, which in turn heightens the sense of self-as-separate.

On closer inspection, we find that the dorsal attention system is an inhibitory filter, in that it filters out what is deemed unnecessary for achieving the goal. It reduces our receptivity to wider reality to help us focus on the task at hand. For this reason, neuroscientists have called the dorsal system the 'achiever mind', as it's continually selectively scanning the environment for what might aid the achievement of the goal. It shapes an outcome-orientated, utilitarian, transactional, outer-focused attention. (Miller)

The dorsal attention system is a powerful tool we need to have available to us as leaders. Nothing wrong with it, except when it becomes too dominant. For then, our attention is hyper focused and in the always-on mode, extracting us from the flow of life and forming habitual patterns of outer-achievement, recognition-reward, anxiety, grasping, addictive-personality, imposter syndrome, insecurity, emotional dysfunction, and fear.

Neuroscientist Iain McGilchrist has extensively studied the two hemispheres of the brain: left hemisphere (abstracting life by narrowing down and focusing in) and right hemisphere (presencing life as it is in full relationality). (McGilchrist, 2009) The more we're in the achiever mind, the more the left hemisphere grasps and homes in on what needs to be achieved, and the less the right hemisphere can presence the relational nature of the systems we are leading and operating within. Our sense of ego 'I' accentuates to the extent that we start to lose our sense of self as immersed in life. This further encourages high beta brainwaves, and thus more anxiety and a greater perceived need to achieve.

In a high beta brain state, we trigger three inner voices that play out in Lens 1's voice in the head. Leadership specialist Otto Scharmer refers to them as the voice of judgement, the voice of cynicism, and the voice of fear. (Scharmer, 2016) There's nothing inherently negative about them. They speak to us all the time, keeping us safe from potential danger. It is only when we get stuck in a vicious cycle of dominant dorsal, high beta, left hemisphere, achiever mind that these three voices can be overly triggered. The patterns of reactivity that any one or all three create can overwhelm us with a rising emotional frustration or anger, leading to an amygdala hijack. As the heat of the moment sends us into a fight-flight-freeze reaction, we either seek to dominate or be a victim. If this pattern becomes a habit, it encourages parent-child control-manage leadership dynamics rather than adult-adult sense-respond dynamics, leaving us stuck in achiever and struggling to find our way to regenerator.

Clinical psychologist professor at Columbia University, Dr Lisa Miller, has comprehensive research to show how this overly dominant achiever mind creates all sorts of problems for us—never feeling satisfied, always insecure, obsessive—which undermine our capacity to adapt to the ever-changing and increasingly volatile nature of life. Instead of learning to flow with life, we are frustrated and distressed. We get stuck ruminating, worrying, and needing to control outcomes. We relentlessly cycle through motivation, reward, insecurity, and fear, draining us and taking us away from our sense of meaning and purpose. We become hamsters on the treadmill of outer-achieving, running fast but never questioning to what end other than a sense of security, recognition, and reward.

When caught up in an overly dominant achiever mind, we are more easily distracted. A major distraction these days is 'digital distraction' which is not just emails and text messages but the always-on streams of WhatsApp, Twitter, Instagram, Facebook messenger, Teams messages, Slack channels, LinkedIn, Medium, YouTube, and you name it. Now, if we are grounded in our true nature, these can be seen as tech communication tools we can pick up and put down, aiding our purposefulness. But when the activated dorsal attention system of the achiever mind feeds on the recognition and reward received each time there's a view or like on a social media post or a message appears in the inbox, then our attention gets caught up in the need to check and respond to the post or message. We're reactive.

These digital distractions pull us in, and we all too easily show signs of addiction to the distraction when in dominant achiever mind. Scientific studies show that our incessant urges to keep checking in, again and again, are fueled by neurochemical dopamine hits in the brain. These short-lived highs do nothing for our real wellbeing. In fact, they do the opposite by creating a creeping sclerosis of the soul, as the voice in the head becomes noisier with the distraction.

USC psychologist Albert Ritzo has researched how a dominant achiever mind is in a constant state of 'impression management' projecting a version of the ego 'I' on to the world. (Kotler & Wheal p101) Harvard Business School professors Robert Kegan and Lisa Lahey have also studied how most leaders and employees today are hooked on this impression management. As a result, most leaders and team members are doing a second job no one is paying them for—the job of managing other people's impressions of themselves, covering up uncertainties, playing politics, and hiding their true selves at work. (Kegan & Lahey) This is destroying productivity, resilience, innovation, initiative, and trust. The root cause? An overly dominant achiever mind.

The dominance of the achiever mind lies at the heart of our myriad crises today. Born from an imbalance in our own minds, when left unchecked it manifests as anxiety, fear, greed, narcissism, individualism, and consumerism. No doubt as leaders we can recall moments of experiencing some, if not all, of these trademarks of the achiever mind. The spiraling and vicious cycles of inward worry countered by outward action, or imposter syndrome countered by impression management. When our outer actions become infused with inauthenticity and impatient grasping motivated by transactional, superficial neediness rather than a genuine purposefulness, right relation of self-other-world unravels as self-as-separate reigns supreme. This is ego-consciousness firmly in the driver's seat of our lives.

The Ventral Network

The ventral attention system is the opposite of the achiever and has been likened to the 'awakened mind', in that it opens our perceptual horizon. It softens the focus on the goal while allowing us to pick up insights, synchronicities, intuitions, and epiphanies. This attention network helps the ego to permeate, to open its 'I' and reduce our sense of self-as-separate. Ventral goes hand-in-hand with the right hemisphere's expansive capacity to presence the wholeness of life, sense the interconnectedness of our selves immersed within life, and perceive the depth of life beyond surface appearances. And so, through our ventral attention network, we can become more intimate with the immanence and more transparent to the transcendence of life. We sense inner-outer nature in this state, and this spacious depth of receptivity provides for a relaxed and flowing sense of self-as-participating. In place of a dominating ego-consciousness in the driver's seat, we find heart-soul consciousness—a more embodied empathic connection with the world—at the helm.

Awakening the ventral network broadens what we perceive as informative, useful, and meaning-making. It's less acquisitive and goal-orientated and more open to insight, new pathways, inner knowing, developmental learning, synchronicities, and inner guidance. It brings us the ability of connecting to something larger in the world. Immanence and transcendence happen through this system, and we gain a greater sense of purposefulness. In concert, this improves our hormonal systems and our emotional outlook, and increases our bodymind's repair and renewal rates. We find it easier to flex and flow with changes in our environment, to bounce back from setbacks, and to learn and move on without getting ensnared in the fight-flight-freeze, anger-blame-judgement victim cycles. We become happier and healthier with the attention of the ventral network.

Research shows that when we are in this awakened mind, the parietal region of the brain emits alpha brainwaves. Beta waves are still present, but alpha frequencies increase. Interestingly, alpha is the predominant resonance we find in nature. As Dr Miller notes, "alpha is everywhere… it's the wavelength of the oneness of all life." (Miller, p215) The 'Schumann resonance' (after the scientist who first scientifically verified it) is alpha wave pulsations found throughout the natural world, referred to as 'the heartbeat of the Earth'. This alpha resonance is thought to be vital for the flourishing of all life on Earth.

I find it interesting that as we move into the ventral's awakened mind, and ease out of the dominance of the dorsal's singular, outward achiever focus, we also find resonance with the Earth. The more we awaken our parietal region to alpha frequencies, the more we attune with life, and the more connected we feel. Our psychological and physiological inner-nature starts to attune with the outer-nature of the Earth, and we rejoin life—a return—and in doing so we rejoice and regenerate. We find right relation. We live in alignment. Our inner bodymind instrument finds harmony with the song of the Earth and Universe.

In this awakened mind we can drop behind the noisy voice in the head of Lens 1 and open into Lenses 2 and 3. We reduce the sense of separation or 'othering' and more easily empathize and connect with other humans, hold space for tensions of difference, listen and share more, and engage in dialogue in an openhearted, presencing manner. We increase our relationality with the systems around us and the interconnectedness with all of life.

It's not that the ventral network is good and the dorsal network bad. This is not to polarize. As depicted by the yin-yang, there is a choice here to struggle with imbalance or to harmonize. Take, for example, early morning routines. Wake up to the alarm, and as soon as those first sips of coffee hit, we flick straight into the dorsal system and dive into emails and social media. Or we rise, perhaps a little earlier and to a different sounding alarm. We feel our feet on the floor, take a few deep breaths, maybe practice a meditation or body movement routine like yoga or chi gung, and make a ritual of finishing the first cup of coffee (or herbal tea) as we take in the day, the weather through the window, the sensation of sunlight on the skin.

There are a host of practices that ease the habitual dominance of the dorsal and bring the ventral on stream more frequently (see the Appendix and my *website*). These practices can be called upon throughout the busy day to help us rebalance our attention systems. For instance, deep belly breathing. Just three deep breaths from the belly at the start of a meeting (or why not also during a meeting) can shift our brainwaves. Through these practices, the regenerative leader can learn to toggle between both the achiever mind's goal driven awareness and the awakened mind's presencing spaciousness.

BRAIN COHERENCE

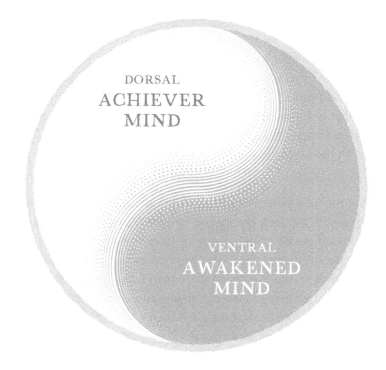

Entering Flow-States and the Potential Pitfalls of Bio-Hacking

In learning to activate the awakened mind more readily during the working day, we experience what psychologists have called 'flow-state' where we feel in flow, simultaneously focused on the task yet open to thinking laterally and sensing systemically. Studies show that when in a flow-state we problem solve far quicker, have enhanced pattern recognition, form connections and trust with others, engender a sense of purpose in teams, and perform up to 500% better in complex, fast-changing environments. Novelty, creativity, heightened perception, amplified connection, and systemic meaning-making all come on stream. Not only are we better at regulating our own nervous systems and overall bio-circuitry, priming us for agility and purposefulness, but studies show that in this flow-state we help other people regulate themselves better. It seems that merely through our presence, our awakened bodymind coherence positively effects those around us to aid their flow. Imagine all the benefits this provides the team and organization in terms of performance, systemic agility, creativity, purposefulness, and innovation. (Kotler & Wheal)

Little wonder then that the corridors of power across corporations and governments have become interested in what's now referred to as the 'Altered State Economy' which is burgeoning by the day. Over the last couple of decades, significant advancements have been made in neurotech. It's estimated that each year at least $4 trillion is spent globally by businesses, governments, and wealthy consumers on a host of technologies and tools to train the brain to reach a higher state of mind. Red Bull's Hacking Creativity Project, the US Navy Seal's Mind Gyms, Google's multimillion dollar mind center, Silicon Valley startups like Consciousness Hacking, research projects funded by NASA and MIT—these are just a handful of the more well-known examples in the US alone. From the military to marketeers, powerful public-private consortia are forming to manufacture the mechanics of flow with tools like transcranial magnetic simulation headsets, brain stimulating ultrasound tools, and nootropic pharmacological investments into mind-melding smart drugs, all seeking to calm the achiever mind and stimulate the awakened mind. What used to be experienced through months of dedicated contemplative practice can now be artificially stimulated in minutes. (Kotler & Wheal)

To what end? one might ask. What's the intention behind the insatiable desire of the fast growing $4 trillion Altered State Economy? The quest for human awakening, freedom from oppression, the cocreation of regenerative futures that benefit all life on Earth? Perhaps some initiatives might hold this intention, but vast swaths of this burgeoning economy are driven by the very power-control outer-achieving egoic dynamic inherent in the achiever mind seeking to be tamed. There are commercial motives too. Studies now show how Americans who have a regular mindfulness-based practice of some kind can save employers an estimated $2,000 a year in healthcare costs while gaining $3,000 a year more for the employer through enhanced performance. (Kotler & Wheal, p175) While there's no mal intent in seeking to enhance performance and efficiency, one does have to be careful of commercial or egoic power-control motives that are manufacturing mindsets.

One danger often overlooked is that of ego-inflation. When short-cut, bio-hacking shifts in consciousness are overused and not adequately integrated into a more enduring process of individuation for the individual, the ego can hijack the increased energy and insight gained as one's bandwidth of meaning-making is shocked into expanding. Meaning that if a more dedicated process of working on one's self has been bypassed, then the ego inflates and takes center stage, and we may feel we are at the center of the universe. We develop God complexes.

Or just as likely, is the ego's addiction to pleasure seeking, getting hooked on the flow-state itself as a blissful experience. Rather than working with the flow-state to engage in right relation and partake in regenerative ways, we become bliss junkies. Just look at how many uber wealthy people seem addicted to the next pleasure high, whether it be the flow experience of extreme sports or the spiritual materialism of attending one retreat after the next. The ego is still firmly in the driver's seat, and we've done nothing to usurp its control over us. Rather than the short-lived highs giving us insights into how we can become more soulful and heart-centered, we merely seek out the next high, remaining firmly in achiever, exploiting our own selves, others, and the wider system of life to fund decadent bliss. Such spiritual bypassing sidesteps unresolved personal issues and unfinished developmental processes. The mundanity of everyday life with its triggers and vulnerabilities is shunned for the next flow inducing experience. The Altered State Economy could well be feeding another consumeristic bubble of illusion, trampling over right relation in the process, and so furthering the degeneration of humanity.

Adult developmental research shows that moving through and up a level of ego stage meaning-making—achiever to regenerator—usually takes at least three to five years. Fasttrack this at your peril. Unfinished business will crop up soon enough, and there is no way round it other than through it. Jung reminds us, "One does not become enlightened by imagining figures of light, but by making the darkness conscious." (Jung, 1973) We must journey inward to integrate repressed shadow aspects of our psyche, and that takes time. To undergo a lasting change in the center of gravity of our consciousness and meaning-making—to upgrade our worldview from Mechanistic Materialism to Quantum Complexity, and our mindset from achiever to regenerator—requires a multi-year psychospiritual death-rebirth journey.

For sure, consciousness raising tools and techniques aid this process, but we can't bypass the journey through bio-hacking. So how might we begin to go about cultivating a more balanced integration of the achiever and awakened mind? Let's first look at some neuroscience and psychology, and then explore a powerful practice that does just that.

Integrating the Achiever and the Awakened Minds

A team of scientists at Yale University have used an advanced brain imaging technique called Diffusion Tensor Imaging (DTI) to identify how the brain's regions and neural pathways are affected by the two different dorsal and ventral attention networks. Their findings show that as we integrate the achiever mind and the awakened mind, we enter what they call 'Quest Orientation'. Dr Miller's research has found that people with prolonged and active psychospiritual practices of connectedness (as opposed to short-lived bio-hacks) are more able to tap into this Quest Orientation. Our perception of life and ourselves within it (our self-other-world relation) subtly shifts. We perceive life as a learning journey, with its tensions, triggers, and challenges being meaning-making rather than things to be avoided or worked around. We open ourselves up more readily to the inner-outer dialogue of life, sensing insightful learnings amid challenges and becoming more aware of synchronicities, insights, and intuitions. (Miller, p170)

This psychological shift pairs with a physiological shift in how the regions of the brain integrate. The left and right hemispheres are more connected, as are the prefrontal cortex and parietal region, and the dorsal and ventral attention systems find harmony, neither dominating the other, both working together. This changes how we perceive ourselves and the world around us and gives us the ability to focus and achieve without losing our innate sense of purpose and connectedness.

As a result of this physiological and psychological shift, our experience of life becomes less grasping, anxious, and outwardly focused. We embrace the ever-changing nature of life and flow within the lively, dancing dialogue of developmental learning. As we make meaning and find purpose from challenges, stresses, and tensions, the voice in the head can no longer spin stories that leave us ruminating and rudderless.

Yes, we still get stressed and doubtful on the journey, but we gain resilience, are more able to embrace complexity, access insight, and learn from challenges. Rather than getting subsumed by fear, stress, self-doubt, and insecurity, we notice the voices of judgement, cynicism, and fear creeping in and can realign and regenerate ourselves with each pitfall as a potential for learning. We become more future-fit, more able to renew ourselves, and can more easily cross the threshold from achiever to regenerator.

This Quest Orientation, where we toggle between achiever and awakened mind, correlates with adult developmental research that shows a significant shift in our meaning-making upon enduring a mid-life crisis, or a journey of inner reorientation and renewal. In adult developmental lingo, this is the shift from 'conventional' to 'post-conventional' ego-stage development which aligns with the threshold crossing from orange/green achiever to teal/turquoise regenerator that we explored in Chapter 2. What greatly aids this threshold crossing is a committed approach to psychospiritual practices.

THE METAMORPHIC SHIFT

Life becomes a creative unfolding soul journey, where we engage with the present moments before us in a more integrated, aware manner. With less grasping and focusing, we invite space for intuition, gut knowing, insights, and synchronicities, all of which give us a sense of inner direction. This is a felt-sense shift inside ourselves, bringing forth a relaxed, open dialogic engagement with life, an orientating to our right relation of self-other-world. This personal change from the inside allows us to be more receptive to the wisdom within and all around us—Nature's Wisdom—and allows meaning and purpose to flow through our lives. The fabric of the world becomes a glowing tapestry woven with wisdom. Our human soul works with the World Soul of inner-outer nature, and we become truer to our dharma, our soul path, and our soul craft.

The most beneficial physiological and psychological state that aids this toggling between achiever and awakened mind is what I call 'bodymind coherence'.

Finding our Bodymind Coherence

As I mentioned in Chapter 1, our physiology and psychology are inextricably linked, just as inner-nature (mind) and outer-nature (matter) interpenetrate at the most fundamental level, with every cell and sinew of our physiology forming part of an energetic 'bodymind'. While every part of the human body exhibits mind, there are three major neurological centers—the head, heart, and gut. Each of these centers have neurological networks in their own right yet are wired as one system. When in coherence, these three centers work together, in tune, and the coherence of these centers encourages coherence across other networks in our body, such as the nervous, lymphatic, and hormonal systems. This coherence also enhances our health, wellbeing, resilience, creativity, insight, and intuition. Bodymind coherence is the key to activating our super-nature.

While the brain has by far the most neurological networks in it, the brain connects directly with the heart and gut which each have their own neurological networks, even their own emotions and memories. Science now refers to the heart and gut as 'brains' because they are powerful sensing-responding organs of perception and core to our overall bodymind consciousness.

The brain in the head exhibits various brainwave frequencies (alpha, beta, delta, theta, gamma) that change with the state of our consciousness. Relaxed and sleepy, we experience more delta and theta waves. Alert, and beta waves are present. In different states of the wake-sleep cycle we can see more calming alpha waves. Gamma waves occur when multiple regions of the brain are active, which can be when we are highly alert or opening into altered states of consciousness.

Hormones like melatonin and serotonin work within the bodymind to help our brainwaves sync with the natural cycles of the day and night. As we wake up and get going in the morning, melatonin drops and serotonin increases, accompanied by a change from delta and theta waves to alpha and beta waves. As we get more drawn into the busy working environment, the achiever mind creates high beta waves, and if this achiever mind's high beta waves are not kept in check with a regular visit to the awakened mind's alpha and theta brain waves, then we find incoherence in the brainwaves across the whole brain and incoherence between brain-heart-gut. Bodymind incoherence exacerbates our sense of fight-flight-freeze and further activates high beta achiever mind.

No doubt we've experienced this vicious cycle when we've gotten stressed, impatient, and frustrated, which exacerbates more stress as we attempt to control, react, transact, and achieve in impatient incoherent ways. We then feel more off-balance, create more upset and reactivity inside ourselves, and possibly also in those around us. Simple practices can alleviate this vicious cycle by enabling coherence.

Bodymind coherence occurs when the brainwaves are synchronized with the waves of the heart and gut. This brain-heart-gut coherence encourages the brain to be available to a wider range of brainwave frequencies (alpha, beta, delta, theta, gamma) and able to toggle freely between achiever and awakened mind. Studies show how this bodymind coherence leads to quite dramatic improvements in health, wellbeing, resilience, empathy, and creativity. In other words, we transform our physiology and psychology together.

Science now clarifies, through brain scans and electrodes over the bodymind, that a practice called 'Heart Entrainment' can quickly and effectively cultivate bodymind coherence. I have found the Heart Entrainment practice to be like a master key and have used it now hundreds of times with leaders from all walks of life and from different geographies and cultures throughout the world with great effect. Through easy to do practices, such as breathwork, energy cultivation, intentionality, and presencing, we can achieve Heart Entrainment within a couple of minutes (see Appendix for a detailed description of this practice).

But like the brain, we need to explore some science of the heart and why it's so central to bodymind coherence.

Cultivating Our Heart-Consciousness

Through the physiology of Heart Entrainment and the psychological practice of bringing our intention and attention into the heart, we cultivate what I call 'heart-consciousness.' This helps us ease out of dominant ego-consciousness and find our way into a more regenerative, self-other-world dynamic.

> "The best and most beautiful things in the world cannot be seen nor touched but are felt in the heart."
>
> —Helen Keller

Recent studies point to the heart being the body's most powerful electromagnetic sensor and transmitter, continually decoding the vast array of electromagnetic and quantum signals radiating in our lived-in environment. The heart is thousands of times more magnetically powerful than the brain. The heart governs our bodymind's sensory, neural, nervous, and instinctual systems; 65% of the cells in the heart are neural cells which are wired into the nervous system, gut, and brain. More information flows from the heart to the brain than the other way around. (Hutchins, 2016)

Practicing Heart Entrainment leads to physiological and psychological changes in the bodymind. Eyes dilate, peripheral vision increases, focus becomes receptive rather than reactive, and brainwaves entrain with the waves of the heart. This is what Heart Entrainment is—the brainwaves synchronize with the heart when the EM waves of the brain embed themselves with the EM wave-form of the heart. As this brain-heart wave coherence occurs, our emotional state becomes more relaxed, with an increased sense of caring and affection, as well as a heightened perception of external stimuli. It's as if we become more alive and present within the moment through our hearts. Heart entrainment also helps our heart rate variability (HRV) and, as we saw earlier with the awakened mind coming on stream, the bodymind starts to resonate with the alpha waves of the Earth. Our heartbeat finds resonance with the heartbeat of the Earth.

As the brainwaves align with the heart waves, the entire body synchronizes as one wave form, with stronger amplitude—a consonance. This affects the nervous and hormonal systems throughout the bodymind. The stress hormone cortisol drops. There is a doubling in DHEA production promoting feelings of well-being, enhancing tissue repair, sexual hormone production, and improving metabolic and memory functions. Notably, the hippocampus area of the brain improves its functioning, stimulating stem cells to produce new neurons, along with neocortex activity in the brain altering as mental chatter reduces. (Hutchins, 2014)

Overall, it seems Heart Entrainment recalibrates our bodymind's center of awareness from the forebrain region to the heart, and we see that heart-consciousness enhances well-being and physiological activity, such as improved repair rates and immune system function. We start to heal ourselves as we open to the perception of the heart with its totalizing bodymind coherence. We literally regenerate ourselves from the inside out. Studies show that this personal coherence has an uplifting impact on others enhancing overall group effectiveness. (HeartMath)

The more often the heart and brain entrain, the easier it becomes to regain entrainment time and again, and the healthier and more resilient we become. With a regular entrainment practice we can rewrite old habits ingrained in us by the dominant achiever mind and rebalance a more integrated achiever-awakened Quest Orientation, so essential for journeying toward regeneration. We re-mind—re-member—a more natural way of being in the world, becoming less addicted to outer achieving and more inner-outer aligned. This is a 'return' to a more animist perception where we more readily feel, perceive, and attend to an authentic communing with others and nature.

Through the quality of our attention and our heartfelt intention, we affect our radiating EM (and quantum) heart field, which not only affects the functioning of our brains and other body organs, but also affects others around us. This is how animist cultures throughout millennia attuned with their neighborhoods—how all our ancestors once lived. We find that it is one thing to cognitively and rationally understand that all of life is holistically interconnected in some way, but it is quite another to know and sense through our hearts—this is wisdom. This heartfelt experience is a profound philosophical, physiological, and psychological renewal—a remembering—urgently needed in leadership today.

While much of this continual and participatory inner-outer dialogue with the world happens beyond the perceptual horizon of our daily, waking awareness, as we develop heart-consciousness we can allow ourselves to become more conscious of these life-force fluctuations. We can perceive subtle fluctuations in our bodymind's capacity for knowing (our 'somatic intelligence') and its less reactive and more empathic emotional response to life's fluctuations (our 'emotional intelligence'). Developing heart-consciousness, therefore, enriches both our intuitive mind and our embodied ability to sense and respond with the world around and within us.

> "Unlike the egoic operating system, the heart does not perceive through differentiation. It doesn't divide the field into inside and outside, subject and object. Rather, it perceives by means of harmony… When heart-awareness becomes fully formed within a person, he or she will be operating out of nondual consciousness… where they will discover the resources they need to live in fearlessness, coherence, and compassion—or in other words, as true human beings."
>
> —Cynthia Bourgeault

Heart-consciousness comes with immediate benefits. There is heightened mental clarity, improved decision making, increased responsiveness and resiliency to change, efficiency of energy use, greater ability to embrace complexity, and increased creativity and innovation. Emotions of general happiness, empathy, compassion, trust, and conviviality increase. All benefits, by the way, are contributors in shifting our organizations toward agile, purposeful, and regenerative businesses.

We start to see the heart beyond a physiological and psychological sensory organ but also a spiritual organ of perception. We go beyond mind-matter and psychology-physiology and into the realm of psychospiritual, as through heart-consciousness we further soul-consciousness. Transcendent imaginal experiences, and non-ordinary states of consciousness enter our awareness, along with an increasing capacity for intuition, insight, imagination, and the meaning-making of synchronicities and clairsentient psychic abilities. Such capacities have been referred to as 'higher faculties' or 'super-sensory' or 'psychic.' Whatever we label them as, they are a natural aspect of becoming more human in this more-than-human world.

Cultivating our higher faculties of soul-consciousness further expands our self-other-world right relation. In distinguishing from the awareness of heart-consciousness to soul-consciousness, I refer to a two-step process of 'activating our super-nature.' First step, heart-consciousness.

Activating our Super-Nature through the Heart and Soul

Step 1: Heart-consciousness

Through the practice of heart entrainment, we gain bodymind coherence, whereupon we ease out of the achiever mind and bring the awakened mind on stream. This lights up different regions of the brain with more alpha brain-wave frequencies, broadens our receptivity, and creates a sense of empathic connectedness. We more readily draw upon different intelligences—the four ways of knowing (see table below). We are no longer limited to rational intelligence but now expanded into integrated intuitive, emotional, somatic awareness.

Step 1 relates to Carl Jung's research into whole-body intelligence and integrating the four ways of knowing.

Jung's Four Ways of Knowing

The intuitive way of knowing is inner insight and intuition and has been related to the element ***fire*** and ***SQ*** (spiritual intelligence). We learn to listen to that soft inner voice that often immediately knows about the rightness of a situation, which is easily overruled by our busy rational mind.

The emotional way of knowing is the ebb and flow of feelings and emotions and has been related to the element ***water*** and ***EQ*** (emotional intelligence). We cultivate this emotional way of knowing by allowing our feelings the non-judgmental space they need, so we may gain perspective on what is underpinning these feelings and how best to respond to them. It is a subtle yet important shift from blind emotional outburst—when we become the slave of our emotions—to informed emotional intelligence.

The somatic and sensorial way of knowing is the sensations we have in our body, the gut pangs, hairs on the back of the neck, butterflies in our stomach, or chest perturbations and has been related to the element ***earth*** and ***PQ*** (physical or somatic intelligence). Our soma (our body) is full of psychosomatic sensations that can inform how we attend to everyday interactions. More and more scientific research is emerging about how this somatic way of knowing works alongside our emotional and intuitive ways of knowing. (Claxton)

The rational-analytic way of knowing is our thinking mind's ability to focus on things and analyze, and has been related to the element ***air*** and ***IQ*** (rational intelligence). This is by far the dominant intelligence we call upon in today's business environment. It is a powerful tool that helps us make sense of, delineate, focus, and compartmentalize complexity.

The rational-analytic way of knowing is but one intelligence within our human repertoire, and a very useful tool for sure, yet when it dominates, it can suppress our three other ways of knowing. When we allow all four ways of knowing—intuitive, emotional, somatic, and rational—to cohere within us, we allow the four elements of our inner nature—fire, water, earth, and air—to integrate in their rightful way. As we integrate these four elements, we open the Eye of the Heart, which opens the bodymind up to the fifth element. Ancient and modern cultures have many names for the fifth element, such as Akasha, Spirit, Source, Universal Mind, World Soul, or Field. The fifth element is where Nature's Wisdom resides.

ACTIVATING OUR SUPER-NATURE & OPENING THE EYE OF THE HEART

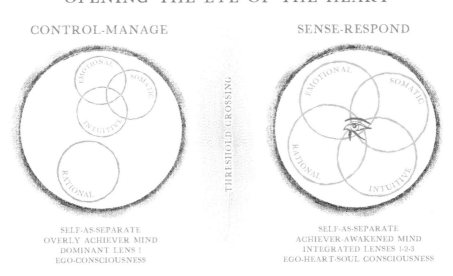

The receptivity of heart-consciousness helps us to toggle between achiever and awakened mind in Quest Orientation. This is both an intimacy with the immanence of life and an opening into intuition and insight, the latter where we start to sense the inner-nature of life beyond the normal five senses. The 'positive gnosis' of phenomenological presencing can aid this intimacy and, as Goethe found through his active seeing, awaken super-sensory faculties as we start to sense the archetypal behind the phenomenon, the inner soul within the outer form. This is a powerful way of sensing and working with the essence, life-force, and systemic dynamics of the living-organization, and brings us to the second step of activating our super-nature, where we cultivate not only heart-consciousness but soul-consciousness.

Step 2: Soul-consciousness

As we integrate Lenses 1-2-3 and become more receptive to the Field through heart-consciousness, we become more conversant with a super-sensory realm—more transparent to the transcendent. In Step 2, we are presencing-in-the-now (intimate with the immanent) and entering the realms behind space-time (transparent to the transcendent) using higher faculties of knowing and by working directly with insight, synchronicity, clairsentience, and soul-knowing. One might say, we are using a more enhanced intuitive capacity.

Accessing this inner realm broadens our perception and invites insights from Nature's Wisdom to come into our conscious awareness. These insights work through sensing our emerging soul craft and then developing and delivering our soul craft. Our 'soul craft' is unique to each of us, a vocation or way of being in service of life whether that be, for instance, caretaking a piece of land, caretaking others, raising a family, being an artist or craftsman, or leading a for-purpose organization. The outer form the soul craft takes is secondary. Primary is the way we engage in our craft through alignment with soul. The more we activate our super-nature, the more we draw from soul and Nature's Wisdom which infiltrates our work with a higher-source energy.

This has the positive virtuous cycle of further enlivening our higher faculties and sensitive receptivity to what's emerging around us, informing the cultivation of our soul craft for the benefit of ourselves, others, and the world around us, and informing our receptivity to the essence, energy, and evolutionary potential of the living-organization on its regenerative journey. We find right relation through our soul craft while being conduits for Nature's

Wisdom. This is a substantively different mode of being and knowing than the vicious cycle of stress and strain associated with the incoherence and imbalance of an overly dominant achiever mind.

With a dedicated routine of practices (like Heart Entrainment, Mindful Meditation, and energy cultivation exercises) as part of a committed psycho-spiritual journey, both psychological and physiological shifts can occur in the bodymind, such as the stimulation of the pineal gland (also known as the 'third eye') located in the mid-brain, just above the eyes around the mid-forehead. An activated pineal gland aids a transmutation of the hormonal chemical melatonin into benzodiazepines, which anesthetize aspects of the achiever mind while bringing the awakened mind on stream. While still considered controversial, some studies indicate that powerful antioxidants are produced by this awakened pineal gland, like pinolines that appear to be anti-aging, anti-cancer, anti-neurodegenerative, and anti-inflammatory antioxidants. They help the body heal and regenerate by amplifying the energy in the nervous system. (Dispenza, p225-275) By continued advancing of energy cultivation and meditation practices, a continued activation of the pineal gland can trigger the production of the chemical DMT (dimethyl-tryptamine), which is the powerful psychoactive hallucinogenic chemical found naturally in the plant ayahuasca. When we are 'opening the third eye', we are referring to the natural production of DMT inside the brain, which is a way into soul-consciousness, and contributes to the whole bodymind effect of opening the Eye of the Heart.

> "If thine eye be single, thy whole body shall be full of light."
>
> —Jesus Christ

While the pineal gland opens us to higher faculties of knowing, this gland also activates the pituitary gland (located in the mid-brain behind the bridge of the upper nose). The pituitary gland produces oxytocin and vasopressin, which provide for elevated emotions of love, wholeness, empathy, and compassion—an expansive sense of the heart region opening. The voices of judgement, cynicism, and fear are quite distant in this state of soul-consciousness. Physiologically, the activated pineal gland acts as a transducer reverberating with the Field, like an antenna connecting our human ego-heart-soul consciousness with higher vibratory realms aiding our access to Nature's Wisdom.

Sensing into our Soul-Consciousness

> "You could not discover the limits of the soul, even if you travelled by every path in order to do so; so profound is its meaning."
>
> –Heraclitus

The soul is frequently thought of as the spiritual essence of the individual, and yet the soul is more like a portal into the spirit realm rather than a 'thing' in itself. By naming it the 'soul' it is easy to objectify 'it'. Instead, think of the soul more as an aperture into a soul-scape, like a frequency channel on a TV set, which is located in the bodymind (immanent) and yet extends beyond the bodymind (transcendent), an immanent-transcendent bridge between the two worlds of outer-nature and inner-nature. When in soul-consciousness we perceive (know) life as inner-outer nature.

The words of the poet help to convey this immanent-transcendent soul-consciousness: (Note – the Swan is a worldwide emblem of the soul)

> "Even this morning, O Swan, awake, arise, follow me!
> There is a land where no doubt nor sorrow have rule: where the terror of Death is no more.
> There the woods of spring are a-bloom, and the fragrant scent 'He is I' is borne on the wind.
> There the bee of the heart is deeply immersed, and desires no other joy."
>
> –Kabir (translated by Rabindranath Tagore)

> "O! the one Life within us and abroad,
> Which meets all motion and becomes its soul,
> A light in sound, a sound-like power in light,
> Rhythm in all thought, and joyance everywhere."
>
> —Samuel Taylor Coleridge

> "Out beyond ideas of wrongdoing and rightdoing,
> there is a field. I'll meet you there.
> Where the soul lies down in the grass,
> the world is too full to talk about.
> Ideas, language, even the phrase 'each other'
> Doesn't make any sense."
>
> —Rumi

This field, land, or dimension beyond duality's right and wrong and ego's doubt and fear, is the mythic 'promised land', the one Life, resonant and rhythmic, which we find through soul-consciousness that lies at the root of regeneration. It's our way into an ever-flowing fecundity of sublime symphony that irrigates our nature and informs our gnosis.

Poets, mystics, seers, and shamans throughout the ages have attuned with this immanent-transcendent soul-scape, existing both here in space-time and there beyond the constraints of space-time in the Field. This Field, the ground of being-becoming, is the realm where psychic energies, archetypal powers, and cosmic forces underpin the potentialities of the life-force. This primal energy flows into our ego-heart-soul consciousness and differentiates through us as personal to our unique nature, yet it is made up of the same psychic energy flowing throughout the entire World Soul. Our very own life-source pervades all of life. We are nature, and nature is us.

> "Unless we see that we are nature and nature is us,
> We will not begin to understand the rhythm of our own body and that nature is the heartbeat of our very soul.
> The soul — the place in us that is sacred, divine, otherworldly, lovely, shy, beautiful, joyful, peaceful, all-knowing, eternal and pure love."
>
> –Lynna Foster

Through soul-consciousness we can sense the transcendent, unlimited aspect of our own essence beyond space-time *and* we can sense the potent purposefulness of this unique soul journey in this lifetime, which is limited by space-time. The unlimited interfaces with the limited through the soul aperture within.

Entering our inner-nature is not some dreamy out-of-this-world experience, but a clear sense of a psychic depth—a clair-sense—an inner dimension beyond the normal realm of everyday consciousness. One way into this realm is through a twilight state of consciousness, which can occur between wakefulness and sleep. Dr Andreas Mavromatis has explored this state as 'hypnagogia' a twilight zone of wake-sleep which allows a receptive opening of the ego into a numinous depth. Such work is usually reserved for the province of the creative—the musician, poet, or artist, for instance—yet for the regenerative leader it's an important way into Nature's Wisdom.

Welcoming in the Twilight Zone

The twilight zone between wakefulness and sleep happens naturally every day when waking up and falling asleep. At the end of the day, our brainwaves slowdown from achiever high beta to beta-alpha as we relax in the evening. Then as we start to settle down for a good night's sleep, the brainwaves slow further to alpha-theta. When in sleep we are in theta-delta, and then the low delta of deep sleep. Often, we might skip through the twilight zone quite unconsciously, perhaps slumped in front of Netflix or sipping a glass of wine after dinner or running some errands. At morning, it may be a quick get-up-and-go routine of rushing out the door, right into high beta not long after the alarm.

On the regenerative journey, we can learn to become more conscious of the wake-sleep twilight topping and tailing the day, allowing the alpha and theta waves of the twilight zone to fructify our bodymind coherence, activate our super-nature, and integrate our ego-heart-soul consciousness. I often provide practices for my coaching clients that encourage an intentional attentiveness to the waking up and falling asleep parts of the day.

Yet the twilight zone can also be accessed during the busy working day through practices like Heart Entrainment and the Creative Imagination Process (explored in Chapter 7), that invite a slowing down of the brainwaves and a purposeful dwelling within the sweet spot of alpha-theta. In this zone, the hormone oxytocin increases our sense of connection, wellbeing, trust, empathy, and peace. We are able to hold an immanent-transcendent awareness of both the outer-nature phenomenal world of normal space-time and the super-sensory synchronistic experience of inner-nature. This is the opening of the Eye of the Heart: the regenerative act of walking between worlds where we bring the darkness into the light and light to see in the darkness. This twilight 'seeing' relates to what the English painter and poet William Blake speaks to when saying, "To the eyes of the man of Imagination, Nature is Imagination itself." This 'Imagination' is not a mere flight of fancy but a sensing into the immanent-transcendent depth of nature. It's a psychospiritual soul-knowing (a gnosis) hence why Imagination has a capital 'I' to convey its profundity and sacredness.

Blake spoke of the significance between 'seeing with the eye' as opposed to 'seeing through the eye.' For Blake, when one sees *with* the eye—which we have a habit of doing in normal waking achiever mind—we see only the outer form and appearance and attend to nature only with our five senses, therefore failing to sense into inner-nature. When one sees *through* the eye—which 'welcoming in the twilight zone' aids—our super-sensory receptivity perceives the spiritual archetypal depth of inner-nature.

> "We are led to believe a lie
> When we see not thro the eye."
>
> —William Blake

As mentioned in Chapter 1, this walking between two worlds can be symbolized by the mythic phrase 'Heaven on Earth.' Heaven, the eternal transcendent inner-nature realm which is beyond normal space-time accessed through the awakened mind's higher faculties and predominantly alpha-theta brain wave zone, and Earth, the temporal normal space-time corporeal world which the waking consciousness of beta waves and our normal five senses operate in.

The twilight allows for insights from the depths of inner-nature to be seen, and Paracelsus's 'light of nature' (known as *lumen naturae* by the ancient alchemists of Europe and the Middle East) is found, illuminating our inner-vision and expanding our consciousness beyond the narrow confines of Mechanistic Materialism.

This experience of Heaven on Earth may feel rather removed from the normal daily cut-and-thrust of business life. Yet through the accessibility of 'welcoming in the twilight zone', it's possible, with practice, to activate this immanent-transcendent experience amid the everyday. For the regenerative leader, this enhances our self-awareness and systemic-awareness to sense subtle perturbations and energy shifts in the living-organization, influencing our interactions. It also greatly aids our thinking-out-of-the-box creativity, pattern recognition and sensing of synchronistic signs informing our decision-making. And the subtle energy that pours into us from opening to inner-nature reinvigorates our bodymind, aids our coherence, and can also enhance the coherence of others we are working with. In this way, we can see how the regenerative leader is working with the right relation of Heaven and Earth, dark and light, sleep and wake, moon and sun, yin and yang, feminine and masculine, awakened mind and achiever mind, to walk through both worlds in the liminality of the twilight zone. On Earth as it is in Heaven, as above so below.

Meditation, contemplative reflection, gentle body movement like chi gung, breathwork, and chanting or more intricate practices like Yoga Nidra (see Appendix), active seeing, lucid dreaming, astral projection (an intentional out-of-body experience), indigenous medicine wheel rites, and the Creative Imagination Process all aid this twilight zone. By slowing down the normal waking brainwaves of beta (30Hz to 13Hz) into alpha (13 Hz to 8Hz) and theta (8Hz to 4Hz), we find ourselves in this liminal land. It's rejuvenating and relaxing, and we find resonance with the subtle energies of nature, Earth, and cosmos here. It's as if we come home, in right relation within our own nature and with those around us. The bandwidth of our ability to work with wisdom widens beyond the limitations of high beta, and we're better able to handle complex interwoven challenges in ways that honor right relation of self-other-world. We find an ease of toggling between achiever-awakened and over time, with dedicated practice, we up-stretch into a new psychological center of gravity from ego self-as-separate into soul self-as-participatory.

Over many years of working with busy leaders, I've found the frame of 'welcoming in the twilight zone' a practical way of learning to open the Eye of the Heart. Clients are often surprised by the accessible practicality of this potent liminality. In the Appendix I provide an introductory framing and practice for 'welcoming in the twilight zone' with more advanced practices best reserved for coaching sessions than the written word.

> "Without union with universal energy there can be no true transformation."
>
> –John P Milton

Our lives are full of tiny, easily overlooked moments when the social constructs of our reality fall away, and the ego permeates. In these moments, we can have a soulful conversation with the world around us, and each brief moment of heart-and-soul consciousness offers a mini threshold crossing for us; an embodied felt-sense of this other worldly yet very much of-this-world feeling. We reach beyond the 'I' perspective of ego-consciousness, seeing beyond its narrowing lens, shifting our way of attending with the world. We may find—if only for the briefest of moments as we begin this journey—that we quite naturally and gracefully commune and cocreate with others in a coherent, authentic, compassionate, and wise manner. In this natural state of awareness, we are genuinely 'being regenerative'.

Essentially, the entrance gate into opening the Eye of the Heart is an imaginal indwelling, a dropping behind one's own thinking mind into the depths of inner-nature and soul through which we find right relation with our own selves and with life. This inner receptivity found through the twilight zone provides the fertile soil in the psyche from which we can bring forth our potential into the light of our everyday interactions. The more we experience this liminal receptivity the more practiced we become at allowing this soul-flow to enter our daily consciousness.

Phenomenologist Robert Romanyshyn talks of such soul moments as, "a tear in the fabric of space and time, miracle… to germinate in the recessed chambers of the human heart… shimmering, resonating, vibrating frequencies which we, with our own poor consciousness, can tune into with only just enough awareness to be filled with longing." (Romanyshyn, p38)

The beauty of this life experience is that when we open up through the heart and soul of our innermost being, we also open our bodymind to the subtler resonances and rhythms of natural grace within and all around us, and the life-force of creation flows unencumbered through us. We are enriched and rejuvenated. We learn that we can heal ourselves while activating our healing potential to help others. While remaining connected to the flow of life, we toggle into the achiever mind when getting-the-job-done is what is called for in the moment and we toggle back to awakened mind when the job is done. Welcoming in the twilight zone in the midst of the day greatly supports this toggling.

As our lives start to center more in the soul and less in the ego, we begin to sense life in a subtly different way. Rather than brief moments of meditation and short-lived tears in the fabric of space-time, we sense that life itself is the meditation. Each moment, day, week, month, year is an invitation to welcome in the twilight zone. For instance, each inbreath and outbreath practiced with intention and ego-heart-soul attention is a way into a mini twilight zone whereupon we pull ourselves out of high beta into alpha-theta when we feel the need to toggle. Also, why not have various times in the day intentionally set aside. Perhaps a ten-minute twilight zone by engaging in a practice like Heart Entrainment. Or a longer contemplative space, such as time away from the office in nature, for an hour or so, where we intentionality welcome in alpha-theta twilight by being at-one with nature in a state of presence and coherence.

There's also the day-night routine of intentionally elongating the liminal space when we rise and fall sleep. Beyond this, there's the weekly routine of welcoming in the twilight zone. For instance, we might decide to reduce the schedule on Friday afternoon to a minimum, and for parts of the weekend reduce the rushing around, with perhaps an hour or two set aside for nothing but sitting in quiet imaginal contemplation. Then, there's the lunar cycle every four weeks, with its ebb and flow, to set time aside around the new moon and full moon for alpha-theta meditative moments. And beyond the lunar-month is the school half-term and full-term breaks, bank holidays, birthdays, and cultural ceremonial moments in the calendar whether it be New Year's Day, Valentine's Day, Spring Equinox, Easter, May Day, Summer Solstice, Autumn Equinox, Halloween, Winter Solstice, Christmas, or other traditional events specific to one's culture. These days do not have to be limited solely to 'outer activities' where we engage in social, cultural, or consumer activities. They can also be time for 'inner events', the moments in the year when we intentionally pause, welcome in the twilight zone, contemplate and reflect, reorientate our being-in-the-world. Then life becomes the meditation, and we find our rhythm with the rapture of reality.

> "Those who flow as life flows know they need no other force."
>
> –Lao Tzu

For the vast part of our human history, we embraced individual and communal practices and celebrations that intentionally sought a welcoming in of the inner realm and its subtle energies into our daily consciousness. It's what shamanic medicine wheel practices found the world over aid with, keeping us centered and in right relation with the life-force and wisdom of nature, Earth, and cosmos. For instance, in Neolithic Western Europe one such indigenous medicine wheel practice is that of the Celtic-Druidic tradition, where we find the honoring of eight sacred moments of the day, eight sacred moments of the lunar-month, and eight sacred moments of the year. This honoring of the 'wheel of life' helps the bodymind find accord with the daily, monthly, yearly cyclic seasonality of nature, Earth, and cosmos.

> "For more than 99% of human history, the world was enchanted and man saw himself as an integral part of it. The complete reversal of this perception in a mere four hundred years or so has destroyed the continuity of the human experience and the integrity of the human psyche. It has very nearly wrecked the planet as well. The only hope, or so it would seem to me, lies in a re-enchantment of the world."
>
> —Morris Berman

The ancient Greeks perceived life as innately flowing with deep currents of wisdom, which they referred to as the Goddess Sophia. To attune ourselves with this wisdom innate within life, is to experience Sophia within us, to be in love with the Goddess. We have a wisdom current flowing through the soul, nourishing and refining our ways of knowing, cultivating our wise experience of life. Through our coherence, deeper wisdom currents of life flow through this bodymind instrument we have, a conduit, a flute through which life plays its wisdom dance. The psyche is opened to the intrinsic numinosity and existential meaning of life which penetrates us informing our soul journey. We become more adept at aligning our different ways of knowing (intuitive, emotional, somatic, and rational) into our everyday living while disentangling ourselves from old habits. Our ego soon learns how to embrace the interests and passions of the heart and soul through a healthy, constructive style of leading and living within a values-centered, purpose-driven work life.

Life starts to be seen for what it really is, a rich 'action research' or 'collaborative inquiry' of learning as we go, exploring and broadening our sense of who we are while more of our soul emerges through us. The good news is this way into regeneration is a relaxation into how life really is. We can either struggle with the dance of life, caught up in the ego-machinations of fear and desire, or we can learn to flow as life flows, and embrace the dance of life with a warm heart and open mind.

Further into the book, we explore our way into soul-consciousness through a process of entering the Imaginal Realm, the twilight zone space between normal space-time and the Field, in order to bring forth the insights of Nature's Wisdom into our unique soul craft. But first, in the next chapter as we move into **Part 2 Understanding**, we turn our attention to the nature of living systems by learning how we might apply our integrated ego-heart-soul consciousness to leadership.

"Tumble with the rock which falls from the mountain. Seek light and rejoice with the rosebud about to open; Be restless with the dog that barks in the night; Labor with the parsimonious ant; Gather honey with the bee; Expand in space with the ripening fruit; Run with the greyhound."

—R.A. Schwaller de Lubicz

"I now see not with the eyes, but by the operation of spiritual energy in the powers. I am in heaven, in earth, in water, in the air; I am in living creatures and plants; I am in the womb, before the womb, after the womb. I am present everywhere."

—Hermes Trismegistus

"To see a World in a Grain of Sand
And a Heaven in a Wild Flower,
Hold Infinity in the palm of your hand
And Eternity in an hour."

—William Blake

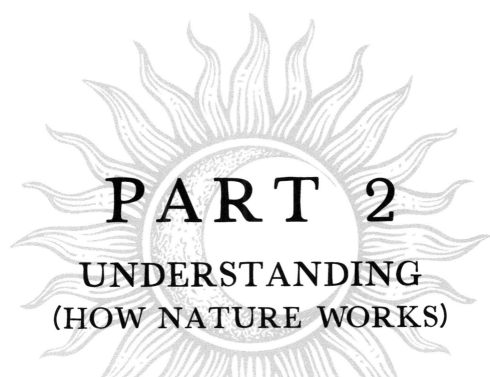

PART 2
UNDERSTANDING
(HOW NATURE WORKS)

The Nature of Living Systems

It's likely that we've been educated to see nature as innately competitive, as separate species struggle for survival in a dog-eat-dog world amid a clockwork universe devoid of meaning. Even our nature programs on TV sensationalize the competitive nature of life. Combat, struggle, and strife, it seems, entice our attention and make for gripping viewing. From this mechanistic perspective, the only point to life is self-preservation through maximization, where one only survives in this world by outcompeting others. The irony is that this narrowed focus on self-preservation and competition is undermining our evolution, and therefore our self-preservation.

> "The creature that wins against its environment destroys itself."
>
> —Gregory Bateson

A hyper-competitive view of life has been applied to everything from the genes in our bodies to the soil beneath our feet, from organizations to the wider business environment, from socioeconomics to civilization itself. Yes, competition and survival are important aspects of life, yet the nature in our own bodies, in life around us, and throughout our organizations, neighborhoods, and cities is far richer, more complex, and inter-relational than what the narrowed Mechanistic Materialism view provides.

What really happens in nature is that the chromosome, gene, nucleus, cell, organ, organism, and ecosystem all evolve in relation with each other through a rich interplay of collaboration and competition. In fact, science now recognizes that collaboration is the overriding evolutionary force—not competition. Interdependency, reciprocity, and relationality are what make life happen, all the way down to the quark strings within atoms and the molecules that make up our living cells, through to the teams within the organization inter-relating within a wider business ecosystem of diverse stakeholders including society and the more-than-human world. Everything and everyone learn and evolve through continuous sensing-responding of energetic exchanges with everything and everyone else. Participation rather than competition better characterizes life on Earth.

Evolution is not a linear chain reaction fueled by separate beings in competition. It's a complex combination of tensions and reciprocal interactions, interpenetrations and inner-outer dynamics that create a nonlinear network within which evolution plays out through emergent sequences that seamlessly connect all life. This nonlinearity of interactions can seem like chaos. However, it is self-organizing and constitutes a higher form of order. No disorder or randomness here, only meaning to be found all the way down. Everything is full of energy and consciousness, and there is no distinction between the physical and metaphysical.

Evolution is developmental. Living systems learn through an emergent network of inner-outer inter-relation. This learning is more complex than say, adapting to change in the environment. It is demonstrating an intrinsic potentiality to become, to realize essence through energy into emergence for evolution. Outer change creates a need—a tension—for adaptation and inner potential creates a need—a tension—to become fully realized. Evolution is fueled by learning and growth, which are both 'inner' (impelled from the essential nature of becoming) and 'outer' (adapting to external changes in the environment).

Contrary to our understanding, outer changes in the environment do not act like mechanical causes to modify the nature of the organism. Rather, outer influences induce the formative forces of the organism's essential nature to manifest in a particular way. It's not the outer influences that are the creative potential, but the inner-nature which creatively responds to the outer change.

Each living system (whether organism or organization) brings forth its wholeness through evolutionary pulsations, sequences, or up-stretches that occur through an emergent process of becoming. This emergent becoming unfolds through the rhythmic, relational tensions of divergence (expansion) and convergence (contraction).

We can start to see life from a new perspective. Life is not some struggle to adapt to external change to survive, by which we evolve through blind chance and random mutation. Life is a purposeful choreography, a dance of inner-outer tensions full of life-force. Yes, competition and survival are key ingredients in the mix, but the foundational ingredient is collaboration.

The very existence of a living system—from organism to organization—is unceasing relationality and exchange, or what one might call 'flow.' A flow of meaning, information, nutrients, matter, and energy; a simultaneous flow of both physical (outer) matter and metaphysical (inner) mind. As human beings, we are not only physiological excitations of flesh and blood, but we are also psychological excitations of psychic energy (essence, drive, directed consciousness). We are physiological and psychological 'becomings'—biological, emotional, cognitive, psychospiritual beings always in a process of becoming due to a continuous flow of energy and consciousness. If this incessant flow ceases, then death is immediate. This flow is not mindless, but full of intentionality. We need only observe a plant growing toward the light, a squirrel learning how to open a birdfeeder, or our own daily errands to notice intentionality innate within life. This flow of becoming is metamorphic in that living systems are continually transforming themselves by encouraging their own being (soul-essence) to evolve amid the incessant flow of energetic emergence, all rooted within the unifying ground of the World Soul.

> "Everything is new, and yet always the old. Nature is forever transforming herself, and there is within her no movement of standing still, yet her laws are unchangeable."
>
> –Johann Wolfgang Goethe

Discovering Our Evolutionary Nature of Becoming

As leaders, we can learn to sense the incessant inner-outer processes of 'human becoming'. This helps us work with the emergent evolutionary dynamics of the living-organization rather than against them. The regenerative leader works with the life-force, essence, and purposefulness of the living-organization within the wider context of the business ecosystem and fabric of life on Earth, all the while steeped within the World Soul, the rhizome ground within which the organization's essence is rooted. That is, the organization-as-living-system needs to be perceived not just as a living system immersed in a relational flow of life, but also grounded within the World Soul of nature. The organization is as much a *part* of nature as we human becomings are. This rhizome ground provides the rootedness of the unchangeable amid the ever-transforming nature of the living-organization. The living-organization's essence is like the soul of a living being. It is unique to the living-organization and also an aperture or connective portal into the transcendent Field that pervades all life.

The regenerative leader knows how to work with the evolutionary dynamics of the living-organization by opening into how inner-outer nature works. Mechanistic Materialism sees only outer-nature (products, structures, outcomes, numbers, results). Quantum Complexity sees outer-nature in a less reductive, more relational way, and more importantly also sees inner-nature (psychologies, systemic energetics, purposefulness, life-force, Nature's Wisdom, World Soul).

This inner beingness is the essence of the living system, which enables the living system to become more of what or who it truly is. The acorn becoming the oak tree, the caterpillar becoming a butterfly, the baby becoming the passionate agent for change, the entrepreneurial start-up becoming a for-purpose regenerative business. The essence gives rise to the evolutionary potential of the living system, which develops to survive and thrive through relational adaptation with the world as it evolves into more of what or who it truly is. The living system is realizing its dharma, or the fuller version of itself, its destiny. Each living system has its own unique dharma, just as each regenerative business has its unique reason for being (essence, purpose, mission) and showing up in the world through its brand, stakeholder relations, value propositions, and culture.

Think of the organizational essence not as a 'thing' to be defined but as a soul-scape that pervades the entirety in which the living-organization inter-relates with outer change. The essence is the creative imperative impelling the inner-nature to learn and adapt to outer change in a way that's unique to the organization. The essence is not only essential for the inter-relating parts but for the whole gestalt—the systemic field of the living-organization. In this regard, the regenerative leader senses the organizational essence through an activated super-nature of knowing that is not limited to a rational-analytic comprehension of a mission statement but draws upon an intuitive systemic awareness and a dialogic sensing into the system.

One might say that a concrete mission statement is a 'reductive unitive essence' that is useful for the convergent order a unifying goal provides for. Whereas the dialogic systemic sensing provides for what one might call a 'holistic organic essence' of purposefulness, an intuitive felt-sense that is embodied through each and every emergent dynamic of inner-nature sensing and responding to outer-nature. It's useful to have a mission statement for sure, but let's appreciate how we also need something more embodied and systemic. We need a guidepost that allows us to sense when the ever-transforming nature of the essence's becoming (through the emergent and evolutionary dynamics of the living-organization) is in flow or not.

While this new evolutionary dynamic that calls upon the recognition of 'essence' might sound more complex than seeing the organization as a machine with a concrete purpose and hierarchic set of commands and controls, this Quantum Complexity view of the living-organization emancipates its life-force from the narrowed lens of Mechanistic Materialism. The machine model cuts the flow of life up into concrete slices so that things can be categorized and compartmentalized, which is a useful tool for measuring and monitoring, yet one that can undermine the reality of the emergent quality of life.

When we mechanize the living system, instead of evolutionary potential and essence, we form neat and tidy mission statements stuck to the wall 'out there' but rarely felt 'in here.' Inauthenticity creeps in, and soon we see our work as just a job—a vehicle for earning money to pay the bills as we edge toward retirement, where we dream that some form of freedom from the mechanization of life might exist. But the expansiveness we desire deep in our hearts, the freedom to feel the life-force pulsating through our veins, is not something to experience outside of work or in retirement. It can be experienced through our enterprising ventures. Afterall what are businesses actually for? Who are they serving? Us. Businesses are here to serve us (and life). Which, alas, currently consists largely of our consumerist egos unmoored from any true sense of purpose or meaning.

So, let's get with the program of life, go deeper than the ego, and see beyond the organization as some kind of clockwork machine to control and manage when in actuality we know it's full of life and is where we spend much of our lives. The messy, unpredictable human relationships next to the coffee machine, down the corridor, in the corporate boardroom, the meeting conventions, decision-making protocols, what's said, what's not said, the informal power plays, the hidden leader networks, tacit knowledge shared through gossip or social media, are how we show up, listen, and share. All of this 'humanity' contributes to either enlivening or stifling the evolutionary potential of the living-organization.

The life-force of the living-organization has a purposefulness that flows in right relation day-to-day, hour-by-hour affected by and affecting the attentiveness of each person within the living system. Creative life-force is realized through the being-and-becoming of the essence, which brings in the immanent and transcendent nature of life. The immanence of the unfolding becoming and the transcendence of being in the world as a soulful presence are two sides of the same coin.

It is here that we must acknowledge the decades of engrained programming. Our vision, both individually and collectively of nature, and the nature of business, is warped, therefore the unlearning process is a crucial step on the regenerative journey.

The good news is that we can take inspiration from living systems within and all around us, for free.

> "Look deep, deep, deep into nature and you will understand everything better."
>
> —Albert Einstein

We have the opportunity to look into nature and explore insights that might aid our living-organization on its inner-outer regenerative journey of being-and-becoming.

Learning from the Networks of Living Systems

It's in our Genes

The machine mindset sees the gene as a unit of selfish ascendency that occasionally, randomly mutates by accident and without purpose. But when we look deeper, we see that genes are constantly changing in highly adaptive ways—splicing, rewiring, and upgrading as the cell engages with its changing environment. Inner purposefulness of the gene is working with tension, in relation with changes that are happening in the external environment. Inner essence with outer change enables emergence.

CELL & GENE IN CONSTANT DIALOGUE WITH ENVIRONMENT

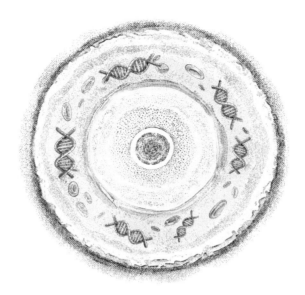

The gene is always adjusting itself while in dialogue with its ever-changing environment, metabolizing, alchemizing, flowing. Yet, all the while, it is maintaining coherence, remaining true to its essence, and not losing itself amid this continuous interplay of adaptation and complex interaction with other cells.

The Buzz of Cellular Life

There are around 37 trillion cells in the human body and each one performs millions of interactions every second. Enzymes and amino acids catalyze interactions, changing the pace and nature of the flow between cells. In fact, 330 billion cells are replaced daily. Just look at your hand. It's not the same hand as yesterday thanks to the continual renewal of skin epidermic cells. It's the same for the cells in each of our organs, bones, ligaments, hair, tissues... everything is continually renewed. Even the non-human cells working in collaboration with our human cells. In the intestines, for instance, there are 10,000 billion non-human bacteria working in communities to help our digestion processes. (Letellier)

Decision-making between cells occurs all the time amid an environment of cycles of creating, repairing, transforming, and evolving. This buzz of life is richly complex and far from random. There is no top-down, hierarchic org chart or bureaucracy of management to instruct these fast-paced decisions. Still, it's not a free for all, out of control mess. These cycles of regeneration are exquisite. The regulation of blood pressure, hydration, muscle tone, cell renewal, and such like happens all the time through sensing-responding to a multitude of changing variables and coherently aligning inner-outer nature in highly adaptive ways. Life is developmental, and the bodily systems have learning baked in.

THE BUZZ OF CELLULAR LIFE

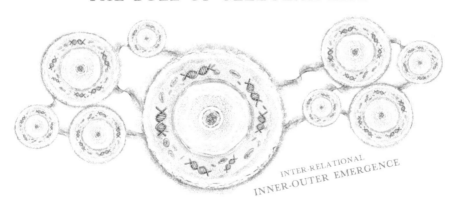

Well ok, the human body is exquisitely beautiful. Fine. But what about the muck and mud of nature outside the backdoor, under the tree, on a wet afternoon, getting my boots dirty? How can that cajole us out of mechanistic thinking?

A Handful of Soil

In a handful of healthy soil there are more living beings working together than there are human beings on the entire planet. Soil is a vast repertoire of hidden life—millions of microorganisms can be found in just a teaspoon of it. The living community in just one small teaspoon of healthy soil includes 100 million bacterial cells operating in complex networks, hundreds of meters of fungal hyphae, 10,000 protozoans, and a similar number of algal propagules, as well as larger microarthropods, nematodes, and worms. Each living being playing an important role in the living ecosystem of the soil. Soil lives in symbiosis with plant life, each helping the other in their cycles of life. The soil provides the vital reincarnation process of death and decomposition into new life.

Bacteria often get a bad rap these days, yet they are essential to soil life, as well as our own bodies and wider life on Earth. Since the Archaeon (some 3,500 million years ago), bacteria have been thriving on Earth through networks and partnerships spanning the entire globe. Bacteria cells reinvent themselves as they attune with their environment through what is referred to as 'autopoiesis' or self-making, which is a form of co-creating with their environment. Bacteria often live in vibrant communities with different cells carrying out different functions while all working together as a super-organism—group of organisms communicating, collaborating, and adapting to their surroundings in a coherent way that benefits the community. (Hutchins, 2014, p79-82)

Bacterial communication is known as 'quorum sensing,' which they use to detect helpful and harmful situations, activate dormant genes, and switch language when needed to obviate disruptive behavior. Communicating throughout the community allows them to form mixed species communities and so increase their diversity and the variety of tasks undertaken, therefore becoming more resilient during times of volatile environmental conditions. If bacterial behavior detrimental to the community is detected through quorum sensing, those 'anti-social' bacteria can be 'tuned-out' of the community 'discussion' and so left with the option of addressing their incompatible behavior or being excluded from the benefits of being part of the community.

When bacteria communities reach a certain size, they cooperatively organize themselves into colonies. It's as if there is a bacterial social intelligence. According to scientist Dr. Stephan Harding, bacteria are deeply sentient creatures that work together creatively with exquisite sensitivity to their environment. (Harding, p167) Interestingly, many self-serving relationships within bacteria communities have evolved into mutualistic relationships as if recognizing the enhanced benefits of partnership. As Harding notes, "The great bacterial web has run the planet to this day, and is, in a way, rather like the unconscious processes that operate key aspects of our own metabolism ... our very own cells are associations of once free-living bacteria that now engage in sophisticated intra-cellular communication." (Harding, p169) A single bacteria has thousands of sensors protruding through its cell membrane informing a continual sensing-responding of the inner cell with outer change.

As well as bacteria in healthy soil, we find fungi, or networks of 'mycelia' as called by biologists. Mycelia are the builders of soil and the grand recyclers of life. Their fine web of cells run through the soil unlocking nutrients from one source and providing food for another. Mycologist Dr Paul Stamets views mycelia as the neurological networks of nature. In his book *Mycelium Running*, he explains that mycelia form vast sentient networks of information sharing membranes. "These membranes are aware, react to change, and collectively have the long-term health of the host environment in mind." (Stamets, p2) Breaking down decaying matter into nutrients for life as they go, they share the nutrients across wide ranges of diverse ecosystems and in doing so help ensure the overall health of these diverse ecosystems.

Mycelia display four modes of activity: exploration, assimilation, conservation, and redistribution. As these sentient networks seek nutrients in the soil they expand outwards in a radial fashion. While assimilating nutrients they also conserve other areas of the wider ecosystem by redistributing nutrients throughout their network. Mycelia networks can, for instance, connect one tree of a certain species, say an oak, with another tree of a different species, say a beech, and share nutrients between them where one tree may be rich in one mineral and the other is deficit. Each tree has millions of root tips which intimately inter-relate with the mycelia. It's difficult, even with powerful magnifying scientific instruments, to notice where the root tip ends and the mycelia begins, so infused they are in each other. Each of the many millions of root tips the tree emanates into the soil senses and responds to vast amounts of information. Much like neurons in our brain, these root tips transmit and receive electrical signals throughout the root network and through the mycelia network across the forest floor. (Rayner, 2013)

The mycelia networkers must learn to simultaneously let go of their communication and nutrient network structures while holding on to current nutrient supplies. Too much holding on can result in gridlock—an overly retentive system that gets caught up in the density of its own integration and so cannot move on. Too much letting go can lead to dissolution and a lack of capacity for sharing, communicating, and learning. Vital to mycelia— or for that matter all of life— is this attunement of holding on and letting go within an ever-transforming context. Giving is essential for receiving. Death provides the opportunity for life. Reconfiguration enables fresh exploration. Letting go allows for thresholds to be crossed and perceived boundaries to be transcended.

There is giving and receiving, sensing and responding, letting go and welcoming in, working within limits while permeating boundaries. Nature never stops networking, learning, and growing through material and energetic death-rebirth cycles of continuous renewal. Death-rebirth, not as something to avoid, but as a renewed flowering of life that connects backwards with its rhizome source and expands forwards with renewed creativity. Living systems stay true to their essence only through this unceasing inner-outer renewal. One might say 'ditto' for our living-organizations.

To fully understand this, we need more than just a 'systems thinking' head-shift out of machine thinking. It's a felt-sense intuitive systemic body-mind-shift, a presencing that invites an immersion into how nature really works.

Life's Unceasing Transformation

Life doesn't do inactivity. In fact, stasis is pathological. Hang on a minute! What about a period of rest or dormancy, like the seed lying dormant in the soil for many months? This too is a time of sensing-responding, waiting for the right conditions to break open. Different aspects of nature operate across different timeframes, a notion which is useful for the living-organization to appreciate. Organizational learning, too, operates across different timeframes. We need more than a binary, strategic three-year plan versus the tactical quarterly plan—we need a rich spectrum of strategy-tactic timeframes that honor emergence while providing much needed coherence and clarity. The rational-analytic mind demands some form of timeframe categorization for its strategy planning and forecasting processes, and that's all good. As long as we remember that we are using this as a tool to aid the life-force of the living-organization's flow with the ever-changing nature of life. Let's not get so caught up in management by numbers to the extent that we begin to believe the numbers are the purpose of the living-organization.

Traditionally we assumed that species would become more competitive as environmental conditions became tougher, but from recent studies it seems many species become more cooperative in stressful times. With the rising interest in facilitation ecology, science is beginning to recognize that evolution is essentially cocreative and participatory— something animist cultures have intuitively known for millennia. Our own bodies are a good example of the extensiveness of interplay and partnering that goes on throughout the biotic world, as only one out of every ten cells within our bodies is a human cell. Without the help of the 'friendly' bacteria within our bodies we would utterly fail at life.

Rather than organisms struggling for survival they thrive through dynamic relationship. It is also worth noting that in times of strife, like the hurricane flooding in New York, we humans, too, transcend perceived boundaries of separation and seek to help each other where possible. And so, even with our culturally habituated ways of thinking so deeply ingrained in separation, scarcity, competition, and combat, there is hope.

Nature's Relationality

Relationships in nature are multi-faceted and dynamic, meaning that two organisms can have many different types of relationships over time, even at the same time. If you look at two trees growing side by side in a forest, they are clearly competing for the same resources in the same location, yet the trees have evolved to live collaboratively together in the forest.

Relationships between organisms can be generalist or specific. In your garden, you may notice that one honeybee may pollinate many different types of flowers and that those flowers may be pollinated by a variety of different insects— a generalist interdependency. Some flowers, however, can be pollinated by only one specific species of insect or bee or bat and perhaps only during very few days (or nights) each year. In this case, the flower and pollinator have coevolved to perfectly meet each other's unique needs—a specific codependency.

What is clear is that purely exploitative organisms can appear to be benign, but they invariably weaken the host, sometimes in a less than obvious way. Conversely, there can be organisms that at first sight appear purely exploitative but can have more subtle beneficial effects on their host or for the ecosystems in which they live. Such subtle benefits sometimes only become apparent in times of strife for the host or the ecosystem. For instance, mistletoe on a tree can undermine the health of various branches and even weaken the whole tree if too prevalent, and yet with its own evergreen capacity for photosynthesis it produces energy that may be given back to the host in the lean winter months. Similarly, fungi on a tree may be exploiting it for certain nutrients which it then shares across its network benefiting the wider ecosystem in turn benefiting the tree.

Likewise, in business it's not always easy to discern which parts of the organization are not overtly adding value (the ones that are merely there for the ride) and those providing a subtle benefit unmeasured by the normal performance assessment process. Cutting dead wood from an organization in challenging times may be prudent, yet damaging a useful web of stakeholder relations in times when greater resilience is needed is not. There is a fine balance between prudent pruning and reductive acts that thwart the organization's ability to thrive amid unceasing transformation. Also, spare capacity in business, as well as nature, is important in times of transformation as it can allow for creativity and innovation to spawn. Much like we explored in the previous chapter how to enhance creativity by welcoming in the twilight zone, downtime between intense projects, 'wintering' moments of reflection, spare capacity to brainstorm and prototype out-of-the-box initiatives, and networking events outside the office, can all help fuel the ever-learning evolution of the living-organization.

Like relationships between organisms, relationships between organizations can take many different forms, ranging from tightly coupled joint ventures to more loosely coupled preferred supplier relationships or associates in mutually beneficial networks with diverse stakeholder communities. Within the organizational boundaries of a business there can be relationships between aligned business units, communities of specialists, close knit teams, and agile cross-functional circles. In fact, without relationships, both within the organization and between organizations, none would thrive. Effective relationships between people thrive through interpersonal links founded on common values, mutual trust, and a cooperative approach to challenges. Finding the right harmony between creativity and productivity is key, as is fostering a sense of trust and sharing across the business ecosystem. This attitude amongst stakeholders emanates from a culture that values developmental learning, cooperation, trust, and creativity, whilst accepting change, failure, novelty, and emergence as a part of life.

> "In organizations, real power and energy is generated through relationships. The patterns of relationships and the capacities to form them are more important than tasks, functions, roles, and positions."
>
> —Margaret Wheatley

The more we recognize the importance of relationality amid unceasing transformation for the living-organization, the more we understand that a strong, ever-learning regenerative culture is foundational for the regenerative business. As mentioned in Chapter 1, I refer to this regenerative business culture as DEE: Developmental (ever-learning), Emergent (flexible and ever-changing), Evolutionary (durable life-affirming intent and purposefulness). We shall explore this DEE culture in more detail in the next chapter.

Nature's Permeable Boundaries

In nature every living organism consists of one or more living cells. The interior workings of these cells are contained within a watery milieu of protoplasm by a fluid semi-permeable envelope called the plasma membrane (or cell membrane). For living cells to stay alive, their envelopes must be sufficiently permeable to allow substances that provide energy to flow into them, but not so permeable as to immediately lose whatever they have gained (like a bucket full of holes). They need, therefore, to sustain an appropriate and variable balance between permeability and impermeability, as a function that is sensitive to their environmental circumstances. For many years biologists thought the role of the cell membrane was passive. More recently there has been increasing recognition of the role of surface 'receptors' (signal-receiving molecules) which reconfigure in response to stimuli and bring about changes in permeability affecting intercellular exchange. So vital is this living cell boundary to the ability of each cell to stay alive and relate in a sustainable and variable way to its neighborhood, that some biologists have likened it to a cell's 'brain.' (Hutchins, 2014, p75)

The presence of a boundary between the inner world and outer world of a living system does not isolate it from its environment as an independent entity but sustains its identity within an ever-changing environment. Life breathes through the continual inspiration-expiration of energetic flows through permeable boundaries. There can be no hardline boundary around any living form, yet there is most definitely a boundary.

Sometimes in our eagerness to dispel the illusion of separation, we seek to do away with boundaries all together, viewing everything as an amorphous 'oneness' where dualism is replaced with monism. In doing so, we replace one paradox with another paradox—we are all the same yet obviously different. In reality, there is no either/or. It's not the presence of the boundary itself that is causing the mechanistic reduction of reality but our power-control ego's desire for a clean cut, hard-and-fast boundary that we can control-manage. Boundaries abound, but hardline boundaries are illusions. There is differentiation and distinctness yet there is no absolute discreteness. It's what naturalist poet William Wordsworth pointed out two centuries ago when he said, "In nature, everything is distinct, yet nothing defined into absolute, independent singleness." (Rayner, 2011, p68)

The living-organization's inner-nature (its essence, values, and cultural integrity) is in continuous interrelation with its outer-nature (its ever-changing market and stakeholder ecosystem). The permeability of the living-organization opens it up to various partnerships, collaborations, networks, and initiatives of exchange and reciprocity. This is not limited to partners, suppliers, ambassadors, and customers but expands to a diverse range of stakeholders, including the social communities and ecological bioregions the business affects and is affected by, and the wider biosphere of the natural world at large with its intricate set of interrelating factors, limits, tipping points, and feedback loops. Likewise, the living-organization's essence, sense of integrity, and purposefulness relies upon team days, all staff gatherings, culture rituals, and communities of practice that prioritize the inner-nature of the organization.

THE LIVING-ORGANIZATION INTER-RELATING WITH OTHER LIVING-ORGANIZATIONS

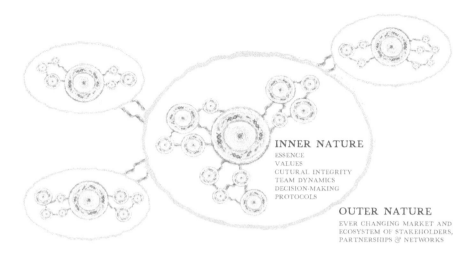

INNER NATURE
ESSENCE
VALUES
CUTURAL INTEGRITY
TEAM DYNAMICS
DECISION-MAKING
PROTOCOLS

OUTER NATURE
EVER CHANGING MARKET AND
ECOSYSTEM OF STAKEHOLDERS,
PARTNERSHIPS & NETWORKS

Life is continually expressing itself through open dialogue with life. Organisms pulsate in a relation of dynamic tension with the world around them. They exist in a constant state of adjusting, rebalancing, and shifting with environmental perturbations. Receptors in the organism convert sensory signals into electrical impulses, and these electrical impulses provide a detectable electromagnetic (EM) field around the organism. Living and non-living aspects of the environment give off a sea of EM wave energy.

Our bodies are in an EM dialogue with their surroundings, though much of this energetic dialogue goes below the radar of our normal conscious awareness. Contemporary philosopher Christian de Quincey notes that, "We are constantly sharing messages with the world around us, picking them up in our bodymind, processing or metabolizing them, and expressing some residue back out. We call this process 'life' ... As the self opens to respond to more environment—whether physical, mental, or spiritual—the experience of self expands, and more of what was not-self is incorporated."
(De Quincey, p77)

The ability of each bodymind to open and filter this continual dialogue is fundamental to how the organism survives and thrives. The health of the organism greatly relates to the electromagnetic interactivity and resonance of the organism with its environment. EM fields influence physiological processes, such as enzyme activity, cell growth, tissue repair rates, and so on. As we have seen, each cell membrane surrounding the cell is a semi-permeable boundary with thousands of pores that open and close depending on what is being sensed. With EM fluctuations, the membrane can either become more permeable and, in turn, more sensitive yet more vulnerable to its environment, or it can become less permeable and, in turn, less sensitive and more protected from its environment. The membrane is detecting and decoding the subtle changes it experiences in EM wave form, by sensing amplitude and frequency. (Buhner, p51-63) In the human body much of this EM sensing and responding is processed by the heart although neuroscience is uncovering new findings on how brain and gut neuron behavior also depend on resonance with EM stimuli, and, as we explored in Chapter 4, we can also experience bodymind coherence through entrainment of head-heart-gut.

Energy cultivation and coherence practices aid the energetic sensing-responding capacity of the bodymind to up-stretch to a new level without affecting the integrity of its inner-nature. We become more sensitive and responsive without becoming too vulnerable and overly sensitive.

For the living-organization we can enhance its overall sensing-responding capacity using what I call 'Systemic Enablers.'

Systemic Enablers

Select a diverse group of people from across different functions in the business—any number from four to fourteen people can work well, regardless of the organization's overall headcount. These are your Systemic Enablers. This group of people ought to be diverse in terms of the functional business areas they represent and their general outlook. Hierarchy is not important here. What is important is the aptitude, perception, and relational engagement each person has with the organizational system. Systemic Enablers ideally have healthy peer connectivity and diverse networks of sharing and collaborating across the business, a strong resonance with the purpose and values of the business, as well as a view not just across the inner-nature (the culture) of the organization but also across its outer-nature (its wider stakeholder ecosystem).

This cohort of Systemic Enablers then becomes a community of practice by embarking upon a transformational learning journey for themselves, as a community group, and for the wider organization. When they convene, they are in service of the organization. Through regular (for instance, monthly) gatherings (circles) the cohort shares their insights on the living-organization using an appreciative inquiry method of positive questioning, deep listening, systemic sensing in, and collaborative inquiry.

Upon identifying and acknowledging systemic patterns, the cohort then learns to discern where and in what way to engage in small systemic interventions— 'organizational acupuncture'—that send positive ripples across the system, no different than the acupuncture pinpricks that align us to our innate healing potential. We repattern relational stuckness into better flow, richer purposefulness, and increased outer impact.

For a case study on how Systemic Enablers can work within an international and fast-moving organization, see *Leading by Nature* which case studies the award-winning natural health and lifestyle brand Vivobarefoot and its journey toward regenerative business.

The magic of nature flowing through the relations as well as in the things themselves is overlooked by the mechanistic worldview. Nature is continually attuning its ability to sense and respond. In opening to this continuous stream of sensory and super-sensory flux flowing all around and through us, we embody this interactivity of nature. In becoming consciously aware of swimming within this ocean of energy, we may begin to experience nature beyond the fragmenting separation of Mechanistic Materialism. There's reciprocity between body and world where the perceiver and environment are not independent but interactive, and where cultural and environmental factors interact and reciprocate with personal factors. As the ancient Chinese Book of Changes, the *I Ching*, notes, "whatever is flexible and flowing will continue to evolve, whatever is rigid and blocked will wither and die." (Wilhelm, 2003)

Embracing Nature's Diverse Rhythms and Tensions

Reciprocal relationships ensure that each living system gains energy and resources through the myriad relationships within its ecosystem. The more reciprocal the relationships the more tolerant or 'playful' the ecosystem is to social, economic, and environmental change. Diversity improves the chances of co-creative relationships. Monocultures, on the other hand, occur when one type of species or one type of organizational or cultural behavior is encouraged at the expense of others, and such monocultures reduce diversity and the chance for reciprocal relationships to form, making their members more vulnerable to volatility, as when a hitherto unknown disease spreads like wildfire through a uniformly susceptible population.

In nature, we find the formations of monocultures at the early outset of ecological succession, following a disturbance or disruption to the ecosystem.

Certain organisms capitalize on this disturbance. These prolific species are referred to as 'weeds' and 'rodents.' Interestingly, these organisms exhibit similar characteristics to human capitalists—short-termism, focus on rapid growth, exploitation of immediately available resources, and inability to associate and sustain themselves in complex reciprocating relationships with others. Just as interesting, many mammalian males tend to exhibit more of these capitalist characteristics than their female counterparts who tend to focus more on nurturing reciprocal relations.

These capitalist characteristics are natural expressions of nature, but when these characteristics dominate to the extent of undermining nature's unfolding richness, then disharmony ensues. Hyper-capitalist, patriarchal, dominator cultures tend toward unsustainability and degeneration. Excessive competition and short-termism destroy diversity and innovation—a lesson it seems that many politicians, company executives and economists have yet to learn. It's about time we started to wake up to the wisdom running throughout life on Earth. We can embrace our ability to work with rather than against each other, and we can harmonize the tensions of our differences through dialogue.

We live in a time of immense volatility, tension, and opposing views. Holding space through dialogue can be an immensely powerful way to allow diversity to work its magic in fueling insight and evolution. Working through tensions of difference enhances organizational and individual learning. At Vivobarefoot 'Field Circles' are hosted every three months where a group of diverse people from across the company come together to sit in circle with a talking stick, which is based on the ancient indigenous practice of Way of Council (see Appendix for a deeper dive on this practice). What arises through this open-hearted and vulnerable sharing are not only powerful insights on differing perspectives (where tensions transmute into crucibles for creativity and a space for empathy and connection to form through differing opinions) but also a collective regeneration. This occurs by the circle's ability to hold space, which affects not only the participants in the circle but sends positive ripples through the whole living system, and often further into the extended business ecosystem of people's family constellations.

The Inner Harmonies of Life

As we touched upon in Chapter 1, there's a hidden language, or grammar, innate within nature, that of harmonies expressed throughout all forms of life from electrons to galaxies, from soil to trees, from human neurons firing to our business ventures. Everywhere we find these harmonious vibratory relationships.

Harmony is formed through contrasting aspects working together and creating a tension. Diverse influences come together and commune in a way that creates the harmonious 'music of life,' a pleasant attunement of differences. The rhythm and resonance these tensions provide invoke the experience of beauty and vitality within us and inform the beautiful proportions and patterns running through nature and the wider universe.

The Golden Section (also referred to as the Golden Ratio) is one such harmonic relationship we find running throughout nature. The Golden Section is where the smaller part stands in the same proportion to the larger part as the larger part stands to the whole. This is also where the Fibonacci Series originates and the Golden Mean, Phi. The Golden Section frequents organic growth, as if the emergence within life itself follows a harmony. From plant leaves to our human bodies, we find Golden Section harmonics, hence its nickname of 'nature's code.'

THE GOLDEN SECTION AND FIBONACCI SPIRAL

Nature's forms work with harmonics to inform their structure and growth patterns. This holds the same for buildings designed using the sacred geometric principles of harmonics and resonance, just like the ancient sites and temples did millennia ago. It's what Goethe points to when saying, "Architecture is frozen music." In becoming conscious of these rhythms and resonances we aid our right relation.

What is sometimes overlooked in seeing harmonious patterns is that there is a union of complementary but differing rhythms within these harmonious patterns. For example, the relationship between the major and minor scales in music, the relationship of the sun and moon, and yin and yang. Harmonies arise through the uniting of differing parts of the whole creating other stages in the relationship whilst still maintaining the integrity of the parts that make up the relationship. This union of differing relationships is vital to life as an opposing yet synergistic energy that drives organic growth. This is what the Hungarian architect Gyorgy Doczi refers to as 'dinergy' (his own word created by combining the Greek 'dia' meaning 'between' or 'through' and energy) rather than synergy, as synergy refers to the joining of cooperative forces, whereas dinergy is the joining of differing forces to create tension.

We find these dinergic tensions everywhere in life. The human body, for instance, is full of dinergic tensions—the double helix of DNA, the brain with its two opposing yet complimentary attention networks, the parasympathetic and sympathetic nervous system. Even the spirals we find in the microtubules within each cell are dinergic. All patterns in nature have a dinergic origin, as this opposition catalyzes rhythmic vibration, which is a pulsation created by an attunement of difference. This harmonic resonance is the basic unity throughout manifold diversity. The flower musically becomes more of itself, unfurling through whole number proportions in space (its harmonious form) and time (its harmonic unfurling growth pattern). Think of how each snowflake is unique yet unified, each blade of grass different yet similar, each fingertip of every human the same kind of pattern yet unique to the individual. All are dinergic tensions.

These dinergies are powered by limits, as it's the limitations in each of the differences coming together that ensures music not noise, beauty not blandness, creativity not combat. This is the nature of nature; its full of dinergic dance powered by limits. Tensions have limits, and cells have boundaries that aid the filtering and resonance of harmonic tensions via permeability (opening-up) or impermeability (closing-in). Similarly, the bodymind gains coherence by activating its super-nature through right relation of it's inner-nature (physiological and psychological vibratory fluctuations) with its outer-nature (eco-psycho-spiritual relational environment of vibratory fluctuations). Likewise, the living-organization aids its emergent becoming and evolutionary purposefulness by working with tensions powered by limits while utilizing permeable boundaries.

By working with the tensions of difference (yin and yang, freedom and order, opening up and closing down, divergence and convergence) life allows for emergence, a flowing dance of unfolding, adapting, and evolving. This goes directly to the root of one of life's perplexing paradoxes: why there is a yin-yang duality in life. Without this tension life would be flaccid. It would lose its vibrancy. The creative union between these seemingly opposing forces is what drives organic growth and allows the life-force to flow.

We are all transmitters and receivers of these rhythms. It's the sharing of the diversities of these wave patterns which gives life its immense beauty and vibrant variety. Through sharing relationships (interacting vibrations) life creates diversity which breeds and supports more life. This is the paradox of reciprocal relationships. In sharing one's limitations with another we complement each other, in turn providing harmony in life, or what Doczi refers to as 'the power of limits.' Limitations interact to provide openness beyond the inherent limitations. This is how life grows, how it interacts with seemingly opposing forces to create new growth, which can then interact with other oncoming forces or factors. The power of limits is the force behind creation.

The primal creative tension of difference or 'dinergic tension' drives life's creative advance through harmony and difference. In other words, integration and differentiation are co-creative. As the writer Reshad Feild notes, "This world requires the creative tension of opposites, and it is here we can see the miracle of multiplicity. Unity is not the miracle; the miracle is in the diversity." (Feild, p53)

Rather like the philosophy of Aikido, we work with the opposing force, transmuting the energy of tension into a movement that enlivens creativity rather than fueling a resistant combat. The tension fosters emergence which enables the life-force of the living-organization to flow. Recall the example of the Field Circles at Vivobarefoot. Rather than the life-force stagnating through unprocessed conflict that projects, blames, and isolates, we work through tensions for insights that spawn emergent evolution.

> "When masculine and feminine combine,
> All things achieve harmony."
>
> –Lao Tzu

The Dance of Yin and Yang

Ancient Chinese physicians studied these seemingly opposing forces in nature. They called them yin and yang—the soft and the hard, the shadow and the light, the negative and the positive, the receptive and the responsive, the feminine and the masculine. By attuning the tensions of these yin and yang qualities of life, one achieves rejuvenation and harmony. Just as 'dia' means between or through boundaries, it is the relationship between or through these tensions of yin and yang that makes for our reality. There exists not either/or, only the challenge/opportunity to find the right harmonic within and through the tension. In certain life situations a little more yang than yin may be useful, while others call for a little more yin than yang. It's the twisting and turning primordial spiral as it attunes. Only when one side of the reciprocal relationship begins to dominate, and so undermines the reciprocity of the dinergic relationship, does disharmony and disease ensue. However, with regenerative leadership consciousness, dualistic competition becomes dinergic reciprocation.

Emergence Arising from Tension

Emergence is the way life unfolds. It's nature's creative advance. All living systems express themselves through the self-generating, self-organizing property of emergence, and organizations are no different.

Emergence is propelled by tensions. Tensions create unease that stimulates and cajoles us out of the status quo and into emergence. These tensions arise between the space of divergence (diverse perspectives, opening up) and convergence (alignment around purpose and values, closing down), and in the sweet spot between divergence and convergence flows emergence. Too much divergence, and chaos ensues. Too much convergence, and rigidity forms.

Living systems thrive on this edge of chaos and order, and it's this edge that enables adaptability and vitality across the living-organization. Dee Hock, former CEO and Chairman of VISA uses the term 'chaordic' to describe this alchemy of chaos (divergence) and order (convergence). Therefore, tension is vital for a healthy living-organization, as plenty of tension ensures plenty of emergence which ensures overall anti-fragility. Hock views this chaordic sweet spot as the essential organizational ingredient for future-fitness—and one that has certainly helped VISA consistently succeed in a rapidly evolving marketplace.

Tension creates the crucible for creativity. Creativity is not something we are born with or can rehearse but it is something we can learn to cultivate by working with tensions. Comedian John Cleese researched what makes people creative. Cleese found that creative people are able to work with two different states of mind—an open state (divergence, playful, expansive, relational, curious) and a closed state (convergence, focused, goal-driven, structured). People require both, the open state to ideate and the closed state to manifest their ideas through planning and focus. This oscillation between open divergence and closed convergence is happening everywhere all the time, in our own lives, in life all around us, and across the living-organization.

Mechanistic organizations tend to honor only the closed state, becoming overly convergent and rigid through bureaucratic and hierarchical decision-making protocols that stymie creativity. But the life-force of the living-organization is stimulated through the alchemy of divergence and convergence. Without this right relation there is no flow.

The Living-Organization's Tension of Divergence-Convergence for Emergence

Divergence occurs through greater levels of self-management, personal freedom, and responsibility, which allow people to adapt quickly and locally to tension and affect change right where it's needed *without* the cumbersome need for chains of command. Contrary to popular opinion, self-management does not mean the absence of structure, workflow processes, or rules. This is where convergence comes in. It is stimulated through clarity of roles, purpose and values, methods of communicating and collaborating, meeting practices, decision-making and advice seeking processes, group dialogue practices, feedback, learning methods, and more.

As well as encouraging self-management, divergence is stimulated across the organization by encouraging diversity of perspectives by working across boundaries, encouraging people to go to the edges of the system, and engage with a variety of departments, specialists, and external stakeholder groups. This includes cross-functional teams visiting frontline operations, liaising with different customer segments, and engaging with diverse groups of people in society to ensure diversity in age, outlook, creed, culture, gender, and sexual orientation. There are practices like stakeholder dialogue interviews, World Café, and Future Search workshops that can help with this. (See the Appendix and my *website* for more on these and other practices).

Living systems deepen their becoming because of unceasing transformation. Life is not about 'defending against', 'coping with' or 'managing' unceasing transformation, but about working with the tensions of transformation in order to bring forth the evolutionary potential of the living system through the tensions. To learn to work with living systems as a regenerative leader—whether it's a living-organization or a community group or neighborhood—we are engaging with systems that are rooted in an underlying rhythmic and tensive composition pervading inner-*and*-outer nature. This is what the ancient Chinese explored through the *I Ching*, the Book of Changes, some four thousand years ago, which recognizes that the ever-changing diversities in nature have an underlying rhythm—one might say, resonance—in which everything is related to everything else inwardly in their spirit and outwardly in their manifestation. The foundation of this inner-outer order is the dinergic dance of feminine-yin and masculine-yang, opposing forces that work together through the power of limits to create emergence in all living systems. By working with this wisdom of nature we can learn to lead and live by it, and so become regenerative.

Nature is founded upon harmonic, dinergic relationships. Living systems thrive through dance, and the regenerative leader knows how to hold space for tensions to work their magic by providing just the right amount of emergence to both unfurl the purposefulness of the living system and adapt to ever-changing circumstances, surfing the edge of chaos. The regenerative leader and living-organization don't merely 'cope' with complexity, they 'thrive' amid complexity.

As our lenses widen, and we open into nature, we gain a deeper understanding that inner-nature and outer-nature are inextricably entwined. Everything in nature, including particles, atoms, galaxies, and supernovas, is the emergent consequence of inner-outer interpenetrations, tensions of interactions, and relationality outwardly and inwardly. This harmony can manifest as viability, resilience, purposefulness, authenticity, profitability, and systemic value creation. Life is regenerative. Reconnect with the rapture of reality and regenerative leadership consciousness flows through us, naturally. This is the beautiful simplicity the other side of all this complexity. Where the soul's wisdom up-stretches beyond the ego's cleverness.

> "Learn how to see. Realize everything connects with everything else."
>
> —Leonardo Da Vinci

It's a virtuous endeavor, one as old as time, to seek inspiration from nature amid metamorphic times. Yet it's all too easy to apply a mechanistic mindset to our acquisition of findings 'from' nature that ignore nature's energetic interconnectedness and leads us to applying the very same level of consciousness to our well-intended solutions that created the problems in the first place.

We must re-member that essentially, we *are* nature, we are infinitely immersed *in* nature, never separate from it or Her. Nature is a participatory affair steeped in consciousness. Sentient, energetic, informational, rhythmic, and held within a depth of dimension one might call 'metaphysical,' 'inner,' 'quantum,' 'Spirit' or 'Source.' From the quark string humming away, the water tumbling down stream, the sapling and Mother Tree, the bee and hive to the leader and organization, we find more than 'systems nested within systems' but 'fields immersed within fields,' interpenetrated with intentionality. And we humans participate in this, whether we're conscious of it or not.

From the moment we wake up, it's convenient to slip into Mechanistic Materialism, regardless of our wish to be regenerative or not. Before we know it, the organization *is* a machine to be managed by the profit and loss statement (P&L) *for* the P&L. Rather than the P&L serving as a useful tool to help the vitality and purposefulness of the living-organization, it becomes the master, enslaving the life-force of the organization. Enter the wasteland of the wounded Fisher King and the dire plight we are inflicting on this planet. Along with an achiever mind cut adrift from any sense of meaning or purpose, grasping outwardly for material happiness while feeling disillusionment, insecurity and disease grow from within.

As Morpheus says to Neo in the film the Matrix, "You have to understand, most people are not ready to be unplugged, and many of them are so inured and so hopelessly dependent on the system that they will fight to protect it."

Through the inner death-rebirth metamorphic journey, we learn to let go of old ways and start to see with new eyes. In doing so, we are cultivating a mastery of ego-consciousness that opens our hearts and minds to learn from *and* attune with living systems. It's this learning from *and* attuning with living systems that we turn to in the next chapter on Living Systems Awareness.

The Three Levels of Living Systems Awareness

Through many years of coaching regenerative leaders and practitioners through death-rebirth metamorphoses, I've found that a powerful way to convey the richly textured shift in consciousness from achiever to regenerator is to frame it in the **three levels of living systems awareness**.

THREE LEVELS OF LIVING SYSTEMS AWARENESS

LEVEL 0 — ORANGE EXPERT/ACHIEVER
SELF-AS-SEPARATE
ORGANIZATION-AS-MACHINE

LEVEL 1 — GREEN INDIVIDUALIST OPEN MIND
LEARNING FROM NATURE
ORGANIZATION-AS-FAMILY

LEVEL 2 — TEAL STRATEGIST OPEN HEART
PARTICIPATING WITHIN NATURE
ORGANIZATION-AS-LIVING-SYSTEM

LEVEL 3 — TURQUOISE ALCHEMIST OPEN WILL
ATTUNING WITH NATURE
ORGANIZATION-IN-SERVICE-OF-LIFE

Before we dive into each Level, which we will do in this chapter, I want to give you an overall picture of the journey, and before we do that, we must acknowledge Level 0. Consider Level 0 to be where mainstream corporate thinking resides—with a developmental color band of Orange to denote an Expert/Achiever mindset that is self-as-separate and organization-as-machine with control-manage leadership dynamics. Short-term profit maximization is a strong imperative here, and there is little sense of purpose beyond profit, market competition, and developing one's particular niche or product offering.

At Level 0 there is faint, if any, comprehension of how we might learn from or with living systems. The leader might be intrigued by nature, perhaps even enjoy walks in nature and watching nature on TV, but the general understanding of nature is anthropocentric and Neo-Darwinian. Nature remains as 'red in tooth and claw.' It's a world of survival of the fittest, evolution through random mutation, where there is no sense of the sacred. Consciousness is an epiphenomenon of the human brain, and nature a utility or escape for humans.

Now that we have a grasp on the system dynamics of Level 0, no further time will be spent at this level, or on how to shift a Level 0 leader into a Level 1 leader. Because this book is written for leaders and practitioners who are already embarking on the journey toward regeneration, and there are (now) ample regenerative, living systems, and bio-inspired books, courses, and seminars available to assist leaders in the 0 to 1 transformation. While the bridging of Level 0 to Level 1 is of the utmost importance and is where the groundswell of mainstream interest in regenerative business tends to focus right now, it is not the main thrust of this book.

We begin at Level 1 with an 'open mind.'

In this first level, we are **gathering at the threshold**. Here, we are learning *from* nature, educating ourselves about nature's design principles, and all the ways in which we can study the natural world. Examining, exploring, and being with nature as 'out there' or 'outer-nature.' In Level 1, human awareness is standing apart from nature, observing the ensemble of forms, relationships, designs, rhythms, experiences, patterns, ecosystems, ecologies, and principles to help open minds and become conscious of how nature 'out there' works and how we might benefit and gain insights 'from' nature.

We move on to Level 2 with an 'open heart.'

We are now **crossing the threshold** of learning *from* nature to participating *within* nature. Here, we immerse ourselves within living systems and are a co-creative embodiment existing 'within' the system. Level 2 involves the inner journey of individuation. The human-nature dichotomy (along with the mind-matter, inner-outer, feminine-masculine fissure) begins to integrate within our consciousness. Heart consciousness comes on stream and is enhanced by psychospiritual practices like advanced meditation and body-mind coherence. The first step of activating our super-nature—becoming intimate with the immanent—happens here.

In Level 3, we experience 'open will.'

No longer just learning from or participating within, here we are **alchemically working with Nature's Wisdom** by *attuning with* nature. It is a learning to find accord with the mystic rhythms of life, as much as an intuitive felt-sensing of the living system as an eco-psycho-spiritual super sensing of inner-nature. Level 3 is working with the 'inner' aspects, or esoteric aspects, of Nature's Wisdom to alchemize inner-outer nature in service of life through our soul craft. We have become more intimate with the immanent and now are becoming more transparent to the transcendent nature of reality.

THREE LEVELS OF LIVING SYSTEMS AWARENESS WITH THRESHOLD

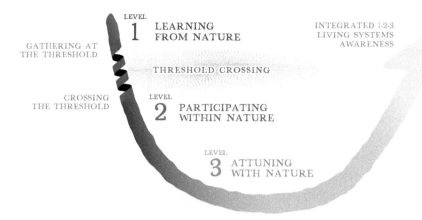

Integrated together, Level 1-2-3 Learning *from-and-within* living systems enables a shift in how we perceive life and our sense of place and purpose within it. It is a 'seeing with new eyes', which is both ontological (a shift in our way of being-becoming) and epistemological (a shift in our way of knowing); both scientific (a shift from mechanistic materialistic science to quantum complexity science) and spiritual (a shift from an anthropocentric experience of life 'out there' to a developmental and metaphysical experience of inner-outer nature).

WORKING WITH NATURE'S WISDOM

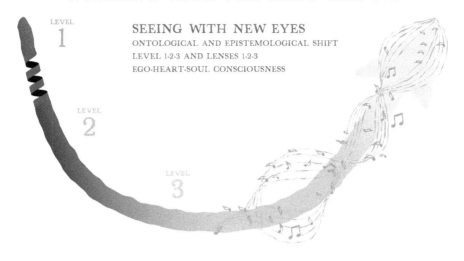

LEVEL 1

SEEING WITH NEW EYES
ONTOLOGICAL AND EPISTEMOLOGICAL SHIFT
LEVEL 1-2-3 AND LENSES 1-2-3
EGO-HEART-SOUL CONSCIOUSNESS

LEVEL 2

LEVEL 3

Level 1 Living Systems Awareness – Learning *from* Nature

We are opening our minds to learning *from* nature by educating ourselves about how nature works, albeit from a largely outer-nature perspective. This can include a wide range of 'door-opening' disciplines such as systems thinking, cradle to cradle, permaculture, biomimicry, circular economics, biophilic design, industrial ecology, to name a few. Opening these doors organizes an important mobilization during the early stages of the regenerative journey. We are whetting our appetite and feeding our minds with myriad patterns, principles, and processes that can be applied by engineers, architects, designers, innovators, creatives, leaders, and entrepreneurs. We can then apply our new knowledge to designing new products, services, processes, structures, cultures and places.

At the time of writing this book we have seen an exponential rise in interest in this Level 1 learning from nature, which is encouraging. Only fifteen years ago—not a long time in the grand scheme of the evolution of human consciousness—I started running workshops on 'Business Inspired by Nature' for corporate executives. Back then it was very niche, groundbreaking even. Today, it's everywhere. We find it in mainstream Sustainable Business, and People & Culture conferences are frequently holding nature-inspired sessions for business leaders. These efforts are heartwarming and show the increasing numbers of leaders who are exploring the L&OD shift from Orange Expert/Achiever organization-as-machine into Green Individualist organization-as-family. We're witnessing mobilization and momentum that perfectly illustrate **gathering at the threshold.**

Level 1's focus is primarily (but not always solely) on 'outer-nature', with attention drawn to the forms, patterns, relationships and structures we find in nature. For instance, we open our minds to how mycelia connect trees underground through a 'wood wide web', a sentient network exchanging nutrients and information. We can observe how termites work together as a super-organism to design intricate structures that regulate temperature, or we can explore how termites work with other species (like fungi) to engage in regenerative farming techniques.

There is simply so many ways we can open our minds into nature—to learn *from* nature. In doing so, we ease out of the heightened sense of human self-as-separate from nature and form a sense of connection with nature, at times, even a reverence and respect for nature.

While this Level 1 perspective aids our right relation dynamic of self-other-world, nature might still be (but not necessarily) observed in an objectified, rational-analytic, head-orientated way. Systems thinking and circular design are tools that go a long way in moving us from linear cause-and-effect thinking to relational complexity thinking, but they can be limited to mapping systems 'out there', forcing us to draw reductive lines between reductive parts of the system that makes up a 'whole.' Although, one might say a 'counterfeit whole', as the system map often overlooks the holistic organic understanding of the whole. No doubt this helps us rationally analyze a complex system, encouraging our left hemisphere's ability to make sense of complexity, yet it may not further our empathic and holistic connection with the system as a whole, nor with the intricate nature of the relationships between the parts beyond cognitive analysis.

Level 1, with its left hemisphere, rational, 'out there' learning, has its limitations, especially when it's not coupled with the learning of Levels 2 and 3. Even though Level 1 is primarily 'out there', we cannot negate that Level 1 learning is certainly an important part of the journey. So, before we up-level, let's explore a few of the nature-inspired principles common to Level 1 to discover how they might aid our regenerative journey.

A great overview of 'outer-nature' principles is provided here by Fritjof Capra, a world class scientist and teacher of eco-literacy: (Capra, 2003, p202)

Nature Inspired Principles

Networks: At all scales of nature, we find living systems nesting and interconnecting within other living systems—networks within networks. Boundaries within and among systems are not boundaries of strict separation but boundaries of identity and interaction. All living systems interconnect, communicate with one another, and share resources across their boundaries.

Cycles: All living organisms must feed on continual flows of matter and energy from their environment to stay alive, and, in turn, all living organisms continually contribute flows of matter and energy to their environment. An ecosystem as a whole generates no net waste, as one species' waste becomes another species' food, allowing matter and energy to transform and cycle through the web of life.

Solar Energy: Solar energy, transformed into chemical energy by the photosynthesis of green plants, is the foundation of ecological cycles. However, there are rare exceptional non-solar ecosystems. For example, deep sea vent ecosystems are driven by energy from Earth's molten core.

Partnership: The exchange of energy and resources within an ecosystem is sustained by pervasive cooperation. Life did not take over the planet by combat but by cooperation, partnership, and networking.

Diversity: Ecosystems achieve robustness and resilience through the richness and complexity of their ecological webs. The greater their biodiversity, the more resilient they will be.

Dynamic Balance: An ecosystem is a flexible, responsive, fluctuating network, a consequence of multiple sense-respond feedback loops that keep the system in a state of dynamic balance. No single variable is maximized; all variables fluctuate in concert around a collective optimum.

We also cannot move on from Level 1 without a brief exploration into the scientific discipline biomimicry, which studies nature as a source of inspiration to solve human problems—*learning from* nature. Biomimesis as a practice has been around for thousands of years, but as a formal design concept it's relatively recent. The word itself, 'biomimicry', was coined by revered biologist and naturalist Janine Benyus (author of the book *Biomimicry*) and originates from the Greek 'bios' (life) and 'mimesis' (imitation). (Benyus) To provide guidance to designers using biomimicry, the Biomimicry Institute has developed a framework based on the conditions under which life operates referred to as 'Life's Principles.'

The Biomimicry Life's Principles

Life adapts and evolves by:
- Being locally attuned and responsive
    - Using constant feedback loops
    - Antenna, signal, response
    - Learns and imitates
    - Resourceful and Opportunistic

- Free energy
- Shape rather than material
- Builds from the bottom up
- Simple, common building blocks
* Running on cyclic processes
* Being resilient
  - Decentralized and distributed
  - Redundant
  - Diverse
  - Cross-pollination, common information system (genetic)

Life creates conditions conducive to life by:
* Optimizing rather than maximizing
  - Using multi-functional design
  - Fitting form to function
* Being interdependent
  - Recycle all materials
  - Self-organization
* Using benign manufacturing
  - Using life-friendly materials
  - Using water-based chemistry
  - Using self-assembly

From biomimicry, we can derive nature-inspired principles that can be specifically applied to regenerative leadership. I call these seven principles of learning from living systems 'The Logic of Life principles.' You might notice that The Logic of Life principles draw from what has already been shared above with Capra's and the Biomimicry Institute's principles, then infused with mine and Laura Storm's regenerative leadership research.

These seven principles provide a good coverage of Level 1 learning from living systems as applied to Regenerative L&OD. We'll now touch on each one, as a general principle. For a fuller exploration of these seven principles see the book *Regenerative Leadership*. (Hutchins & Storm, 2019)

Learning from the Logic of Life's 7 Principles

1. **Life-Affirming:** This is the overarching principle. Life creates conditions conducive to life. The regenerative leader seeks only life-affirming activities and outcomes, being watchful for anything that could be toxic, life-denying, or degenerative.

   Life creates conditions conducive to life. Yes, the overarching principle for all life on this planet is *that* simple. It was Benyus who was first to capture the notion that all life facilitates more life in one sentence: "Life creates conditions conducive to life." Life itself, we learn, is life-affirming by its very nature. Life-affirming explains how diverse species have been able to evolve through billions of years of life on our planet, at times enduring harsh and life-threatening conditions.

   We can look to the ecosystem of a forest, which recycles nutrients and provides the conditions for its species to survive, thrive, and evolve. Even parasites and viruses play their part in the interrelating emergent system. The forest is constantly breaking down the old and transforming it into new growth, while navigating the changing seasons, weather disruptions, and system shocks (like a wildfire). Everything contributes to the complex dynamics of the forest's ongoing adaptation and evolution.

   In nature we find a continuous dis-equilibrium. Nature seeks harmony and allows for rich diversity within a coherence of unity. Perfect balance would bring stasis, which would halt the energy of life and its evolution. To see the greater picture—the Logic of Life—is to see that within nature's imbalance every part finds its place within the whole, every species adapts to its niche, and the overall system lends itself to a coherence within the creative chaos of constant change.

2. **Ever-changing & Responsive:** Change is an inevitable aspect of life that we can embrace for the opportunity and leverage it offers us for learning, adaptation, resilience, and evolution.

   Change is inherent within life. Change occurs all the time, everywhere. We can either be afraid and resistant to change by trying to control it or avoid it. Or we can embrace it as a source of creativity and innovation. We can ride change like a wave. To embrace the ephemeral nature of life is to experience one of life's true joys. No two moments are ever the same. No two days or sunrises or snowflakes are ever the same. As the Greek philosopher Heraclitus stated, "We can never step into the same river twice." Life is a river of continuous change, a song of ever-changing melodies and symphonies.

   In this volatile uncertain age, the ways in which organizational conditions change will only become more complex and more transient, but we have an option. React with increasing fear and create more stress in an attempt to control the uncontrollable. Or embrace the challenge of change and permit the breakdowns of old systems to yield the breakthroughs of the new.

   The mechanistic way of structuring organizations—around hierarchies of bureaucracy and control—decreases organizational agility and creates cultures that reduce the individual's and the collective's capacity to see new potential and to cope with threats quickly and effectively. Regenerative leaders, however, are tasked to structure teams of individuals who can tune in to these transient conditions and make informed decisions as the moment calls for it.

3. **Relational & Collaborative:** Everything in life consists of interrelating, interconnected systems nested within each other. Understanding these interconnections frees our perception from seeing and thinking in silos and broadens our thinking into systems.

   Life thrives through relationships. No man is an island. Yet, machine mentality has encouraged a hardening of boundaries to atomize, control, protect, and maximize our means of life, which has led us to a siloed mentality of separation. However, organizations thrive on partnerships—just like nature. "It's all about the numbers" is a slogan of the Orange Expert/Achiever, and in learning from nature, as we move into Green Individualist, we can now say "It's all about the relationships."

Regenerative leadership encourages permeating boundaries to foster collaboration, shared value, and co-innovation, all the while maintaining respect for security, safety, local customs, and differing cultural values and ownership approaches. This relationality is the lifeblood of adaptive, resilient, regenerative business, and the more we increase the relationality within our teams and across the organizational silos and stakeholder ecosystems, the more we allow the organization to, like nature, be resilient and agile.

4 **Synergistic & Diverse:** The presence of diversity and the ability to work tensions through into synergy and dinergy are vital to life.

Diversity breathes new life. Our organizational systems are made up of tensions of difference, which unleash new perspectives, innovations, and creative energy-flows that allow the living system to adapt and evolve. We tend to view synergy as two or more complementary and cooperative relationships coming together to strengthen the greater whole. While this is often the case, there is plenty of evidence in nature and in human-nature of differing dinergic relations—those that seemingly oppose each other—colliding or coming together for the purpose of releasing new opportunities, new systems, new life.

In the case of humans, the strength of our living system dynamics depends on how open, curious, and compassionate we are in holding such tensions, whether they be derived from opinion, race, gender, background, upbringing, age, sexual orientation, belief, or perspective. This calls for leaders to open their perceptual horizons to embrace diverse perspectives and be more than okay surrounded and informed by views different than their own. No tension in a system signifies no aliveness, no learning, no evolution.

5 **Cyclical & Rhythmical:** The emergent nature of life contains rhythms of cycles and seasons that ebb and flow. The more we understand the pulses of life, the more of Nature's Wisdom we can tap into.

The seasons of life are at the heart of Nature's Wisdom. We see this everywhere we turn—the ebb and the flow of tides, the cycles of the moon, the sun, the seasons, death and rebirth, rest and regeneration. Emergence comes from cyclic rhythm. In fact, emergence unfolds through pulses and phases of development that can be likened to the four seasons.

Spring is the phase of new shoots bursting forth and animals leaving their hibernation and seeking new partnerships—a period of rapid innovation, growth spurts, and development. *Summer* is the phase when growth rates stabilize as plants and animals attune to their surroundings—a period of incremental development through increasing efficiencies and effectiveness. *Autumn* is the phase of harvesting the fruits fertilized in spring and grown over summer—a period of capitalizing on the market position yet remaining aware of change in the air and a need to let go of the current proposition, like the trees dropping their leaves to prepare for a significant phase shift as life conditions change. *Winter* is the phase of breaking down of old ways to make space for reflection and renewal—a period marked by slowing down, taking stock, letting go, and perhaps hibernation during which reorganization, reinvention, rebirth, and renewal occur.

In nature, and in business, each of us experiences these rhythmic phases in our lives. The unfolding, the growing, the harvesting, the letting go, reflection and renewal are perpetual phases of breakdown and breakthrough. The more we learn to become conscious of our own rhythms and cycles of psychological growth and renewal, the more effective, compassionate, and authentic we can become as leaders. These cycles of death and rebirth within our psychology are vital for the emergence of our authentic selves.

This cyclic death-rebirth rhythm has been referred to in living-systems science as 'Panarchy', though myself and Laura Storm often refer to it as the 'Rhythm of Life'.

PANARCHY - THE RHYTHM OF LIFE

6. **Flows of Energy & Matter:** There are innate ecosystem processes that life depends upon, and as such everything flows in a cyclic and interconnected way. Designing and operating with this understanding of energy-flows is what enables us to recycle, reuse, and renew in ways that do not undermine life's ecosystems.

Life depends on flow. Ecosystem flows exist at the biological, psychological, socioeconomic, and ecological levels. At the biological level, life depends upon the flows of water, minerals, and nutrients. We also know that the living system of Gaia (our world's entire biosphere) has natural limits and boundaries that these flows of energy and matter must operate within. There are macro flows (such as the carbon, nitrogen, oxygen, and water) that operate at the global system level and micro flows (and microclimates) that fluctuate depending on the locality.

A fact that is often overlooked by Mechanistic Materialism, is that our organizational and community systems have their own flows. These human systems depend upon the biological ecosystem flows that exist in nature, in conjunction with their own flows of information, resources, relational and psychological energies, and the flows of purpose and meaning. Whereas ecologists study the ecosystem flows at the biological level, we need people within our organizations that can sense system flows of relational energy. As regenerative leaders, we become conscious of the hidden, intangible patterns and interrelations that make up our organizations.

Becoming sensitive to these energy-flows is an opening into the 'inner-nature' of the organization-as-living-system, which edges us toward Level 2 Living Systems Awareness.

7. **Living Systems Field:** As we have already explored, scientific evidence points to an all-pervasive Field that informs all form. This seventh principle of the Logic of Life provides for a sense of the interconnectedness of all life opening us up to inner-outer nature, which brings us into Levels 2 and 3 of Living Systems Awareness.

Life is an interconnected whole. This seventh principle of the Logic of Life provides for a sense of the interconnectedness of all life and recognizes the Field of interconnection. Our lives, our relations, our thoughts, and feelings are all immersed and participating within this Field of consciousness, which is evolving all the time as we participate within it at all times. We can either ignore it, as we have largely done since the Scientific Revolution, or we can become conscious of it once again, just as the ancients were and as many of today's next stage conscious leaders are.

> "There is not anything in the cosmos that is not alive."
>
> –Hermes Trismegistus

At Level 1 Living Systems Awareness, we open our minds to how nature works. We learn to weave living systems thinking in to how we perceive the organization-as-living-system and how we sense the relational, energetic, and seasonal nature of life within the living-organization. Yet much of Level 1 learning resides at the head level, as a rational-analytic comprehension of outer-nature. Level 1 increases our awareness of nature as interrelating systems within systems, but we often stand separate from these systems. That is, unless we begin to shift our awareness inwardly, which brings us to Level 2 Living Systems Awareness of participating *within* nature.

This is the shift in consciousness from a dominant, left hemisphere ego-consciousness that sees self-as-separate (within the worldview of

Mechanistic Materialism) to an embodied right-left-right, ego-heart-soul consciousness (within the worldview of Quantum Complexity). We are no longer gathering at the threshold but crossing it to embark on the inner death-rebirth journey.

To be very clear, the motive here is not to judge, to separate or to prioritize one Level of learning from another, or to categorize one as better or worse. We urgently need leaders who dare to open their minds to Level 1 Living Systems Awareness and begin to fill their dialogue and messaging and boardroom agendas with words and phrases that spark and initiate this Level 1 learning. Such as: biomimicry, circularity, biophilia, cocreation, bio-inspired, nature's intelligence, environmental psychology, ecological consciousness, environmental awareness, eco-literacy, systems thinking, systems design, circular design, cradle-to-cradle.

This Level 1 journey toward regenerative leadership consciousness will likely start with principles and applications such as 'nature as a metaphor.' Learning from bee, ant, and termite behavior or that of a tree, rooted downward while branching outward, for instance. Or frames (like systems mapping and circular design) to help open the mind beyond a purely linear, siloed view of product and process design.

We open our minds beyond Level 0 and beyond its traditional mechanistic mindset in which the majority of our ESG/sustainability and wellbeing-at-work initiatives are often unwittingly rooted in. This exploration of nature's ways and rhythms, of understanding that 'natural connection enhances human wellbeing' is an important opening into the regenerative leadership journey, and aids the shift from Orange Expert/Achiever into Green Individualist. However, it's not until we dare to journey inward and shift our own self-and-systemic awareness that we can cross the threshold that takes us beyond unconscious mechanistic limitations.

Level 2 Living Systems Awareness Participating *within* Nature

In Level 2 Living Systems Awareness we cross the threshold from self-as-separate to self-as-participatory. We are no longer standing apart *from* nature, observing and learning *from* nature out there. Through various practices (like bodymind coherence) the way we attend to life subtly shifts and we become immersed within the system. It's a felt-sense, an embodied experience of opening our bodymind, a heart opening that welcomes in heart-consciousness. The heart, as we now know, symbolizes the center of the bodymind.

In Level 2, our bodymind becomes receptive and open to the systemic dynamics of the system we are in, whether it be in nature or when working in the living-organization. This sensitive receptivity involves a simultaneous self-and-systemic shift in awareness. Rather than the 'systems thinking' of Level 1, we now have 'systemic awareness', which is a fundamentally different way of perceiving, sensing, and embodying living systems. This involves what adult developmental psychology refers to as 'vertical development'—a shift in our meaning-making—and corresponds with a movement from Green-Individualist into Teal-Strategist (a journey we explore in detail in Chapter 8). Here we increase our capacity to feel, intuit, and comprehend the participatory rhythms, resonances, repercussions, and ripples we are reverberating within. We are sensing-responding and participating *within* the system.

As we embrace this Level 2 Living Systems Awareness, we activate our super-nature and open our awareness to the hidden ordering forces, subtle energy-flows, organizational acupuncture nodes, patterns of relationality, and networks of tacit knowledge sharing. Remember the Systemic Enablers mentioned in the last chapter? We sense the essence, life-force and evolutionary potential of the living-organization. This shift in awareness also entails a recognition that the outer-nature of the organization (value propositions, stakeholder relationships, brand) is fully enlivened and authentic when in accord with the inner-nature of the organization (culture, values, essence, evolutionary potential).

We still maintain the capacity to stand apart, by using our left hemisphere as a tool. But through presencing, our right hemisphere finds its rightful place as primary, with a more natural right-left-right hemispheric attention aiding our ability to sense-respond to the developmental, emergent, and evolutionary dynamics of the living-organization.

> "Attention is a moral act: it creates, brings aspects of things into being, in doing so makes others recede. What a thing is depends on who is attending to it and in what way."
>
> —Iain McGilchrist

It is here in Level 2 that we can fully experience the systemic capacity for DEE (Developmental, Emergent, and Evolutionary), but before delving into DEE, let's get to know the quality of presencing that the activating of our super-nature enables. Recall how Heidegger's presencing and Goethe's active seeing both take us into the experience of experiencing— an awareness of the unfolding, a coming into being. We are no longer limited to Barfield's 'alpha-beta' reflexive thinking, which is observing our own thoughts and feelings about the phenomenon or indeed ego-consciousness sensing the system outside ourselves. Level 2 learning is not a dualistic observation of self and system. The experience of experiencing is an immersive, embodied involvement in Barfield's 'final participation', whereupon we are fully within self-and-system, yet retain the capacity to stand back and observe self and system. There is a toggling between left and right hemisphere, dorsal and ventral attention systems. The ego is not dissolved. It is permeated.

Level 2 is a simultaneous ego maturation and ego permeation. This subtle inward shift, this heart-consciousness, is where we enter a more empathic quality that enables us to call upon the rational-emotional-somatic-intuitive ways of knowing within our bodymind while becoming sensitive to rhythmic tensions within and all around us in self-and-system, all the while pervaded by life-force currents and constellations. We return to the rhizome root without being subsumed into the unconscious Field. As humans, we have journeyed through Jung's individuation and expanded our meaning-making to welcome in more of life.

Level 1's ability to map the system using systems thinking is still useful, but we are freed from standing separate. We are now able to be immersed within and thus sense a dynamic depth in the system that permits a conscious holding of space for tensions of divergence-convergence that birth emergence. We not only comprehend the organization-as-a-living-system, but we feel it, as a participatory felt-sense that we intuit due to the receptivity of our presencing. Through tools and practices (like dialogue and deep-listening) we can help ourselves and others improve self-and-systemic awareness and work with the DEE capacities that enable future-fitness. We do not fear change but recognize that change impels development, growth, and opportunity.

This self-and-systemic awareness applies also to life beyond the living-organization, and we sense the relational sentience in our own family constellations, communities, throughout the more-than-human world of local neighborhoods, bioregions, and the whole living Earth (Gaia). This systemic sensitivity might be better named 'ecosystemic awareness' with reference to our capacity to sense-respond to the more-than-human world, not in an 'outer-nature' way but in an inner-outer sensuous intimacy and super-sensory transparency to life and its sentience. We feel inherently part of nature.

The work of ecopsychology is relevant here, as we start to heal the festering psychic wound of human-nature separation that we have endured in the psyche and soul for much of our achiever-orientated living and leading—for much of modern history. Level 2 awakens a (yin) receptivity and (yang) responsiveness inside our psyche and our soul. One might liken this to a spaciousness inside us forming, a space for presencing the unfurling becoming of what is within and around us, in the moment. A space for bodymind coherence, deep-listening, and dialogue for what wants to emerge unfettered by our grasping left hemispheric ego-consciousness. We are living and learning beyond the need to achieve, push, and force. We stand upright, strong in our own soul power, open-hearted, and fully available to sense-respond in the moment.

None of this is easy to convey in words, hence the reason I coach leaders and practitioners through multi-month-long journeys. It takes time to embody the internal felt-sense difference between Level 1's learning *from* nature and the receptive-responsiveness of Level 2's participating *within* nature. Level 2 involves an intuitive consciousness of the multiplicity within the unity of Nature's Wisdom where we learn to dance with a diversity of dialogue through dinergic tensions powered by limits, and before the journey takes us to Level 3 of Living Systems Awareness, we must start to trust in Nature's Wisdom.

Learning from-and-within Nature's Wisdom

All of life—including human society, the organization, and the leader—is immersed in a rhythmic and relational dance. When off kilter with the rhythms of this dance, chaos and fragility ensue. When attuned, all parts find flow and flourish. It's the same for life within the organization as it is for life beyond the organization. Regenerative leaders can live in accord with this wisdom through certain practices of learning how to sense and work with life's subtle ways.

I've spent many years contemplating what Nature's Wisdom is to the human mind, psyche, and soul. Drawing upon my own life practices, phenomena, and out-of-body and near-death experiences, I have framed two sets of three aspects of Nature's Wisdom. The first set is comprised of three aspects that are related to systemic outer-and-inner nature which we open to in Level 2 Living Systems Awareness, and the second set of three takes us inward into the psycho-spirituality of inner-nature, closer to our soul center and into Level 3. I refer to the sets as 'exoteric' and 'esoteric' aspects.

There are other aspects to Nature's Wisdom, and these three exoteric and three esoteric aspects are not meant to be in any way definitive or exclusive. Quite frankly, when we immerse ourselves into Nature's Wisdom, words crumble in the face of awe and mystery. Still, I have found this mirrored outer-inner framing of Nature's Wisdom to be extremely helpful when guiding leaders and practitioners through the inner journey of achiever to regenerator, which is what I am doing here in this book.

The Three Exoteric Aspects

- **Life is ever-changing:** Change is happening everywhere all the time. In everything, there is both stillness and movement. Movement is pervaded by stillness. Stillness gives rise to movement. The evolution of life spawns from this movement arising from stillness. This dance of life follows the pulsating rhythm of arising and expressing and doing (yang) and falling away and reflecting and being (yin).

- **Life is full of tensions:** Tension creates the crucible for creativity. There is tension between the yang and yin, which is what incites nature's creative advance. At times there is more yang, at times more yin. This yin-yang tension creates opportunities for synergy and dinergy. Learning to be comfortable with the uncomfortableness these tensions give rise to is an important leadership skill to acquire. Dinergy, as we have already explored, is where seemingly opposing perspectives, such as a clash of views, may feel uncomfortable yet if worked through something new can emerge beyond the initial perspectives.

- **Life is relational and interconnected:** All life is infused by a Field of consciousness that informs and interconnects everything. Nothing is separate. Everything interrelates in varying degrees. Each manifest aspect of nature, along with ourselves and our organizational systems, is distinct in its own right—holding its own boundaries, essence, and purposefulness—yet all are immersed in this Field. The leadership team is nested within the organizational system, which is nested within its wider stakeholder ecosystem, which is nested within societal and ecological systems. All living-systems, including human ones, thrive through reciprocity and give rise to systemic dynamics—pulsations, ripples, repercussions, flows, and potentialities.

While we might be able to intellectually comprehend the three exoteric aspects, Nature's Wisdom is revealed only through embodied experience. And this is what Level 2 provides for—a shift in our own self-and-systemic awareness that enables us to discern and notice when we are in tune with Nature's Wisdom and when we are not.

When in tune, this aids our capacity as Systemic Enablers to work with the creative and responsive forces of the living-organization through the three qualities of DEE: Developmental, Emergence, Evolutionary. (Hutchins, 2022)

Developmental

The living-organization is constantly learning, creating, renewing, and growing. And it's important to know that by 'developmental growth' I do not mean the maximization of scale, production, and profit. I mean growth through psychological and relational development by becoming more integrated and authentic in our relationships—inter-personal, inter-team, inter-organization, inter-stakeholder. This calls for a greater understanding of authenticity and purposefulness in ourselves as leaders and also across the organizational culture.

Developmental organizations celebrate learning. Everyone in the organization has the opportunity to thrive. This requires an organization and leadership that create psychologically safe yet demanding environments for everyone to learn and grow in ways true to themselves. Such a learning environment allows for plenty of space to reflect, discuss, and share constructive feedback. There are many tools and techniques to help this cultivation of a developmental culture. Leaders can lean on deep-listening, dialogue, coaching conversations, sharing circles, and group sessions away from the normal working environment, such as nature immersions where people can openly reflect and share.

As an example, leaders encouraging coaching conversations through a coaching culture invites people to treat everyday conversations as reciprocal learning explorations. Here we can create non-judgmental, two-way learning through how we listen, speak, ask open questions, and use non-violent communication methods. It's about approaching all conversations with a participatory attitude of listening, exploring, and learning together rather than a transactional culture of identifying, solving, and fixing before something more profound might emerge through the conversation.

Just as helpful as a coaching culture, are feedback methods (like 360-degree feedback and feedback circles). Often, we might project our 'stuff' onto others, so others can see learning areas we may not be conscious of. Becoming more authentic in our relationships, helps serve the living-organization and its creative potential while manifesting life-affirming futures right here in the present moment. The developmental journey starts where we are at now and continues in how we are showing up for each conversation and meeting.

Developmental characteristics: reflection-in-action, coaching conversations, feedback

Emergence

As we have explored in earlier chapters, emergence is propelled by tensions. Tensions create an energy that stimulates and cajoles us out of the status quo. These tensions arise between the space of divergence (diverse perspectives, self-management, distributed leadership) and convergence (alignment around purpose and values, clear roles, responsibilities), and in the sweet spot between divergence and convergence emergence is created. Too much divergence, and chaos ensues. Too much convergence, and rigidity forms.

The living-organization's developmental culture is indispensable because it's a psychologically safe yet demanding environment that permits everyone to embrace complexity and grow through tensions. The culture creates the right space for tensions to be held, observed, and allowed to unfold in ways that provide the right learning and growing environment for diverse people with different stress and anxiety tolerances, thus becoming emergent. However, reduce anxiety all together and you take out tensions, and the organization loses the ability to adapt and evolve.

Our everyday conversations provide creative crucibles for noticing and reflecting inward (self-awareness-in-action) and outward across the system (systemic-awareness-in-action). I have witnessed firsthand how dialogue transforms conversations and shifts leadership team dynamics—how it changes companies. The word 'dialogue' comes from the Greek *dia* meaning 'through' and *logos* meaning 'relating through words.' In dialogue we relate to each other's perspectives by empathically listening and sharing. This is a form of presencing-in-action. By practicing deep-listening inwardly (within our own selves) and outwardly (with others around the circle) we presence. With an open heart we notice the whole gestalt of what is being shared in dialogue and can sense insights about the emergent dynamics of the living-organization.

The more we invite this different attitude into conversations at work, the more emergence flows. Gaining awareness of how we deal with our own and others' anxiety in working through tensions (psychologically safe yet demanding environments) is a continuous work-in-practice each day, in every moment, where mistakes are opportunities to reflect, learn, and grow.

Emergence characteristics: divergence-convergence, tension-transformation, self-management, dialogue

Evolutionary

The Quantum Complexity worldview shows us that the living-organization is adjusting and adapting both within itself and with its external environment through relationships on an ongoing basis. Everything is in unceasing participation with everything else, which is quite a shift from feeling the need to compete, assert, control, and survive. We let go of the personal will's ego-orientated, achiever drive and awaken a deeper purposefulness within ourselves and with life itself, whereupon we find ourselves on our own inner journey.

But what's relevant here is that this individual purposefulness provides a less acquisitive and ego needy 'What's in it for me?' and a more vulnerable, sensitive, and open way to work with the purposefulness of the living-organization. As our dharma (our inner truth) resonates with the purpose of the living-organization, we begin to ask new questions.

How can I best help the organization become a truer version of itself?

Psychological energy that was consumed by the need to relentlessly achieve to better one's career, status, salary, and personal ambition is now flowing into sensing-responding to what genuinely serves the organization and its purpose beyond hitting the numbers.

What is the organization here to do and be?

The more we become attuned with the systemic dynamics within the organization, the more we sense what best serves the evolutionary potential of the organization and the more we acknowledge what is holding it back from serving its purpose. As Brian Robertson, founder of the consultancy Holacracy, explains: (Laloux, p200)

> "The key is about separating identity and figuring out 'what is the organization's calling?'" says Robertson. "Not 'what do we want to use this organization to do, as property?' but rather 'what is this living system's creative potential?' That's what we mean by evolutionary purpose: the deepest creative potential to bring something new to life, to contribute something energetically valuably to the world…It's that creative impulse or potential that we want to tune into, independent from what we want ourselves."

Sensing into the systemic dynamics of the living-organization becomes a vital capacity. The role of Systemic Enablers is key here, but we must remember that everyone in the organization has this latent capacity to sense in if they so choose to cultivate it. Self-awareness-in-action and systemic-awareness-in-action is not just for leaders or Systemic Enablers. It's for everyone to embrace to help the organization become more alive, more adaptive to change, more future-fit.

> "We are all natural sensors; we are gifted to notice when something isn't working as well as it could or when a new opportunity opens up. With self-management, everybody can be a sensor and initiate changes—just as in a living organism every cell senses its environment and can alert the organism to needed change. We cannot stop sensing. Sensing happens everywhere, all the time, but in traditional organizations, the information often gets filtered out…In a self-managing organization, change can come from any person who senses that change is needed. This is how nature has worked for millions of years. Innovation doesn't happen centrally, according to plan, but at the edges, all the time, when some organism senses a change in the environment and experiments to find an appropriate response."
>
> –Frederic Laloux

Evolutionary characteristics: Sensing in, listening to the living-organization's evolutionary purpose

Once we learn to systemically sense in to the living-organization and into life, per se, we becoming increasingly more aware of an 'inner' metaphysical dimension. We are now *attuning with* nature. We are ready for Level 3.

Level 3 Living Systems Awareness – *Attuning with Nature*

With the 'open will' of Level 3, we learn how to work with the three esoteric aspects of Nature's Wisdom, which involves an eco-psycho-spiritual undertaking. I refer to this as 'open will' because our individual ego-will opens into our deeper soul-will, which then opens into the World Soul of nature and universe. In part due to the shift in consciousness that occurs through Level 2 Living Systems Awareness and in part due to a rising soul desire inside us as we awaken.

During our psychospiritual journey, the soul begins to form as a central point of awareness inside the psyche—soul-consciousness, which we are familiar with from Chapter 4. The ego-consciousness of Level 1 and heart-consciousness of Level 2 remain present and active, yet we become more able to center into the soul within, experiencing a stillness and rootedness in our core. This manifests as a spaciousness, a peacefulness, and a trust in life.

Aristotle perceived the soul as an animating presence within us, and as we open into this presence, it's like we step into our power, our sovereignty, right into the core of our being. We feel more ourselves, more 'at one' with life. It's a form of atonement, an unabashed reconciliation and reintegration within oneself. One might say 'at-one-ment' as it comes with a sense of stillness and an ability to be at peace even while cacophony swirls around us.

As we explored in the previous chapter, the soul is an aperture into the transcendent metaphysical realm. It's not a 'thing' but a portal, a vortex in the center of the psyche that opens us into the World Soul. When we center our awareness inwardly into this central point, we activate soul-consciousness. Soul-consciousness is both of the inner-self and beyond the inner-self, as it's experienced through the intimacy of our immanence (like the presencing of Level 2) and also behind all that exists, that which pervades all forms of matter and energy, a transcendent realm that we can experience through our transparency to it.

As we center into the soul, we tap into the inner esoteric aspects of Nature's Wisdom, where we can work with the potent forces and archetypal powers that reside in this inner realm. This is what Level 3 'attuning with' means—to learn to tune in to this inner realm and work with its wisdom. The word 'esoteric' means 'hidden' or 'inner', as opposed to 'exoteric' which is 'seen' or 'outer'. The word 'esoteric' has been warped by Mechanistic Materialism, which as a worldview has cut itself off from the 'inner', as these days 'esoteric' can be assumed to mean 'secret', 'occult' or for a 'select few', but this is not its meaning. This is not what I am conveying. There is nothing secret about what we are sharing here. It's available to everyone who sincerely embarks on the inner journey.

To tap into and work with the esoteric aspects of Nature's Wisdom we need more than our five senses. We use our higher faculties—intuition, insight, imagination, and clairsentience. Activating these higher faculties is completely natural. They are nothing to be scared of, nor do they require one to be part of some weird community, cult, or secret school. Each of us have the inherent capacity to activate Level 3 Living Systems Awareness.

As the spiritual teacher Rudolf Steiner notes, "In actuality, esoteric, or inner knowledge is no different from other kinds of human knowledge and ability. It is a mystery for the average person only to the extent that writing is a mystery for those who have not yet learned to write. Just as, given the right methods, anyone can learn to write, so too anyone can become a student of esoteric knowledge." (Steiner, 1994, p14)

The reality is, we live in a world pervaded by deeper aspects hidden from our normal senses, and through the cultivation of higher faculties, we can thin the veil between the hidden inner realm and the everyday world of outer-nature. This thinning of the veil between outer and inner-nature opens us to more of life and its inner dynamics, so we can more fully work with life. Inner and outer nature are infused—they are at one. Yet our modern human consciousness has become so inured in ego-consciousness that our higher faculties have become impoverished to such an extent that most of us no longer see, hear, or sense what we used to. We are out of range from the inner depths of nature's sacredness.

In opening our awareness into this esoteric inner-nature, we find a truer purposefulness, serenity, reverence, and respect for life. We cultivate a knowing of life from the inside out, which, as Steiner notes, is like "reading a hidden script." "Things speak to us and our inner nature speaks as we observe them." (Steiner, 2000, p211) This is Blake's 'Imagination' which perceives the sacred meaning hidden in life; a way of knowing that opens the book of life right out for us. "True Imagination", writes Maurice Aniane, "actually 'sees' the 'subtle' processes of nature [and] is the capacity to reproduce in oneself the cosmogenic unfolding." (Aniane, p78) We begin to know the nature of life, not through objectified analysis from the outside, but from within the soul, and can start to sense the inherent correspondence of inner and outer nature. The veil thins and mystic rhythms reveal themselves. We see with new faculties, revealing a different order of being-and-knowing—crossing the ontological-epistemological threshold—and finding our wholeness within the wholeness of the world. We re-root down into our sense of place and purpose amid the sacredness of life.

> "Man knows himself only insofar as he knows the world, becoming aware of it only within himself, and of himself only within it."
>
> –Johann Wolfgang Goethe

This way of attending to life, which is an unconditional love of inner-outer nature, helps bring forth what is within us—our birthright, our dharma, our destiny. The seedlings of our soul craft start to sprout with the help of the inner sunshine of soul-consciousness and we learn to become a regenerator.

Entering Level 3 calls upon cultivating inner centering and stillness, much like in Level 2, but this time it's liminal, a blend of the conscious and unconscious mind. Therefore, we invite different brainwave frequencies to work together as we drop behind the high beta brainwaves of daily ego-consciousness into the alpha-theta waves of the twilight zone. As the ancient saying goes, 'The owl of Minerva flies at dusk.' The twilight zone between wakefulness and sleep is our way into the esoteric aspects of Nature's Wisdom.

"He is made one with Nature, there is heard
His voice in all her music, from the moan
Of thunder, to the song of night's sweet bird;
He is a presence to be felt and known
In darkness and in light, from herb and stone.
Spreading itself where'er that Power may move
Which has withdrawn his being to its own;
Which wields the world with never-wearied love
Sustains it from beneath, and kindles it above."

–Percy B Shelley

Nature's Wisdom

The three levels of Living Systems Awareness are not a nice-to-have luxury to contemplate only when on silent retreat or round the campfire. They are the prerequisite for dealing with the root of today's breakdown of civilization and enabling future-fit business. Not climate change, nor capitalism, corporatism, or consumerism—these are not the root. They are the downstream effects of an ungrounded perception of life. Dealing with our myriad crises with the very level of consciousness that created them is unwise. One might say, futile.

When embodied, all three levels of Living Systems Awareness allow us to work with the flows, rhythms, and wisdom that life affords us. The ability for our sophisticated, digitized, and stressed-out organizations to attune with Nature's Wisdom is the next great frontier. This means aligning with life itself. This is what lies before the whole of humanity. Nothing more, nothing less. We must embrace a full-bodied immersive experience into what it means to be human in this more-than-human world.

> "The greatest breakthroughs of the 21st century won't occur because of technology; they will occur because of an expanding concept of what it means to be human."
>
> –John Naisbitt

Adult developmental psychologist Clare Graves, through his painstaking research, saw this latent regenerative potential in human consciousness being born on our watch, and his prescient work is coming true through the exponential uptick of regenerative business, leadership, economics, farming, medicine, and more. Welcome to the wisdom that's fresh yet ancient, momentous yet timeless, alive with dynamism yet born of stillness. Welcome to the Wisdom of Regeneration!

> "Then he clasped his hands together, smiled, and said, 'This could be a good time! There is a river flowing now very fast. It is so great and swift that there are those who will be afraid. They will try to hold on to the shore. They will feel they are being torn apart and will suffer greatly. Know the river has its destination. The elders say we must let go of the shore, push off into the middle of the river, keep our eyes open, and our heads above the water… All that we do now must be done in a sacred manner and in celebration. We are the ones we've been waiting for."
>
> –Hopi Elders' Prophecy

All of life—including human society, the organization, and the leader—is immersed in an ever-changing rhythmic and relational dance. As we have learned, when life is off kilter with the rhythms of this dance, chaos and fragility ensue, and when in tune, all parts find flow and the capacity to flourish. This applies to *all* life. We find the same rhythms for life within the organization as we do for life beyond the organization, and those organizations and leaders who learn to attune with the rhythms and ways of nature are the ones most able to adapt to change.

Jazz musician and philosopher Jouchin-Ernst Berendt notes, "Entering into harmonic relationships is the goal not only of music. It is the goal of atoms and molecules, of flocks of birds and schools of fish and—in principle—of human beings." (Berendt, p119) It's interesting to note that cancerous cells have failed to find harmonic resonance with their local body functions and so fall out of sync, are no longer in tune, and ultimately fall out of right relation causing disease and rhythmic chaos. As the poet Novalis once poignantly said, "Every disease is a musical problem." (Novalis)

Due to Mechanistic Materialism, we've tuned ourselves out of inner-outer nature, which has corrupted our right relation with life and our home, Earth. The modern mechanistic mind has become carcinogenic. Our coming out of tune with inner-nature unravels our right relation of self-other-world, we lose our way, forget our sense of place and purpose, and seek to solve the ache and loss we feel inside by overachieving 'out there' which further impoverishes right relation 'in here'. Enter egotism and consumerism. Enter overconsumption and pollution.

But we can heal ourselves and find right relation once again. To find our tune—to attune with nature—is the goal of life. It's our way into discovering our dharma and our destiny. Campbell said, "The individual has to find what electrifies, what enlivens the heart, this is the salvation of your life. That means putting yourself in accord with nature... When you are in accord with nature, nature will yield up its bounty and every sacred place is the place where eternity shines through time." It's this being in accord with nature that is at the heart of becoming regenerative, and as we've seen, we find wholeness by working through relational tensions and transmuting challenge into learning and growth. (Campbell, 1988)

Our developmental work is to *attune* yin-yang within and without, through inner-outer nature to reveal our own *atonement* of wholeness and wisdom through being in service of and in *accordance* with life. Our *attunement* to nature's inner-outer tensions enables our *atonement* (at-one-ment), our harmony of wholeness within our center. From this center our soul craft unfurls in *accordance* (ac-cor-dance) with our dharma. *Cor* being the Latin for 'heart' and the root for 'courage', as this ac-cor-dance is a courageous, open-hearted dance with life. Our right relation reciprocity reconciles the polarity of the human ego separate from nature, while aligning inner and outer nature through our felt-sense and super-sensory awareness. The wisdom that arises in attunement, atonement, and accordance transmutes our way of living from a mere 'survival of the fittest' into a 'sacred art of living wisely.'

ATTUNEMENT → ATONEMENT → ACCORDANCE

ATTUNEMENT
WORKING WITH DYNERGIC TENSIONS
FINDING RHYTHM AND RESONANCE
WITH INNER-OUTER NATURE

ATONEMENT
INNER JOURNEY TOWARD WHOLENESS
KNOW THY SELF
INTEGRATING SHADOW
CLEANSING AND COHERING BODYMIND
CENTERING IN THE SOUL

ACCORDANCE
COURAGEOUS DANCE WITH LIFE
SACRED ART OF LIVING WISELY

In this chapter we immerse ourselves in the three inner 'esoteric' aspects of Nature's Wisdom, as each are necessary in the shift from the achiever's 'survival of the fittest' to the regenerator's 'sacred art of living wisely.'

Nature's Wisdom

Nature's Wisdom is a universal substratum underpinning all more-than-human and human operations. We live in accord with this wisdom through psychospiritual practices that cultivate higher faculties within us. Then we learn to sense-respond with the inner realm of nature and its inherent wisdom. I have already shared the three outer exoteric aspects of Nature's Wisdom. To recap: 1. **Life is ever-changing:** Change is happening everywhere all the time. 2. **Life is full of tensions:** Tension creates the crucible for creativity. 3. **Life is relational and interconnected:** Infusing all life is a universal field of consciousness that informs and interconnects everything, and within which are systemic dynamics we can learn to sense-respond to.

The three are indeed exoteric, in that they relate to our empirical experience of nature working in the space-time dimension of our physical world. However, each correspond—in subtle ways, as we shall see—with the three inner esoteric aspects of Nature's Wisdom.

Exoteric Qualities of Nature's Wisdom	Esoteric Qualities of Nature's Wisdom
Ever-changing (stillness & movement)	Immanence-transcendence (receptivity)
Tensions (synergy & dinergy)	Inner-outer quintessence (creativity)
Interconnectedness (relational Field)	'As above so below' correspondence (synchronicity)

We are traversing along on our journey and reaching Level 3 of Living Systems Awareness, where alchemy and esoteric aspects are predominant. The inner realm, where we find the three esoteric aspects, is present all the time, right here with us, yet it's shrouded from our normal senses due to our heightened ego-consciousness and the sense of self-as-separate. Once we work with the esoteric aspects, we begin to lift the veil and peer into a world of life that thrives beyond our mechanistic mind and space-time dimension.

The Three Esoteric Aspects

Summary of The Three Esoteric Aspects

1 **Receptivity – Life is immanent and transcendent**. We experience the immanence of life through an embodied, visceral experience when we presence life, in the here-and-now, through heart-consciousness. Rather than an objectified snapshot, a decontextualized categorization of life from left hemispheric ego-consciousness, presencing opens us to the ephemeral relational energies of life. This is the beginning of the breakthrough to the transcendent, unlimited, spiritual depth to life beyond our immediate space-time experience. With practice anyone can become receptive to this simultaneous intimacy and transparency that allows us to tap in to the first esoteric aspect of Nature's Wisdom. There's a nuanced correspondence of the first esoteric quality with the first exoteric quality, as immanent-transcendent

receptivity comes through embracing stillness and movement. It can be emancipating to realize that amid the ever-changing nature of life we always have a way into immanence-transcendence available to us.

2. **Creativity – Life's inner metaphysical realm interpenetrates with the outer physical world.** Our daily consciousness perceives the outer realm of nature, the corporeal experience within normal space-time. There is also an inner realm, the Field, that interpenetrates the outer world. As we cultivate higher faculties with practice, we can learn to tap into and work with this metaphysical dimension. This ability to tap into inner-nature helps our soul—our essence—to work with Nature's Wisdom, giving rise to what the ancient alchemists referred to as 'quintessence', an authentic soulful flowing of inner essence and life-force into our soul craft to enrich outer-nature through life-affirming service. Again, we find correspondence of this second esoteric quality with the second exoteric quality, as the unfurling becoming of our quintessential soul creativity is realized through life's dinergic tensions. We start to see challenging tensions as providing the alchemic heat needed to hone our soul craft.

3. **Synchronicity – Life works with the correspondence of 'As above so below; as within so without.'** All life contains harmonic patterns that convey wisdom from the macrocosmic to the microcosmic and from the spiritual inner realm to the material outer realm. When we find accord with these harmonic patterns, we experience correspondence between the inner-realm and the outer-realm. Here, we sense synchronicities. The infinite and unlimited meet with the finite and limited, and we witness that what lies behind space-time corresponds with an event in space-time. Sensing these sacred harmonics of life enables us to work with the synchronistic and holographic nature of reality. The subtle correspondence of this third esoteric quality with the third exoteric quality is that the synchronistic and holographic recognition of reality is also a deep knowing of life's relational interconnectedness.

1st Esoteric Aspect of Nature's Wisdom
Receptivity – Life is Immanent and Transcendent

In this first esoteric aspect, we are invited into a dual depth of awareness, one which opens up within the immanent dimension (presencing through an embodied, sensorial experience of nature in the here-and-now) and a second within the transcendent dimension (intuitive, imaginal, metaphysical experience into what lies behind the physical presence of nature). By cultivating a receptive attentiveness to both dimensions, we enter an interconnected, participatory conversation with life.

We might have an intimate experience of the immanence of life, say, by noticing the morning dew glisten, the sunset glow, or the leaf twirl in the wind. Such experiences awaken our awareness if we so choose to engage in a phenomenological active seeing with a receptivity of our bodymind. With the example of the morning dew, for instance, one might glance out and see the dew 'with' the eye. Notice the dew glisten, perhaps even comprehend how 'dewy' it is today, may be even notice the clouds and morning sunlight, and start to think about the weather in general. Yet we are observing the dew and weather 'out there' with Lens 1's voice in the head adding its running commentary. When we start to quieten the voice in the head, we may notice the rainbows dancing through the droplets, the Indra's Net pattern across the lawn littered with tiny spider's webs laden in dew. As the voice in the head further quietens, we enter the 'open mind' of Level 1 Living Systems Awareness.

If we remain undistracted in the now, and intentionally relax the bodymind while becoming mindful of our presence, we may start to feel a subtle shift inside us. A space inside opens for deeper breathing, we sense everything more vividly yet also ethereally. We purposefully open into the unfurling becoming of the moment, which provides for a heightened empathic connection and a participatory immersion into the systemic dynamics of what's all around and within us. We start to sense with the full bodymind, not just 'with' but 'through' the eye and 'open heart' of Level 2 Living Systems

Awareness. But this phenomenological presencing does not necessitate a transcendent experience.

We might have a transcendent experience, say through an advanced meditation that opens our receptivity to an otherworldly experience of reality ('negative gnosis') by intentionally connecting deep into the Earth and cosmos while opening our chakras. We feel the expansive bliss of transcendent connectedness. We can also find this through deepening our receptive presence with the morning dew ('positive gnosis') which is what Goethe's active seeing and 'welcoming in the twilight zone' aid. Looking 'through' the eye, the spider's webs, the morning sunlight's rainbows in the dew drops, our open-hearted empathic sense of self-as-participatory, provide for a tear in the fabric of space-time. Our coherency in our bodymind corresponds with inner-nature 'speaking to us' – Steiner's 'hidden script.' A depth of being and knowing awakens the soul that provides for a numinous otherworldly imaginal inspiration. We glimpse a mini-epiphany if only for the briefest of moments as time stands still. While transcending space-time we feel more connected to the world around us and to a sense of meaning beyond the here-and-now.

It's up to us to cultivate the capacity to become transparent to the transcendent *and* intimate with the immanent, and in doing so an alchemy of both a heightened receptivity of physical (sensory experiences) and metaphysical life (super-sensory experiences) strengthens our meaning-making and lands us in the 'open will' of Level 3 Living Systems Awareness.

It requires practice to work with this alchemy of an intimacy of the immanent and transparency of the transcendent. It involves learning to permeate and maturate the ego, an integral part of the inner journey of achiever to regenerator. The ego permeates *and* maturates. It's gained an awareness, no matter how briefly, of life beyond the illusion of separation, and is not overwhelmed by this, but instead finds a surer rooting into the rhizome of regeneration.

This alchemizing is also the vertical development shift not just from Green-Individualist into Teal-Strategist but one shift more into Turquoise-Alchemist. One can quite happily engage as a regenerative leader with the living-organization at Level 2 Living Systems Awareness with the heart-consciousness of the Teal-Strategist. Sure, this esoteric engagement (of immanence-and-transcendence) necessitates soul-consciousness that can be present within Teal-Strategist, but as the name suggests, we find it's more predominant in Turquoise-*Alchemist*.

Before we turn our attention to the alchemy called for in the shift from Level 2 to Level 3 further into Turquoise-Alchemist, let's explore what it means to cultivate this 'intimacy with the immanent' *and* 'transparency with the transcendent.'

Intimacy with the Immanent

Recall the phenomenologists' (Goethe, Husserl, Heidegger, Gadamer, Merleau-Ponty, and others) emphasis on presencing through cultivating a receptive intimacy where the 'other' is not actually separate from us but rather in reciprocating energetic engagement with us through the animating life-force of nature. It's a mutual embrace, not a standoffish observer or the self-reflexive abstraction of the rational mind. As we open our receptivity, by presencing life, we reignite (remember) a perception of nature whereupon we perceive the vivid aliveness of this world.

Recall David Abram saying, "The world is perceiving itself through us." (Abram, p68) I find Abram's description particularly helpful when describing this way of perceiving life, as it's as if we are no longer the perceiver. The 'I' ego permeates and becomes receptive to such a degree that it no longer feels like it's 'me' perceiving the 'world' out there, but rather we are in flow, a mutual embrace. We are in the flow of perceiving, as if the world is perceiving through us. We become a conduit for perception.

In this presencing practice, the superficial separateness created by left hemispheric ego-consciousness has eased, and we are immersed within a vibrant awareness, sensing a vast interconnectedness. This is what Heidegger called a 'worlding', an embodied, heartfelt commingling of felt presences. 'I' and 'world' are not two things standing apart. Our experience is a reciprocal interplay of perceiver and perceived in cocreation with each in the other's aliveness. *This* is intimacy of self-other-world.

Abram notes that many indigenous peoples know their surroundings so intensely that they are sensitive to its private presence, taking care not to offend it, much like Westerns take care not to offend other people in their company. This relation with nature is embedded into their culture and psyche. From this understanding, a kinship of reciprocal respect develops. Rather than life being seen as something to be controlled, it's understood as something to be communed with. We learn to participate in a conversation with life.

Humans are recognized as creatures of distance that maintain the ability to re-present reality and so differentiate with it (Barfield's 'alpha-beta thinking'), while also sensing the sacred unity of the World Soul that we are never separate from. On our 'return' journey toward Barfield's final participation, we gain the capacity, as self-reflexive ego-souls, to step back from the immediacy while retaining a respectful kinship of *comm-union* within diversity. This ability we have as humans to step back, rationalize, and re-present makes it all the more necessary for us to sustain a healthy, permeable human-nature relation through intimacy with the immanent. To do otherwise, we become deluded and dis-eased.

Transparency with the Transcendent

Perhaps on the other end of the continuum, from immanent intimacy, we find transparent transcendence. If we allow ourselves, through practice, we can open further into the realm that is the backdrop to everyday experience. These are the practices that take us to the most inward experiences of nature. It's to this inner realm we shall attend to when coming to the second esoteric aspect of Nature's Wisdom. Should you be curious to know, the second esoteric aspect is not at all separate from this first aspect. The truth is, the two are labeled differently to help our left hemisphere comprehend the intricate qualities of each and both.

But let's linger a bit longer to enrich our understanding of this first esoteric aspect, so we might see that by alchemizing both the immanent *and* transcendent we shift our meaning-making, activate our super-nature, and work with sensory and super-sensory knowing as we tune in to Nature's Wisdom. You've likely come across the caduceus image.

THE CADUCEUS

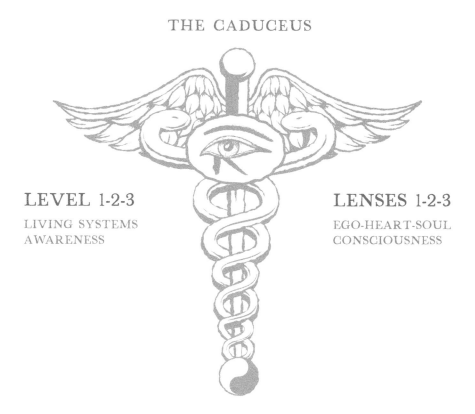

LEVEL 1-2-3
LIVING SYSTEMS
AWARENESS

LENSES 1-2-3
EGO-HEART-SOUL
CONSCIOUSNESS

The caduceus is the symbol for this first aspect of Nature's Wisdom. The twisting pairs represent the immanent-transcendent experiences that are entwining through our bodymind coherence to open our minds-hearts-wills into the Imaginal Realm where soul and World Soul can be found through the awakened Eye of the Heart. We have the techniques and the practices (presencing, active seeing, bodymind coherence, advanced meditation, advanced breathwork, Tantra, welcoming in the twilight zone, and more) to aid us as we journey onward with a renewed sensory and super-sensory awakening.

2nd Esoteric Aspect of Nature's Wisdom
Creativity – Life's Inner Metaphysical Realm Interpenetrates with the Outer Physical World

Quantum scientists have given scientific rigor to this metaphysical order of reality with phrases such as the 'quantum vacuum' and 'zero-point energy field'. Bohm, in his brilliance, found reality to contain both an Explicate Order (our everyday experience of outer physical tangible form) and an Implicate Order (an inner metaphysical transcendent realm full of potential energy that underpins and interpenetrates with the Explicate Order of manifest polarized energy). Through his studies he found the explicate—exoteric tangible immanent—realm of form to be enfolded within the implicate—esoteric intangible transcendent—realm. Through what Bohm called 'holomovement', life and all matter continually pulsate through an unfolding and enfolding movement from the implicate inner realm into the outer manifestations of energy and matter. Whether subatomic particles like electrons, human interactions, Earth or universe, everything is in a constant state of oscillation between the implicate, transcendent realm beyond space-time and the explicate immanent space-time dimension of manifest reality. (Bohm, 1980)

His ground-breaking studies have later been corroborated and further expanded by present day physicists, cosmologists, and philosophers. We now know that this continuous vibratory hum of 'inner' implicate and 'outer' explicate underpins reality. All life is participating within the same Source consciousness, never separate from it. Even when things appear to our senses as separate objects, in reality everything is awash with a field of fluidity that connects and pervades everything. Nothing exists that is separate or disconnected from the transcendent field of consciousness. Quarks and neutrons and all subatomic particles are immersed in this consciousness, and so too are all atoms, and the cells in our bodies, along with the flowers and leaves, trees, rivers, and clouds, even the air we breathe and the water we drink.

Quantum physics has smashed open the clear-cut foundations of objectified mechanistic-materialistic science, and there is now a significant groundswell of robust scientific thinking that acknowledges consciousness as imbued in all things. (Currivan, Laszlo, E.) Nothing, it would seem, is separate from anything else. Nature (including human nature) is a multiplicity-in-unity. The transcendent unmanifest energetic 'inner' field of consciousness (mind) and the immanent manifest 'outer' energetic field of form (matter) are two sides of the same coin.

The 'outer' immanence is the multiplicity we can experience either as separateness through an overly rational-analytic ego-consciousness or as participatory through a receptive presencing experience of heart-consciousness. The 'inner' transcendent spirit realm is the unifying field underpinning this multiplicity, which we can either acknowledge or refute rational-analytically. It's admittedly difficult for rational analysis to discern something intangible and unmanifest, something that is seemingly nowhere and yet everywhere, yet we can reach this transcendent inner realm through practices that open up our consciousness to become more receptive to and conscious of this deeper dimension of reality.

Consciousness, and so meaning and purpose, is seen as flowing through all matter, throughout all nature. Nature is not an ensemble of things. It is animated by a primordial energetic field that in-forms all energy forms. *All* energy forms, including non-matter energy forms, such as sound and electromagnetism (which includes the light spectrum). This emanation of energy from inner into outer works through harmonics, as we have learned, and we have the ability to attune with this animating principle—this life-force—that is beyond the world of form and matter. The Field is animating everything we relate with, from our own bodies to our living-organizations, business ecosystems, social systems and nature's ecosystems. Everything is infused by these immanent-transcendent harmonics.

So, we can start to see how outer matter is a transmission of an unseen inner metaphysical life-force. By going 'in' to the metaphysical realm we can engage with, and become conscious of, this primal force of nature. Earlier, we mentioned Henri Corbin's intermediary realm between the immanence of everyday awareness and the transcendence of spirit, what Corbin calls the Imaginal Realm.

We can lean into this Imaginal Realm through practices that help us quiet our rational-analytic minds, activate our super-nature, center into ego-heart-soul consciousness, integrate Lenses 1-2-3, and cultivate our Creative Imagination. For it's Creative Imagination that enables us to work with both the physical and the metaphysical realms—the here-and-now and what lies beyond. To bring this immanent-transcendent twilight zone of the unseen imaginal into our everyday workings is to work with Nature's Wisdom.

While the first esoteric aspect is depicted by the caduceus, the second esoteric aspect is symbolized by the archer's bow, which depicts the act of holding space within our own ego-heart-soul consciousness through advanced meditation and bodymind coherence practices. We are interpenetrating the outer realm with the inner, allowing for the tension of inner-outer within our Creative Imagination to work its magic and bring forth emergence. The archer's bow is held tense for the arrow to hit the mark. This tenseness is not tightness but rather a flowing intentional attentiveness. It is quintessence, an alchemic act of inner-outer at-one-ment.

We learn to manifest our outer activities of our soul craft in harmony with the inner harmonics of Nature's Wisdom. We work with rather than against or in ignorance of, inner-outer nature. In this regard, our intention held within our own center is to serve life—to be life-affirming—and for our soul craft to be attentive and in service to the world, which is to be regenerative in aiding humanity and life on Earth toward becoming more integrated, whole, and in harmony.

In this second esoteric aspect intention and attention are fused. These two words represent an act of love deep within our own consciousness that catalyzes a flow of life-force that is regenerative and in service of life. The alchemy of attention and intention is life-affirming. We attend to life through presencing, through our soul craft, and through finding right relation, with the intention of permeating our human egos and our manifest reality with the liminal Imaginal Realm beyond space-time.

ARCHER'S BOW

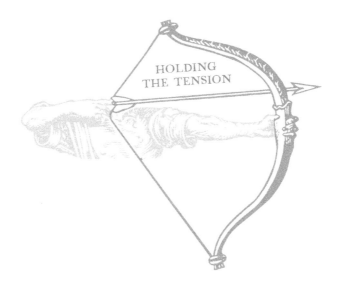

Within the quintessential moment, we access the center point both in space-time (immanent) and beyond space-time (transcendent), the still-point of the turning world, where the harmonic dance of life is attuned with.

> "At the still point of the turning world. Neither flesh nor fleshless;
> Neither from nor toward; at the still point, there the dance is,
> But neither arrest nor movement. And do not call it fixity,
> Where past and future are gathered. Neither movement from nor toward,
> Neither ascent nor decline. Except for the point, the still point,
> There would be no dance, and there is only the dance."
>
> –T.S. Eliot

This 'intimacy with the immanent and transparency with the transcendent' quintessence takes us beyond our once perceived duality and into a non-dual moment. The archer's bow fires the caduceus arrow into the zone of becoming, and we discover our dharma. The caduceus arrow is our attuned bodymind coherence, and the bow is the tension that arises before and through the alchemy of the immanent and transcendent. The zone the arrow is fired toward might appear as a bullseye on a dartboard, but it is actually an opening, a portal into another way of being-becoming in the world.

HITTING THE MARK & OPENING THE EYE OF THE HEART

LIFE AS SACRED
OPEN MIND-HEART-WILL
IMMANENT-TRANSCENDENT
ATTUNING WITH LIFE
SEEING WITH NEW EYES

The holding of the tension that provides for the quintessential moment is both full of aliveness *and* beyond the living, temporal *and* eternal, conscious *and* unconscious, movement *and* stillness. Through the nondualism of the now eternal-temporal moment we can enter into the sacredness of Life. We can expand our meaning-making and enrich our way of being-becoming in the world. We see behind the veil, and life becomes Life with a capital L, just as nature becomes Nature with a capital N. The sacred quintessential experience is always available to us when inner-outer align, and it's here that we find accord with Nature's Wisdom.

> "(S)he who is harmony with Nature, hits the mark without effort and apprehends the truth without thinking."
>
> —Confucius

As Confucius knew some two thousand five hundred years ago, this harmonic moment of inner-outer attunement is where we hit the mark and apprehend the truth without thinking. The bow and archer are at-one, the chord is struck, the music of emergence unfolds in tune with life. We hit the mark effortlessly, in flow, with intention-attention, and active-relaxation. We are like an athlete in the zone, a surfer riding the wave, a musician composing the song. There is no more voice in the head, only flow, a stillness amid movement with a deep trust in life. We have reconnected into the rhizome of regeneration.

This conscious act inside us is an act of sacrifice, of surrender, a letting go in order to flow. It's a ceasing of our thinking, an easing our grasping, and a trusting in life. It's an atonement. We're at-one with an open mind-heart-will, and our ego-heart-soul consciousness is activated by our super-nature which permits the unknowable to come into the knowable. This is a different order of knowing—it's gnosis. Insight is gleaned in the intentional-attentional zone of apprehending the truth without thinking. This zone of quintessence is both in space-time and beyond space-time, and in that regard introduces synchronicity.

Quintessence is a devotional practice. It asks for both attention and intention, alchemy that brings forth a deep love of Life, which has a transmuting effect on the bodymind. The soul is opened, and the spiritual organs of the third eye and hara centered in the Eye of the Heart open. With a higher frequency life-force flowing through us, we are also cleansing the psyche. Quintessence regenerates our bodymind and upgrades our DNA, and with this inherent knowing of Nature's Wisdom we can serve our soul craft. Our newfound space within makes us a vessel for manifestation. We learn to cocreate with the sacredness of life and to aid life-affirming emergence and evolutionary purposefulness. This has a subtle yet profound healing effect on others around us and those we serve through our soul craft.

A useful practice to develop quintessence, one which I have already mentioned, is the Creative Imagination Process. This is a nine-step process inspired by the work of Henri Corbin and his research on Sufi masters such as Ibn Arabi.

The Creative Imagination Process

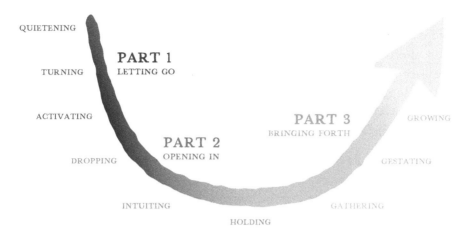

Part 1: Letting Go

1. **Quietening** – Through meditation we start to bring awareness to our own thoughts. Depending on what works for our temperament, we might wish to engage in some energy cultivation work and body movement practices first before then settling into meditation. Such meditation does not limit itself only to sitting in a room or out in nature. We can also learn to move mindfully, whether that be walking or practicing yoga, tai chi, or chi gung, for instance. In this *quietening* stage we allow the ruminating voice in the head to quiet, the rational-analytic grasp of the left hemisphere to ease, and the high beta brainwaves to shift into beta and alpha (as quietening deepens). Soon enough the awakened mind will start to come on stream as the achiever mind quietens.

2. **Turning** – This is an intentional *turning* of the beam of our awareness on ourselves, not on our thoughts, but down into the bodymind. Behind our arising thoughts and emotions, we notice somatic sensations in the body and subtle energy fluctuations. It could be a flutter in the belly, an expansion or contraction in the chest, or a warm sensation or tingling in the legs. It does not matter where or what we feel at this stage of the practice. What matters here is bringing attention into the

bodymind through somatic awareness. For instance, by noticing our breathing perhaps while engaging in rhythmic belly breathing exercises and a body scanning practice, we can sense subtle energy movements in the bodymind. *Turning* opens Lens 1 ego-consciousness into Lens 2 heart-consciousness. Even a deeper spaciousness into Lens 3 soul-consciousness may start to occur.

3 **Activating** – Through bodymind coherence practices like heart entrainment, we work on head-heard-gut coherence. We can engage in practices of intentionally opening and clearing our chakra system with practices like mantras, yantras, and intentional body movement in order to *activate* our super-nature. Brainwave frequencies are no longer predominately beta but have access to a full spectrum of alpha-beta-delta-theta-gamma.

Part 2: Opening In

4 **Dropping** – When we practice bodymind coherence and heart entrainment, we learn to focus on the heart as a psychospiritual organ of perception. This works best when being still, meditating in a regular sit spot whether outside in nature or inside. We focus on the heart region and with slow rhythmic breathing, we intentionally open the Eye of the Heart with bodymind coherence and an activation of the spiritual faculties of the head, heart, and gut. More specifically, we connect the energetic center of the pineal gland (referred to as the 'third eye') and the energetic center of the enteric nerve plexus in the lower abdomen referred to as the 'hara' or 'tanden' (the gut) with the heart. By cultivating a twilight wakefulness-sleep hypnagogic state while in bodymind coherence, we feel energized yet relaxed and can surrender into not knowing. This is a self-emptying, where we *drop in* to a spacious realm behind space-time, and into the Imaginal Realm. It's likely we flicker in and out of this state, sometimes going too much into the unconscious 'night' of sleep, which is when we literally fall asleep as delta brainwaves predominate, or too much into the conscious 'daylight' of wakefulness when beta-waves predominate. This flickering in and out

of the alpha-theta twilight-zone is part of the practice. We get used to surfing the liminality between conscious and unconscious, holding the tension of the bowstring in just the right way in order to hit the mark, to receive insight through the Imaginal Realm. This can sometimes feel like lucid dreaming, when perhaps we are a little more in sleep than awake, yet still conscious of what is happening.

5   **Intuiting** – In the twilight zone we have dropped into a simultaneous emptying and listening space. We surrender intently and notice insights, symbols, imaginal messages, and revelations. Here we are discerning the 'wheat from the chaff', *intuiting* the difference between insights (from the spirit-realm of Lens 3) and psychic stuff like shadow projections, memories, suppressed emotions, and fantasies (from Lens 2). This intuiting comes with a trusting. We must trust the entrance to the portal into the Imaginal Realm by feeling safe, protected, and guided by our Higher Self in service of the sacredness of Life.

I share advanced practices with my clients to aid this trusting, guiding, and protecting aspect as we drop in and intuit the Imaginal Realm. Here, the awakened mind, with its intuitive capacities, is active. With practice the pineal gland becomes more awakened, activating clairsentience— our subtle psychic abilities, such as premonitions, clairvoyance, strong inner knowings, even telepathy. This does not necessarily mean we become 'psychic' and can be as simple as starting to trust our gut more, listen to our intuitive hunches, and learn to sense somatic sensations in the bodymind that pick up on super-sensory information through once imperceptible shifts in the Field. For instance, the inner ear or heart region might shift in pressure when something is not quite right for us, or someone is sharing something inauthentic that we need to be cautious of, or if we are sensing an important connection that is useful for our soul craft. To acknowledge these shifts is a part of activating our super-nature.

6   **Holding** – As we enter the Imaginal Realm, we *hold* the tensions— emptying yet listening, not knowing yet knowing, gaining insight without rationalizing while becoming aware of the insight in our conscious mind. Gently bringing the light of our awareness to bear, but still in

the twilight zone where insights of awareness are not too bright. We are learning to stay still with the insight, recall it, hold it intentionally, allow it to birth. Like a wild deer in the dark woods, we do not wish to scare it off with our glaring flashlight of ego-consciousness. Instead, we endeavor to be in our heart-and-soul and stay for a moment with the wild creature, to sense it, connect with it. This greater discerning is to know which insight to stay with and what is a flight of fantasy or psychological projection. Here we ask: Is what we are sensing from the numinous depths of Lens 3 or residing in Lens 2?

There is nothing wrong with having psychological baggage surface. It's quite natural, and processing this inner baggage is a helpful part of our inner journey toward wholeness. But this is not the purpose of this Creative Imagination Process. Here we are learning to stay with the surrendering, to discern and not be distracted with inner baggage or dreamy emotive thoughts of past and future, to simply hold ourselves open to the Imaginal Realm in the twilight zone. Holding can be thought of as a 'kenosis for gnosis', a surrendered emptying of not knowing (kenosis) for direct insight (gnosis) to come in.

Part 3: Bringing Forth

7 **Gathering** – A flash of insight, a potent symbol, a clear message, or a download of energy, whatever the gnosis is, we are receiving it. Like a womb being impregnated, our psyche is open to the soul-scape, fertile, and ready for insight to come in. If we discern that it's not a flight of fantasy or our shadow stuff, then we welcome this direct transmission from Source to be *gathered* inside our psyche by intentionally acknowledging its presence. In the twilight zone, we bring the light of our hypnagogic partial waking consciousness to the insight. Whatever the knowing—a symbol, sensation, vision, or voice—we hold this knowing in the Eye of the Heart, in the center of our being. We are now receptive and also responsive to the insight. By doing so, without going into the rationalizing head, we can allow the seed to become an embryo, feeling

the gnosis grow, while we remain in the womb-like energy of the twilight zone.

8. **Gestating** – Gathering our knowing around the insight as it embryonically forms, we can gently move out of the twilight zone and into freewriting, drawing, or body movement to help *gestate* the embryo into a more concrete knowing as a thoughtform. To start with, in this gestating phase we are conscious of remaining in bodymind coherence and not rushing into the active achiever mind of rational analysis. With integrated ego-heart-soul consciousness we capture the insight either in written form or through a drawing or other creative outward expression. An act such as writing it down activates the left hemisphere and ego-consciousness, yet let's try and keep ourselves in the heart with freewriting or sketching to help keep the right hemisphere active for a little while longer. We hold the insight with intentional attentiveness, gestating the embryo with our own loving attention and allowing it to birth into manifestation through journaling, drawing, or envisioning to ponder how it relates to our own lives and soul craft.

9. **Growing** – To birth something into a manifest form (to manifest), we naturally need the tools of ego-consciousness to plan, prototype, test, and learn. This is an exploratory phase of sensing how the insight is best brought into our soul craft as an enterprising idea. Entrepreneurial and enthusiastic energy can help it manifest and *grow* through daily actions and intentions, all the while remaining true to heart-soul.

The *Bringing forth* part of the Creative Imagination Process provides for an embodied experience of the seed-flower-fruit process of becoming which is inherent throughout inner-outer nature. The seed essence becomes flower and fruit through the regenerative process of life. It's the creative force impelling all emergent evolution, and it's simultaneously a receptive and responsive dynamic, and lies at the heart of the *Creativity* of this second esoteric aspect. The receptive 'kenosis for gnosis' creates the womb-like space for the fertilizing of the 'seed' of insight. Then the responsive gathering, gestating, and growing brings forth inner-nature into outer-nature. Recall Jesus in Chapter 2 saying, "If you bring forth what is within you, what is within you will save you. If you do not bring forth what is within you, what is within you will destroy you." This bringing forth is what I refer to as receptive-responsiveness, which we shall now dwell on a little more by drawing upon the mythological framing of the Trinity and its inherently alchemic nature.

Manifesting Through the Sacred Trinity

With an awareness of the nine steps of the Creative Imagination Process, we return to our archer's bow. The bowstring is stretched as we hold the tension of stillness inside the twilight zone of wake-sleep. Calm, yet holding the tension. The stillness and receptivity of dropping, intuiting, holding. Until the bow is struck! This is the creative act, the response of gathering, gestating, growing. The receptive-responsive sacred marriage of the tension (bowstring) is held inside our ego-heart-soul consciousness until the pregnancy is just right, for the birthing of the 'sacred child', the new dawn (hitting the mark).

The 'Three' of emergent creativity is born out of the 'Two' of the tension which arises from the stillness of 'One', the oneness of the nondual Field.

The sacred Trinity in the dynamic of one-two-three is what ancient texts the world-over refer to as the animating principle of life. Or as explained poetically here by Lao Tzu in the ancient Chinese text the *Tao Te Ching*:

> "Tao gives birth to One,
> One gives birth to Two,
> The Two gives birth to Three,
> The Three gives birth to all universal things."
>
> —Lao Tzu

Out of the unmanifest transcendent Field (the One), where life-force is yet to be polarized into energy/matter and insight/mind, comes the holomovement of Implicate and Explicate (or the original tone of Nada Brahma or God's Word as per Genesis, "In the beginning was the Word"). This tone or movement arising out of stillness creates a yin-yang, inner-outer, formless-form, corporeal-eternal, immanent-transcendent tension (the Two). It then becomes all too easy to be pulled into the duality of the corporeal world by the ego's voice in the head unless we work with Welcoming in the Twilight Zone (shared in Chapter 4) and the Creative Imagination Process shared above.

The then tension becomes the bowstring to find harmony through dinergy for insight and creativity (the Two become the Three). This brings about the energizing potential of seed-essence coming into being in the world, followed by the centering inward and holding space for the tension to work as a bowstring, to allow a birth or emergence through the tension in firing the arrow (the Three). The arrow is released, newly born, and now we have the new creative insight manifesting into the world of form.

The importance here is that the creative unfurling is rooted in the rhizome of Source, in right relation with inner-outer nature, and so is regenerative. We are not coming up with ideas and acts that are ego-machinations caught up in the very consciousness of Mechanistic Materialism that creates today's degeneration. The creative act—symbolized by the archer's bow, and caduceus arrow entering the portal into becoming—is in right relation with inner-outer nature. At-one with Nature's Wisdom, it's inherently regenerative. Mythologically, this is the Trinity within Unity, or diversity-in-unity, as the Three is not severed from the Field (as is the case with self-as-separate ego-consciousness) but ever-connected to it (self-as-participatory ego-heart-soul consciousness). Our soul craft is ever-immersed in Nature's Wisdom through our regular and committed practice of Welcoming in the Twilight Zone, the Creative Imagination Process, or any other specialized processes.

THE REGENERATIVE PROCESS OF BRINGING FORTH

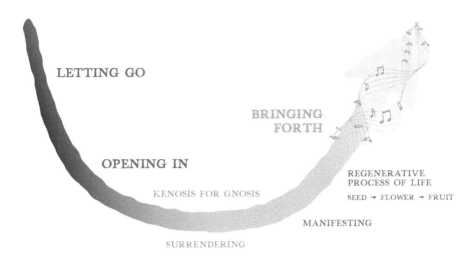

> "Great is the mystery of marriage, for without it the world would not exist."
>
> —The Gospel of Philip

The mystical narrative of the One-Two-Three Trinity is at the heart of creation. A sacred child is born through the marriage of feminine-masculine, yin-yang dinergic tension. From the birthing-becoming into the world, diversity-in-unity unfolds. Diversity-in-unity is Bohm's holomovement, which occurs at fractal levels throughout nature, from the electron to the human to the universe. This is the magic of life, a dance, a musical attunement requiring our atonement, a holding space for the bowstring to birth the Trinity in accordance with Nature's Wisdom. When in harmony with nature, the Three is actually the One, and there is no illusion of separation ego-machination caught up in the Two. The creative act is attuned to the Field, never separate from it, an act which is sacred because it's both limited and unlimited. It's synchronistic.

> "All things that are ever said to be consist of a one and a many, and have in their nature a conjunction of limited and unlimited."
>
> —Plato

TRINITY IN UNITY

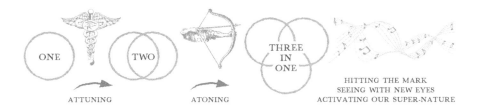

The Three 'return' is always here in us if we so choose to remember. The 'departure' from the One—Garden of Eden, original participation—into the 'initiation' of the Two duality of form creates identity and also limitation. Yet these limits do not mean we divide and conquer and get caught up in the fear or our own ego-separateness. Instead, the tension, the competition, can be a healthy striving toward right relation, which is the very power of limits that impels a birth into the Three. This is a rebirth inside ourselves, our conscious re-membering of our true nature as a spiritual being immersed in this sacred Life. Our rebirth through re-membering is final participation, where we witness a conjunction of limited and unlimited, immanent and transcendent. In Islamic esotericism this birthing or bringing forth is understood as a 'leading back' a returning from outer ego form into the innerness of one's spiritual being, conveyed in the Quran as 'ta'wil' meaning to 'lead back.' It's worth emphasizing that the return is not simply going back to where we started, because the journey of departure out of the Garden of the One has brought forth something new.

Just like original participation, final participation is rooted in the One and yet something has changed since original participation, as the movement through the tension of the Two and the bringing forth of the Three have become a conscious undertaking in right relation with inner-outer nature.

This receptive-creative act—the Trinity—provides for the Four (Lao Tzu's 'all universal things') pervaded by the love and sacredness of Life: Heaven on Earth.

> "One becomes Two; Two becomes Three; and by the means of the Third comes the One of the Fourth."
>
> —Maria Prophetissa

Recall, in the Introduction section of this book, the four overlapping circles of Living, Leading, Culture and Impact. The center of these four circles conveys in practical ways what Maria Prophetissa calls 'the One of the Fourth'. When we undergo the receptive-creative becoming of One-Two-Three we enable: Our *Living* (consciousness & wellbeing) to become regenerative by working with the light of soul and nature; Our *Leading* (ego-stage development of Teal-Turquoise) to become regenerative by working with Levels 1-2-3 Living Systems Awareness; the organization's *Culture* (essence, purpose, values, behaviors) to become regenerative by nurturing developmental, emergent, evolutionary wholeness for all; and the organization's *Impact* (ESG, brand, value-creation, stakeholder ecosystem) to become regenerative as the living-organization tends toward harmony with life. The center-point of the four overlapping circles – the 'Four-in-One' – is *activated regenerative leadership consciousness* emanating through the Trinity of the soul-essence (the One) and the emergence (the Three) of ourselves and through the essence and emergence of the systems we lead.

Insight gleaned from being in-tune with Nature's Wisdom is planted and nurtured within the fecund soil of our soul-scape (and the fecund DEE culture of the living-organization) for ideation to manifest into life-affirming service. The ultimate goal of the regenerative business to serve life is realized in right relation with Nature's Wisdom.

THE PROCESS OF BECOMING

A CONTINUAL PROCESS OF STILLNESS, MOVEMENT, DANCE AND DEVELOPMENTAL GROWTH

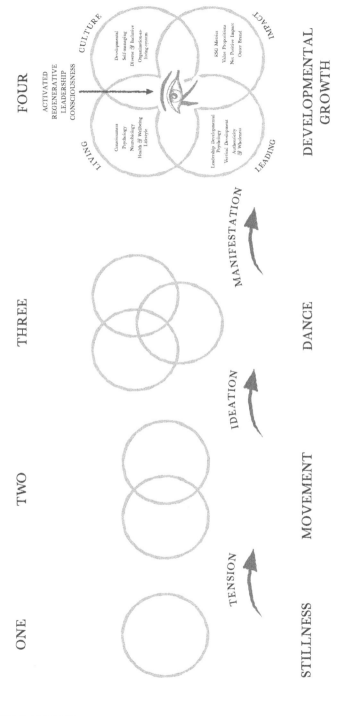

We, and our organizations, become conduits for Heaven on Earth through our manifestations of products and services. Yet, it's a journey, not a holier-than-thou destination. The process of becoming is fractal. It's happening through micro-spirals of death-rebirth One-Two-Three-Four processes each and every day. Sometimes we get stuck in ego-consciousness and yet we learn from mistakes and misfires, tripwires, and wrong turns. Nothing is wasted. All is digested and composted. Though the intent is resolute—to bring forth greater wholeness while rooted in an enchanting love of Life.

In mythology, there's a 'macro' journey (taking many years) and a 'micro' journey (a shift in consciousness amid our daily soul work) of One-Two-Three-Four. The 'macro' life journey is symbolized by the movement out of the Garden of the One, involving a 'fall from grace', a journey of decent into the underworld followed by a heroic undertaking of challenging tensions of disintegration and reintegration, before remembering as a 'resurrection' in becoming who we truly are takes place. In our wholeness, life becomes a sacred marriage of inner-outer, insight-synchronicity.

This is what the Cross symbolizes, a center point where inner-outer, above-below, immanent-transcendent, ego-soul are at-one; an atonement through which Heaven on Earth is realized.

The 'micro' journey happens amid the moment, through our immanent-transcendent state of consciousness. Here, the Garden symbolizes an archetypal sanctuary, both a physical place of creation and renewal (like a sacred grove, sit-spot or temple), and also a temple within the bodymind for meditation and atonement of our ego and soul with the World Soul. The center point of the Cross is realized within the moment through our soul work. An act of creation in harmony with the immanent-transcendent nature of life. We might therefore see the Garden as a state of consciousness that can be realized anywhere and at any time in our lives through our conscious attunement and atonement with life.

When the legendary Native American holy man Black Elk said, "anywhere is the center of the world," he conveyed that we can access the center point of the Cross anywhere regardless of place with the right intention and quality of attention. (Neihardt, p43) We can learn to thin the veil, tap into Source, and go beyond the pair of opposites and the duality of normal waking consciousness. This is how practices like bodymind coherence, the Creative Imagination Process, and Welcoming in the Twilight Zone aid a state of attunement and atonement through which we find harmony with nature, Earth, and cosmos. Out of the Two comes the Three, and the creative life-force pours in from the transcendent realm as we learn to work with wisdom in bringing forth what is within us. The Three manifesting into the Four, while rooted in the One.

Poet Samuel Taylor Coleridge illustrates exactly this when he said, "All opposition is a tendency to reunion," which brings us to the third esoteric aspect of Nature's Wisdom.

3rd Esoteric Aspect of Nature's Wisdom: Synchronicity – Life works with the correspondence of 'As above so below; as within so without'

Through all the three esoteric aspects of Nature's Wisdom, we are cultivating the capacity to work with the unlimited 'inner' and limited 'outer' nature of reality, and here we see how the third aspect overlaps with the other two. It highlights the way inner and outer nature find accord and enable synchronicity to unfold. We are working with creation, as part of creation, while sensing behind creation to bear witness to and midwife the very process of becoming within life.

There is a relationship, a correspondence, between the inner metaphysical realm and outer physical realm. Likewise, there is a correspondence between microcosm (the individual aspects of the everyday world of things) and macrocosm (the universal aspects of the cosmos, solar system, planets, and Earth). This correspondence is expressed through the Hermetic dictum 'As above so below; as within so without' and the Vedic proverb 'As is the individual, so is the universe; as is the universe, so is the individual.'

In both Eastern and Western esoteric traditions, it's often referred to as the 'Law of Correspondence.' We experience the correspondence of inner and outer through harmonic resonance and sense synchronicities beyond the space-time realm that enter into this space-time experience. Learning to listen to these sacred harmonics underpinning and interpenetrating life enables us to work with the synchronistic and holographic nature of reality.

As we've already seen, nature works with harmonics. There are harmonics 'above' in the cosmos and 'below' inside our own nature. Throughout the cosmos, we find electromagnetic and sound vibrations that emanate from and continuously unfold and enfold in holomovement within the inner metaphysical realm. These vibrations follow harmonic laws, the same as music does. As scientist Kepler found, and others after him have corroborated, the planets in our solar system relate to each other with musical resonance, as do their moons. This 'Music of the Spheres' emanates a detectable acoustical wave frequency. It's extremely low and inaudible to the human ear—though the 'inner ear' can cultivate the capacity to detect perturbations within this background acoustical field we are immersed in.

Planetary resonances play out within a vast electromagnetic plasma field that envelopes the entire solar system. Everything participates or reverberates, or one might say 'plays' within the wider cosmos and its electromagnetic and acoustic fields of vibration. (Bamford, p48) This orchestra of sound waves and electromagnetic (EM) radiation from the sun and planets enter the Earth's atmosphere all the time, resonating with the Earth's own frequencies. Our Earth plays its own unique tune within the solar system, galaxy, and cosmos, and yet its tune is affected by the wider orchestra within the wider cosmic vibrations, and so Earth plays along with the orchestra while maintaining its own uniqueness of diversity-in-unity.

Likewise, at the level of the microcosm, all living bodies are EM and soundwave systems. All metabolic processes in life demonstrate oscillatory properties and are harmonic in nature. (Bamford, p47) For instance, in the human body, nerve impulses use bio-electric waves, brain activity resonates with EM fields outside the head, and each one of the trillions of cells in the body has its own EM field. The individual cells are like mini-musicians each emanating their own sound and EM music in ways that resonant with the wider orchestras (energy systems) they participate or 'play' in.

Knowing what we know from heart entrainment, the heart is a powerful EM organ of perception, receiving and emitting EM information all the time. In fact, science is now realizing that the whole body can be conceived as a transducer— transmitting and receiving—that picks up fluctuations in the sound and EM fields we are immersed in. We are not only sensing but broadcasting, via the laws of resonance and harmonic affinity.

Macrocosmic celestial resonances affect earthly resonances which affect our own bodily resonances, and so the other way. We—everything manifest and unmanifest—are all immersed in a 'Song of Songs.' We can become conscious of, and receptive to, these resonant energies as we grow our capacity to sense into the inner realms of nature. We can also learn to screen ourselves from disruptive sounds and EM waves through certain practices (such as bodymind coherence, concentrated thought, mantras, yantras, color therapy, sound healing, crystal healing, and intentional dance and music), which organize the vibratory conditions around and within ourselves.

Much like certain buildings, such as temples, enhance coherence by working with the harmonics of sacred geometry. Or certain music, like classical music, works with tonal sound. We too have bodymind instruments that need attunement by our own conscious selves to help them resonant with terrestrial and celestial harmonies. We can work with the Music of the Spheres, placing ourselves in accord with nature, elevating our individual vibratory soul-song with the song of the World Soul. This aids our capacity to work creatively (open into Creative Imagination) and synchronistically (corresponding events in space-time with nonlocal forces beyond space-time).

Enhanced receptivity enables creativity to come through us from the nonlocal Field, which can then work in sync with the space-time world. Harmonics from inner-nature attune with outer-nature through our right relation of self-other-world. We become more receptive to synchronistic events and epiphanies to such an extent that they become the norm. Inner and outer starts working in tune through us. We begin to understand ourselves as microcosm within macrocosm and so dawns the humbling realization of the importance of right relation with the whole through our own authentic relating with others and world.

This embodied knowing then allows for wisdom to work with us, a gnosis that has existed within humanity for a large part of our history. In ancient times, gnostic wisdom streams are found emanating out of early civilizations like Sumer, Mesopotamia, the Indus, Egypt, and the Far East that go on to form influential esoteric currents in mystical Jewish, Muslim, and Christian traditions pervading the Western world. The same gnosis is present in ancient shamanic traditions the world over. In fact, it's an inherent part of who we are as *Homo sapiens*, or 'wise beings', or rather 'beings who work with wisdom.' Without this inner-outer correspondence, we humans fall out of tune with life and we lose our way. Enter today's malaise.

RECEPTIVITY → CREATIVITY → SYNCHRONICITY

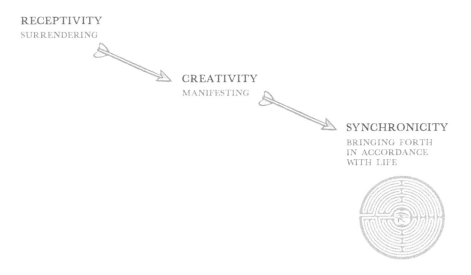

It's quite a humbling and sacred undertaking to work with Nature's Wisdom. We hold space for the transcendent harmonies of the esoteric inner realm to flow into and cocreate with the divergent-convergent-emergent self-organizing relational resonances of outer-nature. This includes the living systems we lead, advise, or coach. Quantum Lens 3 soul-consciousness works with systemic Lens 2 heart-consciousness and then applies the tool of Lens 1 ego-consciousness to birth our becomings.

NATURE'S WISDOM / 233

From the immensity of the Field come energetic resonances or song lines that enter us through our soul-consciousness. These can be insights and messages as we saw in the case of the Creative Imagination Process. They can also be energies and forces that have no specific message, yet in-forming, informational in an energetic sense, they potentialize through us. The bodymind is a conduit—like a flute or panpipe—and through heart-consciousness harmonic in-forming energies enter our soul craft. Through our outer presence, relationality, and interactivity with the system we're working with, this energy manifests into the world of form.

This sacred creative act of working with the inner animating harmonics of life requires a continual strengthening of our own acoustic electromagnetic bodymind instrument. This is not a one-off bodymind coherence undertaking, it's a never-ending psychospiritual routine, as Holderlin's Bread & Wine poem notes:

> "For a weak vessel is not always able to retain them,
> And only occasionally is man able to bear the heavenly fullness."

This way of living and leading requires a foundational practice (which we will get to in this book), and it's far from some dreamy, wishful, New Age way of experiencing life. It's not something to attain on a weekend retreat or a place where you 'get away from it all.' It's a depth of psychic receptivity that remains in us amid the marketplace of busi-ness through a daily practice of working with life— immanent and transcendent, inner and outer. An ongoing alchemizing attentiveness that enables the seed of our potential to flower and fruit into regenerative futures.

To surrender into this imaginal quintessential moment beyond space-time is to die before you die. It's a crucifixion of the knowing mind by the unknowable Mystery, which leads to a resurrection, a rebirth, a re-membering. Many of the world's myths work with this death-rebirth process, which we find at the heart of the spiritual journey, of becoming who we truly are, *Homo sapiens* – beings who work with wisdom.

Every day and every night we are cultivating the conditions in our alchemic vessel (the bodymind) for it to be receptive to direct transmission from the transcendent and find harmonic right relation with the inner-nature of our own ego-psyche-soul. We learn to serve the living-organization and life through this inner-nature conduit. The panpipe with the breath of Source coming into the pipe to play a unique tune. The formless in-forming form.

How we listen inwardly and outwardly helps our receptive right relation with self-other-world. By sacralizing the moment through our intentional attentiveness, we hold space to bring forth the inner into outer. We are simultaneously listening to the music all around and within us, and playing the music, live, on-air, directly broadcasting into this orchestra of life. Our way of perceiving and walking through life is animistic, not in some religious or spiritual 'belief' sense, but through a practical attentiveness to life. Everything is sacred and infused with an animating potential informed by a deep Mystery, and we are co-creating within it, self-as-participatory. We have re-turned back into real life. The mythological journey of departure-initiation-return moves up a spiral through our wholeness as we authentically flow with right relation through our unique soul craft, quintessentially invoking archetypal energies of Nature's Wisdom and so en-chanting life.

A re-enchantment of life is an important aspect of shifting from achiever to regenerator. We are the alchemic agents. Busy at work with tensions within and all around us, recalibrating through figure-of-eight flows of death-rebirth, our essence working with the essence of nature, our soul in tune with the World Soul. The unconscious found through inner-nature lights the dark depths to reveal a wisdom that can be brought into daily consciousness through our Creative Imagination. This is to work with the *lumen naturae*, or the luminosity we find in the depths of inner-nature where the darkness becomes light. This is the radical act of regeneration, being a force of nature by finding accord with the rhythms of Life.

> "This is the true joy of life, the being used for a purpose recognized by yourself as a mightier one… the being a force of nature instead of a feverish selfish little clod of ailments and grievances complaining that the world will not devote itself to making you happy."
>
> —George Bernard Shaw

The symbol for this third esoteric aspect of Nature's Wisdom—spiraling, turning, twisting synchronistic correspondence of 'As above so below'—is the Eye of the Heart within the center of the labyrinth. The labyrinth journey inward and then back outward again, like the U, but winding and unwinding to and from the center, where we find the opened Eye of the Heart through which we re-member and commit to a new way, bringing forth what is deep within us to venture forth beyond the labyrinth into the Way of Nature. Life as a sacred experience rooted in right relation.

Its center reveals the secrets in our soul. We are the ones we've been waiting for. We are sovereign, energized soul-systems capable of working with unlimited energy in serving Life. No external hero required. We're in the driver's seat of our own lives, winding down narrow roads in the dark wilderness with the guidance of wisdom. Corrupt systems that seek to control, manipulate, and impinge on our soul's sovereignty are seen for what they are, negative, anti-life forces debased from the harmonics of life. Through our own inner knowing and harmonic attunement, we can learn to steer clear of them as we journey into our soul craft.

Speaking in Symbols

The primordial symbols, insights, and images we find through the Imaginal Realm are a part of the return. Jung notes, "It is only possible to live the fullest life when we are in harmony with these symbols, wisdom is a return to them." (Jung, 1973) The primordial images and archetypal powers found in inner-nature are a vital compass showing humanity the way out of the ego-illusion it's got itself caught up in. Our regenerative futures depend upon finding our true sense of place and purpose in the world.

This is what the Creative Imagination awakens, as Coleridge notes, "a repetition in the finite mind of the eternal act of creation in the infinite I AM", an accordance of inner-outer nature, 'As above so below', which enables right relation to flow through our thoughts, words, and deeds. We are working as an intermediary messenger, a bridge or conduit, between transcendent (Heaven) and immanent (Earth) through inner unfolding into outer (through

Creative Imagination), and resonating back from outer into inner (through the acts of manifesting our soul craft). This is the labyrinth that spirals both directions, with the centered open eye, that sees 'through' outer into inner and back out again. This is a receptive-creative-synchronistic way of serving life.

For Corbin, Hermes dwells in the Imaginal Realm, the same Hermes who walks with the caduceus as his staff. Hermes is a messenger of the gods, walking between worlds. He is thought to be a Greek version of the ancient Egyptian god Thoth, who works with the rhythms and relationships between all things. Hermes is the conduit for gnosis, helping us gain insight through the Imaginal Realm as a messenger bringing harmonics in from the other side, thinning the veil for us. He is a spirit guide aiding our insight for our own rebirth into a deeper knowing.

The poet, Rainer Maria Rilke, unveils the co-creative undertaking in his *Sonnets to Orpheus*. As 'creatures of stillness' to hear wisdom and form a temple within, the quintessential centering inside that awakens us to all three esoteric aspects of Nature's Wisdom. To activate this depth of listening is to find the 'wakefulness' of Zen, and learn to hear the sound of silence, the very harmonics of creation, the Song of Songs deep inside nature.

> "A tree ascended there. Oh pure transcendence!
> Oh Orpheus sings! Oh tall tree in the ear!
> And all things hushed. Yet even in that silence
> a new beginning, beckoning, change appeared.
>
> Creatures of stillness crowded from the bright
> unbound forest, out of their lairs and nests;
> and it was not from any dullness, not
> from fear, that they were so quiet in themselves,
>
> but from just listening. Bellow, roar, shriek
> seemed small inside their hearts. And where there had been
> at most a makeshift hut to receive the music,

> a shelter nailed up out of their darkest longing,
> with an entryway that shuddered in the wind-
> you built a temple deep inside their hearing."
>
> —Rainer Maria Rilke

Embracing Life in Right Relation

It might feel like hubris to the ego that one might even consider living wisely. Yet it's an act of deep humility to realize that we are always within Nature's Wisdom, albeit not always attuned with it, or rather, attuned with 'Her' as in Sophia. The first step in approaching Her is learning to embrace life as a sacred learning experience. The second is to realize the importance of treating our bodymind instrument rather like a temple. We can create a sacred space—a Temenos—inside our own ego-heart-soul consciousness that allows for our attunement, atonement, and accordance with Nature's Wisdom.

CREATING A TEMENOS INSIDE OURSELVES

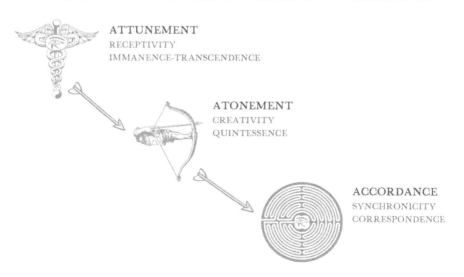

ATTUNEMENT
RECEPTIVITY
IMMANENCE-TRANSCENDENCE

ATONEMENT
CREATIVITY
QUINTESSENCE

ACCORDANCE
SYNCHRONICITY
CORRESPONDENCE

Attunement – cohering the bodymind helps us receptively listen to immanence-transcendence through presence. We work with the primal tension of diversity-in-unity (out of the One comes the Two of yin-yang) and we work with yin-yang tensions to make the music of life sing in harmony through right relation.

The symbol is **caduceus**.

The Esoteric Wisdom Aspect is **Life is immanent and transcendent.**

Atonement – working through any blockages or stuckness in our capacity to find flow of inner-outer nature and allowing the inner darkness to be alchemized into the light of our consciousness, involves a journeying toward wholeness, a process of at-one-ment. The very essence of Self is at-one with the ultimate forces of nature. To be in our center is to open into the Field where Source-energy pours into our becoming. We hold the tension to allow our true nature's soul-consciousness to shine through the world through our soul craft (the Three-in-One Trinity). We are at-one with the inner-outer Mystery.

The symbol is the **archer's bow**.

The Esoteric Wisdom Aspect is **Life has an inner metaphysical realm that interpenetrates with the outer physical world.**

Accordance – finding right relation of self-other-world is a process of becoming, of realizing our soul craft in ac'cor'dance with our soul-dharma with an open-heart in harmonic right relation. Through the open Eye of the Heart, we become a sacred messenger between inner-outer nature. We become aware of our capacity to return to our center within and enter into realms without and beyond. We, like all of life, are in the flows of oscillations while manifesting our fruits (Four-in-One). Life is diversity-in-unity, a developmental emergent and evolutionary becoming in accord with nature, Earth and cosmos.

The symbol is the **open Eye of the Heart at the center point of the labyrinth**.

The Esoteric Wisdom Aspect is **Life works with the correspondence of 'As above so below; as within so without'.**

I fully appreciate that it may be asking a lot for a busy leader or practitioner to digest this rather esoteric chapter, let alone actually embody the esoteric aspects into everyday living. I am aware that what I share here is very close to what some esoteric traditions call White Magic, as we are working with super-natural (super-sensory) powers to serve life through our soul craft. I have had the people I coach ask me whether we need to be careful about getting ensnared into Black Magic by mistake. On the one hand, yes, we do, which is why there are specific practices of intentionality that help ensure we are catalyzing super-natural energies in a beneficial, life-affirming way. On the other hand—and this is what I hope you leave this chapter with— let's not become fearful. What is vital here is the subtle yet profound truth of our intention to serve life.

This is what being a regenerator is all about, pure and simple. Regardless of what soul craft you undertake in the world, as long as you are coming from the right place inwardly then you will be working with love and serving life outwardly. Journeying inward, you learn to discern when the ego or some other influencing force might be distracting you from the path. Soul work is divinely guided, and when we work with our dharma, our unique essence, it aligns our intentions at the soul-spirit level. It's only if the ego usurps our intentions or negative forces come into play that we might drift into something selfish, vindictive, manipulative, or dark that does not benefit the harmonics of life's evolution.

There are negative energies and demonic obstructors of consciousness that we must learn to protect and clear ourselves from as we journey. This is why the inner foundations covered in Chapters 9-12 are so important, as through these inner conditions we ensure we are flowing with the right intention and attention.

I am conscious that this chapter may come across as heavy on philosophy and light on practicality. As said, we shall be turning to practicalities in the chapters head. I feel it's important to provide this mythological and meta-physical basis to activating regenerative leadership consciousness, because without its philosophical anchoring in the mind, heart and soul, we can become unmoored and sucked back into Mechanistic Materialism. In the years ahead, massive change will unfold as the 400-year-old worldview and accompanying socioeconomic system of Mechanistic Materialism goes through its death throes. Riptides and hurricanes lie ahead. Amid fearful times of immense uncertainty, old habits will die hard. Powerful forces handsomely profiteering from the malaise of egoic capitalistic consumerism will try to hold on even tighter. Without a sure footing deep inside of us, the stormy seas of epochal change ahead could leave one shipwrecked. But a new way is coming, unfolding by the day.

> "Thy kingdom come, Thy will be done, on Earth as it is in Heaven."
>
> —The Lord's Prayer

The 'second coming' is not some historic event 'out there'. It's 'in here', in our hearts and minds. It's the capacity to see and hear the kingdom of Earth as it is in Heaven, to sense that the here-and-now and beyond are One. To realize the Song of Songs and to listen to our song-lines is the very experience that Life is simply waiting for us to wake up into and see with new eyes.

This journey is a shift in consciousness, no less. We simply cannot activate a new quality of leadership consciousness with the flick of a switch. No, we must endure a journey of transformation that involves a psychological renewal—a process of *dying and being reborn*, a threshold-crossing from one state of being to the next by letting go of the old while bringing in the new. This crossing morphs how we relate to our inner selves and outer world. The ancient Greeks used the term 'metanoia' to describe such a shift. 'Meta,' like in metamorphosis, is to 'shape-shift' or 'move beyond' and 'noia' relates to 'true understanding', to transform the understanding of our sense of self and how we relate with the world. It's a profound undertaking that affects us in deep and partly unconscious ways. It's not something to be taken lightly, yet without this personal shift in consciousness the looming crises our organizations and societies now face will be unavoidable.

It's to this journey of total transformation that we now turn to in **Part 3 Journeying**, along with some practical steps to gain our sure footing for the future head.

"This above all: to thine own self be true."

—Shakespeare

"The ultimate mystery ground, the transcendent energy source of the universe, is also the mysterious source of your own life."

—Joseph Campbell

"Nature, not the wit of man, gives to knowledge its integral character."

—F.J.E Woodbridge

PART 3

JOURNEYING
(INTO RIGHT RELATION)

The Journey

So far throughout this book, we have repeatedly emphasized the importance of undertaking a journey inward. A journey that involves a process of letting go of the old self—the achiever—to endure the process of individuation, which asks us to traverse through old wounds and suppressed shadow aspects of the psyche, while drawing upon our soul-nature and discovering our way to serve life through our soul craft.

Recall what Jesus said, "If you bring forth what is within you, what is within you will save you. If you do not bring forth what is within you, what is within you will destroy you." The present predicament of Western consciousness (which now engulfs vast swaths of humanity) is the egoic over-active achiever mind, which is tethered to the Mechanistic Materialism worldview. This way of attending to life fails to bring forth what is within us, as it works only at the surface of things. The achiever inhabits life as a separate unit, seeking survival in a world without meaning, searching for security, recognition, and reward through outer achievement. There is no space or time for unearthing what is hidden within, and so what is within—the unconscious—starts to destroy us.

The inner journey, however, brings forth what is within us, and we work with inner-nature to invite our own essence to work with the ultimate forces of nature—the archetypal powers and spirit energies—to wholly integrate. We are tasked to know one's Self and to bring forth into the world of service the elixir of our soul craft, the boon we gain from the descent into the center of our selves.

Make no mistake, this inner journey calls upon courage and may activate confusion, suffering, depression, privation, challenge, and tumultuous tension. Yet it's challenge and tension that reveal a wisdom that otherwise remains buried inside.

> "Adversity reveals genius, prosperity conceals it."
>
> –Horace

The sacrifice endured on the journey crucifies our Selves, dismembering us, down into the descent of our own shadows, wounds, constrictions, and fears. Uncomfortable tensions pull us apart, disorientating and disrupting what we thought we knew of self and world. In disintegrating the old self, the dominant egoic 'I' habits, personas, protection-rackets, and thoughtforms that encapsulate the achiever as self-as-separate in turn disintegrate. It's only through this descent into our own dying that we slough off the old skin. Here, in this inner space, we form a kind of cocoon inside our psyche, which can process the disintegration-reintegration and to birth and nurture the true nature of our soul. Then, as we start to sense into the soul-scape at the center of our being, we find our way of living and leading more authentically in right relation with self-other-world—our dharma. The wisdom of the death-rebirth process reveals our soul powers, the higher faculties that aid our knowing and walking the path back into service.

The ultimate aim of the journey is not to reveal one's Self but for the wisdom to serve others, to serve life itself. By allowing the soul within to come through our integrated ego-heart-soul consciousness we learn to serve life and find flow not only with our own true nature but with how life flows. The achiever becomes the regenerator. When in the center point of our own being, we are at-one with inner-outer nature and form right relation. This is the ultimate purpose of the journey, and it's an act of immense love and truth attained through wisdom.

This process of awakening is a waking up to the realization that the soul inside is eternal and transcendent within immanent nature, and that the individual soul swims within the World Soul flowing through all life. From an off-centered and dis-eased existence comes healing and wholeness. We learn that our individual and unique natures are immersed in all of life, like the holographic fractal symbolized by Indra's Net.

INDRA'S NET

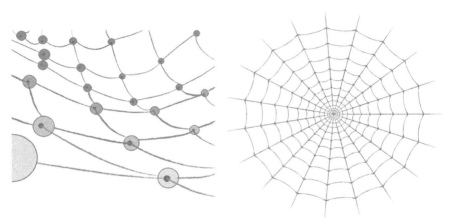

While being an intimately individual journey, this is also a collective journey. We are all participating in this journey as a civilization. Right now, here, on Earth, modern humanity is taking a momentous leap into the Mystery of life, as we shift from Mechanistic Materialism into Quantum Complexity, crossing the threshold from Level 0 into Levels 1-2-3 Living Systems Awareness. As Graves knew, "It's not merely a transition to a new level of existence, but the start of a new movement in the symphony of human identity," whereupon we re-member, we re-embody, the magnificence of existence. (Graves)

Certainly, indigenous peoples, esoteric traditions, and wisdom schools have kept this flame of consciousness alive, hence it's a remembering. But only now are we starting to experience a widespread collective shift of human consciousness, which is taking place across all colors, creeds, and cultures. One might see how the macro-arc of Western consciousness over the last two thousand years or so is itself a journey, albeit outer orientated, that has been taking us further from the inner realm of Nature's Wisdom. Now, with recent findings (such as quantum and complexity science, depth and ecological psychology, neuroscience, and consciousness), we are seeing signs of a return back into the symphony of the Song of Songs.

THE COLLECTIVE U JOURNEY

MECHANISTIC MATERIALISM

DEATH-REBIRTH
RISING DISSONANCE :
GREAT RESIGNATION
MENTAL HEALTH PANDEMIC
ECOLOGICAL COLLAPSE
CONFLICT
SOCIAL UNREST

QUANTUM COMPLEXITY
RISING INTEREST IN :
CONSCIOUSNESS
NATURE CONNECTION
REGENERATIVE AGRICULTURE/
ECONOMICS/ BUSINESS
SPIRITUALITY

This collective journey, when seen as a return movement from achiever to regenerator, contains a fractal of the departure-initiation-return U movement. The departure from the dominance of Mechanistic Materialism with its prioritization of outer achieving is evident. There is a dissonance rising in the world. More and more people are sensing that all is not well with our current socioeconomic approach of capitalist consumerism. The mental health issues that have reached epidemic proportions, trends like the Great Resignation (where people search for deeper meaning in their lives beyond the treadmill of recognition and reward through outer achieving), and the impoverished state of the environment are all signs. These signs are the 'call to adventure', our push to depart from the status quo.

It's what Joanna Macey, David Korten and others call 'The Great Turning', which isn't limited to an outer shift from the dominant-extractive-industrial model to an emergent-regenerative-economy model, but also embraces an inner shift from achiever to regenerator. While the collective journey is paramount, the return of the collective necessitates our own individual journeys of decent, death-rebirth, and return.

Without this inward reorientation the newly forming regenerative zeitgeist can get hijacked by the old mindset, because it's not wholly transformed. As has been said, in place of a genuine metamorphosis, we could emerge as 'caterpillars with wings', a term first coined by living systems explorer Nora Bateson. However, this chapter turns to the journey of becoming butterflies.

Mapping the Journey Inward

There comes a point in one's adult life, often referred to as a 'mid-life crisis', when the dissonance inside us speaks up. At first, we suppress the dissonance, try to ignore the inner nagging and voiced concern that all is not right. We carry on with our days and duties. This inner dissonance gets louder, leaving us with no choice but to question the (achiever) path we are on. *Could there be more to life than this?* Perhaps we get an inkling of something different through brief moments of oneness or mini epiphanies that leave us feeling more fully alive, connected, in flow. Or we recall happier times, often as a child, when we were connected to nature, more connected inside ourselves, more embodied, less in the head, less stressed.

This rising dissonance is our 'call to adventure'. It's time to embark on the journey inward into the center of our being. But this labyrinth journey is full of twists and turns, trials and tribulations. If we dare to venture inward, we will come right up against our own ego, which is the very dominance fueling our achiever mind. Though we can't ignore that voice of dissonance, saying that something's not right with the way things are in our life, and yet we are scared to challenge the achiever mind which, on the surface, looks like it's the only thing that's given us our successes. After all, we've achieved the material things necessary for our survival in this challenging dog-eat-dog world of separation and competition.

If we do find the courage to embark on the descent into our own being, then a truth will be revealed, one beyond the achiever mind's outer gaze. This is the revealing of our divine spark within, that means to live in one's center, for its only through this journey that we can learn to serve life through an integrated ego-heart-soul consciousness. Separateness is still a living function of space-time duality, but separateness is now seen for what it truly is—a duality within the trinity of unity.

The real challenge of embarking on this journey is that none of what we speak of makes any sense. That is, until we are a significant way through the journey, which does precious little to convince our dominant achiever mind that embarking on such a journey is a good idea in the first place. Our ego-consciousness will question us. *How is this in any way useful, practical, or necessary for our way of living and leading amid an increasingly volatile and dangerous world?* Fortunately, we have the capacity to listen inward to hear the rising dissonance inside. And question again, *Do we want to step foot on this journey that takes us down and in, or do we want to stay safe-and-sound on the riverbanks watching the flow but not daring to go in?*

My guess is—because you are still reading this book—that you are no longer on the banks of the river. You are already in it. Which is why the aim of this chapter is not to convince you to take the first step, but to provide guidance for the journey ahead. I coach leaders, practitioners, and people of all walks of life through this labyrinthine journey. While the journey is unique to each one of us, there are way markers along the maze that have proven useful. It's a three-phased journey, and there are nine guideposts I'll offer you along the way.

The Three-Phased Inner Journey: Departure, Disintegrate-Reintegrate, Return

Throughout divergent cultures the world over we find sacred stories of death-rebirth journeys. These myths transcend language. They are metaphors for what lies behind the visible world—a hidden nature so vital for our living wisely on Earth. The inner journey is a quest into the soul. It's a pilgrimage for the mortal ego to embark on, to tap into Nature's Wisdom just out of sight in the immanent-transcendent world beyond the achiever mind. This soul-quest is essentially an initiation to a threshold crossing into a new way of being in the world, where we learn (re-member) how to take part in the sacred dance of life, where we come to play our tune (at-one) within the Song of Songs.

The journey strengthens our receptivity, allowing us to work simultaneously with the inexhaustible energies pouring in from inner-outer nature and those found in the center of our being through heart-and-soul consciousness. It's also a journey of psychological death, disintegration, dismemberment, and crucifixion. A death of the old in order to enter a new zone of experience, to see beyond the veil of the known into the unknown, which requires a bona fide psychological readiness.

The labyrinth we find within is netted with thick cobwebs and meshes made up of our own ego-consciousness. All the 'stuff' we need to work through as we descend into the recesses and shadows of our innermost being. In processing, disintegrating, untying, and reweaving the psyche, we experience a 'dark night of the soul' which can take many months, often years, and cannot be rushed by the achiever mind. Then, through an alchemizing process of disintegrating-reintegrating, there comes a time when we sense the readiness and feel the certainty of our own centering. We start to return from the abyss and back to contemporary life to serve as a regenerator, to help heal and renew society. The details of this soul craft service will be proportionate to the depth of the descent.

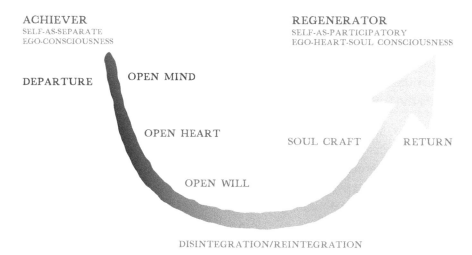

This same three-phased journey, which begins with the *departure* from everyday ego-consciousness and then descends into a death-rebirth process of *disintegration-reintegration* to finally *return* back into the world of service, is the same journey depicted and symbolized in myths throughout the world's wisdom traditions and indigenous peoples. It's a birthright process of making ourselves whole as humans. So important to our learning to live a wholesome life that it ought to be taught at school, but that necessitates the very worldview shift we are beckoning. Because today's dominant Mechanistic Materialism honors only an achiever mind, and it quiets anything that could be seen as a distraction from its goal of outer fixing, even if it (or we) has lost the plot about what to fix.

I use the *symbol* of the labyrinth and the *metaphor* of metamorphosis for this inner three-phased journey. As we depart, we go inward, let go of old ways, and allow the old self to die by entering a 'wintering' descent in to the labyrinth. Metaphorically, in this hibernation phase, we form a cocoon, an inner laboratory for the disintegration-reintegration process to unfold. This involves a dark and mystical reorientation of our sense of self. For in the cocoon stage of a caterpillar becoming a butterfly, it is dark, chaotic, and messy on the inside. Before life emerges anew, it exists hidden and formless.

As our true nature starts impenetrating our psyche, through an alchemizing of our ego-heart-soul consciousness, we gain the courage and conviction to reemerge as the butterfly in service of life. This is a fundamentally different self from the old (caterpillar) self yet is the same being. As humans, this metamorphosis can be quite perplexing for longtime friends, relatives, and colleagues to remain truthfully in touch with someone enduring such a transformation, because as the inner self morphs outer ways of relating with others and the world change. The ego's achiever mind is no longer in the driver's seat. The soul with the awakened mind has found its rightful place as the driver, delegating the ego as a useful tool to aid the soul's destiny.

Through my coaching work, I have given names to each of the three phases of this inward, downward and outward spiraling journey. The first, our *departure*, is when we are 'wintering'. From 'wintering' we enter a stage of *disintegration-reintegration*, which I call 'alchemizing'. And the last stage is our *return* from the inner realms and brings us to 'serving'.

THE THREE PHASED U JOURNEY

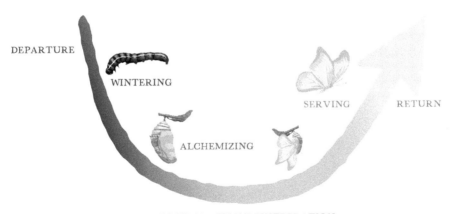

This three-phased journey of wintering-alchemizing-serving has nine stages to it. The nine stages are our friendly way markers on a map for those of us enduring what can often feel like a messy, confusing, twisting, and turning labyrinthine metamorphosis.

THE JOURNEY / 253

THE NINE STAGED U JOURNEY

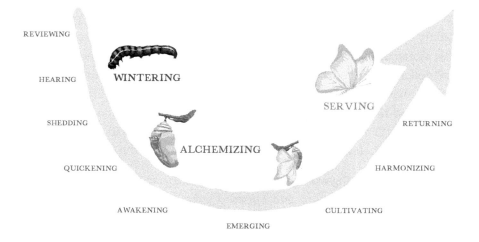

Before we depart on our journey of phases and stages, let's take a moment to pause, to still our minds for a moment, to contemplate this quote:

> "People say that what we're all seeking is a meaning for life. I don't think that's what we're really seeking. I think that what we're seeking is an experience of being alive, so that our life experiences on the purely physical plane will have resonance within our own innermost being and reality, so that we actually feel the rapture of being alive."
>
> –Joseph Campbell

Please spend a few moments reflecting on this quote. Meditate. Journal. Close your eyes to breathe. See what thoughts, feelings, or sensations arise within you before we embark.

Wintering: *Reviewing* → *Hearing* → *Shedding*

Reviewing

Symbol: Harvest Supper
Season: early to mid-autumn
Key words and phrases: dissonance, inner-turn, know thy self

As the achiever leader, we've achieved some noble feats and have gained reward and recognition for our work. Much of which has been driven by a worry and fear that we need to survive, save up. We work and work and then work some more, to protect ourselves from the increasingly volatile and uncertain world. We climb the slippery ladder; we do what needs to be done. Yet there's an exhaustion, a mental, physical, and emotional fatigue that's creeping in. It may also be that we are getting increasingly frustrated with the state of the world. Perhaps we have attended a course or retreat that's opened our mind to another way of living. And this rising *dissonance* bubbling inside is questioning how we are living. *Is there more to life? Am I really living my purpose? Who am I, why am I here?* This can feel like a mid-life crisis but can happen at any time in our lives, from our late twenties to late sixties. Some adults, regardless of age, never entertain such questions, not even in retirement, therefore they never embark on this inner journey.

With dissonance at roiling boil inside, telling us that something needs to change, we start to look in, look out, look around. I call this the *Reviewing* stage because rather than the head-down, overachieving of the last however many years, we pop our head up from the rat race, and we pause. Something is up and we can feel it. If we dare reflect on this inner dissonance, we see that if we continue along this same path of outer-achievement, we may not ever know who we truly are. Still, fear of change is inevitable, and it's easy to put off such a deep review of where we are at in life. But there is a nagging feeling of 'if not now, then when?'

As a start, we acknowledge the fruits of what we have achieved. Rather like enjoying a *Harvest Supper*, we know the season is changing and winter is coming, yet there is bounty to be proud of. Look what the achiever mind has achieved! This acknowledgement of where we are positioned outwardly in our lives can briefly satisfy the dissonance gnawing at us from the inside. Especially when there is an underlying fear of what might be round the corner where the season of life begins to turn wintery. This fear can push us back into the status quo security of the achiever mind, but soon enough a sense of longing and loss, of deep dissatisfaction and disconnectedness, wells up. Turns out that our outer achieving is merely fulfilling purposes that are not properly our own. We are gaining outer fulfillment but at the expense of our inner wellbeing. An unconsciousness is being made conscious, and with it comes the emotions of frustration, anger, despair. Depression might take hold. While we sense a life transition ahead, we continue to fear the unknown.

A coach, therapist or friend can help to encourage us along the path as the ego achiever mind is still in the driver's seat and now panicking about any possible change ahead that might dislodge it from supreme control. This is an intentional *inner-turn*, a choice we are making, so we have the power to bend the beam of our awareness away from outward achiever and dare to illuminate something inward. Looking in, we sense shadowy depths inside. All the stuff we've suppressed during years of outer-achieving is there underneath the surface.

Sure, it can feel easier, far less fearful, to resist the inner turn, but then this *Reviewing* stage remains at a superficial level of 'outer' projection. There are others to blame 'out there' for my dissonance, or there are things I can fix and change 'out there' to bring me fulfilment. This is where the image of the mid-life crisis is trivialized by buying a motorbike or fast car, finding a younger lover, or a place in the sun. We reside at the outer level with our superficial alterations rather than any inward review, and instead of diving down into *Wintering*, we resist and hold on to an achiever lifestyle where the ego is firmly in the driver's seat.

For those of us who dare to go inward—and for some this needs to be thrust upon us through an outer event, such as a loved one leaving us, someone close to us dying, a bad accident, or protracted illness—we are invited into our descent into the inner dissonance. We review what is going on *inside* ourselves and begin to notice how we have got caught up in an imbalanced, lopsided experience of life that has constructed an artificial version of our

Selves. How we've manifested an outer projection that fits in but is not true to who we are. This is not easy to see, which is why it's easily resisted.

This is precisely when the ego senses the possible psychological death ahead and kicks into overdrive with all sorts of anxieties and fears about how the risks of changing anything are simply too huge to even contemplate. All sorts of justifiable reasons abound for delaying the inner change—waiting till the pension, the kids leaving university, or aging parents passing away. All quite sensible (though not super-sensible). The time will never be quite right from the ego's perspective, as the self-as-separate will always be insecure and hooked on the achiever mind. If we manage to work through the anxiety-inducing noise of the ego and pursue our inward reflection, then we shall start to hear something within. Enter the Hearing stage.

Hearing

Symbol: Halloween
Season: mid to late-autumn
Key words and phrases: retreat, listening in, call to adventure

The more we reflect, the more the dissonance inside rises and permeates our daily conscious awareness. The sense that something is not right about our current way of living infiltrates us, and we seriously consider a significant change ahead. We know in our hearts that something has got to change. This provokes a desire to spend more moments in reflection, contemplation, and meditation. Perhaps booking a weekend *retreat* to have space and time away from the usual relationships, activities, and hobbies. We may not know it, but this urge to go inward is us *hearing* the call to enter the descent into our own innermost being. Destiny is knocking, summoning us into the darkness of winter within. We may resist, turn a deaf ear, but the knocks come harder.

Perhaps changes in our outer life happen, like a relationship or job ending abruptly, which may cajole us further into this Hearing stage. Our center of gravity shifts, subtly at first, from the incessant outer-doing of the achiever mind that seeks to fit in to society, norms, conform, be liked, and be acknowledged as a success. We question this ego-version of ourselves as soft song-lines of the soul within us can now be heard. We can't help but *listen in.*

This time of inner shift is symbolized by *Halloween*. The psyche knows the descent into winter is ahead. Halloween can be full of fright. Facing our own demons and going into our dark recesses is scary. And the ego will scream, *To what avail is this inner journey?! Why now?! Why not carry on achieving for a little while longer? Listen to me!* But Halloween is the most liminal time of the year, when the veil between realms is thinnest. At this stage of the journey, the veil between our ego-consciousness and soul-psyche is thinning. We start to hear the subtle voice of the soul asking for a quietening of the ego for a descent into winter.

It's quite normal to refuse the call amid this scary time. Why not continue with the outer ego needs and desires, rather than risk entering a death-wintering process? Because if we consistently resist the call, then our lives may become like the Wasteland of the Fisher King in the Holy Grail legends. Turning away from the soul, and we remain caught at the surface of things and starve ourselves of soul. We come to resent our outer achieving. *Surely there is more to life!* we scream inside, and we get increasingly frustrated, anxious, or depressed with our lot. This is a stalling of the descent. Rather than the inner journey, we choose the comfortable numbness of the status quo.

But the dissonance will remain and rise inside regardless. Do we have the courage to hear the *call to adventure*? If—and it's a big 'if'—we commit to the inner journey, then we can begin shedding what no longer serves us. Enter the Shedding stage.

Shedding

Symbol: a snake shedding its skin
Season: winter
Key words and phrases: letting go, dark night of the soul, cocoon

We have decided to enter a wintering within, a psychological death process where we enter the metaphorical *cocoon*, an inner space where the old self disintegrates. While this cocoon wintering is an introspective stage, it's anything but idle. Many of us may not be able to hibernate in an outward sense by taking time away from work. The chores of everyday life remain, as do the needs of family and friends around us. Yet there can be an inner hibernation process occurring regardless of our outward activity, allowing us to become more introspective as we dare to enter the darkness inside our innermost being.

This begins what has been referred to as a *dark night of the soul*, which can last many months if not years. Shadow aspects of ourselves will need attending to as we sense inward more and more. Anything that is holding us back from a deeper metamorphic unfolding will start to disintegrate. We are learning to let go. *Letting go* of the baggage, stories, and narratives we ruminate on through the voice in the head that no longer serve us. We allow inner stuff to come up inside ourselves as we notice, process, let go, and integrate. We begin letting go of judgements, fears, identities, routines, fashions, habits, hobbies, and even relationships and commitments that no longer serve us. This can seem self-indulgent or self-absorbed, but it's not. It's a process of discerning what is true to our nature and what is inauthentic, having the courage to acknowledge it as something that may have served us until now but no longer does. We see how parts of the old self need now to be shed, like a *snake shedding its skin*.

The phrase letting go feels… apathetic maybe, cliched, or perhaps counter-intuitive in the face of so many challenges and problems to solve in our outer lives, organizations, and social systems. Yet the reality is that letting go is a radical act of the upmost importance. It's a surrendering, rather like the long out breath that follows a deep in breath. It's a release—an opening and allowing.

It's likely that in this wintering phase, we are particularly sensitive to being triggered. This can be seen as a good thing, as the triggers give us a way into seeing our own inner stuff, noticing what we react to, and reflecting on why we are being triggered. We can feel triggered by something, and we bring our awareness into the feeling, notice it, and allow the triggered sensation to just be. We are not trying to fix anything. Only noticing that the trigger brings a conscious awareness into our own inner psyche.

Throughout much of our lives we have been conditioned to hold on to, react to, or suppress any uncomfortable feelings that arise in us, and opening vulnerably to the sensation of an uncomfortable trigger is not at all easy, but it is simple. The voices of judgement, cynicism, and fear become more perceptible, and we start to notice how they are a way into noticing our own deeper nature and the fears and insecurities of the achiever mind and self-as-separate. We ought not judge ourselves too harshly for our old ways of being and doing or we undermine this letting go process. See each twinge of cynicism or pang of fear or defensive or aggressive reaction as a useful learning, an insight from which to gain perspective on what is within us—all our habits, wounds, and shadows. We can feel vulnerable as the old protection-rackets we have harbored to keep us safe from the world—projection, blame, resentment, unforgiveness—are noticed and shed, leaving us unarmored, undefended, and thin-skinned.

Hence the importance of the cocoon, the inner psychological space of non-judgement where we can take a step back from the immediacy of life, from outer-doing, and embrace the inner-being. Important, even amid running errands, doing the day job, and being busy with life. We now observe how and why we do these things. We can observe our attitude, our awareness, and invite a letting go of patterns and relations that are holding us back from our own metamorphic unfolding.

During this wintering, we learn to work with tensions and their polarities and right versus wrong conflict. We hold the tensions before being quick to judge. We open into the inner dimension behind our everyday thoughts and feelings to deepen our receptivity. This may invite an exploration into the more spiritual aspects of life. Practices that aid our letting go and encourage us to get out of the voice in the head and go into heart-consciousness and bodymind coherence can assist us here (see the Appendix).

The inner shedding of old habitual patterns of thought may also correspond with an outer shedding. We may downsize or quieten our way of life or change consumer buying patterns. Even where and how we choose to spend vacation time, weekends, or evenings can be affected. The activities we partake in, the books we read, what we watch on TV, and who we spend time with, all may morph. Life becomes unfamiliar, perhaps messy, even depressive. The coordinates and metrics we used to check our sense of self by (job promotion, salary increase, car we drive, clothes we purchase, holidays we go on, restaurants we frequent) are not so prominent or may have disappeared completely, leaving us disorientated about our sense of self. The old identity of 'achiever' is losing its grasping grip on us.

When coaching clients, I often liken this stage of the journey to 'wading through the marshes' where we feel bogged down at times and the air around is foggy and disorientating, as we squelch and sometimes sink in the bog of our own stuff. It's important to keep plodding, noticing, letting go. This old self disintegration can be a tricky time, and it's easy to get stuck in our own shadow, as well as get sucked down by archetypal forces in the shadow of the collective unconscious. The blame, anger, resentment, hurt, and trauma suppressed throughout our life as achiever are also suppressed in society through many lifetimes of conforming to the self-as-separate system of power-control Mechanistic Materialism. It's quite natural to feel angry and seek to blame the system or blame the 'other.' To a certain extent this anger is an important way to process and heal. Even so, we need to be careful of being subsumed by unconscious forces, getting bogged down in the marsh, our boots now so stuck in the mud that it's hard to move as we sink further into the muck of our own inner shadows.

Having an experienced coach or confidant during this stage of the journey can be invaluable to avoid unnecessary ego escapades of self-victimization, self-absorption, projection of anger or blame on to the 'other', or suppression of the shadow to try and feel 'good enough' again. Discerning what needs to be processed and integrated and what needs to be shed, is not at all easy or straight forward. This is where the labyrinth mythological narratives play out, like facing Medusa or the Minotaur—the dark side within—and not being frozen by fear but enduring a soul quest into our own center by integrating the shadow and the powers it possesses.

After what can feel like a protracted marathon of inner trials and tribulations, we start to learn to work with the inner realm in a more friendly way, no longer scared of the demons and ghouls of our own shadow. We might experience a more active dream life during this time, strange potent dreams, not always pleasant, but which form part of the process of disintegration and reintegration of this dying, shedding stage. Through practices like advanced meditation, bodymind coherence, and the Creative Imagination Process, we can start to drop behind our psychological baggage and activate soul energies. This requires a genuine psychological readiness that enduring the marshes has prepared us for.

Sure enough, as we persist in our plodding through the muck and the mud, the ground underfoot feels steadier, and we move into the Quickening stage, whereupon we start to learn to work with the activating soul energies within. This also signifies an end of the Wintering Phase and the beginning of the Alchemizing Phase.

Alchemizing:
Quickening → Awakening → Emerging

Quickening

Symbol: campfire
Season: late winter
Key words and phrases: integrating, practicing, imaginal, soul-scape

Having traversed the marshes, we've gained a good rhythm of wading through our own shit—processing, integrating, letting go, moving on. That's not to say there are not the odd patches of bog and fog still lurking, but we are now surefooted, a little quicker in our step, and a little brighter in our outlook. The cold dampness of winter lingers, but we sense a little light shining in.

In learning to *integrate* shadow aspects, our psychic powers are released and inner dragons and demons no longer scare us. Now they can be worked with, ridden, befriended, and released into energies that serve rather than scare. Now we can build new habits of noticing and processing that form a new way of being. For instance, learning to sense and work with subtle bodily somatic sensations of something rising in us, whether it be a tension to be held, or a constriction to be released. Our bodymind will register the trigger in some way —a pang of discomfort in the belly, tightness in the chest, twitch in the face, for instance—and once it does, we consciously bring our awareness to the sensation before getting hijacked by the fight or flight response of either wanting to react to it or suppress it. Stay with the feeling inside—notice it. With *practice* we get the hang of this.

At times, when we sense into the inner sensation, memories of past experiences arise and invoke strong emotions. The voice in the head can easily start up with judgements and views on the past memory, but if we can refrain from getting caught up in the judgement, criticism, or fantasy associated with the memory, then opening into these memories can shine a light on our inner shadows and suppressed emotions. What we are practicing here is a conscious re-membering of the experience and associated feelings before gently bringing awareness back to the sensation in the body. This is part of the *disintegrating-reintegration* process where we begin to untangle constrictions inside the bodymind to create more space inside to sense the *soul-scape*, where our inner and outer worlds meet.

Faced with critical choices we learn to discern, to trust our own inner guidance, and sense the soul coming into the bodymind. Synchronicities start to be noticed, illuminating the path while the ego is still wrestling in the labyrinth trying to resist the twists and turns into the center of our being. Sometimes the ego overpowers us, and we end up back in the head, lacerating ourselves with judgement, cynicism, and fear. But the more we practice letting go, sensing into the bodymind, the more we notice and allow, the more we integrate and feel in sync, the more we permeate and maturate the ego. Practice-practice-practice, integrate-integrate-integrate. This is the work of the *Quickening*.

Practices like Welcoming In the Twilight Zone, the Creative Imagination Process and Heart Entrainment become a regular go-to for us, as we learn to open more deeply to the Imaginal Realm and the Field. At this stage, we may still be a spiritual seeker, searching for our own soul-knowing, but we know in our hearts that there is more to life than meets the eye. Some days we feel that deepening trust, and other days we are back in the heaviness of the marsh, caught up in shadow integration. All the while we are cultivating our own courage, discernment, and resilience.

Although it may be unclear at this stage as to 'how' one might bring one's soul craft into the world, the 'what' of the soul craft begins to take shape in an imaginal, unconstrained, dreaming, envisioning fashion. Mood boards, vision quests, writing retreats, silent weekends, nature immersions, journaling, any time away from it all is important here. We let the cocoon work its magic, trying not to force or rush the metamorphosis. Here we stay in the *imaginal* twilight zone, resisting the impatient urge to run (as then we only sink back into the bog) and sustaining a rhythm and routine of regular practice-practice-practice, integrate-integrate-integrate.

While the depths of winter may have passed, conditions are far from springlike, and all about us seems quite disintegrated. The point of turning back on the journey has passed us by. We may often sink our head in our hands and cry *Why can't this all be easier!* We may wish for a get-out or a quick fix, but in all sincerity, we know we need to keep on moving through this inner journey, one step in front of the other, one day at a time, practice-practice-practice, integrate-integrate-integrate. At this stage, we are very much 'in' the transformation. The darkest hour is just before dawn, just as nature can be at its most cruel at this tail end of wintertime.

> "The black moment is the moment when the real message of transformation is going to come. At the darkest moment comes the light."
>
> –Joseph Campbell

In time, things appear less foggy and heavy, with occasional moments of sunlight breaking through the grey clouds to vistas of a mountain range beyond. Sunsets are noticeably later, yet we still appreciate cold evenings around the *campfire* to nurture the hearth within. The campfire also symbolizes the cooking cauldron of our inner stew as we continually practice and integrate, with challenges and tensions providing the alchemic heat for our metamorphic unfolding. Support will show up from weird and wonderful places. We might wish to engage in vision questing nature immersions or feel a need to journal. Seemingly chance encounters or invitations will chime at the right time. Simultaneously challenges will appear to test us, just when we least expect it but most often when we need it.

> *"Support you didn't know to ask for will show up. Challenges you would never have wanted will appear."*
>
> —Bill Plotkin

The Quickening is the harrowing adventure of honing our self-reliance skills, testing our dedication to the path. With no turning back, we may as well embrace the process. Listen to inner guidance as well as seek counsel from outer guides. Daily habits shift – less time in front of Netflix or listening to the news, a hunger to be in nature, away from screens, to listen and take part in spiritual practices and communities. We see the outer drama for what it is, largely a distraction from what's really going on in the world. All the while we are changing. We are also trying to survive. In the midst of all this messy darkness, we find out ways in which we might live and lead that align with this nature emerging within while enabling us to pay the bills. *How might we contribute to the Great Turning while serving the soul and putting food on the table?* we ponder.

What is happening within is a working with tensions, an alchemizing of masculine and feminine energies within, and a dawning realization that the masculine (yang) and feminine (yin) aspects of the psyche serve each other in becoming whole in our soul. This brings momentary insights, shafts of light that illuminate what lies beyond the polarities. A correspondence of inner and outer nature heralds the first signs of spring. Synchronistic moments, déjà vus, prophetic dreams, clairsentience, hunches, intuitions, all occur more frequently. It's as if a secret doorway inside us has opened. Enter the Awakening stage.

Awakening

Symbol: sap rising
Season: Valentine's
Key words and phrases: insight, forgiveness, alchemy

The land underfoot becomes firmer, more consistent, with less of our energy absorbed in the mud of the inner shadow and more in finding out how we might move out of hibernation to begin weaving our soul craft. The *insights* that emerged from the vision questing, journaling, and Creative Imagination of the Quickening stage are nurtured as seeds of insight potentializing within us. Our increased receptivity and capacity to sense synchronicities means we notice messages appearing in inner and outer ways. We learn to read the signs as a sense of our own soul path begins to form.

The cocoon is stifling us a bit, as some days we feel frustrated with all this introspection. Yet introspection is still a useful practice, as is letting go and shadow integration. We must be gentle to keep *alchemizing* the masculine and feminine energies within the psyche. Noticing our moods, biorhythms, psychospiritual energies, sensitivities, sixth sense, and newfound habits is important as we become more sensitive to the energies of those around us, including the wider constellation of systemic energies in our neighborhoods, organizations, communities, and wider systems of change.

Energy cultivation practices become important here. Discerning what's our stuff and what's not. As we start to sense into the 'what' as well as the 'how' of our soul craft, it's only natural for doubts to creep in and old habits to surface. We can use this as an opportunity to go deeper into our wounds— the existential wounds that originate in our sense of separateness from life itself, the primal wounds of our own worthiness and value. *Who am I really? Can I really bring my unique gift into the world and hope to be able to survive, let alone thrive?* Self-doubt is always present, but now we notice it without it subsuming us like it may have earlier on the journey.

We embrace the Fisher King within and find love for all aspects of ourselves and our fellow travelers. We see the old habits of blaming and projecting onto others and find the capacity to be humble and empathize with everything going on around us, knowing in our heart-of-hearts that we are 'all in this together', all struggling with the same human drama. We recognize each person as having a unique capacity to potentialize something of vitality, to participate in the ecosystem. This *forgiveness* and love for our own selves and others helps the melding alchemy within.

Often the wounds we heal and integrate in-form our soul craft, in that the very challenge we have overcome inside ourselves becomes the very learning that can serve others, whether through our servant leadership, wise counsel, capacity to hold space for others, to teach and guide, or to manifest through an entrepreneurial life-affirming venture. The world becomes our oyster. That wound that held us back is now the very grit that creates the pearl, our gift to the world.

Our *awakening* happens every day through the relentless act of learning to grow and give. Each day is seen as a developmental learning journey full of noticing, embracing, alchemizing. We learn to forgive ourselves when we inevitably stumble back into the marsh, and get stuck on our own shadow stuff, just when we thought we were done with it. And we learn to forgive others, as we are now gifted with a hard-won empathy for humanity and all life on Earth.

A spaciousness opens inside. Some days we feel ready to burst through the cocoon, and other days, we are caught up in self-doubt. A trust in life starts to feed us, nurturing the seed potential of our soul craft to grow its first tap roots, drawing from the Imaginal Realm through our own capacity of intention, attention, and energy cultivation. The metamorphic process is now moving into the butterfly stage, and from the outside looking in, we might see the butterfly pushing against the cocoon and wish to help the process by breaking it open. But now is not the time to hurry things. "Nature does not hurry yet everything is accomplished" is the wise adage, and for good reason. Try and pry the cocoon open too early, and the integrity of the butterfly is undermined.

The *sap is rising*, yet the last vestiges of winter can bite back with a vengeance. And we remain connected to the twilight Imaginal Realm to allow insight to start potentializing the outer manifestation of our vision. Creative

Imagination, dreamwork, shamanic journeying, symbolic artwork, creative writing, vision questing, ceremonial sweat lodges and rituals, and sacred medicine journeys can accompany the Awakening stage.

We trust our own inner guidance, to regularly clear our psyche and chakras, to become a 'tracker' picking up the scent of the destiny unfolding. Learning from others but not mimicking or copying their craft. Gaining confidence from other people's stories or the case studies of entrepreneurial ventures and business transformations, but not seeking cookbook approaches or 'how to' guides. Daily personal conversations with helpers, coaches, and our own inner knowing allow the sap to rise. Finally, as winter starts to give way to the warmer sunlight of early spring, we ready ourselves for life beyond the cocoon. Enter the Emerging stage.

Emerging

Symbol: wellspring
Season: Easter
Key words and phrases: new dawn, energy, manifestation

As we emerge from the cocoon, we are sensitive and exposed to the vagrancies and variabilities of an ever-changing and volatile world, sometimes barmy days, sometimes frosty coldness and harsh winds. This is simultaneously an exciting time of birthing new ideas, forming new partnerships and creating new ventures, and a rocky time of highs and lows, false starts, and tripwires. Yet, as life conditions unfold, we become more practiced and confident in our new way of becoming. We are settled and consistent in how we show up as old habits, safeguards, and pretenses die off and inner gifts and deeper insights flower. Before long, there are more spring-like moments than there are remnants of winter.

This bringing forth what is deep within us into our way of being in the world is a profoundly regenerative act. Without it, evolution is retarded, and we drift toward degeneration. It's by consciously welcoming in all of our inner-outer nature and our own evolutionary potential by going through the wintering death to springtime rebirth process that we evolve toward future-fitness and can *manifest* our soul craft into the world of service.

We can hear the song-lines of our soul more readily now and can discern when things feel right and when things feel off. This does not suggest that life is easygoing. In fact, it's no less difficult or challenging than at any stage before, but the way of moving through the challenges has decidedly shifted. We can notice our own selves and how we engage and react, sense our triggers, and acknowledge our projections. Rather than blaming others or suppressing how we experience challenges, we assimilate the learning, transmuting tensions into the emergence they reveal.

This welcome springtime is all about emergence—our emerging potential, our rising life-force coming out of a protracted state of introspection into a more outward manifesting dynamic. We are the *wellspring*, bubbling up from the deep soil into the light of day, and fresh spring water starts to flow into our endeavors.

Still, there are moments of hesitation, of halted flow, when it feels like the slings and arrows of the world are simply too much for our new vulnerable, undefended skin to handle. There is the achiever tendency slinking back in, eager to assert, to make its mark, to attain some early success with our soul craft. Nothing wrong with any of this, so long as we notice it and discern what serves the soul.

Sense the ego as servant and notice its want to usurp. Best to keep an eye out for what could become ego-chicanery pretending to serve the soul but in actuality bringing in the fear-based outer-achieving of old. It will take over by playing up fears of not being good enough, of self-doubt, or judgement from others, which feed a drama the ego can use for fuel to gain a master hold. But this ultimately thwarts the spring emergence and drags out the pregnancy before birth. Cultivating a healthy relationship of ego and soul is important.

In this stage, we work with the light hidden in nature, what the ancient alchemists called *lumen naturae*, and we work with the three outer and three inner aspects of Nature's Wisdom. These aspects become lived conduits, wisdom currents informing our flow (as do the 4 Ds of Dedication, Discernment,

Discipline and Devotion explored in the next chapter). Nature's Wisdom provides the foundation for us to build our soul craft upon the solid foundation of rock, to weather the storms and volatility that lie ahead. We become more visible in an authentic way while serving.

> "Become visible
> While carrying
> What is hidden
> As a gift to others."
>
> –David Whyte

We are beginning to sense the future of the rest of our lives. There is a sacred responsibility to serve the life pumping through our veins. We are now the craftsmen, artisans, and wisdom weavers of our soul craft.

The medieval word *artificer* or 'maker of art' is where the concept of 'artisan', as a creative maker of art, comes from. In Europe, before the advent of industrialization, art had physical, emotional, and spiritual meaning in terms of its contribution to everyday living. Art was the 'right way of making things.' In this artful service of life, the artisan (or craftsman as referred to by social philosopher Richard Sennett) gains meaningful engagement through the act of creating and delivering something of quality and value to self and society. (Sennett) The act of doing something well unleashes an intrinsic motivation and sense of wellbeing within the artisan. Through the creative act, the artisan ensures that the craft flows with creative energy and so is a conduit for realizing creative potential. The total engagement and intrinsic understanding of the task occurs when the artisan dwells in the right way of making things. The artisan or craftsman is transformed by the work. Charles Eisenstein, in *Sacred Economics,* talks of "the one who bows into service," recognizing the sacred nature of such soul craft work delivered with loving attention. (Eisenstein)

It's here in the day-to-day of the soul craft that we alchemize the practical vocational 'outer work' with the psychospiritual 'inner work'. An infusion of outer manifestations with inner energies. The 'Two' of the inner and outer become the 'Three-in-One' of the soul craft's creative manifestation marrying inner and outer worlds: As above so below. Which is what the alchemist Paracelsus meant when saying, "Everything is the product of the one universal creative effort, the Macrocosm and the Microcosm are one. They are one constellation, one influence, one breath, one harmony." (Bamford) It's through our soul work that we find our true place and purpose amid the teleological rhythms of nature, Earth, and cosmos. This embodiment of the sacred meaning of life does not rob us of our self-agency and individuality, but roots us in soul purposefulness beyond the fickle fears and desires of ego-consciousness.

While we may be getting much clearer about 'what' our soul craft is, we are still testing and learning the nature of 'how' the craft is delivered in a way that serves others yet also allows for a way of living. There is no rush to define this delivery mechanism, and yet testing, learning, partnering, exploring is all part of the emerging stage. The achiever energy that lies dormant, from before our wintering stage, gains a new lease of life, back in the saddle yet in service of the soul craft. We have transcended-and-included the 'achiever' into the 'regenerator' in a way that means we do not fall prey to the achiever mind's excesses and imbalances but can include its drive, tenacity, and ambition to get-the-job-done while honing our soul craft value proposition and delivery mechanism.

Soon we start cultivating the way we deliver our soul craft. No longer tentatively emerging into the market with it but mobilizing momentum and gaining traction. This completes the second phase of the journey, and we move out of the bottom of U and into the third phase of Serving, which begins with the stage of Cultivating our soul craft. The energy here is entrepreneurial, curious, and inquisitive, leading us to prototype and perhaps explore forms of investment, whether mainstream investment avenues or less conventional approaches like crowdfunding, the gift economy, or networks of sharing. A healthy tension will emerge between being able to stand on our own two feet through a satisfactory income while serving our craft in a way that does not simply meet society where it's at but catalyzes it in ways that provoke regenerative futures. This emergence stage gives birth to many self-actualizing social entrepreneurs, ranging from the quiet community worker or local healer through to leading a fast-growing for-purpose B-Corp engaging in global markets while remaining true to its soul-essence.

Serving:
Cultivating → Harmonizing → Returning
Cultivating

Symbol: May Day celebration
Season: early summer
Key words and phrases: entrepreneurialism, soul craft, value propositions

The depressive introspection of earlier stages has lifted. As has the murky fogginess of before. This stage of the journey does feel quite different from the stages before, as we have now moved into the outer world of action, and there is fire in our belly, more creative impulse, more yang energy to aid our get-up-and-go. While in many regards this might feel like a celebratory time, such as *the first Day of May*, as we are learning to cultivate our lifework into the world, it's still a time of challenge and immense learning. Bringing our unique gifts into the world is not easy, and any knockbacks and signs of rejection we receive are quite painful as our skin is still thin this early out of the cocoon.

Now, we are clear about our sense of place and purpose. Yet as we come into the market dynamics of the world, it's easy to be affected by the critiques, viewpoints, and judgements of others, especially those who may be perceived as pioneers or experts in the very field we are starting to cultivate our *soul craft* in. Most often there are purists, who uphold an important role of ensuring a certain rigor is applied to the craft, and sometimes the critique of these pioneering experts and purists inhibits our creative *entrepreneurial* flair or the uniqueness we might venture to bring to the table. With the cocoon now well behind is, we might wish for the protection of it, or to hide under a stone for a while amid critique and merciless market dynamics.

The bright sunny climes of early summer are not just benign, they are exposing and testing. Everything is on show, to be revealed. In these early stages of our enterprising venture, we can be susceptible to wanting to fit in, gain recognition from others, and perhaps mold our soul craft to fit around what others are doing. Be wary. Learn to discern what is your ego seeking to be liked and accepted in a new 'clan' and what is your soul search well beyond 'clans' into the immensity of the sea and the space of non-judgmental expansiveness. The more we can learn directly from the people or systems who gain the benefit of our soul craft *value propositions*, the more we gain useful insight on how to adapt and evolve our value propositions.

If we've not mined our darkness and integrated our shadows well enough during the bottom of the U, we get caught in fits and starts of our own ego-soul tussle amid this cultivating stage, and risk becoming ensnared in our own self-criticism to the point of undermining our value proposition. Watch out for the achiever mind, ever-ready to usurp control. Or there is the yang energy of the marketplace—seeking to be active on social media, to cultivate our brand, build a following, gain client references—that can be a trap. Nothing wrong with any of this, though we can learn to discern the subtlety of being 'in' the marketplace but not 'of' the marketplace.

It's all too easy to get caught up in this yang-energy of wanting to achieve, to put the hours in and outperform through sheer work ethic. Remember the wisdom of Lao Tzu, "Know the masculine, yet remain in the feminine." Remember to stay connected to the yin of inner-nature, to call upon Nature's Wisdom and stay connected to the twilight of the Imaginal Realm through keeping up with our daily energy cultivation and spiritual practices. Now more than at any other time through the U, our learnings and trials are being tested out in broad daylight, with no bushel to hide behind. Let's stay connected. Remain true to ego-heart-soul consciousness.

Those slings and arrows from the world can feel painful and confusing. If we listen too much to the ego and its protection rackets, we can forget to hear the song-lines of the soul. Yearning for the dark wintery moments of introspection, perhaps we take ourselves off for the odd long weekend or retreat away from it all to recoup, to regather our energies. This is where the qualities and capacities covered in the remainder of the book help to ensure that this stage of cultivating reveals the success of our soul craft through an authentic way of living and leading rooted in right relation.

In all practicality, we may be still working a day job to earn a living while cultivating our soul craft. Likewise, we may be in a job where we are bringing in more and more of our soul craft into the daily work, yet many activities remain misaligned with our purposefulness. We do not need to be too militant about only doing work that serves the soul. Working on the margins of the mainstream, helping heal and transform the status quo system, requires us to be able to be versatile, get our hands dirty, and flex. We can stay the course, as long as the soul path remains resolutely in focus.

We learn the art of cultivating mini-winters during the summertime of this exciting new life stage. Honing the soul craft goes hand-in-hand with honing our own authenticity, boundaries, daily practice, and sense of right relation of self-other-world. Sensing abundance, being grateful, flowing and manifesting, and knowing when to retreat, take stock, reflect, rest, and rejuvenate. For there are plenty of chances to quieten and watch the ego. To watch how we can feel personally attached to our soul craft, especially as we are so connected to it. To watch how the ego reacts when people criticize or judge us on social media, or a client misunderstands the nature of the work we are doing or is simply not quite up for the soul craft we are offering. To watch the scarcity mindset creep in as we either compare how much we earn now to our previous achiever days or compare ourselves with others we might think of as a benchmark. To watch how the ego might see shortcuts or safety measures, like relying on other experts' models rather than offering fresh insights. And be cognizant of spiritual materialism, a kind of 'sweety-shop' approach to nibbling on new spiritual tools and techniques that seem alluring and offer the promise of shortcuts to enlightenment.

Recall the quote from the Matrix. "There is a difference between knowing the path and walking the path." This is what the Cultivating stage offers us, the hard-won walking of our soul path. Cultivating a way of living *and* working that is regenerative for self-other-world. We *cultivate* skills, narratives, communication styles, and a way with words and relationships that enable us to perform a kind of magic, a magic that manifests from working with Nature's Wisdom. Our twilight zone—whether dreamtime at night, lucid dreaming, journeying, visioning, contemplative or Creative Imagination work—provides insights for the craft and its path. Our thirst for academic learning begins to be replaced by a thirst for practical, experiential, embodied work of engaging in the craft. This inner-outer shaping is crucial for what lies ahead, and our relentless, enthusiastic service amid the fidelity of life provides for an innately re-generative potential that brings a magic into our work. Now we are ready for the Harmonizing stage.

Harmonizing

Symbol: panpipes
Season: mid-summer
Key words and phrases: flow, enthusiasm, sensitive receptor

We are now moving into mid-summer with much promise around us and just ahead of us. This can be a good time, for our inner-nature and outer-nature to start to find alignment and *flow*. It's as if the whole of the inner journey is being rewarded by this stage, as we settle into our soul craft as a way of living and leading both inwardly and outwardly. We feel a rightness in our relation and a profound sense of place and purpose in the world. Having cultivated our soul craft delivery mechanism and differentiated our value propositions, the buds of springtime have already unfurled, the blossom is being pollinated, and there is a hive of activity. A buzz of life all around and within. Our inner connection informs our outer craft with *enthusiastic*, creative dynamism, and the outer work (the connections with others, the feedback we receive, the experiences we work through) stimulates our soul to enthuse more, to open more, and to become more of who we are in the world.

The strategic (outer) mind and the intuitive (inner) mind learn to work together in a certain *harmony*. Just as we learn to work with the outer exoteric aspects of Nature's Wisdom in harmony with the inner esoteric aspects. And as we venture along this life-path, inner and outer start to interpenetrate to such an extent that the notion of 'inner' and 'outer' is transcended, and a quintessence flows through us. We are living our purpose not through our soul craft alone but through each and every experience of life. The sacred moment is the work. To be purely in the moment, whether it be next to a tree at sunrise, in the midst of a keynote talk, holding space for a challenging tension, facilitating a group, or walking side by side with a colleague, is the craft.

Our place in the world is where we are now, whether travelling to a client or working from home. Our place is our sacred space in time that moves with us, because we have potentialized inner-outer and are living life in a sacred manner. The mythological experience is our lived experience. The meditation is life itself. We are *sensitive receptors*.

This learning to 'be' while engaging in our craft is much like a musician whose become proficient at learning an instrument—say the panpipes—and reading the music, and can now play in a way that is full of being, no longer rote, copying a set formula, methodology, or orchestration. The craft flows through us. This is what the *panpipes* symbolize, the self as conduit pipe, tuning with wisdom, playing one's unique melody in tune with the Song of Songs as 'the one who works with wisdom.'

We adapt to each situation by pulling out different tools from our invisible toolkit as each situation unfolds. The way we work with people in offering our service to the world flows more in right relation with our deeper nature. We do not need to protect ourselves from overreach, or over-exhaustion, in the same way as we had to in the earlier Emerging and Cultivating stages, because we have found a flow where the work nourishes and heals not only the ones we seek to serve but also, in the process, our own selves.

Self and craft have become harmonized. Our work-life balance has transcended into work as a way of life. We neither live to work nor work to live. We simply live and in doing so work, and we work and in doing so live. Retirement is no longer a goal, or even a dream in the future, as there is nothing to retire from. We might work less or more, some days or weeks, but this becomes a case of rhythmic right relation, not a trade-off.

Think of the shaman who lives midway between the forest and the village for good reason—to be available for village life, where the craft is crafted and to whom the work serves, but also to be available for the wild, not overly caught up in village life, because the work is also in service of the more-than-human realm. Think also of the 'middle way' of Buddhism which finds a path through the duality of doing-being, science-spirituality, left-right hemisphere, head-heart, masculine-feminine, inner-outer, self-system, rational-intuitive, human-nature. We too are both rooted and flowering. Aware of our essence-seed, the emergent process of budding, the flowering through enthusiasm and the fruit for evolution. Anchored in a trust in life, confident in our service, and sensitized to our right relation of self-other-world.

We can feel and work with the harmonies of life. Letting go is no longer an activity we need to do but a way of experiencing life in an ungrasping, harmonizing, improvisational way. Within the interconnectedness of everything, and a sensitive receptivity to right relation, we open our senses and super-sensory capacities to the Song of Songs immersed in Source. We embody a visceral experience of the holographic nature of life, sensing when we are in tune with it or not. There is the sacredness of life in all we do, from washing the dishes to designing the business strategy.

The learning journey is not 'done', rather it's just begun, as we are now fully committed to the path of the soul. It's our destiny that beckons us forth, and this work totalizes our very being. We are now fully immersed, on stage, live, on-air, bathed in full sunlight, naked, exposed to our vulnerable authenticity, in every moment. We are fully 'in' the craft, which is our way of living in harmony with Nature's Wisdom.

At this Harmonizing stage, the growth of our craft is no longer about size, reach, or impact. While this remains relevant, growth now becomes about growing down-and-in, becoming more deeply connected into the invisible realms while bridging two outer worlds through the craft—the current conventional world that is breaking down with the potentialized future world emerging. We neither resist nor insist. We watch events unfold, whether it's world news or a client's business being hijacked by backward thinking. Our passion and purpose are very much enthusiastically in us, yet we can stand back a little from the immediacy of unfolding situations, as we begin to see the wisdom in everything, even what seems like a backward retrograde movement.

This stepping back from the immediacy is not to be confused with complacency. It's more that we have learned about right timing, and how everything has integrating alchemizing potential in it. Whilst at the previous stage of Cultivating it felt like we've finally placed our hands firmly on the steering wheel of our own lives', finally feeling like we've found the path and are in control, at this Harmonizing stage we transcend this sense of control. Immersed in a multi-dimensional Mystery beyond comprehension, we are certainly beyond steering wheels. But we can learn to fly.

Gratitude and abundance become core qualities which lighten the load of what can become an increasingly committed way of life as our soul craft totalizes our being. The importance here is the sacred manner with which we work. From mid-summer, we go into high summer and late summer, all while deepening our harmonizing of evolutionary potential and purposefulness. Inner soul virtues (which you can learn about in Chapter 11) are savored here in an ever-spiraling process of becoming more of who we truly are; a 'squaring of the circle', an infusion of Heaven and Earth, a sacralizing of this life experience. Heaven as a place on Earth, our place, the center point, where energy from the Field pours into our purposefulness.

> "Take your practiced powers and stretch them out
> Until they span the chasm between two
> Contradictions… for the god
> Wants to know himself in you."
>
> —Rainer Maria Rilke

We are only human, and mistakes are part of this life-journey, so let's not paint the picture that this Harmonizing stage is some idealistic utopia whereupon we have perfected life. Not at all. We are 'in it', in the shit, making compost from it, growing new ideas, adapting amid eddies and undercurrents, tests and tripwires, innovating our inner-outer soul craft all the while. No perfection here, only harmonization in a world full of tension and transformation. Soon, the whole of this book becomes integrated into our own unique way of living and leading in business and beyond.

Synchronicities abound. As we explored in the previous chapter, synchronicities are a form of harmonization, a correspondence of inner and outer, coming together in tune, in the moment, a space for grace to enter.

Amazing. As I write this, a Peacock butterfly lands on my tea mug where I am sitting against a Scots pine during an unseasonably warm mid-autumn here in the British Isles. The shamanic significance of the butterfly is metamorphosis and a spirit-message from inner-nature. At this time of year, as I write this, and as the butterfly flits around me for a good minute or two, landing on my tea mug and then pen, to me it symbolizes a threshold crossing ahead, a hibernatory energy signaling a next level morph round the spiral of ever-becoming, whether that be in the 'how' of the soul craft or a new stage of life beckoning.

How apt, while writing about synchronicities, to see this beautiful butterfly hover and land repeatedly, speaking to me of gratitude, abundance, synchronicity and metamorphosis. As we are now turning to the last phase of the journey—the Returning stage—which is a threshold crossing, the ending of one labyrinth journey and the beginning of another. As we arch around the U, we enter another spiral and arc back to the beginning again, seen with new eyes, at a vantage point higher up the spiral. This Returning stage of autumn is quite different from the Harvest Supper autumn of our earlier Reviewing stage, yet it does involve a reviewing of sorts, and signifies the end of summer and an impeding Wintering looming ahead. Endings for new beginnings.

Returning

Symbol: owl
Season: autumn
Key words and phrases: reviewing, wisdom, Elderhood

Depending on where we are in our life stage and age, we prepare ourselves for either another Wintering stage—a psychological death and U journey into rebirth—and we begin again, at the beginning of this chapter, with *reviewing*, but this time at a more expanded level of meaning-making. Or we prepare ourselves for *Elderhood*, which is the last stage of our life before preparing for physical death.

If it's a *return* to the Reviewing stage, then casting our mind back over all the stages we've been through can be helpful, particularly reviewing the fruits of the summer period just gone with its years of soul craft service. We cast our mind back over all the learnings from the Emerging, Cultivating, and Harmonizing time of weaving our work in the world, the people we've met along the way and perhaps partnered with or aided in some way, the clients we've served, the communities we've engaged with. We cast our mind back over the myriad learnings, the richness of the whole U journey from when we departed at our previous achiever stage way back many years ago before we even endured a psychological death-rebirth.

Sit with all this reflection for a while, and all sorts of gems arise, treasures we hold dear, and insights that help us as we start to prepare for our next round through the labyrinth spiral, down the U again for another psychological death-rebirth. More prepared than the last metamorphosis, and yet this journey is still largely unknown with deeper aspects of our soul-scape waiting to be discovered through the wintering with its marshes followed by the emerging signs of new shoots and verdant leaves. Once again, a meta-morphing of our soul craft awaits us.

Something might have changed in our lives to catalyze this readiness for another death-rebirth. Many people today avoid the death-rebirth process of metamorphosis completely in their lives, choosing to live by what today's egocentric culture has handed them rather than veer off-piste into the hinterlands of the soul. And many people who do engage in the death-rebirth mystery of life only do so once, during a mid-life transition. Some though, have a soul that seeks more from the metamorphic process this lifetime around, and may be pulled by their destiny into another round of the U, transforming their soul craft significantly in the process.

We could be embarking on a complete revolutionary change to our soul craft or a significant upgrade on how we work with soul and World Soul to serve life-affirming futures. Regardless of whether it's a revolutionary or evolutionary shift in our craft, we can spend quiet, reflective moments casting our mind over all that's happened since our shift out of the dominant achiever mind. This Reviewing is preparatory for the imminent descent.

If, however, we have managed to progress through to the Harmonizing stage and are entering the later phase of life (mid-fifties onward) then the soul-calling toward Elderhood may start to tug, beckoning us out of the enjoyable Harmonizing stage and into Returning.

Regardless of our age, or our stage of progression through the U, all of us face the ultimate threshold of physical death at some point (or points—if we include near-death experiences). Death is a return to Source, beyond the Imaginal Realm, where the soul relinquishes the bodymind instrument and yet retains the learning gleaned from this life-journey within its astral body which may then reincarnate into a physical bodymind and have a physical rebirth.

Elderhood, however, does not necessitate a readying for death, nor a retiring from the market and craft, but involves a lessening of outer intensity and a deepening of inner intensity. This inner intensity brings up all sorts of stuff from the inner psyche, soul, and Imaginal Realm. We thought we'd processed all this suppressed shadow stuff during the earlier Shedding stage, but fragments of suppressed psychic energy, memories, trauma, and wounds remain.

In this Returning stage, we once again bend the beam of our awareness inward, much like the Reviewing, Hearing, and Shedding stages before, but this time with our sensory and super-sensory skills heightened. With this inward intentional attentiveness, suppressed psychic energies can start to loosen and release. This can come with a revisiting of old stories, traumatic events, childhood memories, nostalgic experiences, revisiting places we used to frequent, seeking out old friends, having recurring dreams of past aspects of our lives. We are working them through in our psyche, a form of shedding and alchemizing (disintegrating-reintegrating) occurs.

This stage can last many years, and as we get older, it can take the form of grieving ahead of death, a preparation for a saying goodbye to the life experience in this bodymind this time round. Yet this grief is not a heavy depressive burdensome kind of grief that drags us down. It's a grieving that releases an inner power and fuels a deeper love for life and service. It helps us appreciate the bodymind instrument for what it has channeled, manifested, and catalyzed during this lifetime. It's a simultaneous grieving and celebrating of this life experience, this unique bodymind, the people and places, the experiences, the learnings. Much *wisdom* is gleaned from this reviewing of our life journey, which is then insightful for how we wish to serve as an elder. *How do we wish to spend the rest of our life? How might we serve life from this vantage point of Elderhood?*

I have given Elderhood a capital E because this form of conscious service from someone who has endured a deep and lasting death-rebirth journey from achiever to regenerator is a sacred undertaking to commit to serving life, sharing wisdom and insights, and helping pave the way for the next generation and others of any age embarking on their own death-rebirth journeys.

The entrepreneurial drive of Emerging and Cultivating is no longer, and yet our experience of what works and what doesn't is invaluable to others we might guide through their own soul journeys. Practices that help us here include embodiment and somatic practices that aid the release of subtle yet deeply embedded constrictions and stuckness in the bodymind's energy network. This allows the life-force to renew aspects of our selves ready for a deeper form of service through Elderhood.

We become simultaneously settled in our local neighborhood and curious about global events unfolding. We simultaneously live day-to-day amid the practicalities of everyday life and deep in the womb of the world, attuned into planetary and cosmological rhythms. There is no need for us to retire from our soul craft, and yet we might choose to spend more moments in contemplation or engaged in advanced energy cultivation practices. These advanced practices can then inform our soul craft and it might well be that we start to attract a different kind of clientele or customer who are interested in this more advanced soul experience.

Like the CEO or CxO becoming the chairman or coach, the soul-elder helps steady the tiller for the organization to sail the necessary evolution in consciousness into regenerative business while also keeping an eye on the profitability and day-to-day vitality of the organization amid a volatile marketplace. Long-term thinking molds with short-term practicalities. We listen and work with the hidden ordering forces, systemic relational energies, and constellating patterns within the organizational system we coach, guide, or advise as an elder. We become the *Wise Old Owl*.

The metaphysical aspects of Nature's Wisdom become potent. We open more receptively and responsively into life with greater intimacy, joy, authenticity, and flow. We work with (and within) the infinite Field of potential, and the intrapsychic reconciliation of inner-outer through creative wizardry using psychic powers, intentionality, healing, and insight to provide guidance. We may also become more attuned to Earth's energy system and work increasingly with the evolution of consciousness, not just of humanity, but of Earth (Gaia) as a living system. With practice we learn to merge our energy field with the universal energy systems, which can make us extra sensitive to energy shifts going on in the world. However, with our advanced practices of centering and grounding, we can hold space for these seismic shifts and help others to navigate them.

In Elderhood, we dwell in the center of things, whilst noticing the struggle at the surface of the wheel. Tending to the cosmic rhythm embedded in the holographic nature of the systems we inhabit whether organization, community, society, bioregional, or planetary, we work 'As above so below, as within so without'. No longer a wise adage, or even a meditation to contemplate, but our way of life—in constant correspondence with the Mystery of humanity, nature, Earth and cosmos.

When a client, or anyone for that matter, spends time with us they are more likely to intuit coherent patterns of meaning in their life, helping them see and hear more clearly their own soul's song-lines. This aids people's advanced meaning-making, catalyzing their own U journeys and making sense of what can often seem like rising confusion, cacophony, chaos, and catastrophe in the world at large.

There has been a degenerative trend over the last two millennia, which greatly accelerated over the last four centuries, specifically in Western civilization, affecting much of humanity today. This trend has witnessed a loss of touch with how to remain in tune with nature, Earth and cosmos. The ancients had ceremonial practices to enable this subtle yet profound connection to flow through society. Indigenous peoples today hold on to vestiges of this ancient way. However, humanity, as a whole, has lost it. (Plotkin, p394-441)

Elderhood brings a Return to this sacred knowledge, and so giving the name of this stage Returning a second connotation. It's a remembering of who we truly are, a return to ancient wisdom, born again into modern civilization. The elder's role is to aid this re-turn by re-integrating humanity back in accord with the cosmos. This is vital for the evolution of humanity and of Earth. Earth's evolution is intimately entwined with humanity's evolution in consciousness.

To finish this last stage of the soul journey, I call upon the wise words of soul craft specialist Bill Plotkin who refers to the elder as 'sage'. He notes, "The sage embodies and animates an inspiring and heart-opening affection, both innocent and wise, that sweeps every being with its orbit. Death, too, as a final passage of life, is a gift of grace. When death arrives for the sage, there is no resistance, because he has already merged with grace. The sage's dying is a final concentration within his being of the presence of grace. For the sage, death is a celebration, a final journey with the Mystery." (Plotkin, p422)

> "And now having moved through the stage of emptiness, and also having seen God in the World of Nature, the individual can see God in the world of men. Enlightened mingling in the marketplace with winebibbers and butchers, he recognizes the inner light or Buddha-Nature in everyone. He doesn't need to hold himself aloof nor to be weighed down by a sense of duty or responsibility, nor to follow a set of patterns of other holy men, nor to imitate the past. He is so in harmony with Life that he is content to be inconspicuous, to be an instrument not a leader. He simply does what seems to him natural… in doing so, helping others become part of the Harmony of the Universe."
>
> –D. T. Suzuki

The 4 D Foundational Pillars for Regenerative Living and Leading

The way in which we anchor our way of living and leading during our metamorphic journey is key. With so much going on in the world right now, we can (and we must) develop our own practices to stabilize ourselves as we cultivate higher levels of receptivity and responsiveness to change. The foundation we build is a crucial aspect of regenerative living and leading.

As Jesus noted in the Gospel of Matthew, the wise person builds on rock, the fool upon the sand. Today's levels of volatility and turbulence are on track to markedly increase, and as leaders amid these times, we must remain steady in our endeavors. In this chapter, we explore the four pillars that are the bedrock of a foundation that is connected to the substratum of Nature's Wisdom, so that we may construct our everyday lives with the proper supports to live and lead in the transient and turbulent business environments. The four pillars are the 4 Ds: *Dedication, Discernment, Discipline,* and *Devotion*.

Dedication

Anything in life worth attaining requires practice, patience, commitment, and dedication. Whether it's playing a musical instrument, becoming an athlete, or mastering a craft, we must dedicate ourselves to it both outwardly and inwardly.

Outwardly, we dedicate space and time in our schedules to engage in the Work. Work with a capital W, as it is sacred soul craft Work. This 'life Work' is not to be confused with 'just a job.' It is understood as our journeying toward wholeness by realizing our dharma and discovering our unique soul's purpose in the world. This Work is nurtured and nourished every single day.

Even if we are working a full-time job, where only aspects of our soul craft can shine through, when we can dedicate a few moments of each day to intentionally attending to our soul craft, we prevent stagnation. This could be as simple as sending out emails, nurturing our network, posting relevant notes on social media, or a more significant action, such as designing and developing a value proposition with a business partner. The point here is not *what* we do, but the *way* we do it. We do it with dedication and full of intentional attention to the soul craft we are developing as we stay the course of right relation with self-other-world. Daily acts, practiced with intention and integrity, ensure our dedication to the budding soul craft and create unseen ripple effects into outer-nature.

Inwardly, we dedicate space and time for inward reflection, contemplation, and meditation on the very essence of our being—the soul—and wider bodymind and its coherence. When such practices are done daily, such as advanced meditation practices that bring awareness right into the center of our being, like the Creative Imagination Process, we experience a more centered awareness that brings focus to the soul craft. We cultivate space inside ourselves to invite an inward inquiry on what and how things need to be done to allow our soul craft to develop further. We can inquire or sense-check daily, perhaps a few times per day if our schedule allows.

The more practiced we become at stilling ourselves and finding bodymind coherence, the quicker we can undertake mini sense-checks throughout the busy day. Even a three-minute sense-check can work. However, for most of us, five or ten minutes is more adequate. These practices shift awareness into the center of each of the three 'brains'—gut, heart, and head brains. We go into each region and sense for any stuckness. *How is the bodymind feeling? Am I sensing dis-ease or coherence?* We breathe intentionally and sense any tension that needs to unfold in our body. *Where can I sense subtle energy flows in my bodymind?*

When we dedicate ourselves to a daily practice of bodymind coherence and energy cultivation, we can cultivate an internal spaciousness for tranquility in the midst of volatility and familiarize ourselves on how subtle somatic sensations feel in the bodymind. This aids our practice of opening into the Eye of the Heart and activating the third eye and hara to sense what it is to connect behind all thoughts and feelings, and beyond into our soul-scape and Imaginal Realm. Through these practices, we learn to listen to the soul.

The more we open inwardly and outwardly, the more we can sense-respond to the eddies, undercurrents, flows, and riptides, and we come to learn that inner dedication has an immediate effect on our outer-nature. Our ways of showing up, relating with others, and serving our soul craft in the marketplace of business take on a calm coherence and super-sensory capacity to flow with right relation, despite the cacophony and confusion that persists. The inner-outer dedication we bring to our way of living and leading increases the potency of what we channel through our 'way of becoming', our dharmic path inward and outward through the labyrinth. We become a wayfarer, navigating our path, learning with each step, dedicated to each day and night on our soul journey.

Whilst we each have our own unique destiny path and dharma, there exists a universally shared foundation, a 'ground of dedication', upon which all individual paths are rooted through the substratum of Nature's Wisdom. This ground of dedication becomes our common anchor as we open wholly into life by opening fully into the eternal center within. We can then walk and dance the path of our own soul journey by gleaning insights from Nature's Wisdom. Our inner-nature informs the way we experience outer-nature.

Such are the fruits of working with the three esoteric aspects, which guide an inner sense of receptivity-creativity-synchronicity that informs our gnosis, or insightful knowing. Yet, it's through traversing the path of our budding soul craft each and every day, that a new level of gnosis surfaces. This is the lived, embodied knowing of working with the *lumen naturae*, the hidden light within nature, which shows us signs and synchronicities as we learn to activate our super-nature. As mentioned in the previous chapters, through centering into the soul, we open the bodymind to energies from the Field. We are kindling the spiritual light within ourselves, brightening our own soul-consciousness, by working with the spiritual light hidden within nature. For it is *lumen naturae* which illuminates our path like a torch in the deep dark forest. Rather than the labyrinth being a nightmarish fumbling around in the dark, doing our best to avoid the disorientating meshwork of ego nets and tripwires, it can be seen as a twisting, turning, whirling dance into our own destiny. And we consciously enter the dance by cultivating higher faculties of knowing that help us discern the beat and find the rhythm. We learn to flow as life flows.

The more intentional we are with our inner-outer awareness, the more we learn to decide between what serves the design and delivery of our soul craft and what is superfluous distraction or even mal intent from others (perhaps fueled by judgement, cynicism, fear, jealous, rivalry, or a need to control). We know to routinely scan the systemic sphere, noticing what's opening for us to walk through, what's hesitating or tense needing us to hold space, and what's a red light saying, 'wrong way ahead, turn around.' As we dedicate ourselves to a daily practice of centering inward, we learn what we need to delve into—mining lead for gold—and what we need to let go of—separating wheat from chaff. Hence the importance of the second D—Discernment.

Discernment

To discern is to notice, to become conscious of, what is insightful for our learning and what is mere distraction. 'Separating the wheat from the chaff' is discerning what is valuable for developmental growth from what is not. At one level, we might take the approach that everything in life is of use. Each interaction, emotion, perturbation, thought, reaction can be useful reflection for our ultimate growth. This has a truth to it. However, as we build the foundation to support the bodymind, psyche, and soul, we can learn to practice a quality of inner awareness to notice mental gyrations, shadow projections, archetypal forces, soul perturbations, bodymind constrictions, and intuitive insights.

Some of what we pick up on internally is what resides on the surface of things (the mental gyrations, reactive ego aversions, shadow projections), and we witness how the ego shows up in a number of ways (the 'poor me' victim mentality, the 'who am I to?' imposter syndrome, and the voices of judgement, cynicism, and fear). As we journey through the Wintering descent down the U, we get behind these habitual triggers of ego-reaction and learn to sense what lies down within the psyche and soul. Our first discovery is that of the psychological energies beneath the surface reactions, and next comes what lies underneath even those—the archetypal and primal powers that stir the soul and the World Soul.

Discerning between what is 'wheat' and worthwhile for us to digest and process and what is 'chaff' or the surface ego husks that can be let go of helps us harvest our own learnings as we journey. This second D is a vital part of the Shedding stage, and yet is also an invaluable tool available to us at any time in our lives, no matter what stage of the journey we are on.

The heart, gut, inner ears, third eye, in fact the whole bodymind, when cultivated through dedication, become an exquisite instrument for discernment. We can rely on it to act as an early warning radar, constantly scanning our inner and outer nature, to communicate to us what is informative and worthy of further exploration and what might be distraction. As we dedicate ourselves to live more receptively and attentively to the stillness and movement in our lives, we enhance our somatic sense perception in the bodymind, now able to pick up on the subtle shifts in inner-outer nature that prove useful for our soul journey and the cultivation of our soul craft. It may be a tingle in the toes or hands, hairs on the back of the neck standing up, constriction in the throat, a heart perturbation, or sudden change of pressure inside the ear. To a certain extent, as I said earlier, everything is 'all good'. Even malignant distractions can be decomposed into compost. The journey ahead is not a quest for purity or a defense up against anything misaligned. Yet, having the capacity to discern what feels aligned, and what doesn't, helps us avoid the rabbit holes.

To practice this level of discernment, one requires an embodied knowing of when something is in flow with our essence and when not, when we are in right relation and when we are not. That is to say, when we are 'in place', rooted in our wholeness, which is not a geographical or space-time place, but an internal sense of place and purposefulness. This is self-other-world right relation regardless of immediate surroundings. Our soul has a unique psycho-ecological niche in the world, an aperture into the World Soul, and it's not only fed by the World Soul but reciprocally feeds into the World Soul. This nonlocal aspect in the core of our being is a sense of a rightness of place and purposefulness, a rootedness into the world *and* a connection into the transcendent realm. A spaciousness beyond space-time. By dropping into the Imaginal Realm through the Creative Imagination Practice, we experience a coming home, no matter where our locality.

Practicing the inner capacity to notice when we feel 'in place' and are flowing with purposefulness is how discernment forms our inner foundation. We are learning to sense when we are in our own soul essence and when we are in the collective unconscious with its archetypal energies. The further within we go, the more we can learn to discern what is our 'stuff' and what is part of the collective trauma and healing of our ancestry, society, and wider humanity. These archetypal and ancestral energies contain collective trauma that can manifest as existential pain, frustration, anger, loss, grief, and a sense of separation born from a wound endured through centuries of violating right relation of self-other-world. Becoming more receptive to the Imaginal Realm opens our psyche and soul to all these energies, and so comes with an increasing need to know what is relevant for our learning process and what could subsume us into the abyss without the chance to serve our soul craft.

There is a fine line between the alchemist and the crackpot. The crackpot has failed to discern the psychic energies pouring in from the unconscious ones, which may overwhelm the ego. The alchemist, however, has learned to alchemize energies through the stage of disintegration-reintegration and can separate the wheat from chaff, thus we find ego maturation coming hand-in-hand with ego permeation.

While words do no justice to the journey into the hinterlands of the soul, what's vital to share here is the importance of having a discipline of practice in order to discern and stay dedicated to the journey. Hence the next D—discipline.

Discipline

This is not a mechanistic, regimented discipline that enforces an outer structure and schedule onto our lives like a straitjacket, nor does it act like a Sergeant Major hounding us to stick to it no matter what. No, not *that* kind of discipline. The kind of discipline we need on our journey is a compassionate, whole-hearted, courageous discipline that builds on the foundational pillars of dedication and discernment. One that ensures that we flow from our own 'ground of dedication', practicing a regular discernment of our sense of place and purposefulness so that we remain both rooted and evolving.

This discipline is a routine noticing of our own ego machinations, and we begin to see beyond them by noticing that, perhaps, much of what's significant is rarely accidental. While we might well experience a short-lived epiphany, as if by chance, or a shock that ruptures the boundaries of our ego for a period of time, the inner journey is not simply about one-off shocks. It's a ritualistic practice of walking the path toward simultaneous ego permeation and ego maturation.

With my coaching clients, I often refer to this as the practice of 'noticing, noticing, noticing, integrating, integrating, integrating'. Rather than the ego's tendency to go to the surface of things, where it gets ensnared in voices of judgement, cynicism, and fear, we learn to drop down below the surface and attend to what lies behind the trigger. This is a quality of discipline that embraces life as a developmental journey, where each day is the crucible for our learning. Notice the foibles and mis-takes we make during everyday life.

Notice our tendency to judge our mistakes, and in noticing the self-judgement learn to smile at our own voices of judgement, cynicism, and fear. Notice how as soon as we notice it, the voice in the head quietens and loosens its grip over our attention. Rather than being consumed by reactivity we can open receptively into the moment—we can presence life. This is the Work—an increasing intimacy with the immanent and a transparency to the transcendent.

As we discussed in the last chapter's Shedding stage, the act of letting go requires noticing and allowing, the latter which calls upon an inner relaxation. A surrendering, the long out breath that follows a deep breath in. This relaxed allowing is a release. When we feel triggered by something, we bring our awareness into the feeling, then give space for the triggered sensation to just be. We notice it, then we allow it. To let go and presence, we need to cultivate the courage to notice the behaviors of the voice in the head of Lens 1, and not let it run the show. This becomes a practice of dedication-discernment-discipline.

There's a subtle difference between the 'exoteric letting go process' (an in-the-moment noticing and allowing) and the 'esoteric letting go process' (that we find in the Creative Imagination Process). Esoteric calls us to go further into quieting the bodymind, by dropping behind our thoughts and entering into the Imaginal Realm where we can become more transparent to the transcendent and receptive to insight. It's an advanced meditation that requires the discipline of continually letting go of the thinking mind to get behind Lens 1, going into our deeper nature of Lens 2, and then beyond Lens 2's raft of emotional patterns and memories as Lens 3 then becomes clear in the Imaginal Realm. Until we have the discipline to go beyond ego-consciousness, we will not have the insights to alchemize the transcendent and immanent within ourselves, which aid our ego permeation and maturation journey.

Discipline takes Practice

I have honed a host of powerful practices through my leadership coaching that help us become more receptive to the Field's life-force that flows through each and every situation. Specifically, these practices enable bodymind coherence, integrate the three lenses, and activate our supernature, and all are safe to undertake, accessible, easy to remember, relaxing, and rejuvenating. Consequently, this makes them suitable for the busy leader to recall and modify as part of a personal practice amid a packed schedule.

These practices draw from ancient wisdom traditions, such as Tantra, Shamanism, Daoism, Druidism, Alchemy, Zen, Sufism, and Buddhism, and I have had the great pleasure of either training with or working alongside master guides including Tai Chi Masters, Sufi Sheikhs, eastern medicine professionals, shamanic practitioners, and advanced spiritual healers. I also draw upon my own empirical experiences, which I have gleaned over my career of advising organizations and coaching leaders through their inner journeys toward regenerative leadership. I, too, am constantly sensing into what works and what doesn't, refining methods and practices as I go. I, too, am dedicated, discerning, and honing my discipline.

I have summarized the action and effect of a few practices I use with leaders here, but you will find more information, demonstrations, and recordings about these and other practices on my *website* and in the Appendix.

1. **Chi Gung** is a time-honored practice thought to have originated in the Far East many millennia ago and today it's practiced by people all over the world. The practice consists of gentle body movements to cultivate presence, relaxation, and energy flow in the body.
2. **Heart Entrainment** is a simple sequence that allows the brain waves in our head to synchronize with the EM waves of the heart. While centering our awareness in the heart region, and catalyzing physiological and psychological shifts, the practice also brings awareness of the heart as a powerful organ of perception.
3. **Opening to Nature Guided Meditation** is an activity that involves going outside and sitting on the ground for five minutes, or more. This practice begins with deep breathing exercises, followed by a Presencing with the Heart practice, and ultimately embarks on a visualization meditation that invites our bodymind to open into Nature's Wisdom.

4. **Body Scan (or Yoga Nidra)** is an ancient practice that develops the discipline of noticing and easing out of Lens 1's voice in the head by consciously attending to different parts of the body. Body scanning increases bodymind coherence as we become more conscious of the gut and heart regions.

As for myself and my own discipline, I have been practicing a whole host of various routines for over fifteen years now on a day-to-day basis, and some of them for longer. A particular one that I find very useful is Energy Cultivation, which I learned from John P Milton through a Sacred Passage training with him in Colorado, where I spent thirteen days and twelve nights sleeping under the stars on Mount Crestone. Energy Cultivation is a meta-practice, in that it's a sequence by which we understand other inner practices that help us cultivate the flow of energy through our bodymind. The sequence for cultivating energy flow is: Bodily Form, Inner Intention, Presence, Relaxation, and Breathing. This sequence can be practiced while undertaking a body movement like chi gung or, for instance, in a meeting without any outward action. We simply become conscious of our bodily form (posture, somatic sensations, inner constrictions), attend to our inner intention to deepen our presencing of the moment here-and-now, mindfully notice our quality of presence, purposefully relax into the flow of the moment, while breathing deeper from the belly (see Appendix for further detail).

There is no one-size-fits-all discipline, and you will find that different days, seasons, and years call for certain conscious practices over others while still some remain a constant—and knowing this *is* the discipline.

'Conscious' is a key word here. It's all too easy to engage in, say, a yoga practice with the music on, and be consumed by the voice in the head for much of it. Or, say, engaging in guided meditations using a mindfulness app, which can help settle the mind but give little space for a deeper soul-connection within. Listening to music, going for a jog, walking mindfully, or reading poetry can all form part of our discipline if they right us from distraction and bring us back to our place, our center, our ground of dedication. Remember: it's not 'what' we do, it's the 'way' that we do it!

Still, I try not to be too overly prescriptive in my schedule or rhythm from day-to-day. Being playful with the discipline is important, otherwise the journey can start feeling too much like hard work or forced, and before we know it the ego will rebel against the routine, or the achiever mind will engage. Even today, after more than fifteen years, I will skip the odd day of doing meditation or energy cultivation practice, and I notice how my body-mind coherence is subtly affected by this skip-in-practice. The noticing of this subtle shift in the bodymind is as much the discipline as is the discipline of engaging consciously in practices.

Our disciplines—practice, practice, practice; notice, notice, notice; integrate, integrate, integrate—are designed to be joyous and expansive, not heavy and burdensome. They are meant to create more inner-outer coherence in life, not another avenue for mechanistic, ego-consciousness. For instance, I sometimes read a couple of paragraphs from the *Tao Te Ching*, which I have at my bedside, and then sit with the words in my mind's eye as I breathe consciously for a few moments. I do not feel I have to do this, but rather I enjoy doing it. The simple yet sacred words of the *Tao Te Ching* remind me to embrace an unfurling, ungrasping receptively to life. Here is a short paragraph,

> "Open yourself to the Tao,
> then trust your natural responses;
> and everything will fall into place."

These three lines sum up the whole Work! This whole book could be conveyed in just these three lines! Yet the question remains, *How to open to the Tao?* This is why we have frames to turn to, such as the 4 Ds, which, in this case, serve as a foundation to ground our journey so that we may foster our trust in life and trust in our own natures.

With dedication and discernment, we now have the discipline of walking the path each and every day. We might see how this discipline is multifaceted, as it's not only a practice of noticing and letting go, and it's not only a practice of learning and integrating, but also a discipline of noticing the effects of our presencing and the supporting root of our groundedness. It's the clarity to know when we are clinging, impatient, or restless, and when we are centered, in our place and beyond space-time.

As the *Tao Te Ching* notes:

> "Why should the leader
> Flit about like a fool?
> If you let yourself be blown to and fro,
> You lose touch with your root.
> If you let restlessness move you,
> You lose touch with who you are."

The discipline is to be in the field of activity and movement yet able to sense the stillness behind all movement. To be working with the yang while remaining in the yin. Dancing to the beat while being present to the song. The discipline to remain rooted amid busi-ness requires discernment and dedication and an open-hearted, full-bodied devotion to the path. Hence the final of the four Ds—Devotion.

Devotion

Dedication, discernment, and discipline can start to feel a little heavy, or at times empty, and that's where the fourth D comes in. Devotion is a remembering of the awesomeness of being alive on Earth, and an immense gratefulness, respect, and care for life. Devotion provides for a sense of duty, but it's not a burdensome, ethical must-do. It's a dutiful responsibility to care for life and be devoted to this path of deepening into life, of deepening our love affair with life. The devotion to the labyrinthine journey of opening the Eye of the Heart in our center. The devotion to following our dharma, trusting in life, and its sacred text for our unique soul journey.

> "Every person's life is a sacred text."
>
> —Novalis

This devotion is a loving embrace of this life experience, which is an experience that is immanent-and-transcendent, simultaneously of this world and its outer-nature and of its metaphysical inner-nature. It's a sense of reverence, respect, and love for the immensity of the Mystery of life's exquisite learning journey. This devotion first aids our soul opening, and then is enfolded into our soul opening to produce an inner power, emblematic of a channel of golden white light cast from the World Soul and shining straight through to the core of our being so we remain aware and aligned in our soul-scape.

Sometimes, when we enter this more spiritual side of life, we might fall prey to shunning the everyday experience, alienating ourselves from life itself. We tell ourselves that we must focus solely inward and ignore the distractions of everyday life experiences. I call this approach 'spiritual materialism', which is no better than Mechanistic Materialism. It's not devotion. It's a trick of the ego. Having a devotional attitude toward life is to choose to reconnect with life more fully, inwardly and outwardly.

The higher faculties we develop enrich this loving embrace of life. The calm contemplative moments, where we still ourselves amid the motion, help our presence—our existence—become more peaceful and receptive in each moment. Inner tranquility is not a stepping away from life, but an ability to discern the essential from the nonessential and to not allow outer influences to pull us from our center and distract us from our soul path. We are becoming increasingly intimate with our life experience, in fact more so because of this receptivity, as we can now disentangle ourselves from the incessant voice in the head. Ego-consciousness is a certain attentiveness to life, whereas integrated ego-heart-soul consciousness is a devotional and deepening love affair. Not in some Hollywood romance kind of way, but a true and wise love that radiates from the core of our being.

> "By love He can be caught and held, but by thinking never."
>
> –The Cloud of Unknowing

When learning to cultivate this devotional attentiveness, I sometimes refer my coaching clients to the ancient Greeks' three qualities of love—*Agape*, *Eros* and *Philia*.

Agape is the transcendent Field which resonates throughout the universe, seen as the all-pervading Mother Goddess who nourishes the soil of authentic being that informs our soul-becoming. *Eros* is the passion that gets us excited about life, the vital presence that invokes us to change beyond stasis, the evocative energy that cajoles our emergent becoming. *Philia* is the com-passion of the reciprocating way we relate in life. These three qualities of love can be understood as: Receptivity (Agape); Responsiveness (Eros); Reciprocity (Philia).

When we find ourselves becoming overly passionate, to the extent of becoming overly eager, lusting, desperate or pushy, then our desire to relate has an impatient, desperate patina. A heightened sense of 'I' and a grasping at things from a perception of scarcity, fear, and competition can be seen as a warning sign that our responsive desire has become unmoored from love's receptivity—Agape. By re-awakening to our soul's silent depths, our responsiveness can re-attune with this receptivity and so re-gain the empathy required for reciprocity. Eros flows once again within Agape, thus ensuring our way of relating is attuned with Philia so that a grounded love of life flows through our compassionate relations.

We find our devotional way of experiencing life through this receptive-responsive-reciprocating relation of love that finds rhythm and flow through each and every evolving moment, always attuned to Nature's Wisdom through our own atonement, which then informs our accordance with the deep rhythms and harmonic laws of nature.

> "Thou Nature art my Goddess
> To Thy laws my services are bound."
>
> —Shakespeare

One might sense the duty of having one's 'services bound' to nature's laws, yet this duty is through a devotion dedicated to wisdom (Sophia). When

Pythagoras was referring to himself (purported to be for the first time in Western history) as a 'philosopher', he was marrying the two Greek terms *philia* and *Sophia*. A 'philosopher' is a lover of wisdom who is devoted to a dedicated way of living in right relation with Nature's Wisdom. Neither a yearning immanent Eros nor a purely transcendent Agape, it's an accordance of Agape-into-Eros-into-Philia which flows back into Agape again (Three-in-One).

This came to be known throughout early Western history as 'the Pythagorean way of life' and influenced esoteric streams in the West for centuries to come. A continual attuning with transcendence-immanence to allow for our inner-outer atonement with the wholeness essential to our sense of place and purpose. It's with this devotion that we serve our soul craft in accordance with life—our services bound by Nature's Wisdom.

In the next chapter we turn to the 5 Es to guide us as we learn to walk the soul path.

The 5 E Dynamics of the Process of Becoming

While the 4 Ds provide a solid foundation for our journey of becoming a regenerator, we must also remain conscious of the dynamics that come with realizing our potential along the journey. This is the energetic 'process of becoming'. Here we have the 5 Es—Essence, Energy, Emergence, Evolutionary, and Enthusiasm. Each represents a certain dynamism fundamental to the revealing, the unfolding, and the regenerating potential essential for the leader and the organization.

As we have seen all living systems—our selves and organizations included—are flowing systems that endure continuous, fluctuating movement. Right at the heart of this movement, the center point, is stillness. It is stillness that pervades and informs the movement. That is to say that essence informs energetic emergence.

The center point of our ever-changing and enduring bodymind is the soul (an eternal center beyond space-time), and the soul is also an ever-changing, always learning and evolving fluctuating movement. The stillness of the soul is not stagnant but full of life, and, as we have already conveyed, the soul is not a 'thing' but an aperture of spaciousness found within the immensity of the dynamic World Soul. Likewise, the World Soul is also not a 'thing' but a vast realm of stillness and movement, full of inner powers and forces that interpenetrate the outer-world.

The life-force flowing throughout the World Soul, our soul, and our body-mind is the same life-force that permeates all living systems and the same life-force that permeates our planet Earth and the entire universe. We call it 'life-force', but more apt would be 'life-forces', as it's more like a swirl of idiosyncratic harmonic energies, morphic fields, archetypal powers, and resonances that our modern minds are only just beginning to comprehend.

Life-force is an animating principle that affects all life, in both inner and outer nature. It's flowing inside us at the most fundamental level and inside everything all the time, through every aspect of reality. This continuous movement of and through inner-outer gives life its dancing dynamism, which is the living regenerative potential that we can learn to tune into through essence-energy-emergence-evolutionary-enthusiasm.

Let's explore each of the 5 Es through two dimensions—self (leader) and system (organization).

Essence

Self

What is our individual, essential nature? Underneath all the habits, acculturations, norms, family conditioning, and personality traits, what is unique to *my* essence? It's a powerful inquiry to ask oneself: *Who am I, really? Why am I here? What are my deepest and most profound gifts? To whom or what do I serve?*

> "The one who looks outside dreams, the one who looks inside awakens."
>
> –Carl Jung

The capacity to sense in to one's essence comes through inner attentiveness, stillness, and an embodied knowing. Only then can we start to work with the grain of our own nature, rather than struggle against it. As we've already explored, this is an opening into a deeper receptivity with life and with our own inner-nature, a vulnerability that leads to authenticity.

> "To run from vulnerability is to run from the essence of our nature."
>
> –David Whyte

System

The taproot that nourishes the living-organization draws upon knowing its essence and regularly bringing our intentional attention to this essence. This involves learning to cultivate the systemic-sense of when activities, projects, and missions are working with, rather than against, the essential life-force of the living-organization. We can sense into the living system dynamics of the living-organization through the three levels of Living Systems Awareness, which go beyond the simple use of nature metaphors (such as imagining the organization as a certain creature or tree). We go deeper, sensing into how the living-organization behaves, getting to its shadow aspects as well as its more overt behaviors. We know the historic journey, including pivotal shifts, trauma, and unconscious bias that cause the habits and patterns that warp the way the living system adapts to change.

The organizational essence is more than a mission statement. Its essence answers: *What is the organization's unique gift or service to the world? How does it genuinely serve society and our life-affirming futures? Why is this living-organization needed now, and what makes it unique from other similar product or service providers? Who are the guardians and stewards of this unique essence? How might these guardians describe the essence? How often do these guardians come together to sense in to how the living-organization is attuning with its essence?*

The analogy here might be one of a parent earnestly listening to their child, looking into their eyes, and connecting at a soul level. This is more than interacting at the everyday, reactive, largely unconscious level while engaging in daily errands, getting ready for school, tidying the room, and so on. All too often we are superficially engaging in errands and to-dos while busying ourselves in the living-organization. We are getting the job done, but rarely are we consciously connecting with the organization-as-a-living-system with its own unique essence and life-force. So, we run the risk of conditioning the organization into the very mechanistic mindset we are then wanting to transform with our regenerative business initiatives. The more we sense in and consciously attend to the essence of the living-organization, the more we notice its unique energetic patterns, rhythms and flow. Hence the second E—Energy.

Energy

Self

Life is full of stillness and movement, essence and energy. This energy is the very life-force of nature. It impels the essence of each living system to unfold. It fuels the process of becoming. Energy fuels emergence.

We can learn to work with this life-force. Rather than achieving, controlling, opposing, we find coherence and connection, letting go of what's not serving our potential and welcoming authenticity in order to flow more fully. Such is an act of surrendering that involves a trust in life. The more we practice this surrendering process, the more we become sensitized to the life-force and can discern when we are off kilter and off balance. Interestingly, we may find dissonance or tension arising within us as we shift from achiever to regenerator as old habits are challenged and released.

Some transformation-based teachings purport that dissonance or tension is a sign that something is wrong and suggest that we avoid situations that trigger us or create discomfort; however, I have found through my leadership development work that this is far too simplistic. In fact, dissonance and tension can become the very crucibles that catalyze our development, as uncomfortable as it may feel to the ego. And so, developing a level of discernment is crucial to sense the difference between negative energy that ought to be handled with due care and dissonance that upsets us while presenting a challenge for us to work and learn through.

As we deepen into our essence, we begin to witness how our inner-being informs our process of becoming in terms of how we perceive and experience the energies and fluctuations of the outer world. Recall Gandhi's insight, shared in the Introduction, "As one changes one's own nature, so does the attitude of the world change toward oneself."

Practicing bodymind coherence and energy cultivation is a vital aspect of learning to work with energy and notice inner-outer alignment. Inner-outer alignment enables energy to flow more readily, and we learn to work with the life-force flowing through our selves, through situations with others (such as team dynamics) and through the living-organization. This kind of life-force energy resonates at a soul level and encourages spontaneity, curiosity, and aliveness. We find an active yet relaxed presence and purposefulness in our experience of life when in tune with this energy. We are more available to our own selves (our authenticity, truth, and intuition) to others (listening attentively, holding space, and sensing-responding) and to the living-organization (deep listening, systemic-awareness, Systemic Enablers).

We can open into the dance of life, full of stillness and movement. This dancing with life involves a sensitivity and surrendering that enhance our systemic-awareness—the capacity to sense the wider relational system we lead and operate within and its hidden ordering forces, patterns of behavior, historic conditioning, habituated responses, and energetic networks of participation, learning, and evolution. As we begin to realize that life itself is developmental (ever-learning) so too are our living-organizations.

System

The living-organization thrives on relational energy affected by how people show up and engage with each other. Complex Adaptive Systems research into the complexity of human organizations shows the importance of allowing processes of human relating through structured (convergent) and unstructured (divergent) engagement. Structured being meeting conventions, check ins, feedback processes, appreciative inquiry frames, developmental coaching conversations and unstructured being office gossip, watercooler moments, WhatsApp, Teams, and Slack chats, out-of-office socials, networking, informal tacit knowledge sharing.

Systemic leadership coaching can help here. While conventional executive coaching focuses on the leader as an individual actor, systemic coaching seeks an understanding of the ever-changing relational field with its relational tensions and developmental dynamics. As mentioned earlier in Chapter 4, an approach I have found particularly useful for helping the sensing-responding relational energy of the living-organization is Systemic Enablers. Upon identifying and acknowledging systemic patterns, Systemic Enablers can discern where and in what way to engage organizational acupuncture, the small systemic interventions that send positive ripples across the system, just like acupuncture pinpricks do in aligning us to our inner healing potential. We re-pattern relational stuckness into better flow, richer purposefulness, and increased outer impact. This helps the living-organization tune in to its essence and flow with the energy of its life-force unfolding in right relation amid a changing business context. Enter the third E—Emergence.

Emergence

Self

Emergence is the way life unfolds. All living systems express themselves through the self-generating, self-organizing property of emergence. Our selves as leaders and our organizations-as-living-systems are no different in their need to creatively adapt by way of emergence.

Rather than fearing change and struggling to survive in a dog-eat-dog world, we open up to opportunities, recognizing that change and tension are what impel development and growth. Our attitude toward self, others, and the living-organization is more in harmony with inner-outer nature. Fundamentally, this opening into the emergence of life is a process of letting go and surrendering in order to work with the essence-energy-emergent flow of life. We have touched on this letting go in previous chapters, and here we build on that with the three level micro-meso-macro framing of letting go.

Micro Level

The micro letting go process is like the frontline of transformation. It's the daily noticing and surrendering of our own reactivity so that we can align and flow with life. It's the life learning revealed through everyday challenges. Each tension and trigger, and the resistance it creates within us, becomes the crucible for opening up to more of life. Noticing and relaxing. Each twinge of cynicism or pang of fear or defensive or aggressive reaction is in itself a useful learning for us, an insight from which to gain perspective on what is within us—our habits, wounds, and shadows. Learning when to surrender and what to surrender to, when to stay one's course and when to yield one's position to the dynamic of life. This revolves around learning to find our center and work with the essence and energy within.

Meso Level

The meso level process involves the leader learning to hold space for the transformation of the organization-as-a-living-system by releasing the control-manage tendencies driven by fear and reactivity and beginning to sense-respond by listening and allowing the system to become more developmental and emergent. The leader begins to sense the dynamics of the system to reveal then heal system blockages and blind spots. Nurturing regenerative ways of working help the system become more purposeful, adult-adult, self-managing, diverse, and inclusive. Deep listening, holding space, dialogic circles of sharing, liberating structures, Systemic Enablers, non-violent communication methods, giving and receiving feedback, coaching conversations are all part of the meso level letting go process. You can find more about many of these systemic processes on my *website*.

Macro Level

The macro level happens not daily or weekly but over many months and years, and it involves the metamorphic journey, where we transition from achiever to regenerator. Adult developmental psychology shows us that as we gain greater self-awareness (facilitated through the micro level) we gain greater systemic-awareness (facilitated through the meso level) and eventually gain greater worldview awareness (facilitated by the macro level). As we journey toward regenerator, we begin to see how the whole journey is one of letting go to surrender to how life really is, life beyond the habituated and acculturated patterns, wounds, shadows, and projections we all too often get caught up in.

System

The living-organization is in a state of constant flux, full of complex emergent processes of human relating. It's emergent by nature. These energetic relationships participate and inter-relate across the system. Small interventions in one part of the system can have great influence on other parts of the system, just as releasing stuckness through acupuncture enlivens not just the localized area that was stuck but the flow of energy throughout the whole system.

Upon learning to recognize the organization-as-a-living-system, we enhance our capacity to navigate the emergent systemic dynamics of the living-organization while transmuting tensions into adaptation, innovation, and growth. Instead of communicating through control-based bureaucracy, we work with the right rhythm of divergence-convergence for emergence. We start where we are at, with each day framed as a learning journey that invokes the growth, adaptation, and evolution within us and the living-organization as we transmute tensions through listening, noticing, reflecting, and sharing.

Emergence is propelled by tensions. Tensions create a dissonance within that cajoles us out of the status quo and into emergence. These tensions arise between the space of divergence (diverse perspectives) and convergence (alignment around purpose and values). The sweet spot is where living systems thrive on the edge of chaos and order, because it's this edge that enables adaptability and vitality across the living-organization.

As the life-force of the living-organization, emergence is fast becoming the Holy Grail for organizations to evolve amid volatile times. Hence the fourth E—Evolutionary.

Evolutionary

Self

Evolution is not a chain reaction or a blind process of random selection, but a flow-response that sensitively and seamlessly connects all life. Everything is in continuous participation with everything else. Tensions of emergence reciprocate and interpenetrate across networks of relationality, in complex and unpredictable ways. There are nonsequential evolutionary dynamics at play that we can learn to work with rather than push against.

To truly comprehend the participatory essence-energy-emergent nature of evolution is not a head-based rational-analytic reductive-scientific activity but an embodied felt-sense, a shift into Levels 2 & 3 Living Systems Awareness, which invokes a transformation in consciousness, no less. Whereupon we let go of the personal will's ego-orientated, achiever drive and step into a purposefulness found within ourselves and also within life itself, as discovered on our inner journey. It's what Gandhi gestures to when saying that as we change our nature, so the attitude of the world changes toward us. Our relational dynamic of self-other-world shifts as does our inner-outer nature dynamic. When we are immersed within life, we can sense the evolutionary potential of the living system unfolding.

What's relevant here is that the purposefulness we awaken within provides a less acquisitive and ego needy "What's in it for me?" and a more open vulnerable, sensitive availability to work with the true purposefulness of the living-organization. Our inner truth, or dharma, then resonates with the purpose of the living-organization, and we begin to ask:

How can I best help the organization become a truer version of itself?

Psychological energy that was consumed by the need to relentlessly achieve to better one's career, status, salary, and personal ambition now flows into what genuinely serves the organization and its purpose beyond hitting the numbers.

System

For the organization, the evolutionary shift in focus is from profits to purpose. For sure, profit is vital for any business, yet healthy profits flow from purpose—not the other way around. I like the analogy of breathing. We need to breathe to live and yet breathing is not our reason for living. The organization needs to live by generating healthy profits, yet that's not its reason for living.

What is the organization here to do and be?

We sense the evolutionary purposefulness of the living system by receptively listening to what wants to emerge while tuning into its underlying essence. The more we become attuned with the systemic dynamics within the organization, the more we sense what best serves the evolutionary potential of the organization, and the more we acknowledge what is holding it back from serving its purpose.

An apt example comes from the healthcare service provider Buurtzorg, with its active commitment to sharing its own hard-won innovations on cultivating an effective self-managing culture with competitors. Because Buurtzorg sees its purpose to improve neighborhood care, helping competitors improve does not undermine the organization. Rather, it helps serve its purpose for system-wide impact. It's this kind of capacity to collaborate across organizational boundaries without the fear of competitiveness and associated need for protectionism that the business world now needs to ensure its future-fit ability to work on interwoven systemic challenges, such as the Climate Emergency, reversing nature loss, and tackling rampant social inequalities.

We can also proactively scan the future horizon. In *Leading by Nature*, I unpack a comprehensive methodology that includes foresight, back-casting, scenario-planning, system mapping, stakeholder interviews, and other tools for Systemic Innovation by identifying emerging trends that resonate with the evolutionary purpose of the organization. This combined capacity of anticipating the future horizon a few years hence while being ever-receptive to the emerging future right before us ensures evolutionary fitness: future-fitness.

Enthusiasm

The final of the five Es is quite different from the previous four, in that it describes the fervent inner-outer dynamism flowing through the whole process of becoming a regenerative leader. The other four Es all feed into each other: sensing into essence, cultivating coherence and flowing with energy, working with emergence, tuning in to evolutionary fitness. And throughout all four, we find the soulful, energetic attentiveness of enthusiasm.

The word enthusiasm comes from the ancient Greek *en* which means 'in' and *theos* which means 'divine.' It means to 'be in the divine.' To be enthusiastic is to live within the divine current, the life-force of our soul-essence connected with the current of World Soul through our soul craft. The regenerator learns to treat each moment as sacred with enthusiasm coursing through all layers of inner-outer connection. For the ancient Greek's *enthusiasmos* meant to work with the subtle energies flowing within nature.

Enthusiasm is what drives the regenerator, and it depends on an embodied way of attending to life, an intimacy with the immanent and a transparency to the transcendent. Enthusiasm is not a New Age positive psychology technique, nor is it a creed or moral code, but a way of becoming that embraces each day as a learning journey, each day as a portal into reconnecting to our flow with life. Through this intentional attentiveness we create a sacred space-time—a *temenos*, a profound sense of place and purpose—through which the regenerative potential of essence-energy-emergence-evolutionary dynamics unfold, harmonizing the metaphysical forces emanating from the spirit realm of nature with the world of form. To live with enthusiasm is to unite one's own nature with the field of nature—this harmonizing effect lies at the heart of regeneration. It's an awakening of awe, a being seized by the soul in flowing with the Mystery of life.

The ancient Egyptians, for whom regeneration was a key principle, knew how vitally important this inner-outer harmonizing effect is to the regenerative life. Cultivating this enthusiasm for life across the living-organization's culture is no mean feat, yet it allows for a future-fitness that fosters developmental growth mindsets for high-performing purposeful teams with a depth of connection into what really matters—authenticity, wholeness and service to life.

To nurture this brewing authenticity, wholeness and service inside our Selves as leaders, we learn to work with the four soul virtues of the next chapter.

The Four Soul Virtues of Regenerative Leadership

Now that we have the bedrock of the Ds and the dynamism of the Es to steady and fuel our process of becoming, we can look inward and receive guidance from the four soul virtues.

Before I introduce you to these inner qualities, it is important to acknowledge the profound degree to which we have been conditioned, shaped, and reformed (some might say deformed) through the process of growing up and being taught to succeed and conform to societal norms. So many years of living with Mechanistic Materialism, steeped in head-based education, reductive managerial thinking, and ego-orientated social conditioning, and the natural gifts we had as a child become warped or abandoned. We've reconciled our Self to the collective norms in exchange for the approval of others. We've drunk the societal Kool-Aid.

This acculturating process is part and parcel of living together in society. We learn to get along by observing norms. There's nothing wrong with this acculturating process per se, as long as we don't lose connection with who we are along the way. But often we do, hence the importance of embarking upon the inner journey of knowing thy self during adulthood, which involves remembering and reclaiming the gifts that are our birthright and integrating lifelong learnings, experiences, shadows, and wounds.

As leaders, we need to reach a level of awareness that enables us to identify what moral codes and ethical values we have appropriated through our external conditioning. Then, during our death-rebirth process, we can slough off what no longer serves us, meanwhile gaining trust in our inner-nature and life itself. This is not to say that adopting values and insights we've picked up along the way is not a beneficial aspect of our journey, as external values, behaviors, and beliefs can have a positive evolutionary effect on us. However, we must know how to separate the wheat from the chaff. Discern what enhances our process of becoming truer and what is cloaking our deeper nature, thereby unintentionally blocking authenticity. The lived values that are congruent with our inner-nature make themselves known to us as we journey inward. They are either true in our heart and soul or not. I call these soul-centered, lived values *virtues*, to distinguish them from the adopted values we have picked up along the way. Virtues emanate from within us (Lenses 2 & 3) and inform how we show up, listen, and act as a leader (integrated Lenses 1-2-3).

Many of the organizations I've worked with pride themselves on being values led, meaning they put aside time to comprehensively identify, revisit, and refresh their organizational values. These values are usually worked through during off-sites and company-wide conversations before they become enshrined in the company's values charter and communicated through staff meetings, the company website, onboardings for new joiners, year-end reports, and on stage at external conferences. This is all good. Yet, when it comes to coaching senior leaders within many of these values led organizations, I frequently find top team execs secretly struggling to genuinely live the values on a day-to-day basis. The problem I've noticed is that when company values are engaged with as something to achieve *out there*, and not lived *in here*, they unknowingly activate the achiever mind and ego-consciousness of Lens 1 and tune out the more integrated and embodied Lenses 1-2-3 ego-heart-soul consciousness of the awakened mind.

Many leaders also consider that company values can come across as ethical obligations or shallow fashion statements asserted by whatever the latest trend assumes is fitting for the day. Or they see how values change each time a new CEO or People & Culture Lead enters the organization. People then feel obligated to do whatever appears right in order to please. Inauthenticity creeps in as we start to suppress aspects of our deeper nature to conform, and before we know it, the company values subtly subvert the inner journey.

So how might we go about exploring values that can be lived within us in a way that aids Lenses 1-2-3 integration and helps us metamorphose from achiever to regenerator?

We can turn to the four foundational soul virtues. No matter what the company values may be or any personal values you might find that work for you as you realize your soul craft, the four virtues sit underneath the surface, at the soul level, and work with any personal and organizational values you develop.

The four soul virtues are: balance, patience, courage, and purposefulness. One might say that balance and patience are more yin-orientated and courage and purposefulness are more yang-orientated. Either way all four integrate yin-yang and invoke an integration of yin-yang within us. Each of these four virtues form a dual function in that they aid us on the inner journey of becoming who we truly are and they aid others while we show up more fully in our relationships, making the virtues both personal and relational.

They enable us to relate authentically and holistically, attuning with the essence of the parts and the whole. They influence how and what we know and the way we apply this knowing. They are conduits for wisdom in the world, transforming ourselves, our teams, our organizations, and the wider society from the inside out. The more we wake up to and live into these four virtues, the more they realign us—keep us true—to flow as life flows. Amid these transformational times, the virtues manifest future-fitness right into the heart of our everyday conversations, meetings, and decisions. Exploring these virtues can help you become more intimate with your deeper nature—noticing and sensing what feels alive for you, what feels challenging yet true for you, and what you may wish to find your own words and insights for as you sense how these virtues play out within your unique individuality and life-path.

I invite you now to enter into a contemplative mode of reflection as you read each virtue. For the explanations here are merely ways in and are meant to encourage your own contemplative reflection. They are not meant to limit or define. Mull over, contemplate, and if you like journaling, then journal about what each stirs within your core. Sense what resonates and what triggers. What intentionally sparks your imagination in reflecting on how each virtue is showing up through how you currently live and lead? Feel into them. Read them once and then again.

Slow down.

In truth, I recommend spending a couple of days with each one, before moving on to the next.

Take your time.

The Virtue of Balance

In the early stages of our inner journey, we bend the beam of our awareness inside to our bodymind. We become familiar with when we feel in right relation (balanced) and when we feel off kilter (imbalanced). Balance is finding that sweet spot. It's not a static thing. Balance is alive, it's dynamic. It's a state of in-betweenness, a sense of resonance, both inwardly and outwardly, personally and relationally. It's a way to experience life, and we can sense balance in each moment of our lives as a feeling of being in right relation.

Balance can be checked in two ways: 1) during a meditative practice of scanning inward; 2) a quick inward scan amid the heat of the moment.

Meditative Scanning Inward

As we become more dedicated and disciplined with bodymind coherence, through meditation and body scanning practices, we become conversant with how it feels to be balanced and imbalanced by learning to sense somatic cues—subtle sensations in the bodymind. When balanced, we sense an uninhibited flow of energy and a healthy dose of both yin-receptivity and yang-responsiveness. This is an active relaxation feeling. When imbalanced, we sense an overly-yang energy in the bodymind (gasping, excited, slightly pensive, tense, impatient, a slight forward-leaning urge) or overly-yin energy (passive, introspective, introvertive, depressive, flaccid, and retreating urge).

As we practice sensing in to the bodymind, we find unique telltale signs. For instance, when imbalanced we might notice one nostril is more blocked than the other, perhaps a mild headache, shallow chest breathing, heightened emotions, gut is tight, slightly constipated, or tense shoulders. When balanced we might notice both nostrils feel open, breathing is deeper and more rhythmic, both inner ears feel clear, the gut relaxes, the heart region feels expansive and open, emotions are regulated, and digestion is smooth. Practice, practice, practice; notice, notice, notice, and soon we tune in to our body's sensations and its telltale signs.

Now, be careful not to judge a somatic energy, as judgement will take us straight into Lens 1 and reduce our scanning sensitivity. No need for any judgement or critique about any imbalance. Instead, stay with the inner sensation. By calling upon one of our energy cultivation practices we can find a way to re-balance without judgement. A few rounds of deep belly breathing, for instance, is easy enough to do while remaining in an inward meditative scanning state. I have found the times of sunrise and sunset particularly beneficial for undertaking a body scanning sense-check. These conscious moments can form an enjoyable and effortless yet nourishing and rejuvenating daily practice topping and tailing a productive workday.

In-the-moment Scanning

As we become practiced at sensing the difference between balance and imbalance in the bodymind, we increase our attentiveness to this bodymind guidance system throughout the entire day. We sense the resonance of what is unfolding within everyday interactions by noticing our somatic sensations. The same as we can intuitively dance or sing in rhythm and in tune with the music, we can sense the resonance of situations and adjust how we hold space (yin) or intervene (yang). Not only are we sensing the yin-yang balance inside our bodymind (self-awareness), but we are also sensing the yin-yang balance in the relational energetic system we are immersed in (systemic-awareness).

I enjoy sailing and so quite like the analogy of the tiller handle on the boat that moves the rudder in the water as the boat sails through waves, undercurrents, tides, and winds. We continuously adjust the tiller this way and that, responding to the changes, and with practice, through an embodied and intuitive sensing, we learn to sense what feels right—what keeps the boat afloat, balanced. We learn when to be a little more yang or a little more yin.

Finding this right relation between how much effort we bring into a situation (yang) and how much allowing of what wants to unfold (yin) is what we call 'a balancing act.' At first glance, it might seem antithetical to be simultaneously applying effort while allowing space, or being in control while letting go of control, but it's this tension of yin-yang that gives rise to a quality of attentiveness that continuously adjusts to life. *When does one plan in preparation and when does one allow for spontaneity? When does one assert a view and when does one listen and reflect? When does one get through as much work as possible during the day and when does one take moments of reflection and rejuvenation between meetings?* Notice these polar urges we have within us. The urge to initiate and progress something (yang) feels different from the energy to presence and allow things to unfold (yin). Each situation may ask for a different balance point of this yin-yang tension, and as the situation unfolds, we can discern the rhythmic nature of the tension and how the resonance may change, inviting in a different yin-yang balance.

Having the awareness and bodymind coherence to sense what is naturally occurring can easily be obscured by our own (and other's) desires, energies, urges, and stresses. Lens 1—with its ego stories, judgements, fears, and insecurities—can get in the way here, just as someone else's charismatic Lens 1 can manipulate and obscure our own truth. This proves the importance of opening into more of Lenses 2 & 3 with bodymind coherence, so we know when we are interrupting the situation with our own baggage or lack of presence and when we are tuning in to the emergent nature of the situation.

By understanding what we're feeling beneath the distracting cacophony of the everyday, we know when it's time to renew ourselves. Rather than progressing mindlessly toward increasingly agitated, restless, impatient, forceful, oversensitive, depressive, unsure, defensive, or withdrawn states, we have the courage and self-determination to take time out, to sense inwardly, and to rejuvenate and find a more coherent and balanced state of awareness. We then experience a co-creative, vitalizing, convivial, and compassionate awareness that flows through our relations and interactions.

Here are a couple of these yin-yang tensions experienced every day.

YANG	YIN
Outer responsiveness	Inner receptivity
Active doing	Reflective being
Reductive focus	Relational expansiveness
Movement	Stillness

Neither side of these yin-yang tensions is more right or preferable than the other. Each situation invites us to sense when the right moment is to bring in more of one side than the other. For instance, it may be that we are getting pent up, overworked, or burnt out, so it's time to take a break, do some exercise, or take some time off. Or we are lounging, letting time pass, or procrastinating, which may call for a need to refocus, respond to emails, or set a course of action.

The virtue of balance is very far from being a utilitarian functional goal. Though it is highly useful for us to effectively navigate everyday turbulence with grace and ease, lightening the load of our schedules in the process, it's not something we need to schedule in and achieve. Our inner coherence informs inner-outer balance which enables right relation resulting in richer regenerative outcomes. Our receptivity and authenticity inform our activity and intervention. Yin informs yang, and balance is found.

From the perspective of Lens 1, this can feel like a juggling of one thing against another, a trade off to 'achieve' a work-life balance. This perspective can become clunky, forced, and mechanistic. We stop one activity only to insert another. We blindly follow an app on our phone that tracks how much exercise we've done or when we should take a break. However, as the inner journey integrates the perspectives of Lenses 2 & 3, we gain a more nuanced awareness, and balance no longer feels like a quantitative, scheduled trade-off measured by a metronomic routine. While an app may be a useful tool that helps enforce a scheduled discipline, we can learn to become conscious of what inherently feels right for us during each day and each situation.

As the virtue of balance works through us, it becomes a qualitative dynamism. Balance is lived uniquely through a blend of our individuality and the systemic relationality each situation affords. We cultivate this inner sense of what feels right by developing intimacy with our bodymind. As we journey inward, we become more aware of body sensations, fluctuating energy levels, intuitions, insights from dreams, premonitions, and imaginations that emerge from our deeper nature and the Field. At the same time, we become more sensitive to the relational dynamics as they unfold and interrelate systemically across the organization and business ecosystem. This increased self-awareness and systemic-awareness provide an enriching, empathic capacity to sense resonance within and all around us. The resonance of each unfolding situation informs us of where and how balance might be found—through listening and holding space or through stimulating and encouraging action.

Resonance-sensing is not merely picking up on the contents or facts of an unfolding situation, but also about the inner qualities of energy affecting the wider relational system. Living into the virtue of balance invites noticing when something feels out of tune, not quite right, inauthentic or agitated, and may need some encouragement or patience from us.

The Virtue of Patience

While the virtue of balance invites a resonance of the unfolding space-time nature of things, the virtue of patience invites an inner serenity with the natural rhythm of the way things unfold. It's a letting go of the grasping at life. Patience is not a task we force upon ourselves when situations require us to pause or hold back. It's a way of experiencing life. Like all four virtues, patience comes with lessening Lens 1's dominance and its expectant, urgent, and anxious need for certainty.

> "Nature does not hurry, yet everything is accomplished."
>
> –Lao Tzu

A useful way to cultivate the virtue of patience in our lives is to notice how impatience shows up in us. As impatience arises, we can learn to let go and allow in patience. Impatience is prevalent in business today and prevalent across much of society. Social media alerts, multi-channel instant messaging, short-termism thinking, a hurried rush through the day, meeting after meeting, an incessant feeling of moving on to the next thing, a 'just get on with it!' mentality.

Humanity is rife with impatience, because we have lost ourselves in the demands of Lens 1, which has corrupted our experience of life. We want tick-box exercises, complete to-do lists, and to find quick-fix solutions to control and secure outer achievements.

Reflection-in-action helps us to discern the subtle difference between purposefully acting because the moment is right and Lens 1's ego-urge to react impatiently. When we act hastily, we create imbalance and lose a quality of awareness as we pull ourselves into Lens 1 and out of the more integrated Lenses 1-2-3 awareness, but we can learn to sense this lack and its associated loss of spaciousness and timeliness. The moment closes in on us, our rhythm and flow are lost, heightened sense perception evaporates, and we feel hasty and hurried. Impatience can drain our energy levels and narrow our awareness. If we so choose, we can let it go instead of caving into its reactive urge, allowing a spaciousness to arise.

As the letting go process is *noticing* then *allowing*, likewise, here we notice the urge of impatience, bring our awareness to the inner sensation, then allow it to be without acting on the tension or constriction it creates. This isn't easy when the uncomfortable feeling within is urging us to just do something—anything! —but collateral damage is incurred when the ripples of our impatient urges upset the natural flow of things.

Patience works with the fullness of time. Impatience is starved of time. Even though Lens 1 asserts that our hurried impatience saves time, this is an illusion. The ego might think that hurrying things along means we have more time on our hands for other things, yet this mindset then fills time with the same hurried impatience—or worse, boredom that stems from our addiction to the incessant grasping at life. How many of us rush work while longing for time off only to fill our time off with activities to pass the time?

Contrary to popular opinion, we do not need more time in our lives to do more things. This is an unfriendly and degenerative relationship with life. What we need is to experience life in a more timely and spacious way. We need to allow ourselves the patience to love life. Rather than pressing, grasping, and shoving at life, we are invited to engage in a more sensate experience, one which feels more embodied, plentiful, rhythmic, flowing, and reciprocal. We learn to savor each challenge as a learning experience that heralds an ever-deepening intimacy with ourselves and life. We no longer seek to control situations. We dance with life as it unfolds.

The ancient Greeks explored different qualities of time—*Chronos* (linear quantitative clock-time) and *Kairos* (rhythmic qualitative flow-time). Lens 1 works with chronological time, and Lenses 2 & 3 work with kairological time. Today's busy, tightly scheduled, impatient business world has all but forgotten kairological time and yet nature works with kairological time. Birds don't wake up with alarm clocks, flowers don't need schedules to unfurl themselves, and bats don't need wristwatches to appear at dusk. They sense when it's the right time due to the resonances and rhythms they are attuned to.

Chronological time is a useful tool that helps us get things done, but kairological time is a rhythmic river flowing through life informing us of the right time to act and the right time to wait and to practice patience. In the heat of the moment, we find an intimate, attentive dance of relational rhythms and tensions. This wisdom is of the utmost use to us amid an increasingly turbulent and complex context.

While balance orientates us around right relation, patience orientates us around right timing.

The Virtue of Courage

As we mentioned previously the root of the word courage is 'cor' meaning 'heart' in Latin, and it's through the heart, rather than the head, that we awaken our inner-nature and allow this depth of ourselves to work in tune with life. The more courageous we become, the more our inner-nature and outer-nature align, and the more we engage in Nature's Wisdom.

We may have experienced moments in life when we have transcended the ego boundaries of Lens 1—perhaps at a time when we were inwardly compelled to help someone or something by putting ourselves at some perceived risk or challenge. In that situation it's likely that we had to cross a threshold by overcoming a fear so that we could act on what is right for something beyond ourselves. This overcoming of fear can happen in two ways: 1) ambition and 2) courage.

Ambition involves the ego's goal-orientated achiever mindset of Lens 1. This ego-drive for achievement requires outer recognition and reward—whether it's acknowledgement and praise from others, accolades and awards, brand enhancement, social media likes, the warm acceptance of one's views by others, or material gain such as a promotion, bonus, or pay raise. Ambition achieves things, sometimes at great personal cost, and therefore it might appear to be like courage, especially when the passionate purposeful fervor of the ambitious act serves a cause greater than oneself. In fact, many beneficial acts are undertaken thanks to the ambitious drive of progressive change agents and pioneering leaders. There is nothing wrong with being ambitious.

We might be helping another person, a group of people, or engaged in a social or environmental change initiative when being ambitious, but we are not always courageous. Ambition is when our Lens 1 ego-awareness and its desire for achievement and need for recognition is dominating our deeper nature. As we become more practiced and experienced on the inner journey, we start to notice and discern a felt sense in our bodymind, a subtle difference between when the gravity of our awareness is centered in Lens 1 and when it's centered in a more integrated Lens 1-2-3. When the gravity of our awareness is more in Lens 1, we feel outwardly driven, hurried, impatient, mildly agitated yet also excited. We are hyped-up. There is a certain buzz about it, which can be addictive; however, our capacity to sense resonances and rhythms that inform us of right time and right relation begins to wane as the yang-drive for ambition takes us over and we lose inner yin-yang alignment.

Charismatic leaders driven by strong moral convictions aimed at helping to serve a better world are often driven by strong ambition. Their strong ego-drive pushes things through business-as-usual bureaucracy and persuades others to commit to making things happen that incite change. This purposeful ambition enlists followers while marching onward over the edge of status quo comfort zones and conditioned norms. It provokes outward advancement and makes change happen. Yet, it's still achiever orientated.

As we progress on the inner journey, we become well-versed in allowing a strong Lens 1 ambition to permeate more readily with Lens 2 & 3, and that's when courage starts to flow. Here we draw from our inner-nature and the limitless Field. Ambition, on the other hand, draws only from the ego's personal willpower, which heightens a sense of separation from life that tunes us out of the limitless Field. Ambition needs to be fed by others' recognition and reward. Courage is fed by life.

The virtue of courage might first make an appearance through fleeting moments in our lives, such as when a situation unfolds, and we feel the compulsion to help another. Courage can also be cultivated as a lived practice where we learn to access its heart-soul current of consciousness more readily during our everyday leadership. Journeying from achiever to regenerator requires courage—the courage to cultivate our inner truth, to not wear others' masks, and to be congruent with our soul-purpose, nature's ways, and natural limits and potentials. In coming to terms with our own foibles, we notice patterns of fear and insecurity within us. These can be revealed and released, or at least acknowledged as our own inner stuff in place of projecting them on to the world out there.

Courage asks us to trust in life instead of trust in our ego. As a leader, we still need the strong ego-will and ambitious drive to make things happen, but only as tools for an integrated Lens 1-2-3. Through embodying the open-heartedness of courage, our sensitivity in the moment responds to an inner-outer connection with life and is not limited to the wants of our personal will. Acting from courage, we are immersed in life.

Open-hearted awareness, bodymind coherence, and inner-outer sensitivity enable a rightness of will—a willfulness emanating from our integrated wholeness. Living into the virtue of courage is not quick and easy. It's the practice of a lifetime, but sure enough with practice we become more open-hearted, more inner-outer attuned, and more courageous. While balance orientates us around right relation, and patience around right timing, courage orientates us around right will.

The Virtue of Purposefulness

It might be self-evident by now that each virtue is a lived quality of ego-heart-soul consciousness that calls upon our inner-outer alignment and integrated Lenses 1-2-3. Likewise, purposefulness is a way of intentionally living with inner-outer attentiveness. Purposefulness is different from 'purpose', which is seen as a statement of intent or outer goal to achieve. Purposefulness is a way of becoming, an approach to flowing more intentionally and attentively with life, a way of learning, adapting, and evolving while living our dharma or soul-purpose.

Purpose is a much-used word in management lingo these days. As we lead the organization-as-machine through its shift into organization-as-living-system, the outdated, top-down power-over relationships that subordinate and disempower employees morph into co-creative participatory and developmental relationships where leadership holds space for others to work through tensions while engaging in learning, critical thought, challenging discussions, diverse perspectives, and conflict transformation. We no longer find conformity through control. We find aligned engagement through purpose. People feel psychologically safe enough to embark on their own inner journeys and bring their whole selves to work, and the living-organization becomes a cauldron of differing perspectives and creative tensions. What allows these tensions to be worked through is a common purpose that provides community coherence.

For the living-organization, purpose is not a static thing to define through an outwardly orientated mission statement focused primarily on the binary value the organization exchanges with its customers and other stakeholders. Instead, purpose is lived by the organization through both its outer stakeholder propositions and relationships and its inner culture, day-to-day behaviors, and developmental learning (the DEE culture).

Put another way, regenerative business is not limited to a focus on sustainability metrics and outer impact but includes the inner culture and ways in which people feel permitted to journey toward their own individual achiever to regenerator journeys, if they so choose. Otherwise, the business is simply busying itself with making change happen 'out there', and this would be the very achiever dynamic we are seeking to move away from masquerading under the label of 'regenerative business.'

I see this lot these days, and it's likely a result of the tendency to gather at the threshold rather than cross the threshold. Let's notice this mistake and learn from it. Otherwise, before we know it the achiever mind will be back in the driver's seat, cut adrift from Nature's Wisdom, and 'regenerative business' will be reduced to 'sustainability on steroids.' Noticing our own purposefulness is a great way to assess when we are in achiever or regenerator.

Purposefulness working with balance is the sensitive hand on the tiller while sailing close to the wind. We can sense what micro adjustments are needed this way and that amid changing weather and sea conditions. Each day offers chances to notice when we are attuned to the unfolding context, fully present, authentic in the moment (balanced) verses when we have slipped out of tune with life and feel inner resistance and reactivity pulling us back into the control-manage dynamic of Lens 1 (imbalanced).

Purposefulness requires us to embrace daily interactions as opportunities to become more vulnerable, authentic, and present and less distracted, unbalanced and impatient. No one ought to expect us to be perfectly balanced and undefended all the time, as situations will inevitably challenge us, yet we can notice what triggers our imbalances and inauthenticity. Each email interaction, difficult conversation, boardroom presentation, conflict tension, budget adjustment, or disagreement becomes our learning edge that we attend to purposefully.

Living in this purposeful flow necessitates an open stance and perceptive curiosity that filters and interprets life experiences with trust—trust in oneself and trust in our sense of place and purpose within life. This trust in life is a courageous inner awareness that invites us to immerse ourselves, undefended, whole-heartedly into whatever unfolds. It requires us to let go of the worries, judgements, distractions, and desires for control and certainty of Lens 1 and asks us to open into Lenses 2 & 3 to emancipate ourselves from the illusion of separation that Lens 1 creates.

By holding the intention to be attentive to the present moment—to practice letting go, to be mindful in becoming aware of our presence, to simply notice our breathing—we allow a limitless life-force to come in from the Field. We enter our own center-point of the soul. Life *is* the flow of activity inviting us to become attentive and intentional in how we experience every moment. Every challenging event or conversation is a learning lab for us to become more masterful in our purposefulness. By purposefully setting an intention to be more present and attentive as we enter a meeting, or a difficult conversation, we can help ourselves become intentionally open and attentively curious to what emerges. Our inner psychic energy flows into our outer environment and the life-force of the Field energizes us to provide our own sensation of flow. This is living in harmony with life. As we open and give our energy, so we receive energy.

While courage orientates us around right will, patience around right timing, and balance around right relation, purposefulness orientates us around right energy.

Flowing with Others

Make no mistake about the importance of how we show up each day, regardless of whether we are CxOs, team leaders, or external facilitators. The living-organization is a complex adaptive system constantly emerging and adjusting in nonlinear inter-relational ways. The relationship ripples we invoke through how we speak, listen, hold space, and act, no matter how minor they might appear, all form part of the systemic energy of the living-organization flowing throughout the relational system.

By living these four soul qualities we are learning to read our own responses to our experiences (self-awareness) and we are learning to read other people's and the system's responses (systemic-awareness) to everyday emerging experiences, decisions, interventions, and contextual changes. By becoming more sensitized to life and trusting, we receive the guidance we need to lead the living-organization in its own process of becoming more authentic and life-affirming.

The more we show up with balance, patience, courage, and purposefulness, the more we create the right conditions for others to drop their ego-armor. Clearer about our own inner-nature, we become clearer about the nature of what is emerging around us and a truer co-creation can emerge. The 'other' may be a colleague, customer, supplier, shareholder, competitor, regulator or the goods and services we work with, the wider supply chains, communities, and sources of nature that provide these. Nature's Wisdom reveals to us that nothing is separate, everything interrelates. In the 'other' we find what is within us.

As leadership specialist Parker J Palmer notes, "Every 'other' we work with has its own nature, its own limits and potentials, with which we must learn to co-create if we hope to get real results. Good work is relational, and its outcomes depend on what we are able to evoke from each other." (Palmer, 2004, p109)

Personal refinement enriches community development. We evolve as a leader through acting and responding more authentically and holistically in the world. This is an inner-outer process of becoming more of our deeper nature—with its unique gifts and learnings—and attuning with Nature's Wisdom. It's an intentional journey of becoming more conscious, more attuned with life, and more in right relation at right time with right will and right energy.

Cultivating Soil Conditions

There is a fertile inner-nature that allows for a continuous regeneration inside ourselves as we journey, and so way down deep below the surface, we must maintain healthy soil conditions.

After many years of the dominant achiever mind and a worldview of Mechanistic Materialism, it's quite likely that our inner-nature has been superficialized by a dominant ego-consciousness. Metaphorically, we now have a thin layer of nutrient deficient topsoil, depleted from years of over extraction and limited regeneration. This thin layer of soil can easily be washed away by the heavy rains and winds that lie ahead on our journey.

Think of the five soil conditions we explore in this chapter as mental-emotional-intuitive-somatic bodymind habits that help us nurture a rich, regenerative garden of our own inner-nature. Imagine weeding, digesting, composting, fertilizing, and renewing the inner psyche to create these soil conditions.

We live in a world with so much volatility, not just on the outside (due to rising societal breakdown) but on the inside as we go through the winding swirling labyrinthine journey. It's all too easy to be constantly triggered by the ego's voices of judgement, cynicism, and fear. If our inner soil is thin and weak, we can become uprooted, unmoored from our own center-point, tossed this way and that by the winds of change. What a rough and bumpy ride as we journey, one that will surely cause a rising fear within, tempting us to turn back, to turn away from the inner work and to resist the path. Thin soil can also increase the risk of being subsumed by the inner demons of the labyrinthine unconscious within, lost in depression or a psychological crack-up that delays or derails the inner journey.

While the five soil conditions do not negate the need to receive experienced advice along the journey—whether from a seasoned coach, friend, advisor, teacher, or therapist—when cultivated with the inner qualities of the last three chapters (the Ds, the Es, and the virtues), these soil conditions help ensure that we grow from the interiority, inner-outer integration, and integrity within the bodymind. We keep our journey rooted in the rhizome of regeneration.

These five soil conditions are: Dance, Respect, Spontaneity, Gratitude & Listening. Let's dig in.

Dance

As we've learned, the whole of reality is underpinned by a natural law of harmonics and resonance. Through our right relation with both the inner and outer nature of life, we find our unique rhythm with life while serving our soul craft. As any professional dancer knows, the art is to remain still while moving, to be centered inside while fully immersed in the movement. This involves flow, the ability to be simultaneously active yet relaxed. To be in step, on time, in the beat, totally aware of the now, yet also conscious of the choreography, the musicality, the tempo, energy, and dynamism of the dance of life's ebbs and flows.

> "In all stillness there is movement. In all movement there is stillness."
>
> —Martial Art proverb

Life is always fluctuating. Change is the only constant. As the Presocratic Heraclitus knew, we can't step into the same river twice. Life is a river of emergent unfolding. Stasis (inactive equilibrium) is largely absent from life. While the ego might quest for equilibrium, everything is forever oscillating, like the water flowing downstream, this way and that, up and down, side to side. No straight lines, fixed points, or perfect repetitions, only dynamism, rhythm, and flow.

It's not only life outside of us that is ever-changing. It's also life within us, within our own bodymind thoughts, feelings, sensations, and intuitions. All are ephemeral within an eternal transcendent dimension. By stilling ourselves inwardly, we can learn to work with this inner-outer dance.

By practicing the inner art of working with the twilight zone we learn to work with wisdom. Like the owl seeing in the dark, we access higher faculties that help us through our own dark night of the soul as we journey. Recall the old saying, "The owl of Minerva flies at dusk." We find that our way into wisdom is through the twilight zone, a dance between achiever mind and awakened mind, and a dance of presencing immanence and centering transcendence. This brings a profound sense of meaning into life. Everyday moments become meaningful moments for our process of becoming. We are simultaneously the dancer within the dance of life and allowing the dance to flow through us, as a conduit (the panpipe) for the tune.

Recall the three esoteric aspects of Nature's Wisdom as an attuning-atoning-accordance—a 'cor' dance—a rhythmic inner-outer dance found through a deepening into heart and soul. We learn to be in the eye of the storm, at the center of the wheel, while the world turns. Stillness in movement, for wisdom weaving, in love with life.

> "Stillness is what creates love,
> Movement is what creates life,
> To be still,
> Yet still moving –
> That is everything!"
>
> —Do Hyun Choe

Applying twenty years of research related to the optimal human experience called 'flow', psychologist professor Mihaly Csikszentmihalyi has uncovered how people can transform stressful, troubled, or tedious situations into enjoyable flow-producing activities. The essence of his findings revolves around cultivating a certain state of mind. He notes, "of all the virtues we can learn no trait is more useful, more essential for survival, and more likely to improve the quality of life than the ability to transfer adversity into an enjoyable challenge." (Csikszentmihalyi, p200) He found two simple tools we each have at our disposal that enable this ability to transfer adversity into enjoyable flow-producing challenge: intention and attention. We aid our soil condition of Dance by working with intention and attention amid daily life.

Let's use the metaphor of a river. There are two different dimensions to the river flowing. 1) Movement: We are immersed in the river flow. We go downstream at pace, enjoying the immersive experience of when we are in flow with our work and life. We are watching and relating with the banks on either side as we flow downstream. When in-flow we notice the riverbanks and yet can let go of them, not getting caught up in sideshow cacophony, ego distraction and judgements of self and others. 2) Stillness: We step back from the immediacy of the flow by accessing the center-point within and sensing the transcendent oceanic oneness of the Field behind the whole river and its banks. While being immersed in-flow in the detail of daily life, we gain perspective on the river flowing intently toward the oceanic World Soul.

When we see with adjusted eyes—connected into soul-consciousness—we realize the banks of the river and the river itself are simultaneously a rich lived-experience and something we can transcend or drop behind. We can be fully immersed in the flow of the work and have the conscious capacity to step behind it all and so notice when we get too caught up in the heat-of-the-moment or the cacophony of confusion on the riverbanks pulling us out of our flow amid rising volatility and challenge.

With tools like bodymind coherence and the Creative Imagination Process, we can dance with the transcendent ocean and the immanent river flow. This is the twilight zone of Three-in-One where we step beyond duality while also being in duality. Awake and active yet not ensnared in high-beta stress about the busy riverbanks, instead flowing with bodymind coherence and full-spectrum brain waves to gain perspective while presencing, sensing the immanent and transcendent in everything. And so, the owl of Minerva flies in us—we work with wisdom.

Regarding the first dimension of this flowing life-experience, we can work with intention and attention which aids are ability to flow with the river. Rather than struggling against the stream we become intentional in our flow. Our attentiveness depends on how able we are to be present to the unfolding situation without getting distracted by the voice in the head (Lens 1) and the unintegrated shadow projections and constrictions we may have in our deeper nature (Lens 2). And although we may like to believe that external circumstances create problems for us (someone taking an argumentative tone or being late for a meeting), on closer inspection inner disturbance is created by our own judgement of and reactivity to the external situation. It's up to us to notice our distraction from present moment awareness. This is where intention can help us. By holding the intention to be attentive to the present moment—to practice letting go, to be mindful in becoming aware of our presence, to simply notice our breathing— we improve our flow capacity. Instead of getting caught up in distractions from the riverbank, pulling us out of the stream of our own integrated consciousness, we allow a limitless life-force to come in from the Field.

By purposefully setting an intention to be more present and attentive as we enter, say, a meeting or a difficult conversation, we can help ourselves become more intentionally open and attentively curious to what emerges. As well as being conscious of our intention and attention, we also practice the ability to connect into the center-point within, the soul-scape. This opens us to the second dimension, the oceanic World Soul that realizes the immediacy of the river and its banks of interactivity for what it really is, a sacred learning journey. We take things less personally, we lighten up, and we learn to lovingly embrace the tumbling twisting turning flow dance. Then, the tensions work their dinergic magic and impel emergence. With our own inner stillness into oneness, we find rhythm with the two of the tension to bring forth the three, the creative undertaking that emerges through the tension.

Instead of struggling against the stream, we dance with the harmonic music life's tensions create.

> "Polarity is the loom upon which reality is strung."
>
> —Mayan proverb

This flow dance with life draws from a rootedness inside the Self of ego-heart-soul consciousness that works with intention and attention. This is the soil condition of Dance, which allows for us to embrace inner-outer nature as the dance of our lives.

> "Dance dance where ever you may be
> For I am the Lord of the dance said [S]he
> And I'll lead you all
> Where ever you may be
> I'll lead you all in the Dance said [S]he."
>
> —Sydney Carter

Respect

To be in right relation is to be grounded in respect for self, for others, for life. Our self-other-world relationality is grounded in respect. Respect is the rhizome that ensures our dance is of the right timbre, tone, tempo, and tenor with the life that flows around and within us. Respect is the rootedness that enables right relation. Respect calls upon both self-awareness and systemic-awareness.

Self-awareness

By knowing our own selves, and connecting with our own essence, we open to life beyond ego and better see the authenticity and essence in others. We can connect with others at a soul-level as well as an ego-level. Often where the ego sees difference and will judge or critique as either good or not good, friend of foe, the soul sees beyond into the essence behind personas of difference. This allows for a quality of attentiveness that holds space for the other and allows the other to ease out of their ego and drop deeper into themselves and the relational field between us. A reciprocating respect forms.

Systemic-awareness

By deepening our awareness of the interconnectedness of everything and the energetic relational nature of the living-organization or community, we are relating with and opening to all three levels of Living Systems Awareness. Recall open mind (biomimicry and systems thinking) open heart (systemic dynamics and constellations), and open will (eco-psycho-spiritual interpenetrating fields within fields). This systemic respect is a reverence for all life. As we experience the interpenetration of each and all, there is no separation. There is only a dancing diversity-in-unity. This respect is life-centric.

As well as being all-encompassing and life-centric, this respect is relationally specific in that we can hold a certain respect for a particular person, creature or place nested within the universal respect of all places, creatures and people. For instance, one might have a sacred sit spot in nature or a meditation shrine at home which commands a certain respect in terms of how one enters the space and conducts oneself in the sacred space. Like entering a church, temple, or other consecrated place of worship, we hold a certain reverence when present. This right relation with a sacred space does not detract from our respect for other places or life-forms beyond that specific space. It enhances it, for as soon as we leave the temple or our nature sit spot, we don't then drop litter and kick the soil in an unconscious habitual way. To see any place as sacred helps us to see everything as sacred.

Imagine if the many millions of people on pilgrimages throughout the world each year realized that the whole journey of the pilgrimage is sacred. Not just an external destination to achieve, but the whole way in which we treat the journey. Unfortunately, these days most pilgrimage sites have massive cleanup operations due to the tons and tons of waste litter strewn all along the trails. For many, the pilgrimage has been hijacked by the achiever mind and its need to reach the destination out there. The point of the journey is trampled over.

"The point of the journey is not to arrive," I often say to my coaching clients. The soul journey is not about 'achieving' a destination. The destination is the journey, and learning to respect self-other-world on the journey is the whole point. We might, say, sit next to a tree in an intentional way, asking for permission, thanking the tree, sitting and becoming conscious of the tree as a sacred living being with physical and metaphysical presence. This is a mark of respect. And yet we may also begin to see how forming a sacred space in such a way is something that we can also apply to everyday life, like meeting someone new, a soul as well as a physical body and persona, that commands our respect, like the tree.

We might see each sunrise and sunset as a sacred undertaking worthy of our respect. We might notice a customer or supplier as worthy of our respect. It might then be easy for the ego to judge, *Is the customer or supplier worthy of our respect? Are they ethical or conscious? If so, how conscious, how progressive?* which affects the respect we might feel they deserve from us. This is the ego of comparison, the left-hemisphere attention creeping in. Soon comes a sanctimonious feeling of superiority and judgement. This is not respect, nor does it nurture the soil conditions within ourselves. It's the ego uprooting us from right relation. Let's learn to notice these complexities of difference and learn to appreciate differences as ways into exploring diversity-in-unity.

Respect is an underlying soil condition that invokes a sensing-in to the life-force, dharma, and soulfulness in each and all, regardless of their ethical alignment, creed, viewpoint, or choice of behavior. Respect is not a trade-off. There is no need to respect one customer or supplier more or less than the other.

Over a decade ago now, I guest lectured at a world famous and well 'respected' college revered for its progressive courses on sustainability, ethics, and such like. During a one-week residential course I was teaching, after a couple of days in, I sensed a rift forming between two camps of participants—a staunchly environmentalist group of about ten or so participants who saw business as a dirty word and another camp of about ten or so participants with careers in business. Rather than a respect for differences, leading to a richer understanding across the groups, a polarization was developing; an air of acrimony with judgement and cynicism formed between these two camps.

As the first two days went on, I could see how the two camps had started to eat breakfast, lunch, and dinner as separate tribes, with little sharing between the groups. On the morning of the third day, I altered the agenda by holding a circle of dialogue, using a talking stick, and encouraging a speaking and listening from the heart, for each to share their deeper sense of self, and what had driven their life decisions so far. What had brought them here to this point in their lives, and what might they see ahead of them in life unfolding. Within an hour of open-hearted sharing, which included plenty of welling up and tears, the acrimony had shifted into empathy. People got up and hugged each other, and from then on, the two tribes were no more. We were one cohort full of difference yet of a shared humanity, learning together with respect for our uniquenesses.

Some years later, I spoke at a conference in Copenhagen, and a lady came up at the end who I recognized—she was from that course years earlier. She shared how that course, and in-particular that sharing circle, had impacted her life decisions from that moment on. Cultivating a respect for others during that course enlightened her more than any course content and helped her find respect for her own gifts while uncovering her true life-path. From the resentful anger-fueled, blame-orientated environmentalism of her earlier years, now, she shared with me briefly, she was no longer dogged by cynicism and judgement of others. Her energy had been freed to fully dedicate her life-force to enabling regenerative futures in her local community while working with corporates, non-profits, local authorities, and community leaders in unison. I could see tears well up in her eyes as we both recalled that circle many years ago.

Respect is an unassuming word with immense potency.

Spontaneity

To take a step out of certainty into the space of uncertain possibility is to embrace spontaneity. To wonder, to be curious, to be in radical astonishment of being alive. Spontaneity is a welcoming of naked authenticity in the moment, a sense of enjoying life as it is, and enjoying ourselves for who we truly are. To act on one's own accord, through deep accordance with life, freed from acculturation and egotism. This is an authentic act of our true nature, in the moment and freed from social conditioning, ego hijacks, imposter syndromes, victim mentality, and status quo thinking.

Activating our super-nature invokes this spontaneity, an exploratory inquisitive curiosity that sparks creativity. This spontaneous curiosity is not born out of a need to acquire knowledge. It's an opening into the life-force of what wants to emerge, exploring with an open-heart beyond acquisition. In fact, the need to know can often lead us down the ego-path of a quest for facts and things to ascertain. This need for certainty stymes our spontaneity and creativity. As when we start to think we know, it prevents our open stance so important for insight. The capacity to be receptive to the ever-becoming nature of life is a relaxing of certainty and control.

Some of the esoteric traditions of the West have used the term 'kenosis' which is the practice of surrendering to life through an opening of the heart. This enables an unguarded vulnerable spontaneity which provides for our ability to truly sense, intuit, and know what is emerging in the process of becoming. This is the exact opposite of Mechanistic Materialism's quest for certainty through control-manage dynamics that undermine the ability to know the truth in an embodied way.

Spontaneity is a humble, curious reverence for life as it really is, ever-unfolding, never the same. This is a playful, childlike approach. Not at all naïve but fresh, alive, and ready for adventure—freed from restriction. It's an ability to hold space, not in some kind of forced or constrained 'held' way, where we need to impose patience on to our ego-will, but in an open-willed, connected, unexpectant aliveness.

The presencing-pause of this spontaneity allows what wants to emerge to flow unencumbered by our expectations, judgements, and critiques. It's a radically creative act, a quality of inner-outer attentiveness that creates a reverberation of the inner with the outer, the unmanifest with the manifest, a tantric yin-yang energized harmony. It aids the birthing of our becoming and creates the soil conditions for us to move readily from the insight born from stillness to an out-of-the-box, open-minded, free-willed, respectful, and humble dance with life.

Just like we find a spontaneity and freshness in ourselves when we fall in love with another, when we fall in love with life, this spontaneity becomes a soil condition that fertilizes our process of becoming in service of life.

Gratitude

It's beneficial to cultivate 'an attitude of gratitude' by reflecting on everything we ought to be grateful for in our lives. For instance, a regular ritual of listing out all the things one is grateful for—ranging from the sunlight, soil, food, and water through to the trappings of modern life and our friends and family. Yet gratitude can reside at the ego level as a scanning of our outer-nature, leaving our connection to inner-nature untouched.

What we are working with here is an attitude of gratitude that emanates from the inside out. By understanding how the inner-outer nature of reality works, we find an immense gratitude for life as an exquisite learning experience of the meaning-making dharmic journey of our soul craft. It's when we are engrossed in the soul craft that we find our flow and a feeling of abundance. We can still have the very real and pressing needs of material survival and financial security, yet there is a knowing that in flowing on this dharmic path we can trust in life and feel able to express gratitude for what arises on the path. This soul-gratitude lightens our tread, eases our load, and infuses our enthusiasm, so our soul-service becomes an act of celebration in, and for, life.

There is an old expression, 'when the student is ready the right teacher appears.' When we embrace a more synchronistic awareness of life by working with the three esoteric aspects of Nature's Wisdom, we notice on our soul craft journey that 'when the leader is ready the right Work appears.' Whether its clients we work with, communities we serve, studies we engage with, people we help when cultivating one's soul-service, often the very projects and clients that turn up for us are revealing the very aspects of our soul craft we are ready to progress. Our process of becoming matches the path's unfolding.

This comes with an immense gratitude for the Mystery of Life. We let go of the distracting nagging voices of judgement, cynicism and fear, and step more fully into an appreciation for life. This gratitude shows that everything in our lives is in divine order right now. Then, the soil of our soul is nourished from the inside out by this gratitude for life easing our flowing dance into mastery.

Listening

The most powerful way for us to connect with the essence of another person and with nature around us is to listen outwardly, and the most powerful way to connect to our own essence is to listen inwardly. Cultivating a practice of deep inner-outer listening is such a powerful part of regenerative leadership. I call this inner-outer deep listening 'regenerative listening', and it's a sacred art which enriches our relationality with self-other-world, aiding right relation.

Over the twenty-five or more years I've been advising businesses and their leaders through various transformations, I've witnessed time and again the power of regenerative listening. When I am asked to name THE one most important thing a leader can learn on the regenerative journey, I always respond that without doubt it's the capacity to listen, and listen deep. One cannot truly lead, in a regenerative way, without cultivating this soil condition of 'regenerative listening.' This might be the last of all the capacities I've shared in this book, but it's the most important by a long shot. And it's super simple (though not necessarily easy).

> "Listening moves us closer, it helps us become more whole, more healthy, more holy."
>
> –Margaret Wheatley

At the individual level, regenerative listening starts with the capacity to be still, and go into our center-point of stillness from which Nature's Wisdom enters. By becoming more able to enter stillness amid everyday life, we welcome in sacredness. As we've already discussed, this is an act of love and comes with a deep receptivity and a responsive reciprocity. It's a simultaneous expanding and deepening of our awareness as we slow down the mind and tune into the wholeness of life. From a narrowed achiever focus we open into a holistic spaciousness more available for spontaneity and dance.

Because of the dominance of the achiever leader, most business school courses and most leadership coaching and training are currently dedicated to how one is seen, comes across, presents, and communicates, with precious little in comparison on how to listen more deeply to self, to others, and to life. We are largely outwardly focused in communicating when in the achiever mode, projecting ourselves out there to achieve an acceptance from our audience, the 'other'. Learning to listen is the way into connection, compassion, respect, and flow. Through regenerative listening we connect with the 'other' at a heart and soul level.

We offer others, life, and also ourselves a great gift when we listen regeneratively, as we savor the moment, what's said and not said, the gestalt or holistic relationality between oneself and the other, and even the super-sensory Field. We become fully present to all of what this inner-outer unfolding relationality affords us, gifting this presence to the other through our deep listening. The other will sense this quality of regenerative listening, and consciously or unconsciously they will ease a little and drop their judging ego-guard and open, as their bodymind will feel the undefended, heartfelt connection of our listening. We are conduits for Nature's Wisdom, in service of life, when we are listening to each other.

Each conversation becomes an opportunity for practicing, and also a gift to others, therefore a form of abundance, gratitude, and flow. As we give, so we receive. The more we practice regenerative listening, the better at it we become. It's like a muscle when going to the gym. The bodymind can become an exquisite listener, holding space for grace and wisdom to flow through our right relation. As we practice, we might notice our inner ears subtly shift, or our heart region expands. And when we speak from this place, the voice might shift in its tone or timbre, and the space between self and other may subtly shift in its intimacy yet spaciousness. Inner-outer nature start to come closer, and the world feels more vivid, more here, more available. Insight comes in and is planted within the fecund soil of the soul, nurtured by our regenerative listening.

Interestingly the six letters of 'listen' are the same as 'silent.' We must silence the achiever mind to truly listen.

And we do not need to be outwardly still to be inwardly still, as in we do not need to sit opposite someone when regeneratively listening. We can listen in this inner-outer way while walking, for instance. In fact, I have found coaching while walking in nature a great way to engage in regenerative listening. As we practice regenerative listening more and more, we begin to realize that life is the meditation, and we are always immersed in stillness if we so choose to listen.

The Master Key

Taken together, the chapters in Part 3 of this book—the nine-staged inner journey, the foundation of the four Ds, the dynamism of the five Es, the four soul virtues, and the five soil conditions—all form a masterful practice that unlocks the way we walk our path through the death-rebirth journey. Think of this as your master key, the one that unlocks all doorways on the labyrinth journey ahead.

THE MASTER KEY

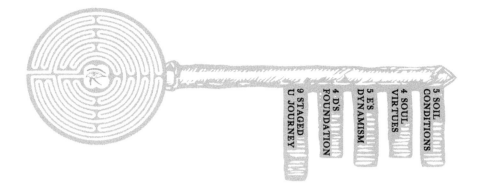

The primacy here is not the content. It's not the 'what.' It's the 'way.' Life is the developmental learning that hones our unique yet unifying Way of Nature. No book chapter, study course, or developmental model can fully explain this unfolding path for us. We must walk our own path, learning with each step, for it's in walking this path that we cultivate trust in life, the capacity to sense truth as a lived dynamic, and a deep reverence for inner-outer nature.

> "The arbiter of truth is life itself."
>
> —Henryk Skolimowski

Epilogue
Mastering the Art of Regenerative Living & Leading

Shakespeare's Hamlet explores this vital question, a question we might pose to ourselves:

"To be, or not to be?"

That *is* the question of the day. *Not to be* is to live inauthentically, to follow the socially conditioned path. *To be*, is to enter one's own energy field and be animated by the wisdom of life, which involves overcoming the egocentric self-as-separate and awakening the heart and soul within. Though a more relevant question for our day and age might be, "To become, or not to become…" as the regenerator journey is a never-ending unfolding process of becoming who we truly are.

The difference between becoming or not becoming is determined by our capacity for wisdom each and every day. *How do we embrace the learnings? How do we hold the tensions? How do we catch our fall? How do we work with grace, grit, and strife, with courage, creativity, and compassion?* As we journey, it dawns on us that our response to these questions depends on another question, or rather a lived inquiry: *How unconditional is our trust in life?* The response determines how much of life we let into our process of becoming, and how much wisdom we have available to work with.

Such an unconditional approach to life necessitates an embrace of death. We come to perceive life as a continual act of dying, and the process of becoming a regenerative leader as a constant shedding. We welcome a never-ending surrendering into life. This is what the symbol of the crucifix inspires. It is not the outer, historic act of punishment, but the inner psychospiritual power unleashed through dying before you die.

We endure this crucifying life experience through love: love of nature with its ever changing yet forever repeating sunrises and seasons; love of our human kith and kin, as we are all brothers and sisters in this life drama, where even our perceived enemies are instruments of destiny. To love thy neighbor as thy self no longer becomes a trite moral statement but an embodied experience found through embracing the ground of all being and sensing the eternal amidst the temporal, the unity within diversity. The love of life then flowers within. We learn to integrate suppressed aspects of our own nature and become compassionate with our own selves by listening deep inside. We learn to live into our soul sovereignty and authenticity, rather than be distracted or swayed by the judgements and views of others. The love of life then flowers within.

Mastery starts with the courage to live one's own life instead of imitating others. As the old saying goes, "You can't wear another's hat." A coach or guide can help cultivate this mastery by observing, from outside of the field of one's own death-rebirth process, the unique yet universal themes and motifs playing out during one's life-changing regenerative journey.

One aspect I love most about my own soul craft of guiding leaders and practitioners through the regenerative journey, is when a coaching client experiences 'Aha!' moments. Time and again, I've observed what lies behind these 'Aha!' moments. They are not just an intellectual comprehension—a lightbulb moment happening in the head—but each 'Aha!' is an embodied experience, a subtle shift felt inside the bodymind. Each a mini release of somatic energy, the sense of which is contained in muscle memory for good and available to be recalled in any instant amid the heat of challenging times ahead.

It's easy enough to read pages in a book, even to test out tools, but to enliven the core themes of Nature's Wisdom into the daily experience of living and leading is not that easy, and not for the faint hearted. It involves letting go of much of what we thought we needed to succeed, peeling back the onion layers of self-protection, insecurity, and over-achievement to find our center, listen to our soul, and let in spirit. The very meaning of life deepens, and we're no longer ensnared in social mores and ego-desires. We are now freed, rooted in our true identity and grounded in nature's rhythms.

It does not matter if we serve life in some socially perceived 'minor' way (like cleaning toilets) or in some socially perceived 'major' way (like leading an organization with thousands of employees), we are engaged in the field of life, and our interactions have repercussions. Our status, role or leadership position is *not* important. The way we do what we do *is*. The enthusiasm, compassion, and wisdom that flows through us as we relate to our own nature, to others, and to the world around us, is what heralds the energy of regeneration. As we walk the path, the Wasteland of imbalanced achiever-focus turns into the Holy Grail of real life lived from the heart.

We don't have to wait for society to transform. Instead, we can unlock the wellspring inside to connect to the wisdom in life. By enduring a death-rebirth process, we descend into the ground of our own being, which opens and reorientates us into Nature's Wisdom and readies us for our return to the field of society, within which we become an organic part of the evolution of human consciousness. We, as individuals, are aiding society's regeneration process of becoming future-fit. Enduring the death-rebirth journey awakens us to the inner-outer nature dynamics inherent in life, which leads to ego maturation and permeation. We become more sensitized to, and able to deal with, the subtle proportions and resonances of the holographic grammar of life. As we activate our super-nature, self- and-systemic awareness becomes a deeper order of magnitude. This is the very death-rebirth journey that shows us how to become more intimate with the immanent and transparent to the transcendent nature of life. We develop a sensitized way of working in right relation with inner and outer worlds and open the bodymind to the energy and wisdom that inform our ability to sense signs and synchronicities and gain intuitions and insights that illuminate the path ahead.

No one can walk the path for us, and no number of self-help tools, leadership courses, or weekend retreats can shortcut it. Though an experienced coach (think sherpa guide) can offer advice about when to rest or push on, when to ignore or listen to others, when to drop one's guard or discern with due diligence, when to read into signs looming ahead or be extra vigilant to what's right before us. All has proven to be very helpful, especially when the journey involves significant life-changing commitments with repercussions for not just our own selves but those around us and the ones we seek to serve, but you are the only one who can walk your soul path.

To endure death-rebirth and realize one's essence and craft is not the end but the beginning. And as we begin, we realize that the transmutation of the whole social order is not desirable but inevitable. The forces of egotism, control, fear, and separation are laid bare. Like the emperor with no clothes, the crowd already knows. The secret's out. There's no turning back from truth. The reform to regeneration is already in motion, rooted in the redemption of the sacred. Life is the constant reminder and learning laboratory of our process of becoming, as we cultivate the embodied sense of the electrifying effect of our lives when we're in right relation.

In today's dominant worldview of Mechanistic Materialism, the individual and collective capacities of regenerative leadership consciousness have scarcely been tapped. Although we are living in a revolutionary moment with profound consequences for humanity and all life on Earth, the main energies and powers that enable the revolution to unfold at scale have yet to appear over the horizon. It's like we're at a party, where many people have gathered, but the DJ and the guests of honor have yet to arrive.

The forces that are going to shift the dial on the revolution toward regeneration lie latent in the inner world where soul, spirit and wisdom reside. Due to the sheer dominance of Mechanistic Materialism today, some hundred years after the profound scientific discoveries of quantum reality from numerous first-rate mainstream scientists, the power residing within the inner dimension has yet to animate the party. Perhaps until now the evolution of human consciousness has not been ripe enough and the human's bodymind instrument has not been strong enough, to hold the spirit energy needed to shift achiever into regenerator. But now, we are ready for the party to really rock. We've just found our dancing shoes and the courage to step into the light of the dancefloor.

The reality is, the actualization of a new worldview and socio-economic system can't form solely from the intellectual, rational abstraction of the current crises. All a reductive scientific analysis of our current state can do is aid our acceptance of the need for a new way. In itself, analyzing and rationalizing does little to energize the revolutionary metamorphosis humanity needs. It may gather us at the threshold—invite us to show-up for the party—but does not lead us through the threshold—enliven us to dance the night away.

The revolution starts in our hearts and souls, not in our heads. It starts with how we perceive and attend to life. Do we see nature as simply 'out there', an ensemble of things, a utilitarian set of resources, or clever design forms and patterns we can copy for human-centric design challenges? Or do we see nature as steeped in consciousness, animated by resonances and rhythms of right relation that invite us to access a wisdom which informs our living, leading, organizing, designing and implementing of solutions that serve life?

In looking to the ancients, we can see that embedded in our psyche is an inherent understanding of Nature's Wisdom, a wisdom that is not removed from life. The very act of living is a sacred undertaking of working with this wisdom. For our ancestors, daily life was not separate from the sacred but a ceremonial way in which we attuned our bodymind instrument in right relation with the resonances of nature, Earth, and cosmos. And now, modern day findings are aiding this revival of ancient knowledge, helping usher in the birthing of the new worldview of Quantum Complexity that appreciates consciousness and energy as integral to humanity, nature, Earth, and cosmos. We are all here to love wisdom and to love life, fully. While this might sound philosophical, its radically practical.

Rebirthing into Nature's Wisdom

The journey, practices, and themes covered in this book aim to help us cross the threshold into a deeper way of experiencing life that is at once ancient yet cutting edge. For instance, a dedicated engagement in the three levels of Living Systems Awareness will activate an individual and collective metamorphosis. To learn from outer-nature's forms, patterns, processes, and designs (Level 1), to embody a participatory systemic-awareness of inner-outer nature dynamics of the living-organization (Level 2), and open the bodymind's ego-heart-soul to the subtle energies of inner-nature (Level 3) through various practices and methods. This threshold crossing is what the next few years ahead invites, to not only intellectually understand how nature works, but to immerse ourselves in a rebirth into Nature's Wisdom by proficiently integrating all three levels of Living Systems Awareness. With an integrated practice, we cross the threshold and undergo a lasting up-stretch in our leadership developmental psychology, thus expanding our meaning-making and strengthening our soul-connection. As well as increased resilience and productivity, we become more purposeful, centered, and authentic. We upgrade our creativity, empathy, resilience, and agility. The meaning of life comes alive in us as we learn to see inner-outer nature not *with* but *through* the eye. Through this soulful activation of our super-nature, we become more future-fit and regenerative for ourselves, those around us, and the organizations we serve.

All this talk of consciousness, psychology, wisdom, and spirituality might well distract us from the fact that any form of regenerative living and leading without a healthy dose of celebration, joy, and playfulness is doomed from the get-go. As Jesus said when he got up from the Last Supper, before entering the Garden, "Let's dance!" Soon enough we notice the radiance in everything and feel compassion for all, the energy pours in, and the party gets underway.

Let's now remind ourselves of some of the tools we have at the ready as we rev up the revolution:

- **DEE Regenerative Business Culture** – Developmental, Emergent, Evolutionary

- **Regenerative Leadership Dynamics** – Self-awareness & Systemic-awareness
- **Nature's Wisdom** – Three Exoteric aspects (Stillness & Movement, Tensions, Relational Interconnectedness) & Three Esoteric aspects (Immanent-Transcendent, Inner-Outer, As above so below)
- **Flow of Life** – Divergence, Convergence, Emergence
- **Rhythm of Life** – Figure-of-eight rhythm of spring-summer-autumn-winter
- **Logic of Life** – Seven Life Principles of Life-Affirming, Ever-changing & Responsive, Relational & Collaborative, Synergistic & Diverse, Cyclical & Rhythmical, Flows of Energy & Matter, Living Systems Field
- **Music of Life** – the harmonic and resonant nature of right relation as an underlying grammar for regenerative living
- **Power of Life** – Dinergic tensions powered by limits, framed: mythically as Trinity in Unity, or Three-in-One; metaphysically as Agape, Eros, Philia; and practically as receptive, responsive, reciprocity
- **Three Lenses** – Lens 1 (voice in the head), Lens 2 (deeper nature), Lens 3 (the Field)
- **Three Levels of Living Systems Awareness** – learning from nature (outer-nature), participating within nature (inner-outer nature), attuning with Nature's Wisdom (inner-nature)
- **The Master Key** – The three-phase nine-stage inner journey of Wintering, Alchemizing, Serving; four D foundational pillars – Dedication, Discernment, Discipline, Devotion; five E dynamics of the process of becoming – Essence, Energy, Emergence, Evolutionary, Enthusiasm; four soul virtues – Balance, Patience, Courage, Purposefulness; five soil conditions – Dance, Respect, Spontaneity, Gratitude, Listening

All of this taken together provides an expertly packed 'backpack' for the regenerative journey ahead. And alongside these frames and processes, we've also got a host of methods and practices available to us, many of which are found in the Appendix and on my *website*. Another great many are mentioned throughout the book, such as bodymind coherence, activating our super-nature, the seven levels of leadership consciousness (with specific focus on orange-green achiever and teal-turquoise regenerator), Welcoming in the Twilight Zone, the Creative Imagination Process, deep listening, dialogue, Systemic Enablers, organizational acupuncture, micro-meso-macro letting go. Each one aids our becoming. As we wake up and fall in love with the Earth, we become more intimate with the immanent and more transparent with the transcendent.

> "There's a revolution that needs to happen and it starts from inside each one of us. We need to wake up and fall in love with the Earth. Our personal and collective happiness and survival depends on it."
>
> –Thich Nhat Hanh

The next few years ahead are vital for the trajectory of humanity. Do we continue down the pathway of technospheric distraction, triggering tipping points left, right and center, or do we wake up to the rapture of reality and step into what it truly means to be human? Over the next few years, the leaders, and practitioners serious about the future of their organizations, their children, and life on Earth must immerse themselves into the inner meaning of life to truly fall in love, each and every day.

As we enter arduous times ahead, it's worth remembering that forgiveness creates space for compassion. Society today is caught up in egotism, and the egoic narratives of judgement reign supreme. It's all too easy to project, polarize, blame, point the finger, and create enemies amongst us. Then, it's war rather than compassion we activate, violation rather than right relation. By finding stillness within, we settle the ego's judgmental nature. It's from the still water on the lake that we see the eternal reflection in life, and this sense of the eternal invites in empathy and compassion. Life is the learning lab for our self-noticing. When are we in an imbalanced ego-consciousness, of labelling, fragmenting, polarizing, blaming, fearing, and desiring? And when can we cultivate the courage to listen, connect, hold space, and see tensions of difference as crucibles for creativity?

As the current worldview dies, the true extent of the widespread exploitative power-control dynamics inherent in the current system will become more blatant. It's only natural to feel resentment and frustration. But the dying of an old way can also allow for hospicing and healing. Creating the right space and energy for the new to emerge is of a different order of being than blame, vengeance, and retribution. For the doorway through which inexhaustible energies of regenerative potential pour into us is found through love, compassion, and wisdom.

A 400-year-old mindset is dying and a new one is struggling to birth, and we find ourselves participating in a great leap of human spirit into which we enter the dance of life by becoming conscious of what's invisible to the eye.

The good news is, the primary undertaking for humanity's revolution in consciousness has nothing to do with AI, business innovation, social ethics, or government politics but is about learning to find accord with Nature's Wisdom. Then—from this rooted place of right relation within the rhizome—we can call upon technologies, innovations, ethics, and political systems in ways that genuinely serve all life.

Entering this revolution is exactly what the soul yearns for, to ride the wave of Mystery, to be in touch with both the here-and-now and the eternal experience of life's true rapture. This revolution is nothing other than emancipation, our individuality dancing with the All, a return home to our soul's birthright. Welcome to the Dance of Life.

Appendix

Compendium of Practices and Further Notes

Receptive Responsive Reciprocity

Experiential practices are powerful due to what they evoke in us, hence the importance of dedicated practices, well facilitated workshops and interventions, and clearly there is only so much that words in a book can convey.

With that caveat, here is a mini-exploration aimed at helping convey the different dynamics we are learning to become more conscious of cultivating in our regenerative living and leading: **receptivity** – an opening up to what is arising within and all around us; a tuning in to, or sensing in to, what is emerging both within and beyond ourselves; **responsiveness** – cultivating our ability to sense and respond authentically to what we are being receptive to; **reciprocity** – upon responding to something or someone in an authentic open-hearted way, both parties are enriched in some way, say though a dinergic tension which manifests mutual learning.

Receptivity comes about through a mindful active-relaxation, a relief and release, an opening up and letting go, so that we can simply 'be' in this moment, attentive to what 'is' without trying to analyze; just feeling, perceiving, being, without thought judgements. By simply opening our awareness up to the here-and-now we provide an invitation for our awareness to transcend the self-imaging, self-justifying ego, even if for the briefest of moments.

There are tried-and-tested techniques to help develop this receptivity such as Mindfulness, Vipassana, Yoga Nidra, Heart Entrainment, and Transcendental Meditation, and in the pages ahead, some easy to practice techniques suitable for the busy business environment are offered. More advanced practices are reserved for bespoke coaching journeys or immersions where various practices can be aligned with one's own inner journey.

> "Meditation is the tool for stepping away from the ego. It is returning to the ground of being from which existence springs. It is the wave remembering that it is not different from the ocean."
>
> –Rashid Maxwell

The good news is that cultivating receptivity is a returning to our natural awareness; it is a remembering of who we truly are; a beginning of walking the path of knowing thy self. The more we practice and develop this, the more our capacity and ability to tap into it grows. We learn to sense how it feels within us when we tap into this authentic, heartfelt-soulful connection. The more we cultivate this awareness, the more we learn to trust its wisdom, in turn the more we become fearless within the moment and courageous in our response.

Responsiveness is our ability to sense and then respond to 'what is' in a soulful way. As we allow for our receptivity to deepen with practice and trust, our ability to relate authentically, empathically, and creatively with others heightens. Receptivity provides the foundation for our heightened responsiveness.

While contemplative practices such as meditation and yoga help develop our receptivity, we need to be able to sustain this receptive-responsiveness amid our busy work schedules. Finding the right level of receptive-responsiveness for the situation we are in requires continual attunement of our ways of knowing: sensing with our guts and hearts, cognizing with our heads, intuiting with our souls. Some situations may require a more rational, analytical, and definitive response while others a more heartfelt empathic listening and sharing, for instance.

A useful metaphor here is of learning to swim (or ride a bike). As we gain confidence in our ability to swim, so we allow ourselves to let go of the side for longer and longer periods, freeing ourselves to immerse fully, unimpaired in the art of swimming. It is not easy to let go of old ways so deeply conditioned in our conscious and unconscious psyche and it requires courage and determination. If at first, we don't succeed, try, and try again. Soon, like riding a bike or swimming, we become proficient enough in the 'new way' that it starts to become instinctual and our overactive ego-consciousness with its anxiety eases its incessant control-based reactions and routines. Our way of attending becomes less encumbered by our 'old way' and our creative potential flows freer. We then begin to deeply sense the co-creative, unfolding, and emergent venture of life. Yes, it is useful to have plans and clear ideas of where we are going and what we are doing, yet this also needs to be balanced with an openness and adaptability to what emerges.

Reciprocity is the way we interrelate with our ever-changing environment. Upon being responsive to what is emerging, we then engage in relationship with the situation empathically and authentically, in a fully-embodied, coherent way, allowing a reciprocating dynamic to unfold. All living systems, including human ones, thrive through reciprocity. Reciprocity is the life-blood that nourishes us; whether it's the small interactions of a smile and supporting comment, or a warm 'hello' and 'thank you', or detailed constructive feedback after a demanding project, each interrelation can be undertaken with varying degrees of heartfelt integrity or cold, judgmental aloofness or defensiveness. The 'way' we interrelate affects the paths that open up or close down from that interrelation.

As the former CEO of Hanover Insurance Bill O'Brien noted, "The success of the intervention depends upon the interior state of the intervener." How open, authentic, and heart-felt we are with our reciprocity will determine the level of flow we experience, and vice versa. The more we are in our soul-flow the more our interrelations will be undertaken in a synchronistic soulful way, and the more we will reap the benefits of what we sow. Yes, there will always be the really difficult situations that seem to be undermining us or pushing our buttons, where our ego is in heightened alert to defend 'self' against 'other'– again this is a useful learning experience in which to practice remaining true to our deeper ways of knowing, sensing and responding without reacting overly defensively or from our base emotions of blame, anger, jealousy, fear, frustration, or resentment.

If we start to try to control or dominate the flow of exchange during a conversation or emerging situation, we will impede the flow and undermine the greatness of what could have been possible. Aligning our pulses and rhythms with the emerging field of our teams and stakeholders is the artful adventure of life. We learn as we go and mistakes are inevitable, providing us the opportunities to learn and improve.

Embodied Practice of Receptive Responsive Reciprocity: To begin with, two people pair up as partners, a short distance apart with legs astride and touching hands. One of us chooses to be assertive 'leader' and the other yielding 'follower'. At first with a rocking to and fro linear motion, then perhaps transforming into a circular motion, the two of us move together. A rhythm develops, as with a swinging pendulum, but the movement is dependent on the leader's self-centered awareness and associated effort, regardless of what the follower may be experiencing. So, the movement could not really be called a 'dance' in the fullest sense, in which each is equally and vitally involved in partnership. The follower might as well not be there. If the leader is tired, the movement will be tired. If the leader is full of energy, the movement will be energetic, but creatively restricted and fatiguing. If at some stage, however, the leader becomes sensitive to the movement of the follower and attunes to this to 'follow the follower', the result is a mutual effortlessness where each is alive within the influence of the other. Both of cocreate without a predefined trajectory and so improvise in a continually innovative way.

To flow in such an open, mutually inclusive way requires an attuning of our bodymind awareness both to each other and to the co-evolving movement. Correspondingly, the dance itself responds to our ever-changing receptive-responsive dynamic. If, for example, while we are dancing co-creatively—with neither trying to lead and both following the communing flow—one partner becomes more assertive, the other may respond either by becoming more yielding or by becoming more resistive. The dance either loses its co-creative fluidity or it becomes tense and jerky. By the same token, if both partners remain passive, the dance won't happen at all. Here, we can sense how reciprocity emerges from a depth of receptive-responsiveness within each partner, and yet the reciprocity emerges beyond either of the two partners, within the dance itself, a synergistic dynamic which both of us flow within.

Another simple yet powerful way of illustrating co-creative reciprocity in groups is when people have to cocreate something without talking to each other. Something we tried once, with a group of workshop participants, was to gather people into groups of four or five and ask them to open their arms and hands out, palms up, so their fingers are all touching in a circle. Then a heavy lump of clay is placed in the middle of the circle of hands of each group, so everyone in each group is co-participating in holding the clay together. Then they are requested to begin molding the block of fresh clay together in silence, while having to also stand up and hold the heavy block between them. As improvisational molding unfolds, each participant adds their own creativity without explicitly knowing what the others have in mind. There is no overarching plan or predefined destination, and yet the participants have a lot of fun creating a group exhibit they are proud of due to a shared sense of inclusive involvement and teamwork. A deep bonding amongst the group forms without words being spoken. This can be a useful team-building exercise.

Pairs or Team Mindful Reflection Practice

Here is a simple exercise in becoming mindful of how we are experiencing the moment. We ask colleagues, team members, or workshop participants to get into pairs. When in our pairs, we are going to share in a non-judgmental way 'what' we are attending to within the moment. For the first three minutes we are going to share back and forth with our partner what is instantly coming up for us, starting each sentence with *Now I am aware of...* So, we simply share what we are aware of in that moment, with no long pauses between sharing so that it is spontaneous without us overly thinking about what we are going to say. One person shares one sentence, and then the other shares one sentence, going back and forth until the three minutes are up.

Then, during the next three minutes we are going to share in our pairs starting each sentence with *What I am NOT aware of is...* We instantaneously recall situations, thoughts, sensations, people, places, and such like, that we were not immediately noticing but are now residing on the edge of our awareness, on the fringe of our consciousness. Again, we do not leave long pauses between our sharing so we are spontaneous while recalling things on the periphery of our awareness.

Finally, for the next three minutes, we share starting each sentence with *I choose to be aware of...*sharing what we choose to be aware of in this moment, again with no long pauses as we take it in turns, back and forth in our pairs sharing a sentence at a time.

This simple yet revealing exercise gives us first-hand experience of the conscious choice we have over what we are attending to and how we are able to transform our stream of thinking. If the pairs are part of a larger team or workshop group, the pairs may wish to feedback to the group as a whole about their findings, feelings, and learnings.

Mindfulness Meditation Practice

The state of mindfulness is an active relaxed receptivity and responsiveness, where we are open to life, in clear awareness, and so can sense and respond to the vividness and ever-changing nature of our life experience. We have more energy and consciousness available to us when we've quietened the grasping ego-need to judge, critique, and polarize our experience into right or wrong, pleasant or unpleasant. We become more accepting of life as it is, more available to a broader range of sensations and responses of the bodymind.

Mindfulness has roots in many of the world's wisdom traditions, and one such tradition is Buddhism where the Pali word 'sati' means 'clear awareness.' This clear awareness frees the mind from distraction and suffering. The thought-forms of Lens 1's voice in the head pull us out of the present moment and lure us into analysis about past and future. This distraction takes us out of the clear awareness of presencing, and instead our awareness is caught up in an egoic sense of self-as-separate (dominant ego-consciousness) usually with high-beta brainwave patterns associated with fight-flight-freeze.

Mindfulness is not a passive state. While relaxation aids mindfulness, it requires an alertness to notice our thoughts and ease our attention out of being caught up in the voice in the head.

The more we practice mindfulness the more we cultivate our capacity for an expansive nonjudgmental awareness of presencing. With this quality of intentional attentiveness, we are fully immersed in the moment and have more life-force energy available to be receptive and responsive to what's arising in our midst. Less conscious energy is diverted into the voice in the head, and more is available for an intimacy of the immediate phenomenological experience—whether it be noticing the sunlight coming through the window or listening to a colleague intently. We can sense the expansive spaciousness and stillness behind the ever-changing flux of life. This ability to sense stillness within the movement of life aids our intimacy with the immanent and transparency with the transcendent nature of life. It's a way into Nature's Wisdom.

This provides for a greater sense of meaning, equanimity, humility, and freedom to emerge in one's life experience. Being less disturbed by the voice in the head's incessant worry, fear, and grasping desire, we are more available to sense-respond to life with an open loving stance of ego-heart-soul consciousness working together in adapting and learning with life, rather than a control-manage reactive stance founded in the fear-desire dynamic of ego-consciousness.

Here is a six-step mindful meditation guide. Allow at least fifteen minutes for this exercise.

Step 1: Sit comfortably in a chair, on a meditation cushion, or outside on the ground. Imagine a cord gently pulling upward from the crown of your head, like a puppet string, so your spine eases upward slightly as you straighten the back in a relaxed open way. No need to force anything or overstretch. Feel at ease with the back relaxed yet erect and shoulders back to open the chest slightly in a way that feels comfortable.

Step 2: Close your eyes and start to notice your breathing. We tend to breathe from the chest, usually. See if you can breathe deeply from the belly, noticing the sensation of the belly expanding with each inbreath and relaxing with each outbreath. Inbreath and outbreath through the nose and notice the sensation of the breath flowing in and out through the nostrils. No need to purposefully count your in or out breaths.

As an aside – there is another practice in this Appendix that revolves around counting your rhythmic breathing, but here we are only noticing the sensation of deepening our belly breathing without any counting. Breathe as naturally and spontaneously as you can while expanding the belly with each inbreath.

Step 3: Notice somatic sensations, by bringing awareness inward into how the body feels, the sensations of sitting and breathing. Notice if there is tightness in the body anywhere. Engage in a gentle inward inquiry. *Where feels relaxed or tense, where feels comfortable or uncomfortable?* No need to judge any sensations as good or not good. Only notice the sensations and how they feel, while also maintaining awareness of deep belly breathing.

As an aside – there is a separate practice below here in this Appendix for a more detailed body scan, but here we are just spending a few moments noticing how the body feels which aids a deepening of inward awareness.

Step 4: Notice thoughts, by observing how easy it is to get caught up in the voice in the head. Whether it be a thought about something you've just remembered you need to do or a thought about a noise or activity outside that you hear, no matter what the thoughts are, just notice them coming into the mind.

Step 5: Notice the capacity to let go of thoughts. Let's use the metaphor of cars going along the pavement in front of us. Each thought is like a car passing us by. We can get into any of the cars passing by and then travel along on a journey inside the car, symbolizing the narrative of a certain thought-form generated by the voice in the head. We might end up along the journey somewhere, now thinking about something completely different that we've become engrossed in, as the thoughtform has taken us on a wild goose chase of different memories, worries, and feelings, as we travel in the car. We can notice how easy it is to succumb to the invitation to get into a car and be whisked along with the thought-form narrative. When we notice our engrossment in a thought, we can get out of the car, and move back to the pavement of witnessing thoughts arising and passing us by. Before we know it, we are unwittingly entering into a new car, a new thoughtform takes us on a ride with emotions, criticisms, judgements, fears about past or future, taking us out of the presencing of now. Simply noticing this tendency of the voice in the head is all we have to do. Notice when we are caught up in thinking and then let go by bringing ourselves back to sitting, breathing, being here now, freed from the thought and associated feelings of worry and attachment.

Step 6: Building the muscle of mindfulness, by noticing the tendency of the voice in the head, noticing the capacity to step out of each thoughtform, and the ability to witness thoughts pass by without getting caught up in them. By realizing that we have the capacity in our consciousness to release ourselves from our own thoughts, we can start to practice the act of noticing and letting go. Noticing and letting go are what build the muscle of intentional attentiveness inside our own mind. This is the way into mindfulness. The more we practice the better we become at it.

There's a growing body of scientific evidence showing the positive effects mindfulness has on our neuroanatomy. The more we are able to notice and let go of thoughts, the more we can be conscious of easing out of the dominant achiever mind and into the Quest-orientation of achiever-awakened mind.

Conscious Breathing Practice

The simple act of being conscious of our breathing can bring about a profound shift within us, as it allows for coherence of our head, heart, and gut.

It does not matter if we are standing in a queue, sitting at our desk, or sitting in a meeting, we can learn to practice conscious breathing wherever and whenever, doing it discretely if we do not wish to bring attention to ourselves while we are doing it. All we are practicing is counting in our heads while we breathe in and out and also learning to sense the feeling between the in-breath and out-breath. Here are two techniques: the four-fold breath and sine-wave breathing, both of which achieve the same thing.

The four-fold breath: First off, we get comfortable with breathing in deeply from our belly area whereupon we start to fill up our lower lungs first, and then as our lungs fill, we expand our upper chest area to ensure we fully fill the upper part of our lungs as well. To start with, we can sense it as two parts of our in-breath, and as we get more used to it, we can allow this to be one deep and continuous in-breath.

Secondly, we get comfortable with holding our breath after that deep in-breath, but not forcing or straining our lungs, rather feeling ourselves lifted upwards by our lungs and relaxing into the expansive feeling of the breath within us. Then, we get used to starting to release our breath calmly, and allow our lungs to fully empty on the out-breath. As we sense the end of our exhale, we relax into the feeling of being completely without breath and welcome this space of no breath with a pause before gradually beginning the inhale, again from the belly and then from the upper chest, as before.

Now we are comfortable with the flow of in-breath, gentle pause, out-breath, gentle pause and in-breath again to continue the breath cycle. We now bring in a 4-4-4-4 timing. We count internally to ourselves 1... 2... 3... 4... as we are breathing in, and then count 1... 2... 3... 4... as we pause before the exhale, and on a count of 1... 2... 3... 4... we breathe out fully. Finally, we pause at the end of the out-breath on empty with the fourth count of 1...2... 3... 4... The next inhale starts the next round of 4-4-4-4.

Let's try and do four or five of these cycles of controlled breathing. As we get more comfortable with this controlled breathing, we can do ten or so rounds, but four or five rounds is enough to start rebalancing the sympathetic and parasympathetic aspects of our autonomic nervous system, in turn helping cohere our three 'brains' – head, heart, gut – and overall bodymind sensory, cognitive, and nervous network. Try it out. It costs nothing and yet has immediate benefits on our awareness and outlook, as well as enhancing the connectivity and plasticity of our neural networks, while promoting a general feeling of wellbeing.

Sine-wave breathing: Another variation of conscious breathing, which is slightly different from the four-fold breath is sine-wave breathing. Here we visualize our breathing in and out as following a coherent sine wave pattern—smooth and evenly regulated crests and troughs of the wave. The movement from the trough of the wave rising up to the crest is our in-breath, with the top of the crest being a gradual shift of our in-breath moving into out-breath. Rather than holding the in-breath, we are going to be a little gentler in our movement of breath and sense ourselves slowly shifting from the in-breath into the out-breath with a slight pausing to elongate the shift from in to out. Vice versa as we go down the wave from the crest to trough with our out-breath, fully exhaling and then slightly pausing before our in-breath as we go up the wave cycle once more.

We are going to count to five on the in-breath and likewise on the out-breath. The more relaxed we are, the more we may find it easy and natural to elongate the breathing in and breathing out parts of the wave (perhaps counting to seven rather than five or counting slower). Let's say we breathe in through the count of five and then, when our lungs are full, we sense ourselves going over the crest of the wave in our mind's visualization. As we go over the crest, we gently move from the end of the in-breath into the beginning of the out-breath, which can happen over the count of 1... 2... 3... In our mind we are counting to three while holding our breath in, and on the three, we start to move into the out-breath and then begin the count from one through five again, just like with the in-breath. When we get to five our lungs are fully empty and we sense ourselves going through the trough of the wave as we go through the count of three again and then start the in-breath on the three, to start us off on our count of one to five again with the next wave. So to clarify, we are counting to five on the in-breath and out-breath and counting to three inbetween the out-breath and in-breath, though it is more of a 'relaxed pause' at the crest (in-breath into out-breath) and trough (out breath into in-breath) rather than a 'forced holding.'

The slight difference of this practice compared to the four-fold breath technique is that on the count of three, at the crest and trough, we subtly sense the shift from out-breath to in-breath and vice versa rather than purposefully holding no-breath at the end of the out-breath and in-breath cycle like we did in the four-fold exercise. In this sine-wave breathing, it is only on the count of '2' during our 1... 2... 3... crest and trough movement that there is no-breath movement at all. It is a more gentle and subtle shift which brings our awareness into the transition between in and out-breath.

To expand a little: when we are at the crest, after breathing in through the count of five, we then count one as the in-breath softly seizes, count two when at the crest when there is no breath in or out, and then count three as we gently minutely start the out-breath. It's a wave. And vice versa for the trough of out-breath going into in-breath.

Whether its four-fold, sine-wave, or another technique, the more we practice conscious breathing the more we get used to bringing conscious awareness to our breath. Then, the more we can apply this in the busyness of whatever we are doing. Regardless of what we are up to, we are always breathing and so can always be reminded of the inner sensation of this respiratory rhythm. We may start to get used to catching ourselves when we are stressed, irritable, impatient, or defensive and so practice a couple of conscious breaths to ourselves while noticing our tension easing. For instance, in the midst of a stressful yet important decision-making meeting we may apply this conscious breathing to enhance our head, heart, and gut coherence to activate the innate generative wisdom sources within us, rather than operating solely out of an ego-grasping, left hemispheric, firefighting, reactive, defensive mode.

Bodymind Coherence

This section has three parts which can be treated as three distinct practices though when done together stimulate bodymind coherence.

Part 1 – Heart Breathing: Whether you are sitting or standing, first off become aware of your breath. As you breathe in and out, feel your lungs move up and down and your stomach in and out. Feel the breath in your nostrils, cool as it comes in, warm as it goes out. Let's embark on a couple of rounds of conscious breathing to settle our awareness and bring our attention into our bodies while allowing grasping thoughts to ease as our awareness deepens. If the situation allows, we can place both hands over our heart area, one hand above the other, so one is covering the lower heart region and the other the upper heart region of our chest. If the situation does not allow, then we can simply imagine we are placing our hands over our heart area and bring our attention into our heart region as we do so.

Then, with our imagination, we breathe in and out through the heart area (as if breathing through where our hands are placed over our heart). Do a few rounds of this heart breathing, breathing in and out deeply and consciously as we focus on the heart area. This 'heart breathing' amplifies our heart-awareness while helping our bodymind cohere within us (improving our sympathetic and parasympathetic network alignment as well as our left and right hemisphere coherence). We may notice a subtle shift in how we feel, perceive, and attend to what is emerging around us. A simple yet profound shift in conscious from head to heart occurs within us no matter how fleeting.

Part 2 – Heart Entrainment: Let's find a space where we can be free to relax uninterrupted for four minutes. This could well be the office toilet or nearby park bench, unless our organization happens to have dedicated quiet spaces which, alas, is still the exception rather than the rule. But times they are a changing! When comfortable, we start with the practice of heart breathing (as above).

Then, when we feel ourselves breathing deeply and calmly in and out through our heart region, we use our imagination to recall a memory and feeling of something we really love. This might be, for instance, a memory of a pet we have or once had, a favorite song, a walk in nature, swimming in the warm sea on holiday, playing with our children, a special memory of a time in our lives when we felt really happy and alive—it does not matter what it is, only that it invokes a feeling of love within us. While still doing our heart breathing, we conjure up this feeling of love, and re-live this loving feeling with our imagination—really feeling it in our heart. Then, we allow this loving feeling to start to expand from our heart region throughout our body. Feel this loving feeling spread into our legs and arms, our toes, fingers, and spine, our neck and head, all over our body. Allow ourselves to indulge in this feeling, immerse ourselves in it, as we continue with our heart breathing. Feel every cell and sinew in our body being washed and cleansed with this feeling of love.

As we allow ourselves to relax into this feeling of love, we undertake an affirmation, which we can either verbalize softly out loud, or if the situation dictates, we can simply say it in our mind. *I am able to fully love myself.* Repeat this statement over and over at least five times to ourselves while we are still heart breathing and still feeling this expanded feeling of love. Next, relax and sit for a few moments or for as long as our situation allows us. Again, notice how our perception, awareness, and way of attending to 'what is' in our lives at this moment has subtly shifted compared to how we were before we undertook the exercise.

As we practice this exercise more and more, we can change our affirmation to be something related to an improvement we would like to see occur in our relations with our work environment. As long as the affirmation has a loving intent (for example, *I am able to lovingly accept my boss for who she is* or *I am able to compassionately listen and empathize with my team members*), it will help reprogram subconscious patterns of behavior within us, allowing us to cultivate heart-awareness within ourselves while helping alleviate our ego reactions to situations.

Part 3 – Head-heart-gut Coherence: Like with the heart entrainment exercise, we find a space where we can be free to relax uninterrupted for at least four minutes. We start with the heart breathing and then move on to the heart entrainment exercise, as above. Then, rather than doing the affirmation, we consciously bring our feeling of love into our head and notice what thoughts arise; we notice these thoughts without getting overly involved in them while being conscious of maintaining our loving feeling. It is quite normal for judgmental or anxious thoughts to creep in, and as this happens, we simply notice them and cultivate the feeling of love again while bringing our attention to our heart breathing. Bringing our awareness back to our heart breathing provides a great anchor.

As we move our conscious awareness from the head back down into the heart region, we remain in the heart for a few breaths and sense what it feels like, and then we move this awareness down into our gut region and sense what it feels like to be in the gut region (our navel area and abdomen), noticing any emotions, feelings, thoughts, sensations—but resisting the temptation to judge or form opinions about these subtle sensations. We just sit with the sensations.

It is normal to sense some background fear or anxiety, yet we try not to react to these feelings or suppress them. Let them be. We use our heart breathing to bring ourselves back to the feeling of love if we are starting to get caught up in other emotions. We then move our attention, and feeling of love, from our gut back into our heart region and allow it to remain there for a while and notice any subtle differences in feelings and felt-sensations. This particular activity can be a useful one to undertake at the end of a stressful day, perhaps following some light stretching exercises such as t'ai chi or chi gung movements.

The more we allow ourselves to feel this awareness of our subtle body sensations, the more we are cultivating our heart-awareness and our overall bodymind somatic awareness, learning to sense what it feels like to be in our head, heart, or gut. This not only allows us to free ourselves from the ego-chattering ruminations of our thinking head, but also to start to release old tensions, habituations, psychic wounds, projections, and held beliefs that have become suppressed within unconscious 'shadow aspects' of our psyche and encoded in our bodymind. By cultivating this awareness, we can allow aspects of our shadow to emerge into the light of our waking consciousness and so begin to integrate more of our psyche. This helps our intuitive, emotional, somatic, and rational awareness to blend, alchemize, and cohere into an enriching gnosis, helping us become wiser in our receptivity and responsiveness to life situations.

Body Awareness

What is often referred to as 'somatic awareness' is fast being recognized as an important tool for leadership and organizational development. Somatic awareness is about learning to bring our attention out of our heads and into our bodies. Our soma is our body. By re-orientating our awareness away from our incessant ego chattering, discursive mind into our body sensations, we develop a more embodied experience of mind integrated into body.

The more we learn to listen to our soma, the better we are at developing our inner sense by feeling the subtle sensations of our body-tingles in the hands, cool air movement around our nostrils, throat constrictions, eye movements, heart pangs, gut reactions, and such like. Rather than noticing and reacting upon or suppressing these feelings we open our attention to them. We bring our conscious awareness into these sensations. By allowing our awareness to go into the arising experiences within our body, we enter a way of knowing that is pre-judgement, freed from the discursive conceptualizations of our thinking mind. With this, we find a spaciousness within us, a distancing from our ego-chatter, and a softening and deepening of our awareness.

As we learn to bring our awareness into our bodily sensations, we can start to touch reality as it is, experienced by us prior to judgement, reaction, and apprehension. We start to re-member the continuous flow of energy within us and the deeper array of experiences which lie within us all the time, yet much of the time unnoticed or suppressed by our busy thinking mind. This awareness helps us to experience a more embodied sense of presencing, a continual communing with our world through these felt-senses, intuitive insights, and emotional sensations. This aids the activation of our super-nature.

Studies now show us that our hearts, gut, and bodymind networks sense and respond with our environment in a variety of ways (sensorial, electromagnetic, quantum) triggering felt-senses, constrictions, tensions, energy releases, and a variety of sensations which, as we become more conversant with them, can enhance our ability to make wise complex relational decisions quickly.

It takes time and practice to develop somatic awareness, in part because we have become culturally anesthetized; our systems of education have prioritized the rational-analytical thinking head to such an extent that it's a cultural norm to ignore or suppress our somatic awareness. As business coach, Julio Olalla, insightfully notes, "The dominant epistemology of our times fundamentally reduces learning and knowing to exercises of a disembodied intellect. This way of knowing is at the heart of the huge crises humanity is facing right now. A deep and lasting transformational learning requires in each of us a shift in the dynamic coherence of our linguistic, emotional, and somatic being." (Strozzi-Heckler)

Through simple practices such as breathing into parts of our body and holding our attention there in a receptive way, we can start to develop intimacy with our somas.

Somatic Exploration

Let's find a quiet space where we will not be disturbed for ten minutes and can feel safe and comfortable enough to lie on the floor. We need to make sure we are warm enough; perhaps placing a rug or blanket over us as we lie down because the body cools down as it relaxes during this practice.

Now, let's lie down, get comfortable, and relax.

Feel the weight of our body on the floor as we lie here, feel our breathing in and out of our lungs as we undertake a couple of rounds of conscious breathing.

We are now going to do a quick 'body scan' which we do by scanning our awareness over our bodies, moving our attention from our toes up our legs, hips, up the back and chest, each arm, and then neck and head. Then, while breathing deeply, we sense into any tensions, pains, or sensations in our body and allow our awareness to go into those places. We are not trying to force or control or manage anything but allow our awareness to notice a tension or sensation and see what emerges. Perhaps the sensation may change slightly or memories may be invoked in our mind or the sensation may remind us of something. We can play with this practice for a while, bringing our awareness back to the sensation each time it drifts off.

When we feel ready, we can scan our body from toes to head again and sense into another area of our body, perhaps our back or neck or a place that is feeling tight or tense; once again, simply let our awareness go into that feeling for a few moments. We gently inquire into the sensation and see what comes. This is a relaxing and easy way to start relating with our body sensations.

At this point, we can either get up slowly and gently to end the practice, or, if we have the time and space available, we can stay lying down and start to engage in some contemplative questions with ourselves and sense the body sensations that may arise upon us asking these questions while attending to our body. Here are a couple of questions we might wish to ask ourselves while sensing into how our bodies feel as we ponder the question in the mind in an open, non-judgmental way for a few moments. A first question might be, *How do I experience the feeling of loving myself?* We gently ask that question over and over a couple of times in our mind and then scan our body and sense what it feels like for the body to respond to the question. We might sense subtle shifts, tensions, or sensations in certain areas, if so, let's go into those areas and explore while gently holding the question in mind.

After a few moments, we might ask the question, *How do I experience love for others?* And again we feel into the body, asking our body the question, sensing any subtle sensations. Then we could ask, *How do I experience freedom?* And again we feel into the body, asking the question and sense. We are mindful of when our attention wanders off into discursive thoughts, memories, or stories, gently bringing our attention back into our body sensations.

Next, we can ask, *How do I experience happiness?* And again we feel into the body while asking our body the question. And finally, *What is my soul craft?* or, *What is my soul-calling?* And again we feel the sensations, going into the sensations for a few moments, just being with the sensations in our body in a relaxed, receptive way. There are no right or wrong sensations or feelings, whatever we experience is right for that moment. When we are ready, we can finish off with a couple of rounds of conscious breathing before sitting up slowly and gently.

Conscious Walking

This activity is best done outside with bare feet, but it can also be done with shoes on, or inside, say in a corridor or long room with plenty of space ahead of us. Firstly, we stand still. We feel our body standing upright on the spot. We feel the sensations, our hands, our feet, the weight of our body on the soles of our feet. We breathe consciously and deeply a couple of times and do a quick body scan with our attention, starting from the feet and going through all our body to the top of our head.

With intimate awareness of our body, we gradually lift one leg up as if taking a step but in slow motion, becoming conscious of how the leg feels as we lift it up, sensing the weight going on the other leg as we maintain balance, sensing our leg stretching out and then the feeling of slowly placing it down again as we step forward on the foot. Feel the rest of our body moving forward and our weight shifting as we maintain balance.

Next, we take another slow step with the other leg, again feeling the body sensations, the balance and weight distribution, our back posture and our arms moving slightly. We take a couple more slow steps maintaining our awareness in the body, noticing our balance and felt-sensations. And then we start to quicken the speed of the steps just a little bit with each step, until we are beginning to walk faster than we usually would, still feeling the body movements and sensations keenly within us. Then, we start to slow the strides down gradually, slower, and slower, feel the balancing, the weight shifting. Eventually we are so slow in our steps that our movement is very gradual, as slow as we can go without losing balance. Then we stop. We scan our whole body again with our awareness as we stand still on the spot, noticing any sensations.

We then go about our normal business while being mindful of the conscious feeling of our strides as we walk. In this way, the everyday act of walking becomes a practice for cultivating somatic awareness and mindfulness.

Yoga Nidra

This is an ancient practice of full-body deep relaxation that cultivates a state of consciousness between being awake and asleep, a state where we become increasingly aware of our inner body awareness and enter the alpha-theta 'twilight zone.' It can help promote healthy sleeping, enhance our general wellbeing, and helps us tame our ego, all while gaining access to deeper wisdom.

First, we find a warm and comfortable space where we are able to lie down undisturbed for at least fifteen minutes. This exercise can be done in bed, as it helps promote sleeping when practiced before going to sleep, but also during the day too it can be undertaken as a way of helping get ourselves into a creative more soulful space rather than sending us to sleep. This practice can be a great thing to do as part of the 'Welcoming in to the Twilight Zone with John Cleese' practice described in the next section of this Appendix.

We lie down on the ground with a rug or blanket over us, and we settle ourselves comfortably. Feel our body resting and the sensation of the floor or bed beneath. Feel the sensation of our clothes against our skin and feel our lungs rising up and down as we breathe. Bring our awareness to our breathing, notice our lungs filling and emptying, and take a couple of deep breaths in and out, and feel the body starting to relax. Notice any tensions and sensations, becoming intimately aware of how the body is feeling overall. We then scan through the body from toe to head swiftly with our awareness. We can take a couple more deep breaths and then bring our attention into our left foot, with specific focus. Let's really feel the left foot with our awareness, feel the sensations. We imagine what it's like to be inside our left foot.

Now we are going to move through our different body parts with our awareness starting with the big toe on our left foot, then moving to each individual toe, then to the sole of the foot, the arch and then the ankle. We move our attention to our shin on our left leg, then to the back calf, up to the front of the knee, and the back of the knee, up our thigh to our left hip, and then up the left side of our body to our armpit. Next, we sense our left shoulder, our biceps, then triceps, our elbow and then our left forearm, wrist, palm, back of the hand, thumb, first finger, second finger, third finger, fourth finger, and fifth finger.

Now, we bring our attention to our right foot and start with the big toe and move along the toes, the sole, arch and ankle, up the leg, thigh, hip, side, armpit, arm, hand, and fingers as per the left side, ensuring we touch each part with our conscious awareness catching ourselves when we drift off, always bringing our attention back to the body.

When we have finished the right side, ending with the right fingers, we then bring our awareness into the base of our spine and our buttocks, and then we move our awareness all the way up the spine, sensing all over our back as we move up the spine, up to the neck. Then we focus on the neck, back of the head, top of the head, forehead, left eyebrow, right eyebrow, nose, tip of the nose, left cheek, right cheek, left ear, right ear, lips, tongue, chin, throat, collarbone, left side of the chest, right side of the chest, diaphragm, feel it moving up and down with our breathing. We bring awareness to our heart area, to our stomach, to the organs in our stomach region, then lower abdomen, down to our sex glands, then base of the spine and buttocks.

We then feel our whole body, we feel its aliveness as we breathe into every part of our body. We do a quick body scan to feel all around the body, notice the subtle energy flowing freely, and feel every part of our body alive with this energy. Now, we take a few deep breaths and relax into this feeling for as long as time allows.

It is quite normal to fall asleep while doing this exercise, and if our schedule allows that's fine as it's rejuvenating. The more we practice it, the more proficient we will become at remaining in a conscious yet deeply relaxed, spacious state without falling asleep. This stimulates changes in our brainwave patterns and our bodymind vibrations so that general coherence, greater intuition, and soul-consciousness are cultivated. It's a powerful practice to get used to and has profound benefits for us while costing nothing.

Welcoming In the Twilight Zone – Introductory Practice with John Cleese

As mentioned in Chapter 4, when we slow down the brainwaves from high-beta achiever mind into alpha-theta awakened mind we enhance many leadership qualities, including empathy, creativity, insight and systemic-awareness.

The famous creative John Cleese once gave a talk on creativity to a large business audience which is both witty and well-researched and provides an introduction into the twilight zone in the midst of the day. The essence of Cleese's talk is that we all have natural creativity within us. It's part of what makes us alive, and we can learn to cultivate this creativity while enhancing our ability to call upon it in constructive ways at work.

We all exhibit what John Cleese calls 'open mode' and 'closed mode' ways of being. The open mode (predominantly right hemisphere and awakened mind) is relaxed, expansive, more inclined to humor, curious for its own sake, playful, and unbounded. The closed mode (predominantly left hemisphere and achiever mind) is action-orientated, anxious, impatient, focused on getting-the-job-done, ticking the to-do list, firefighting, reacting rather than being creative, and exists in more of a 'doing' imperative than a 'being'.

Cleese notes that most of the time in our working environment, we are in the closed mode, and the more we can allow ourselves to bring in our open mode the more creative, innovative, and adaptive our work style and team dynamics will be.

To get into the open mode Cleese suggests we need five things: Space, time, more time, confidence, and humor. Let's briefly explore these.

We create *space* in our schedule, taking *time* out for at least an hour but no more than an hour and a half. We find a quiet space for this specific period of time where we cannot be interrupted or disturbed. An 'oasis-of-quiet' is created by setting boundaries of space and time.

We sit comfortably and start to ponder the problem at hand. To start with, and perhaps even for the first fifteen minutes or so, our ego-chatter will race about in our minds and we will feel the need to get on with pressing matters which we have just remembered need to be done. This is quite natural and we need to sit through this head noise with dedication yet relaxation. Hence *'more time'* is needed as it can take a while for us to start opening beyond the grasping grip of our ego mind to allow the 'open mode' (more soulful, intuitive, and embodied mode) to start enriching our awareness as our ego-chatter begins to settle down and subside.

We rest against the problem gently in our mind, exploring the problem in a friendly non-urgent yet persistent way, while resisting the urge to go with any immediate 'solutions' that start to crop up. Having a note pad on hand can help us as we can jot down some of the things that come into our mind as well as unloading ourselves from the burden of having to remember the errands and things to do our racing ego-consciousness starts to fixate upon.

We may well find it uncomfortable to sit with the problem while solutions start to crop up, which is why we need *confidence* in ourselves and this process, because the longer we sit with the problem, the more creative, innovative, and original our solutions become. Learning to tolerate this discomfort and mild anxiety of not having a fix to our problem, while resisting the temptation to grab an early solution that crops up, allows us to maximize our pondering time and ensure more insightful solutions emerge. Hence the 'more time' and 'confidence' of Cleese's five things, because it is through embracing more pondering time with confidence in ourselves to stay open, rather than grasping at first-come solutions, that ensures richer creativity. Also, we need confidence to play and explore beyond the usual boundaries of what we might deem sensible, logical, or suitable.

This is where *humor* comes in. Whether we are on our own or with one or two other people, lightening up our mood with humor allows a more expansive open mode to form along with more playfulness in our explorations, as the more outrageous our explorations and the more 'mistakes' we make the better. In fact, in this playful period there are no 'mistakes', as anything can be explored, and if we are with other people, we need to ensure we do not judge the others' suggestions or frown or dismiss suggestions as that is a sure way to curtail creativity and playfulness. The more we giggle, laugh, and loosen up the better. Then, more novel and insightful solutions will start to emerge after about an hour of this play.

We need to be aware that sometimes solutions will pop up from our unconscious depths after the session, perhaps in the shower the next morning, for instance. So, we ought to leave some 'cooking' time to allow our deeper unconscious to mull over things and bring up gems from our depths after the event.

Once we have a solution we are happy with, then we need to revert to the closed mode to start to implement it. It is no good still being in the open mode when we are trying to focus on project managing the implementation of the solution. Yet, we ought to regularly make space in our schedules for such an oasis-of-quiet regardless of whether we feel we need specific creative solutions. This allows us to nurture the open mode within us, while ensuring a coherence of our left and right brain hemispheres on a regular basis and enhancing our ability to toggle with ease between achiever and awakened mind. We can enrich our perspective throughout our working week, and welcome in wisdom.

Here are some questions to aid reflection on open-closed, left-right hemisphere, achiever-awakened toggling during our daily work-life.

Can you sense periods at work when you get stressed, reactive, and defensive to the detriment of what you are trying to solve or work on, and perhaps also to the detriment of others you are working with? Note how often per week you feel like this.

When you practice the conscious breathing and heart entrainment exercises above do you sense a shift in your awareness and mood? Describe this subtle shift. Try and think of some descriptions you would apply to this subtle shift in feeling. *Could you envisage it helping you de-stress in times of challenge?*

Are you able to create an oasis-of-quiet in your schedule once a week? Note what is preventing you from making it happen. *Can you work around these preventions if you set your mind to it?*

Can you sense what it feels like when your awareness is more in the closed-mode achiever left-hemispheric orientation (narrowed-down, reductive, focused, and solution-orientated) compared to when your awareness is more in the open-mode awakened right-hemispheric orientation (expansive, playful, creative, empathic, intuitive and relational)?

Are there particular activities that you undertake during your week which require more of one mode than the other? List the different activities you regularly undertake in a normal week and map these to the two different states. Perhaps some of these activities require an integration of both states simultaneously.

What natural passions, strengths, talents and callings do you sense within yourself? List them out and ponder on them for a while. *How can you allow these to flow more readily into your work-life?*

Are there times during your daily experiences that you can sense the ego-soul dynamic within you? Sense when your awareness is more ego-dominated by projections, judgements and thought-chatter or when it is more soulful, expansive, compassionate, and insightful.

What activities or practices could you start to bring into your routine? Reflect on how you might shape your daily routine and weekly schedule differently within the bounds of your obligations to allow for a more integrated ego-heart-soul consciousness to start developing within you and your work style. *Are there any practices, exercises or techniques friends or colleagues have mentioned that intrigue you?*

Soulful Space at the End of the Day

Rich meals accompanied with alcohol and coffee after a hard day's work are seen as quite the norm in business life these days, especially when sharing a meal with business colleagues, clients, or networking after an evening event or staying at a hotel while away on business. But this is the last thing our bodymind needs before bedtime. We ought to allow enough time for the meal to digest well before we start to wind down ahead of retiring to bed. Ideally, we make time in our schedule for some light exercise before going to bed. Instead, try out something different by getting changed out of our work clothes into something more comfortable and go for a ten to twenty-minute walk in the fresh air or perhaps a light jog and a stretch. After this, we might take a shower as a way of letting go of the busy day before getting ready for bed. Then, we can do some gentle exercises for a couple of minutes (longer if possible). For instance, some gentle yoga postures or some chi gung or t'ai chi movements. These gentle movements help us bring our awareness into the body while our thinking mind starts to quieten down.

Upon getting into bed, we remain sitting upright in a comfortable posture with our back straight and our legs crossed (or whatever feels most comfortable). We then engage in a few rounds of conscious breathing. This calms us down and allows our sympathetic and parasympathetic body systems to cohere. We can then dedicate some quiet moments of reflection to run through the day from start to finish, briefly going over the interactions we had, the emotions and experiences, noticing when we got caught up in a particular event or exchange that occurred and the tensions and felt-senses it provoked within us. It can be useful to have a journal or notebook by the side of the bed to jot down the key points of the day in terms of what went well, what we learned, what we could do better in the future, and what was particularly uncomfortable or challenging. Or we can just sit with this reflective exercise without the need to write anything down.

Once we have adequately reviewed the day, do another few rounds of conscious breathing to allow our thoughts of the day to lessen their grip on our awareness. And, when we feel more still, we can place our hands gently over our heart area while doing conscious breathing that morphs into a few rounds of 'heart breathing' as if we are breathing through our heart area.

It is a great practice to then think of things we really love, as well as the everyday things we are grateful for in our lives. These can be universal things such as the air we breathe, the sunlight that gives us warmth and makes the plants we eat grow, the natural beauty of the world, the food and shelter we have, our loved ones, and the little things that make us smile. If we start to struggle with what to focus on in terms of grateful things or notice our mind getting caught up in thoughts of the day, we just bring our attention back into our breathing through the heart and feel the warmth of our heart and a feeling of love flowing through our entire body. At that point we can then either lie down in bed and start to focus on the energy sensations and feelings in our body (as per the Yoga Nidra practice explored early) or remain upright and engage in sitting meditation for a few minutes by noticing our thoughts appearing in our thinking mind while developing deeper awareness of the stillness beyond the thoughts. Soon we will feel ready for some quality sleep which will rejuvenate us far more than if we had gone to bed with a full stomach of rich food and wine, beer or coffee.

If this pre-sleep flow of fresh-air > body movement > reflection/journaling > conscious/heart breathing > bodyscan > sleep may feel a little overwhelming to begin with, then feel free to find an easier to remember flow that works for you, such as movement/stretching > bodyscan > sleep. The additional detail provided above is not meant to put you off but invite you in to a whole host of micro-practices you can start to play with around bedtime, and of course also upon wake-up in the morning. Naturally this often requires adjusting our schedule. I have noticed how many leaders on the regenerative journey start to go to bed earlier and wake up earlier as they progress on the journey, though this is not a prerequisite to advancement.

Twelve Principles of Natural Liberation with John P Milton

I had the real pleasure of spending two weeks with the legendary John P Milton some years ago when undertaking a solo Vision Quest and Sacred Passage training with him in Crestone, Colorado. John is a pioneering leader in nature-connection and environmental movements, having spent over sixty years of personal training with varied teachings from many of the world's traditions, and hosting many wilderness expeditions for leaders, as well as hosting his own Sacred Passage programs on spiritual connection in nature. He has developed unique practices for uniting inner and outer-nature through training in Buddhist, Taoist, Vedantic, Tantric, and Native American traditions, and he incorporates t'ai chi, chi gung, and yoga in his work. As well as being a founding father of the environmental movement in the early 1960's, he's been instrumental in introducing the vision quest to contemporary culture. I thoroughly recommend his training programs and also his beautiful and practical book *Sky Above Earth Below*, from which this précised Twelve Principles of Natural Liberation originates, distilling the essence of many Earth-connected traditions.

> "In an era long before indoor churches and temples, people communed directly with sacred Spirit out upon the body of the Earth, embraced by the vastness of the sky above and the loving ground of the Earth below. Nature was experienced as a flowing creation of the Divine – a sanctuary of the wild where one could recognize life's sacredness... To assist contemporary culture in walking the same path as the ancient wisdom cultures, I have distilled a series of twelve central principles."
>
> –John P Milton

1. The fundamental truth: All forms are interconnected, constantly change, and continuously arise from and return to primordial Source. At the deepest level all forms, including ourselves, are a magical display of the boundless, formless Source that is our true essence. We have the choice of either resisting this fundamental truth, and suffering; or surrendering into this truth – and dancing with the flow.

2. Commit yourself completely to liberation in this lifetime: This principle recommends you dedicate all the fruits of your life and path to the greatest possible benefit and service for all beings.

3. Relax and surrender to life: Learn to de-contract and relax your body, your emotions, your energy, your thoughts, and mind. Let go of old ideas, judgements, emotions, and structures; your own expectations; your need

for approval or acceptance; and your idea of progress. Trust yourself to unwind and empty completely and remain open to now.

4 Remain in now: Become aware of your distractions. Meditate regularly to notice the flow of your distractions. As gaps naturally appear between thoughts, as open spaces arise between emotions, rest in the gaps. Let the clarity of your pure awareness settle naturally in itself. Enjoy the bliss of now.

5 Cultivate union with universal energy: As you relax, you free the body-mind to the life-force. When you combine present-centered awareness with relaxation, you can deepen your awareness into deeper and deeper levels of body, emotion, and mind. Find a peaceful, natural place outdoors where the energy is clear and renewing. With some practice, you should be able to feel this regenerating quality directly. Be totally present with the clear, relaxed intention to receive Nature's gifts of life-force. Then absorb the healing energy of Nature through intention, presence, and relaxation. Learn to renew your life-force during daily activity. Without union with universal energy there can be no true transformation. (See Energy Cultivation sequence below to aid this).

6 Go with the universal flow: Ultimately, over a lifetime of practice, one can gain energy mastery, or the ability to flow in complete union with universal energy. One's experience of the creative dance of form and energy is pure bliss manifesting in the field of Source awareness.

7 Rest in the radiance of your open heart: In cultivating energy mastery, you realize and experience life with unconditional love. Through the natural deepening of this openhearted radiance, the separation between self and other gradually dissolves.

8 Active compassion arises naturally out of unconditional love: Expressive kindness spontaneously arises, moment by moment from your heart essence, which brings peace and happiness to life.

9 Cut through clarity: Moments of luminous clarity, may be powerful, like a thunderbolt, or subtle like the sound of a leaf falling to touch the Earth. Powerful or subtle, it cuts through distractions—all obstacles—to direct experience of Source, laying bare pristine awareness of inner-outer nature.

10 Return to Source: By finally cracking open the ego's seed coat that's been blocking off Source, we sense the underlying reality. We sense Source as the most fundamental, simple, complete, and perfect actuality that is who we really are. The closer one approaches Source, the more synchronous events become. When Source is accessed, extraordinary creativity occurs.

11 Pure Source awareness is – to remain in recognition: Remain in continuous, flowing recognition of the formless light pervading life. We sense all forms, inner and outer, as the natural display of Source's pure creativity.

12 Serve as a warrior of the open heart and liberated spirit: The key is to bring each of these principles into creative interaction with the challenges of everyday life. The deeper one rests in formless Source, the vaster the creative upwelling of freshly evolved forms – forms in the service of the whole and all its parts.

Energy Cultivation with John P Milton

Energy Cultivation is a powerful practice sequence that I learned from John P Milton when undertaking Sacred Passage training with him in Colorado, where I spent thirteen days and twelve nights sleeping under the stars on Mount Crestone. Energy Cultivation is a meta-practice, in that it's a sequence by which we understand other inner practices that help us cultivate the flow of energy through our bodymind. The sequence for cultivating energy flow is: Bodily Form, Inner Intention, Presence, Relaxation, and Breathing.

Bodily Form: Through somatic movement practices like chi gung, t'ai chi, or yoga, we can open energetic conduits (meridians) in the bodymind and open to the life-force or 'chi' in nature.

Inner Intention: Hold a clear life-affirming intention inside ourselves when wishing to cultivate the life-force in our bodymind during body movement energy cultivation practices.

Presence: Notice the mind, notice the emotional state, let go of distractions and find a quietening presence form within us during the somatic movement practices.

Relaxation: Remind oneself to let go of any constrictions or distractions by giving ourselves permission to relax and surrender to the now.

Breathing: Deepen into a rhythmic belly breathing and notice each breath as it massages our inner organs and flows between inner and outer. Relax and release daily tensions, then bring attention to the main energy centers – either the seven chakras or the three 'brains' in gut, heart, and head. Breathe deep, move with intention and relaxed attention, and allow the life-force of nature to enrich you.

Contemplating Developmental Moments & Synchronicities

This practice helps us contemplate and reflect on meaning moments and synchronicities experienced so far in our lives. In reflecting on past synchronicities, we can start to become more conscious of challenging times, break-down and break-through moments, and synchronicities as special meaning-making moments in our lives. Neuropsychologist Lydia Cho at Harvard Medical School's McLean Hospital has studied how an enhanced perception of synchronicity comes together with increased intuition, better mental health, and personal resilience.

For this exercise, have a piece of blank A3 card and some pens (colored if you wish) next to you, ready to draw. Allow at least twenty minutes for this exercise.

Step 1: Quieten through the mindfulness or bodymind practices above. In time, after say five or six minutes of engaging in the mindfulness or bodymind practices, we start to notice a quietening and slowing down of the ruminating voice in the head. Listening to relaxing music can help with this quietening stage. In time, our brainwaves slow from high beta into beta and then alpha-theta, and our awakened mind is activated along with a more expansive perspective that allows more insight and turns down the level of emotional reactivity.

Step 2: Reflect on life so far, by casting one's mind over the following life stages:

1. from as early as one can recall to about eleven years old, the memories of life, the good and not so good, the enjoyable and the challenging, whatever memories come up for you, all the way up to starting secondary school
2. from the start of secondary school all the way till the end of education (which may include higher education like university for some people) before finding one's first job
3. from the time of starting your first job all the way up till the present moment, including all the different jobs, life experiences, relationships, personal life experiences, and such like.

Allow memories to come up, but do not get overly consumed by certain memoires. Keep going back to the exercise of scanning through, being mindful of not getting overly engrossed or emotional about various aspects of our life path. This exercise is not psychotherapy where we delve into past wounds but more a scanning process where we notice memoires, remind ourselves of moments in our life, and then move on to scanning other experiences in our life.

Spending about four or five minutes on each stage of life, and once all the stages have been scanned up until the present day, then scan back over your whole life again. This time with particular attention to pivotal, challenging, break-down and break-throughs, upsets, or synchronistic moments, like an epiphany, a chance encounter, a fork in the road, a real challenge, or lucky break. It does not matter what the event or challenging time was. It's more about acknowledging the times in our life that felt particularly pivotal to our life path.

Step 3: Draw your life path so far, by picking up the pens and A3 card at your side. Start to draw a road or pathway symbolizing the journey of your life so far, and mark up the moments of challenge, loss, disappointment, door-closing, door-opening, lucky break, chance encounter, something breaking down like the end of a relationship, accident or health issue, something breaking through. Map the most pivotal and meaning-making moments along the road of your life. It can be useful to think of between three to six meaning-making moments. By all means be artistic and use different color pens as this playfulness can engage the right-hemisphere and open-mode, yet the exercise is not actually about testing our artistic talent.

Step 4: Reflect on the developmental learning and any synchronicity associated with each life hurdle. The developmental learning might be how one's life has changed, how the tensions of the challenge reveal learning experiences that equipped us further down the line or took us down a different path that informed a richer life experience in some way. Synchronicities are numinous moments that may have felt other-worldly like strangely unique and timely chance encounters, messengers or déjà vu's, where the timing or nature of something happening felt opportune in revealing new insights, connections, doorways, and horizons. Social justice leader Walter Earl Fluker calls synchronistic experiences "moments of ecstasy when I'm most myself." For him, they provide a golden thread running through our lives. For neuroscientist Lisa Miller, "The more we open to the guidance of synchronicities, the better we can engage life as a creative act, living in a way that allows life to reveal itself." (Miller)

Reflect on how your life changed, what has spawned from each of the meaning-making moments, how might have they become stepping stones that have helped the unfolding life quest of finding our dharma, our more authentic soul-nature beyond ego-achiever. The overall invitation here is to notice how life challenges can often end up informing our life's meaning in rich ways if we so choose to see the developmental insights. This can help us live into life as a learning journey, rather than try to control, protect, and avoid certain outcomes. Instead, we flow with the learning each day and stage of life brings.

Cultivating Listening Skills

Active and deep listening is when we give our full attention to the conversation, becoming aware of not just the words but of the feeling being conveyed and any non-verbal cues, such as body gestures, facial expressions, tone of voice, and what is arising in ourselves as gut feelings, intuitive senses of rising emotions, and such like. Psychology professor Albert Mehrabian's research shows that much of what we communicate is non-verbal with on average 55% of our communication coming from the body, 38% coming from sound and tones, and only 7% coming from the actual words. As we journey toward regenerative leadership, we learn to tune into everything, verbal and non-verbal, sensing into what is being conveyed with receptivity to reflect and respond wisely.

This active and deep listening can be consciously brought into how we listen and engage throughout the day in all our meetings and conversations. When in a meeting, we can catch ourselves, notice how we are being, what is going on in our head, the type of inner dialogue, the judgements, the frustrations, and opinions that form in us. We can make a note on this either mentally or by jotting it down, journaling as we go.

We can utilize every interaction as a practice to sense into when we are being fully present, really tuning into what is being said with our full attention and when we are allowing judgements, emotions, distractions, and such like, to fill our awareness.

When we sense this ego-chatter, we might ask ourselves the following exploratory questions: *Am I judging others? Am I rehearsing what I am going to say? Am I getting caught up in ruminating head-chatter? Or am I being receptive to 'what is'? Can I sense all my ways of knowing, my intuition, my felt-senses, my emotional intelligence as well as what is going on in my thinking head? Can I allow myself to sense a deeper stillness beneath the noise of my thoughts and feelings? What can I pick up and tune-in to beyond my immediate thoughts and judgements?* The more we practice this self-awareness throughout our workday, the more we cultivate a deepening of knowing thy self.

Here's a simple yet powerful practice that helps develop our deep listening with others. It's a practice I often use to great effect during leadership team immersions.

We find a partner to pair up with for this exercise (a team member or stakeholder we are working with, or even our spouse or neighbor). We sit opposite each other, get comfortable, relax, and warmly look at each other in the eyes. We aim to maintain this eye contact throughout this exercise. One person is going to speak first, for three minutes, and the other person is going to listen without interrupting. Then we are going to swap over, with the other person speaking for three minutes.

We can explore personal reflective questions such as: *What do I most deeply and profoundly love? What would I like to change about my life? What are my greatest fears?*

Or we can explore work related questions such as: *What is really concerning me at the moment at work? How do I feel about the changes afoot in my work area? If I could change two things about my work life, what would they be? What is holding me back from improving my work-life? If I could have any job within the organization, what would it be and why? What is the deepest and most profound purpose my organization ought to have?*

If time allows, it is great to start with general personal questions first and then explore more specific work-related questions in further rounds. Once the pair is clear on the question they are going to speak about, they agree who is going to speak first for three minutes, while the other listens attentively and fully.

The listener should refrain from any bodily queues that could influence the speaker such as smiling, frowning, or nodding. We listen with a blank yet open and warm expression and maintain gentle eye contact throughout. We remain aware of how present we are while listening, catching ourselves when caught up in distractions, or thoughts about what is being said. We keep bringing our attention back to fully listening.

As said before, this act of listening is a form of meditation in itself, as it helps us free ourselves from ego-chatter and remain present. This helps us become more receptive. The speaker will, either consciously or unconsciously, sense this deeper awareness opening between us allowing for a deepening of authentic heart-felt sharing. The speaker knows there is space to say whatever comes up without fear of interruption or judgement.

When we are speaking it is important for us to tune into our bodymind, feeling into our heart and gut to sense what wants to be spoken through us regarding the question. This is not about answers or right or wrong responses but a general inquiry, and whatever comes up is absolutely fine. This helps the speaker cultivate somatic awareness while speaking—learning to listen to the heart and gut and how this informs us. We speak spontaneously and freely as we go with pauses and spaces for stillness as and when it feels right. It does not matter if the speaker says little or gets into a flow and pours out a lot, nothing is right or wrong here and all is beyond judgement.

The facilitator calls time after three minutes (or if no facilitator, the listener calls time). Then there are a few seconds of stillness before we swap over. In this space between swapping over, the pair can show gratitude, smile, say thank you before the next session starts, and the process is repeated over again.

This deep listening practice can also be adapted for three people, where we still share as a pair sitting opposite each other with a third person taking notes and then providing feedback at the time of change-over. We rotate round until each of the three people have taken part in all the activities (listening, feeding-back, speaking).

This practical embodied experience of reciprocated sharing requires no training or budget, just some basic ground rules, yet has a profound impact.

Dialogue through Way of Council

One of the most essential of human qualities is our heartfelt relating with others. Yet, so often in today's machine mindset we find ourselves very far from this kind of communication. For instance, how often do we really listen to the other person with all of our attention, without getting distracted with thoughts of past or future, or how what is being said affects me and my priorities for the day? Techniques such as deep listening and dialogue can help us cultivate this attentiveness so that we can learn to walk our personal and collective paths with loving, attentive, conscious steps. The dialogue practice I explain here is 'Way of Council' which, like deep listening, I often use to great effect on my leadership immersions.

Way of Council Practice

Through the ancient practice of Way of Council groups of people come together to share within a communal atmosphere of non-judgment and acceptance. In Council, people sit in a circle and commit to being fully present, freed from distractions, judgements or opinion forming, listening intently, and sharing open-heartedly with each other without preparing or rehearsing our responses.

There is a beacon or talking piece (which may be a stick, a stone, a ball or whatever feels appropriate). The person holding the beacon artefact is the only one allowed to speak, everyone else round the circle listens with complete attention and presence. Then, when the talking piece is put back in the center or passed round the circle, the next person to hold it speaks, knowing they will not be interrupted or judged. Here are some basic ground rules:

- When speaking, we speak from our heart and gut, not from our head. We do not rehearse what we are going to say, we allow what comes up within us to come out. We talk from the 'I' perspective, about what is going on for me, not using words such as 'you' or 'they', and we do not bring in blame or projection on to others. We simply talk about what is going on for me, how I am feeling and the challenges or opportunities I am experiencing. This 'first person' speaking allows us to take responsibility for what we are feeling and saying without accusing, judging, or projecting. We are also conscious of the time available for the circle, by being concise in our speech and not rambling too much or speaking for too long.
- When listening, we listen with our whole bodymind, being present in the here-and-now, so that our attention is fully absorbed in listening generously and open-heartedly to what is being said. The act of listening in such a deep and fully present way is beneficial in and of-itself, as the act of listening to another helps us remain mindful, coherent,

embodied, and present. We catch ourselves when thoughts of past or future distract us, and when emotions or judgements triggered by what we are listening to form in us along with associated thought patterns. We continuously bring ourselves back to the act of fully listening each time our attention wanders. This helps keep our heart open and helps a social field of collective wisdom to resonate within the group, which further enhances our heart-felt listening and speaking. This attentive listening is powerful and cleansing for everyone in the circle.

- There is a natural ego tendency to wish to rehearse what we are going to say, so we come across as fluent and intelligible—our ego not wanting to trust what might emerge from our heart and gut. But we let go of the ego grasping desire to rehearse. This helps us build trust in our other ways of knowing beyond the rationalizing head. It also frees us to be fully present in the moment and enjoy being here-and-now, listening attentively, rather than rehearsing in our head while others speak. When we speak from this deeper heart and gut place a more cathartic and soulful sharing occurs, which enriches us personally and the circle collectively. We may well feel fear when it's our turn to take the talking piece, our ego afraid that what may come out will be critically judged by others. This is part-and-parcel of trusting ourselves and trusting the circle of people who are dedicated to being open and attentive as best we all can be without judging, just listening. This learning not to rehearse while having trust, is a surrendering process, a form of 'kenosis', by letting go of predefining thoughts to allow something deeper to emerge. It is a great way for us to practice becoming more comfortable at bringing in more of our heart and soul-consciousness into our work-life.

- The talking piece acts as a beacon of attention. Our attention follows the talking piece and we give whoever has it our full attention.

- No criticism or judgement about other's sharing. We do not critically analyze what another has just shared when we come to speak, yet we may refer to another's comment in terms of how it affects 'me' and my feelings. So, we share how what has been said relates to what is going on for 'me' without getting dragged into me-versus-you judgements or criticisms. This helps cultivate self-recognition within us, helping us notice when we are tending to blame, defend or project as opposed to

open-heartedly share about what is going on for me without projecting on to others.
- Silence is always permitted while holding the beacon, and we can pass the beacon on without saying anything at all if we wish.
- What is said in the circle stays in the circle. General themes may be captured and shared by means of informing our work in general, but people's specific sharing remains confidential and not specifically quoted beyond the circle without permission. This especially relates to gossip. Learning to respect the confidentiality of the circle by holding back on gossiping about others is once again an important learning for us, teaching us to respect each other's perspectives and become more self-aware about our tendency to gossip.

As a practice, Council is applicable to all social interrelations from family discussions to executive board meetings. For indigenous cultures, where collective decisions are regularly made through this circle of shared dialogue, it's acceptance rather than consensus which is paramount—an empathic understanding of the differing views occurs even if everyone is not in agreement with the final decision. This way resentment does not build up and then corrode the community. Differing opinions are healthy and ought to be celebrated as it is diverse opinions within a community that provide for the resilience needed for long term viability.

This ancient communication method of Way of Council is similar to other methods of dialogue. These techniques are aimed at helping us stay in touch with our authentic selves while embracing deep listening, empathy, and non-judgmental conversation. This is all aimed at helping us notice and curb our ego-reactivity while bringing in deeper receptivity and compassion amid our often-stressful work environment. With practice, we learn to replace our ego-patterns of defending, judging, blaming, withdrawing, manipulating, or attacking with a deeper natural compassion and innate human desire to share from the heart with authenticity.

Circles of Trust

Leadership specialist Parker J Palmer has provided a detailed study guide in his book *A Hidden Wholeness* on how to best host communities of solitude or 'circles of trust', as places to nurture our soul within groups. Group sizes can vary from around half a dozen to about a dozen people who form a circle. It is preferable if these people are familiar with Way of Council or similar sharing circle dialogue practices and so understand the ground rules of speaking and listening from the heart. Parker J Palmer suggests people commit to meeting for one to two hours every week for about ten weeks.

The circle is an invitation to do 'soul work'. We are sharing about the challenges and opportunities going on in our working lives right now for us in a heartfelt and authentic way, sharing our fears and failings as well as our joys and successes with kindred spirits on similar journeys. We learn to cultivate trust in what is emerging within us and the confidence to share it openly in a space free from judgement, interruptions, and opinion-forming.

We start and end with a couple of minutes' silence (longer if time allows). Stillness is valued throughout the circle, so after someone has spoken, we allow a pause to reflect before we jump in with what we wish to share. We do not offer advice to others following what they have shared, we simply listen and where we feel it appropriate, we may offer a question to help each other into deeper speech. These questions don't come from a place of personal motive and instead are in service of what is emerging within the circle.

The primacy here is not the content, the 'what', but the 'way', the soulful heartfelt sharing, without specific agendas or outcomes in mind. We are creating space to open up and allow the soul to come through. It's simple yet has profound enriching benefits for all involved. As a group we take confidentiality very seriously, ensuring what is spoken in the circle stays in the circle.

Story Café and World Café

This is an effective way of hosting small groups (Story Café) or large groups (World Café) in dialogue. We gather a group of stakeholders around tables of four seats per table (no more than five per table) and start by discussing a topic that everyone feels involved in. The discussion itself follows a dialogue approach, in terms of listening intently and sharing in an open and heartfelt way without interrupting each other. Let's say we start with the discussion: *Share a time when we felt fully alive in our lives*. Each of us then shares a short story about it.

At the beginning of the discussion, when everyone is clear on the question or topic being discussed, we start the process with a minute's silence and perhaps some conscious breathing to develop our conscious awareness and receptivity. Then each person, in silence, jots down their own story. After three minutes of this, the first person shares their story within the table of four, the other three listen attentively, without interruption, like we practiced in the deep listening exercise. After three minutes we move round the table with another person sharing their story and the other three listening attentively. We repeat, until everyone has shared.

We have no need to sell our stories or present them in inauthentic ways, although to start with there may be that tendency, as we wish to make ourselves look good in front of others, but as we gain experience in this kind of sharing our desire to put on a show dissipates as our deeper authenticity starts to come through. We learn first-hand the importance of this sharing as a gift where it deepens our perspectives of ourselves and others while increasing our team empathy, reciprocity, and wisdom. As we get more comfortable with this authentic sharing, we may wish to discuss questions related to the challenges in our organization, for instance, sharing what makes us feel alive in our workplace and how we might encourage more of it.

With World Café, we have a large group with more than two or three tables of people and, after a couple of rounds of discussion amongst the tables, people are free to leave their table and join another table where space allows. A table host stays on the table but all others are free to move around to experience slightly different sharing with different people. The questions evolve as the session develops. The hosts then share the insights with the overall group.

Social Presencing Theatre

This is an improvisational embodiment activity where groups of people gently move together while bringing attention to the sensations in our bodies. This art form or social technology has been co-created by Arawana Hayashi, Otto Scharmer, and members of the Presencing Institute and is now being used to great effect in organizations of all shapes and sizes.

Either in pairs or small groups (utilizing the Social Presencing methods of Duets, Village, Field Dance, Stuck Dance, Case-Clinic, Seed Dance, and 4-D Mapping) participants move together in improvisational, unplanned, spontaneous ways, or as Otto Scharmer would say, engaging with "an open mind, open heart and open will." (Scharmer, 2016)

Through this practice, we learn to cultivate awareness of our body sensations (our 'somatic awareness') while also sensing the social field we are in as a group while moving together (our 'social awareness'). We simply experience what emerges for us as we explore our movements within this social sphere. This has the immediate impact of cultivating our attention, inner-listening and moment-to-moment mindfulness and general awareness which helps set the right groundwork for unlocking fresh ideas, seeing things from a fresh perspective, while letting go of old mind-sets constraining us.

It helps us become more aware of others as we engage our embodied awareness in relation to the movements of others within our group. It helps enhance our connection and inter-dynamics, highlighting motives and needs, as well as cultural and unconscious biases. It also helps us cultivate a sense of the social field of our group with any tensions or emotional reactions it may invoke within us.

Once the groups have become comfortable with relaxing into the bodywork and feeling into our gentle movements, the groups can then consciously start to frame certain themes or case-study situations we wish to explore.

For instance, how we feel at work in different situations, or envisioning different future scenarios.

This felt experience and group learning affects the participants by fundamentally changing perspectives and relationship dynamics within teams and across stakeholder groups. It helps foster greater authenticity, connection, receptivity, stillness within movement, systemic awareness, sharing, and trust in groups, while allowing the groups to be more open to the generative wisdom of the social field and our individual somatic awareness.

Arawana Hyashi notes, "When the body and mind stop fighting or going in different directions, then we can relax and feel less restricted. We appreciate and fully use all our senses. We can accurately perceive whatever situation we find ourselves in. We can pay attention to details and to the whole simultaneously. We develop a panoramic awareness that lessens the sense of separateness between our self and others." (Presencing Institute website)

Through these Social Presencing exercises we directly sense and embody how to open ourselves up to fresh thinking, innovation, and co-creativity beyond the abstractions, habituations, and ego-chatter of our thinking minds. It helps us shift our awareness from our individual perspectives or 'group-think' patterns into exploring new insights, opening up new fields of exploration while shifting perspectives through what is emerging freshly within the group.

This shift or deepening of our perceptual horizon also assists our general shift from what Otto Scharmer refers to as 'ego to eco', a shift from an 'I' centric perspective to a deeper awareness of the inter-relational systemic nature of our social field. In other words, it helps cultivate a shift from organization-as-machine to organization-as-living-system whereupon we perceive the 'inter-being' of our relations within our teams, wider business context and more-than-human world. Hence plenty of time to debrief after each Social Presencing Theatre session is recommended as it is during these sharing sessions that insights are often revealed, and our felt-sensed experiences and deepening awareness is honored within the team.

These embodied group practices allow participants to develop a felt understanding of Otto Scharmer's Theory U-journey of moving through phases of awareness to let go to let come the emerging future in our organizations. Scharmer's five phases of the U-journey are: co-initiating (tuning into our inner-sense while listening to others around us to sense what life is calling us to do); co-sensing (connecting with others and sensing the emergence within the social field and wider systemic business context); presencing (embracing stillness, being receptive to the generative wisdom, and learning to adapt in open-hearted ways); co-creating (prototyping the future within our teams); and co-evolving (embodying the future within our organizations in artful and wise ways that attune with the shifting context). (Scharmer, 2016)

Appreciative Inquiry

This is a systemic approach for organizations that originated out of David Cooperrider's and others' work in the eighties and has since been evolved into different blends. One recent flavor is W-Holistic Appreciative Inquiry, developed by authors of *Flourishing Enterprises* Professor Chris Laszlo and Judy Sorum Brown, which focuses on the whole human being within the frame of systemic transformation.

Fundamentally, Appreciative Inquiry (AI) is a living systems inquiry approach rooted in positive questioning and collaborative inquiry. It is 'appreciative' in that the line of inquiry is about recognizing the best in people, affirming past and present strengths, successes, and potentials, while recognizing the things that enhance vitality and excellence. It is an 'inquiry' as an act of questioning in an open and appreciative way.

Through this inquiry we seek new potentials and possibilities. It is a systemic discovery of what gives 'life' to the living system of the organization; an exploration into sharing the stories of when the organization is most alive, most effective, and constructive (economically, socially, ecologically). It is the art of asking positive, open questions in a way that reveals the greatest potential of the organization. David Cooperrider frames questions that point to the overall spirit of AI:

> "What would happen to our [L&OD] change practices if we began all of our work with the positive presumption that organizations, as centers of human relatedness, are 'alive' with infinite constructive capacity?"
>
> "How can we better inquire into organizational existence in ways that are economically, humanly, and ecologically significant, that is, in ways that increasingly help people discover, dream, design, and transform toward the greatest good?"
>
> – David Cooperrider

There are four stages to AI: Discovery, Dream, Design, and Destiny

Discovery is the stage where we gather stories and insights from across the business and wider stakeholder ecosystem. This can be through hundreds of interviews framed through open, positive questions with interviewers who have been trained in the art of AI to discover the potential, and art of the possible, within the organization.

Here is an example Discovery question taken from work at GTE, a 67,000-employee telecommunications company: "Obviously you have had ups and downs in your career at GTE. But for the moment I would like you to focus on a high point, a time in your work experience here where you felt most alive, most engaged, or most successful. Can you tell me the story? How did it unfold? What was it organizationally that made it stand out? What was it about you that made it a high point?" (Cooperrider)

The act of undertaking these interviews and of people sharing positive stories has a transformative effect in its own right. It is 'generative' in that the very undertaking of this intervention helps move people forward, generating the future as we go. As David Cooperrider notes, "As people throughout a system connect in serious study into qualities, examples, and analysis of the positive core—each appreciating and everyone being appreciated—hope grows and community expands." (Cooperrider)

Dream is the stage where all the insights and stories are gathered and themes or examples are shared so that we can start to tune into any themes about what makes the organization alive. Areas of visionary propositions are developed and form threads within an interwoven 'convergence zone' forming the 'positive core' of the new dream to be realized by the organization. Again, the undertaking of this process further enhances and enriches collaboration amongst different stakeholders across the organization, who start to develop a widening and deepening awareness of the new world emerging. Then we ask questions about this emerging future, such as: *What is the world calling us to become? What are those things about us that no matter how much we change, we want to continue into our new and different future?*

Typically, about four days of workshops on appreciative analysis, planning, and articulation of the different business directions is undertaken. From this, a vision of a better world for the organization, and a powerful purpose and statement of strategic intent forms.

In the **Design** stage we start to plan the redesign of the organization through prototyping and future search planning. A good question to ask here is, *What would our organization look like if it were designed in every way possible to maximize the qualities of the positive core and enable the accelerated realization of our dreams?* We begin rapid prototyping of the new ways, innovating, and collaborating as we go, and people vote with their feet, joining-in on innovations which they are passionate about, prototyping through co-creative processes.

In the **Destiny** stage we focus on how to deepen the chosen prototypes into full scale across the organization, what the implementation plan is, and the governance and task forces needed to make it all happen.

Laszlo and Brown have enriched this AI approach with contemplative and artful activities to ensure personal and organizational gnosis deepens through the process. This is called W-Holistic AI, where additional emphasis is placed on cultivating our soulful awareness within each stage.

By example:

Discovery – at the beginning of each interview or group gathering of stories (e.g. Story Café or World Café) a few minutes are dedicated to contemplative presencing, such as conscious breathing and silent reflection. Then the interview or sharing is undertaken with deep listening exercises to deepen the soulfulness of what emerges.

Dream – We explore our soul purpose by inquiring into what is our deepest and most profound personal goal of 'what I live for' and then apply what comes from this to the emerging themes and future scenarios we wish to create for our organization.

Design – Expressive artful exercises are undertaken where we express moments of creativity and aliveness in our lives by sharing these experiences through dance or drawing, and then share this in the debrief, and apply this creativity to how we approach the design phase.

Destiny – Contemplative explorations show how our ways of being need to relate with and enrich our ways of doing in the new world of our organization. We explore what regular practices and artful undertakings, group activities and off-site sessions we need to factor into our ways of working and our governance approaches.

Insights from Leaders on the Journey

While gathering insights for this book, I asked some of the leaders I coach who are already immersed in the life-changing inner journey of metamorphosis to share some of their key insights thus far as these insights may benefit other leaders embarking on the journey. Here are the main themes that arose, along with anonymous quotes from some of the coachees:

- **Letting go**. "Learning to let go of externalities and simply to be allows new life to flow in and through us."
- **The importance of seasonality**. "Seasons are part of nature and life. There is an inevitability about them and nothing we can do will change them. Adapting to seasons is not only an important part of leading but also life. There is comfort in knowing that spring always follows winter. New life needs death in order to emerge. In recognizing the cyclical

nature of life's moments and seasons, we can start to work with them rather than against them."

- **Ways of knowing**. "Too often we only use one aspect of knowing, i.e. the rational mind. I am learning to listen to other ways of knowing: the body, intuition, the heart, the soul. Attuning to these other ways of knowing is an important life lesson–particularly in the Global North where the other ways have been programmed out of us."

- **Learning from (and within) nature**. "I think I have always had some connection with nature, but our culture hasn't encouraged it. There is so much out there if only we observed and listened more with the eyes and ears of the soul."

- **Organizations as living systems**. "Viewing the organizations I lead as living systems/beings is not only helpful but essential to leading them, especially in these VUCA times. Seeing the ebbs and flows and sensing the mood throughout is a lesson I am still learning and putting into practice."

- **Our wounds heal us and others**. "Rather than thinking of past crap hindering our development and integration I have learned that they are the place of strength and what makes us that unique person with a unique gift to the world."

- **Sensing the 'Grace of life'**. "So much of what we often think of as 'life' is the visible, the measurable, the tangible, the easy to understand. But there is more that lies below the surface. There is a flow, a force, an energy – the 'Grace of life' in my mind – a current that is so vast and unstoppable, yet so invisible. To acknowledge it is vital. To sense it, flow with it and stay with it inside is challenging. I believe it requires an awareness and an observance that is so often clouded by the daily noise of life."

- **Becoming more conscious of stillness and movement**. "The ego demands movement. Mine asks me all the time, *What have you got to show for your life?* It is really rather unhelpful. Physically, practically I am always on the move. I rarely sit, in peace and quiet and reflection. Why is that? 'Work to do....' I have become better at understanding and listening to how I feel. When I feel ready to move emotionally—in spirit, in relationship—and also when to 'hold' where I am. To not force change, or jump to the next, to be impatient. I am beginning to trust that I will know when it is time to move again. I know I need to stop, listen, and feel for those signals. I think this is where help from a coach is very useful. The check & balance reflection on what space is being held and why; a thing to hold or a thing to die; a time to change or a time to grow."

- **Embracing the 'marsh'**. "Being introduced to the concept of the necessary stages of metamorphosis has opened my mind to the necessity of endings as part of the shift I'm seeking. Embracing the 'marsh' as a natural and helpful part of the process has been enlightening."
- **There's magic in action**. "Small steps create momentum, both personally and energetically. Exploring thoughts and feelings uncovered in the coaching conversation is a step in itself."
- **Asking the big questions and creating space for deep thought**. "The key one for me has been, *What are you afraid of?* I have realized that I've been afraid my whole life. I now know how important it is to create space for deep thought and reflection, which I've not been very successful at. It's way too easy to be 'asleep at the wheel' in a busy life and it takes concerted effort to create the space to change that."

Regenerative Organization Reflection Tool

This tool was first published by myself and Stephanie Paterson, an experienced employment lawyer and partner of Ramsay Paterson. You can find the original version of the Reflection Tool online on my *website*.

The questions provided in the sections below offer a framework for reflection on where you are at on the Regenerative L&OD journey. Co-authors Stephanie and I, call this a 'Reflection Practice' that can act as a catalyst for: 1) intentional self-reflection, 2) dialogue with others, 3) planning organizational change.

You might wish to think of this Reflection Practice as a three-step flow:

First, take some time out to pause and reflect on these questions, seeing what comes up for you.

Second, share the Reflection Practice with others in your organization and dialogue together to see what themes emerge.

Third, start to home in on areas for potential change that can help your organization adapt and evolve toward a more regenerative and developmental culture.

You may find this Reflection Practice more meaningful if you consider each section in separate sessions, therefore focusing on one aspect at a time.

Reflection Session 1: Purpose

Often, we come to think of profit as a prime mover, but it's not. The purpose of the business is its 'reason for being'. Think of profit as the air we breathe— we need it to exist, yet breathing is not our reason for being. Likewise, for the organization. It has a purpose beyond hitting the numbers, a reason for being that galvanizes and coheres the organization amid volatile fast-moving climates.

→ What is the driving purpose of the organization?

→ How does this purpose contribute to the flourishing of life (i.e. make a positive difference to people and planet)?

→ Was it this current purpose that inspired the creation of the organization at the outset? If not, what inspired its creation?

→ Do you have a sense that the organization has lost sight of the founding purpose over time? Or has the organization's purpose strengthened/ evolved over time, if so, how?

→ Have there been any key events or periods of transformation that have affected the organization's purpose? What are these and what was their impact?

- → How far does the organization's purpose influence: its culture and everyday behaviors? governance? internal processes and procedures? interactions with external stakeholder? (existing and potential customers, suppliers, partners, investors?)
- → Are suppliers or external partners chosen in terms of how they relate with the organizational purpose?
- → Is there a tension between being true to the driving purpose and being profitable? If so, how is this tension held by different members of the leadership team, the board and (if different to the board) owners?
- → How clear is everyone within the organization on its purpose? Do you sense that this purpose inspired them to join the organization and continues to inspire their commitment to the organization?
- → Are there any regular activities to engage teams across the organization (and stakeholders beyond) in understanding the organization's purpose?
- → Within the organization, how do you ensure that the organization's purpose is meaningful to teams and to individual roles?
- → How far do you involve everyone across the organization in breathing life into the purpose (and ensuring its continuing influence)?

Reflection Session 2: Culture and Values

If the purpose is your organization's 'why', think of its culture and values as the 'way'—the way people behave while delivering the purpose. Culture and values guide the organization and its people as they go about their business day to day.

- → Does your organization have defined values? If so, were they defined by the founder/board/the leadership or co-created as a reflection of the true character of the organization as a whole?
- → How would you describe the values and behaviors of the organization in your own words? Is this very different to the defined values?

→ How far do the organization's values influence: its culture and everyday behaviors? internal processes and procedures? interactions with external stakeholder? (existing and potential customers, suppliers, partners, investors?)

→ How deeply do people across the organization understand the organizational values and what these mean to them on a day-to-day basis?

→ Are any efforts made to understand individuals' values and how these may be connected to the organizational values?

→ Are there any regular activities to engage teams across the organization (and stakeholders beyond) in breathing life into the values?

→ Is there a tension between what happens in reality and any defined organizational values and external public relations messaging of organizational culture? If so, how is this tension held across the organization? Are people comfortable to call out behaviors, decisions, and processes which don't align with the values?

→ How do values and culture differentiate across geographies? How does any differentiation and localization interrelate with global organizational culture (if applicable)?

→ What is morale like in the organization? How do you know? How do retention levels compare with similar organizations? Are there pockets of higher turnover or lower morale, and of higher morale? Why is this? How is this related to, for example, leadership, employee engagement, team spirit and personal development?

→ Are personal awareness and wellbeing activities (such as mindfulness, nature connection or exercise) embraced as conducive to personal and organizational vitality?

Reflection Session 3: Decision Making

The day-to-day decision-making processes and protocols greatly influence both the tactical and strategic vitality of the organization.

→ How would you describe decision making—on a scale of 1 being dictatorial parent-child top-down through to 10 being self-managing adult-adult networked teams making decisions locally without hierarchical approval?

→ Is there a tension between top-down decisions and more distributed collective decision making? How is this tension held in the business? Is there any rationale behind the different approaches or is it dependent on the individual personalities of leaders?

→ How far are different people across the organization given a voice in decision making processes? Is their voice encouraging, welcomed, and embraced? Are there any systems in place to ensure that diverse perspectives are fed into decision making processes or is it dependent on the preferences of individual leaders?

→ Are people given the space to challenge leaders' ideas and decisions and to be genuinely heard? Do they feel safe to do so? How do you know?

→ Have you experienced any differences in the quality of decisions and engagement of those affected where decisions are made in a more distributed (less top-down) way? Or at least where those affected have been given a genuine voice before decisions are made?

Reflection Session 4: Collaboration and Innovation

In this fast-paced, ever-changing business environment the ability to innovate and collaborate across teams and also between organizations greatly influences the future-fitness of the organization.

→ Would you say the culture is one of embracing experimentation and ongoing organic learning or one of prescriptive cook-book approaches? Or perhaps it is a blend of both?

→ What's the attitude toward failure and mistakes? Are they seen as an opportunity for learning, or something to be feared and perhaps even covered up (perhaps because of the possible consequences)? Or something in between?

→ Are there mind-sets that resist sharing between departments, functions, and teams? If so, why do you think this is?

→ Is creativity and innovation seen as the province of a select group of people or is it disseminated throughout the organization?

→ How do you engage a diverse range of people (internally and externally) to maximize creativity and innovation?

→ How often do teams of diverse stakeholders get together for the purpose of enriching collaboration and innovation without pre-defined targets and outcomes?

→ How are suppliers or external partners engaged with—on a scale of 1 being tight prescriptive management and 10 being fluidity aligned through a shared intent?

→ How are 'competitors' perceived and engaged with? What about wider stakeholders such as local communities, pressure groups, think tanks, social media forums, thought leader networks, industry bodies, etc.?

→ Is attending peer activities, networking events and other related activities outside the organization viewed as healthy or as a distraction and poor use of time?

Reflection Session 5: Interpersonal Relationships and Tension Transformation

The organization is made up of complex processes of human relating. The capacity to work with tensions and transform mis-understandings or differences into creative potential, helps the organization continuously learn, adapt, and evolve.

→ Do people openly engage in authentic and meaningful conversations about their feelings, intuitions, instincts, passions, and tensions? Are they encouraged to do so or given space to do so?

→ Is such openness and vulnerability modelled by leaders?

→ Are people encouraged to—and feel safe to—provide ad hoc informal feedback? Is this in all directions (between team members, leader to teams, teams to leaders?)

→ Is conflict always perceived as negative or are tensions sometimes perceived as healthy in terms of growth and learning? How are people supported to approach conflict in a constructive way?

→ What percentage of people are experienced in any of the following: giving and receiving feedback, dialogue, active or deep listening, non-violent communication, restorative practice, and coaching conversations?

→ Are there team away days and/or nature immersions? How often and how are they facilitated?

→ Across the organization, are there any brewing tensions just under the surface? How do you know? Is this sensed or heard?

→ Is 'positive news' encouraged through the sharing of positive stories and the rewarding/recognition of sharing, assisting and being appreciative of others' contributions?

→ Are there activities for people at the personal and collective level to learn to be more self-aware of egotistic behaviors, unconscious (or conscious) biases, and personal limitations or masks, and how to get beyond these?

→ If tensions and conflict become destructive or damaging, how is this resolved?

Reflection Session 6: Working Environments

Over the last couple of years, hybrid working and the capacity to embrace different working requirements has created a new world of work.

→ When working on-site, are there quiet places intentionally allocated in the building where people can go to reflect, let go, and revitalize? Whether working on-site or remotely, is time and space scheduled for creative thinking, brainstorming, and contemplative activities?

→ Whether working on-site or remotely, is time and space encouraged for people to relax and chat together, to build and strengthen connections and mutual understanding?

→ Are in between times kept sacred for quiet, reflective time or are busy diaries viewed as the norm with back-to-back meetings? (whether in person or online meetings/calls)

→ Does the working environment enhance creativity, collaboration, and flourishing or deaden it? What about creative spaces, white board areas, casual meeting spots? How does this translate to a hybrid or remote working model if that's relevant in your organization?

→ Is there an awareness of infrastructure, spatial design, and layout in relation to personal and organizational effectiveness? Are personal preferences and differences considered? For example, do working environments accommodate neuro diversity and other particular needs?

→ How flexible is the approach to working arrangements? (e.g. place and times of work) How far is the approach based on trust, balancing individual needs and preferences with operational needs?

Reflection Session 7: Leadership Mindset

The way we show up as leaders has a great effect on those around us and the overall vitality of the living organization. Ways of leading that are incongruent with the organization's values and ethos can undermine trust and disempower people, greatly affecting organizational future-fitness.

→ How do leaders perceive growth for the organization? What about transformation, innovation, reconfiguration, and renewal?

→ How is power distributed across the organization?

→ What proportion of the leadership team would you say view the organization as a living, evolving entity and what proportion perceive it as a machine?

→ How self-aware are the organization's leaders of their influence on the culture and values of the organization?

→ How far and how consistently do leaders model regenerative behaviors and ways of being to enable others to thrive? Where there are inconsistencies, and are these through conscious or unconscious choices? For example:

- To what extent do leaders truly listen to others?
- How far do they encourage the views of others?
- To what extent do leaders model creating space—for rest, thinking, creativity, etc.?
- How far do the leaders reflect the purpose and values of the organization in their day-to-day interactions and in their decisions?
- How do leaders practice self-awareness, taking time to reflect and sense if their behaviors and mindset are supporting or damaging a regenerative approach?
- How do leaders practice patience in their approach, in their decision making and reactions, and embracing natural ebbs and flows?
- Do all leaders welcome 360-degreee feedback and actively seek out feedback from those around them?

- Do some leaders have an understanding of systems thinking and the interconnected nature of social, economic, and ecological challenges at both local and global levels?

→ To what extent do leaders invest in their own personal growth as leaders, taking time to become more self-aware and better understand how to model regenerative behaviors and ways of being?

Supporting Comment on the Application of Ego-Stage Adult Developmental Models in Chapter 2

In drawing upon adult developmental psychology and the various models of levels of consciousness applied to ego stage development, one draws upon extensive research with thousands of leaders and practitioners. I have compiled a few different adult developmental models together into the seven levels summarized in Chapter 2. I have found all the underlying research of these different models to be rigorous. That said, I wish to sound three notes of caution:

1. **The map is not the territory.** Any model that maps out levels of adult or leadership consciousness is merely a guide for noticing the signs on our own unique journey, and we must not limit ourselves by getting so absorbed in the model that we start over-identifying with certain stages.

2. **Ascension appeals to the achiever.** Any ascending stage-based model will most likely engage our progressive and aspirational nature to seek advancement to later and higher stages from earlier lower ones. In doing so we may start to turn our nose up at earlier stages, or worse, create a sense of superiority of later or higher over earlier or lower. The ethos of developmental models is to help us integrate our own selves to better relate with others and the wider world rather than segregating and critically judging others based on different stages of psychological maturity. Watch out for the ego's achiever-nature seeking categorization, separation, and a need to move up a level for outer success. Whereas the

soul inquires with curiosity into the nature of leadership consciousness, discerning insights from developmental research to aid a deeper and truer expression of potential to unfold. Draw upon the research to aid our soul-inquiry rather than ego-achievement.

3. **Darwinian evolution is a hallmark of Mechanistic Materialism.** The Darwinian interpretation of history as experiencing an evolution of contemporary higher forms of consciousness from past lower forms is linear, mechanistic, and reductive, rooted in the very mindset we are seeking to move beyond. We have been acculturated in this view and so might take it for granted that previous societies and ways of living are backward compared to today's advancements in modern technology, science, art, and medicine. The historic shifts in worldview and accompanying mindset from Animism to Greco-Medieval to Mechanistic Materialism to Quantum Complexity might well have come with an ascension in technological prowess, but not necessarily with a straightforward linear ascent in consciousness. As we move into a Quantum Complexity worldview, we begin to see the oversimplifications of a Darwinian view of the evolution of human consciousness. One starts to sense the spiraling nature of consciousness, that pulls forth yet also harks back to ancient wisdom, integrating aspects and insights that draw upon historic learnings and draw from a realm beyond the Newtonian space-time construct of linear past-present-future. Many of today's developmental models are still caught up in the Darwinian view that human consciousness has evolved linearly from a primitive childhood of the ancients dominated by superstition to the adulthood of our present-day maturity. One might wish to reflect for a moment on whether today's fickle celebrity culture of Instagram and reality TV is more mature or infantile than the ancient Greeks of some three thousand years ago or the Egyptians of some six thousand years ago. It's all-too-easy for the mechanistic mind to assume ancient ways are more primitive or limited than our own, yet it's wiser to keep an open mind to traditions which have a deeper sense of inner-outer nature connection than contemporary consumerist culture. Perhaps there are aspects of consciousness that have changed over time and other aspects that are renewing themselves in non-linear ways. Perhaps we'll never really know how human consciousness actually

evolves. Suffice it to say, be cautious of seeing things in the Darwinian light of ancient childhood to present day maturity.

These three notes of caution do not aim to limit the insights gained from drawing upon developmental ego stage research when examining the shift from achiever to regenerator. Instead, they aim to ensure a curious soul-inquiry into one's own embodied experience of human development and meaning-making rather than an ego-infatuation with different levels of consciousness.

Vivobarefoot's Approach to Regenerative L&OD

I've had the real pleasure of coaching a variety of leaders within the living-organization of Vivobarefoot, an award-winning natural health and lifestyle consumer goods business. Over the last four years I've worked with Vivo, its organizational living system has undergone a significant transformation. Much of its business including culture, sustainability, brand, organizational structure, and value propositions has significantly evolved. The number of employees has tripled in that time and both revenue and profit have markedly increased. All while enduring myriad supply chain shocks from pandemics, wars, terrorist strikes in the Suez, not to mention BREXIT, the cost-of-living crisis, the environmental crisis, and general market turbulence—all affecting business performance and planning.

There have been (and no doubt will continue to be) many challenges and developmental opportunities for Vivo as it continues its never-ending Regenerative L&OD journey, and the way Vivo has applied regenerative leadership to its culture is quite unique making for an interesting case study to aid others on the Regenerative L&OD journey. For a full case study of Vivobarefoot's regenerative business journey see *Leading by Nature*. Here, I provide some of the images myself and Vivo's Head of Transformation, Ashley Pollock, shaped up with the help of the Vivo design team. These images are printed onto wooden boards that aid the immersive learning experience all staff take part in during regular leadership immersions at the Future Fit Leadership Academy's center of Springwood Farm amid 60 acres of secluded ancient woodland near London.

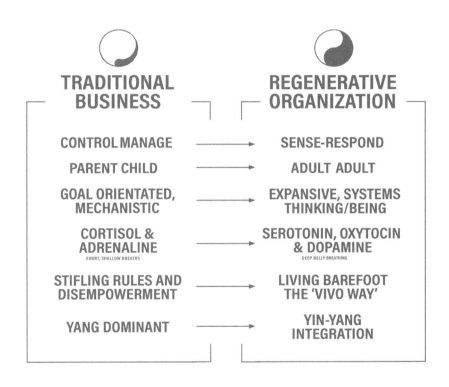

LEADING FROM YOUR WHOLE SELF

TRADITIONAL BUSINESS		REGENERATIVE ORGANIZATION
CONTROL MANAGE	→	SENSE-RESPOND
PARENT CHILD	→	ADULT ADULT
GOAL ORIENTATED, MECHANISTIC	→	EXPANSIVE, SYSTEMS THINKING/BEING
CORTISOL & ADRENALINE SHORT, SHALLOW BREATHS	→	SEROTONIN, OXYTOCIN & DOPAMINE DEEP BELLY BREATHING
STIFLING RULES AND DISEMPOWERMENT	→	LIVING BAREFOOT THE 'VIVO WAY'
YANG DOMINANT	→	YIN-YANG INTEGRATION

BENEFITS
- FEELING WHOLE
- SENSE OF SELF-WORLD CONNECTION
- SENSE OF MEANING
- INNER PEACE
- VIBRANCY & ENERGY
- CREATIVITY
- EMPATHY
- RESILIENCE
- EMOTIONAL INTELLIGENCE
- INTUITION
- COMPLEXITY THINKING
- NAVIGATING UNCERTAINTY
- SYSTEMIC AWARENESS
- CAPACITY TO LISTEN, LEARN & COLLABORATE

VIVOBAREFOOT

APPENDIX – COMPENDIUM OF PRACTICES AND NOTES

YIN x YANG

WHEN THESE TWO ENERGIES ARE IN HARMONY, ONE CAN EXPERIENCE A DEEP SENSE OF INNER PEACE AND ALIGNMENT WITH THE NATURAL FLOW OF NATURE.

WE ARE NATURE

YIN
FEMININE / 'BEING' / SENSING IN / LISTENING / RELAXING / REFLECTING / COACHING CONVERSATIONS / DEVELOPMENTAL FEEDBACK

YANG
MASCULINE / DOING / TALKING / TEAM STRATEGY / WORK-FLOW PRIORITIES / MAKING LISTS / TAKING ACTION / MAKING DECISIONS

NATURE IS US

Yin is associated with feminine energy, being, connection, rest, darkness, the moon and cooler temperatures.

Yin energy: calmness, introspection, stillness, nurturing, receptivity, rest, relaxation, and inward focus.

Yin behaviours: intuition, listening, patience, flexibility, reflection, and introspection.

Yang, is associated with masculine energy, doing, light, the sun, and warmth.

Yang energy: assertive, action-orientated, outward focus, brightness, passion, movement, and stimulation.

Yang behaviours: being decisive, active, assertive, outgoing, and goal-oriented.

NATURE WORKS

THE THREE KEY QUALITIES OF LIVING ORGANIZATIONS

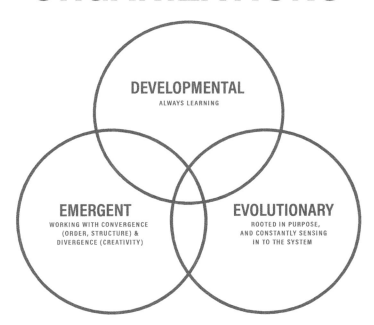

DEVELOPMENTAL
ALWAYS LEARNING

EMERGENT
WORKING WITH CONVERGENCE (ORDER, STRUCTURE) & DIVERGENCE (CREATIVITY)

EVOLUTIONARY
ROOTED IN PURPOSE, AND CONSTANTLY SENSING IN TO THE SYSTEM

DEVELOPMENTAL
Courageous conversations
Feedback, coaching culture
Encouraging 'learning' & 'growth' zone
Partnering with People Team

EMERGENT
Leading amid self-managing
Clarity on roles and responsibilities
Seeking advice & feedback in decision-making processes
Agile-hybrid ways of working
Living our values: Dance, Diversity, Simplicity

EVOLUTIONARY
Vivo's essence
The living barefoot culture embodying barefoot model
9 Pillars of Wellbeing
Nature and human-nature connection
Resilience
Yin-yang balance
Seasonal dance
Succession planning

VIVOBAREFOOT

APPENDIX – COMPENDIUM OF PRACTICES AND NOTES

WHAT IS SELF MANAGEMENT?

MISSION ALIGNED
You know where we are going, and why, and have a plan on how you are going to help us get there

AGILE
Good at navigating priorities, making decisions, embracing failures, learning & adapting.

You look for and give timely and constructive feedback

LEADERSHIP
With less 'management' we need a lot more courageous leadership, and we all need to be leaders at every level

EMPATHETIC, OPEN, VULNERABLE
You don't wear a myriad of masks - you're you and you let others be them.

Embrace diversity and invite in all perspectives

MOTIVATED, ENERGISED
You naturally lean into projects and deliverables when you need to, and keep yourself motivated

Innovative & entrepreneurial - you make things happen

CROSS-FUNCTIONAL
You collaborate XF, bringing the right people in at the right time

Being open to other's opinions and collaborate XF to build the best solution

MAKE GOOD DECISIONS
Knowing when to keep moving forwards and when to ask for help

Knowing you have a voice, but equally knowing when to use it

RESILIENT
You are able to find a yin-yang balance within work and life, working with stress and tensions and navigating life toward more ease and joy while learning and growing, and becoming able to weather the storms of life.

IT IS NOT
- COMPLETE FREEDOM TO DO WHAT YOU WANT
- AN EXCUSE FOR A SELFISH PURSUIT OF WHAT SUITS YOU

VIVOBAREFOOT

Seven Ways to Think Regeneratively

What is explained through the seven ways covered in this concluding section of the Appendix has already been covered in detail throughout this book, but the concise framing of these seven ways provides a reflective summary to end on. The first six of these ways to think regeneratively were published in the Great British Brands 2024 edition, written by me and edited by Country & Town House Editor Lucy Cleland (see this link for the full article: *https://www.countryandtownhouse.com/culture/regenerative-business/*) The seventh, whilst not published in the article, makes the set complete here.

1. Think in Systems, Networks, and Relationships

Since the Industrial Revolution, we've been conditioned to think mechanistically, viewing our businesses as something to manage and control in a top-down fashion with push-pull, carrot stick levers, exploiting assets (including 'human resources') for short-term returns. This system—of business as machine—tends to undermine the future-fitness of the organization in increasingly volatile and fast-moving climes. When power and control reside at the top, decision-making becomes far removed from the customer, and employees too can feel disempowered, robotic, and inauthentic. In fact, Harvard Business School research tells us that most leaders and employees are doing a second job no one is paying them for—that of managing other people's impressions of themselves, covering up their weaknesses, playing politics, hiding uncertainties. This is not a recipe for success but is undermining our individual and collective brilliance. Therefore, it pays to begin to think of the organization less as a machine and more as an ecosystem full of human connectivity—between employees, customers, suppliers, partners, advisors, investors, social media advocates, families and friends, local communities, ecologies, etc.—with a reciprocity that thrives on trust. As a business leader, reflecting on and tuning into the inter-relational nature of these systems helps to sense where there's flow, impasse, or latency waiting to be realized or opportunities for transformation. Rather than chief executive officer, think chief ecosystem officer, one who is constantly scanning the relational systems to sense where there's emerging potential.

2. Recognize that the Inner and Outer Aspects of the Business are Inextricably Linked

The 'inner-nature' of the living-organization is its culture—not some HR charter or values poster on the wall, but the day-to-day ways in which people show up, share, exchange tacit knowledge, gossip on social media, cocreate, and connect in and out of the office. The 'outer-nature' is its brand, external communications, PR, stakeholder relationships, and impact on various groups outside the business. Both natures are connected so it will show up clearly in either aspect whether or a business truly values authenticity, encourages courageous conversations, gives constructive feedback, and offers developmental learning, or if keeps within the machine mindset. Successful businesses will be those that synergize the inner and outer aspects so that all elements feel deeply connected.

3. Think Circular Not Linear

A vital part of future-fit business is the widening of the business lens from merely transactional (i.e. from a focus on selling stuff to customers in a linear one-way process) to participatory and circular (where customers re-engage with suppliers for recycling and upcycling services). Take Vivobarefoot, which recycles worn shoes, thus keeping them out of landfill, and engages with customers—through offering 3D foot-scanning for customized shoes, and hosting online courses, tools and coaching, such as learning to run and breathwork. More often, the value we attribute to such exchanges is not limited to the price tag on the good or service. The organizations with the best ability to work with these relationships and exchanges across the board will be the most adept at navigating the emerging business landscape.

4. Think Inter-generational and 'Glocal'

Amid the short-termism of many business decisions, many of us think individually about the kind of future we're leaving for the next generation. While regenerative acts (such as composting, not wasting food, or helping our neighbors) can happen at home, they can happen in our businesses too. Asking whether a business venture is enhancing life as opposed to just reducing its negative impacts does not distract us from our business endeavors but deepens the creativity we unleash for doing things that provide proper value for the world.

For example, Vivo is transforming its operations, supply chain, and organizational culture toward the principles of regeneration. Therefore, as well as making its products far more sustainable, it has evolved into being a natural lifestyle brand, where opportunities such as rewilding experiences are offered. And by acting 'glocally' (with local and global awareness), it supports a variety of initiatives involved in regenerating local ecosystems, which sparks all sorts of synergies and reconnects company success with social and ecological progress. Globally, it is involved in networks and conferences that work on society-wide solutions, such as the B Corp movement and United Nations COP conferences. This 'glocal' perspective challenges a narrowed view of wealth-creation limited to maximizing short-term financial returns for shareholders, to thinking of wealth more holistically, in terms of regenerating community, nature, society and our home, Earth, upon which we all ultimately depend.

5. Think Life-centric

As we get used to seeing the organization-as-living-system, we start to value the importance of learning from life itself, in recognizing that nature thrives through ever-changing inter-related systems within systems, just like our living-organizations. We participate in this life-centric reality whether we're conscious of it or not. Each unique individual employee's essence finds its tune within the team essence, within the wider organizational essence that finds its tune within wider systemic interplays (business ecosystem, society, Earth). When we open to life in this way, we realize that humans are immersed in a web of relationships, and to harm any of them is to damage our own selves and undermine our home. This life-centric sense of interconnectedness can inform how we lead and operate in business and beyond, which dovetails with the seventh way. Think interconnection not separation.

6. Think Tensions, and the Power they Unleash

Learning to be comfortable with the uncomfortable is an important leadership skill. Tensions between individuals are inevitable but handled correctly by working through them rather than suppressing them, can create crucibles for creativity. We can also learn from seeing how nature's creative advance is impelled by tensions. There's the primary tension of yin-yang, for instance. Yin represents stillness, inner-being, receptivity, and compassion, and yang represents movement, outer-doing, responsiveness, and assertion. We need both in business. Sometimes we might need a little more yang, sometimes more yin. There's also the divergence-convergence tension. Divergence is opening-up, creativity, exploration, etc; convergence is bringing-together, cohering around a sense of purpose, having clear roles, and suchlike. Too much divergence and chaos ensues, while too much convergence leads to rigidity. Getting that tension just right is essential to allow for emergence. All living systems express themselves through the self-generating, self-organizing property of emergence. Businesses are no different. Living systems thrive on this edge of chaos (divergence) and order (convergence), and it's that edge that enables adaptability and vitality across the living-organization.

7. Think Interconnection Not Separation

Essentially, we *are* nature, we are ever-immersed in relationality steeped in consciousness. Separateness is an illusion we have created in our own minds. In reality, everything interrelates with everything else—energetic, informational, rhythmic, held within a depth of dimension one might call 'metaphysical', 'source', 'the field' or 'quantum'. From the quark string humming away, the water tumbling down stream, the sapling and Mother Tree, the bee and the hive to the leader and organization, there's not just 'systems nested within systems' but 'fields immersed within fields', and all interpenetrated with intentionality. Think, Indra's Net or living systems reciprocating across both tangible and physical and intangible and metaphysical dimensions. Mind and matter interpenetrate—there is no separation. As the great scientist Albert Einstein noted, the greatest illusion in life is the illusion of separation.

> "And I know one thing.
> We are not born to avoid dying by lying low and playing safe.
> We are born to live.
> We are born to leave the garden more beautiful than we found it."
>
> —Mac Macartney

References

Abram, D., (1997) The Spell of the Sensuous, Vantage Books

Anderson, R., & White, R., (2009) Confessions of a Radical Industrialist, Random House

Andrews, T., (2021) Sacred Sounds, Llewellyn Publications

Aniane, M., (1976) Notes on Alchemy, Issue 6, Spring

Avens, R., (1984) New Gnosis, Heidegger, Hillman, and Angels, Spring Publications

Bamford, C., et al (1980) Homage to Pythagoras, Lidisfarne Books

Barfield, O., (1988) Saving the Appearances, Wesleyan University Press

Baring, A., & Cashford, J., (1993) The Myth of the Goddess, Arkana

Baring, A., (2013) The Dream of the Cosmos, Archive Publishing

Bateson, G., (1979) Mind and Nature, Hampton Press

Bateson, G., (2000) Steps toward an Ecology of Mind, Chicago Press

Beck, D., & Cowan, C., (1996) Spiral Dynamics, Blackwell

Beck, D, et al., (2018) Spiral Dynamics in Action, Wiley

Benyus, J., (2002) Biomimicry, Harper Perennial

Berendt, J-E., (1983) The World is Sound, Destiny Books

Bergson, H., (1946) The Creative Mind, Citadel Press

Berman, M., (1981) The Reenchantment of the World, Cornell University Press

Berry, T., (2009) The Sacred Universe, Columbia Press

Biomimicry Institute *https://biomimicry.org/*

Blake, W., (1961) Complete Poetry and Prose, edited by Geoffrey Keynes, Nonesuch Press

Bohm, D., (1957) Causality and Chance in Modern Physics, Routledge

Bohm, D., (1980) Wholeness and the Implicate Order, Routledge

Bohm, D.,, (1996) On Dialogue, Routledge

Bonansea, B., (1969) Tommaso Campanella, Catholic University of America Press

Bortoft, H., (2012) Taking Appearances Seriously, Floris Books

Bourgeault, C., (2008) The Wisdom Jesus, Shambhala

Bourgeault, C., (2010) The Meaning of Mary Magdalene, Shambhala

Bourgeault, C., (2016) The Heart of Centering Prayer, Shambhala

Bragdon, J., (2016) Companies that Mimic Life, Greenleaf Publishing

Brown, B., (2011) Conscious Leadership for Sustainability, unpublished dissertation

Buhner, S., (2004) The Secret Teachings of Plants, Bear & Company

Campbell, J., (1988) The Power of Myth, Doubleday

Campbell, J., (1990) The Hero's Journey, New World Library

Campbell, J., (2004) Pathways to Bliss, New World Library

Campbell, J., (2008) The Hero with a Thousand Faces, New World Library

Capra, F., (2002) The Hidden Connections, Flamingo

Capra, F. & Luigi Luisi, P., (2014) The Systems View of Life, Cambridge University Press

Chittick, W., (2008) Sufism, One World

Claxton, G., (2015) Intelligence in the Flesh, Yale University Press

Coleridge, S. T., (1817) Biographia Literaria, Princeton University Press

Cook-Greuter, S., (2010) Postautonomous Ego Development, Integral Publishers

Cooperrider, D., (2021) Prospective Theory, NRD Publishing

Corbin, H., (1969) Alone with the Alone, Princeton University Press

Csikszentmihalyi, M., (2002) Flow, Rider

Crawford, M., (2009) The Case For Working With Your Hands, Penguin Books

Crouch, C., (2004) Post-Democracy, Malden

Currivan, J., (2017) The Cosmic Hologram, Inner Traditions

Curtis, A., (2002) The Century of the Self, BBC4

Darwin, C., (1859) On the Origin of the Species by Means of Natural Selection, J. Murray

Dawkins, R., (1989) The Selfish Gene, Oxford University Press

Dawkins, R., (1999) Unweaving The Rainbow, Penguin Books

De Botton, A., (2004) Status Anxiety, Hamish Hamilton

De Botton, A., (2009) The Pleasures and Sorrows of Work, Penguin Books

De Quincey, C., (2002) Radical Nature, Park Street Press

De Saint-Exupéry, A., (2002) The Little Prince, Egmont

Dillard, A., (1982) Teaching a Stone to Talk, New York, HarperCollins

Dispenza, J., (2017) Becoming Supernatural, Hay House

Doczi, G., (1981) The Power of Limits, Shambhala Publications

Einstein, A., (1923) Sidelights on Relativity, translated by Jeffery, & Perrett, Dutton & Co

Eisenstein, C., (2011) Sacred Economics, Evolver Editions

Eisler, R., (1988) The Chalice & The Blade, Harper & Row

Elkington, D., (2021) The Ancient Language of Sacred Sound, 2nd Edition, Inner Traditions

Eliot, T.S., (2001) Four Quartets, Faber & Faber

Emerson, R.W., (2008) Nature, Penguin Books

Emoto, M., (2007) The Miracle of Water, Simon & Schuster

Eriugena, J. S., (1976) Periphyseon: On the Division of Nature, Book III 678c. Bobbs-Merrill

Evola, J., (1975) La Tradition Hermetique, Editions Traditionnelles

Feild, R., (1990) The Alchemy of the Heart, Element

Fisher, A., (2013) Radical Ecopsychology, Psychology in the Service of Life, Suny Press

Freke, T., & Gandy, P., (2008) The Hermetica, Tarcher Cornerstone

Freud, S., (1933) New Introductory Lectures on Psychoanalysis, W.W.Norton

Gallup, (2017) State of the Global Workplace, Gallup Press, p22

Gebser, J., (1985) The Ever Present Origin, Ohio University Press

Gimbutas, M., (1973) The Beginning of the Bronze Age in Europe and the Indo-Europeans, Journal of Indo-European Studies 1

Gnostic Gospel of Thomas, cited *http://www.gospelofthomas.info/essays/stone.html*

Godwin, M., (1994) The Holy Grail, Viking Studio

Goethe, J., (1988) Sautliche Werke, ed. K. Richter, 21 Vols, Carl Hanser Verlag

Goldman. J., (2022) Healing Sounds, Healing Arts Press

Goodchild, V., (2012) Songlines of the Soul, Nicolas-Hays

Graves, C., (1974) Human Nature prepares for a Momentous Leap, The Futurist, p72-87

Greer, M.J., (2007) The Druid Magic Handbook, Wieser Books

Grof, S., & Bennett, H., (1993) The Holotropic Mind, HarperCollins

Griffin, D., (2001) Reenchantment without Supernaturalism, Cornell University Press

Griffiths, J., (1999) Pip Pip, Flamingo

Griffiths, J., (2006) Wild, Penguin Books

Gunderson, L & Holling, C (2002) Panarchy, Island Press

Haisch, B., (2006) The God Theory, Weiser

Hall, M.P., (2005) The Secret Teachings of All Ages, Penguin

Hamilton, R., (1990) Earthdream, Green Books

Hamel, G., & Zanini, L., The $3 Trillion Prize for Busting Bureaucracy, MLab report, March 2016

Hargreaves, P., (2021) The Fourth Bottom Line, SRA Books

Harding, S., (2006) Animate Earth, Green Books

Harner, M., (1990) The Way of the Shaman, HarperCollins

Hart, W., (1988) The Art of Living, Vipassana Research Institute

Hartshorne, C., & Reese, W., (2000) Philosophers Speak of God, Humanity Books

Hawkins, D., (2012) Letting Go, Hay House

Hawkins, P., (2017) Leadership Team Coaching, Third Edition, Kegan Page

Hawkins, P., & Turner, E., (2020) Systemic Coaching, Routledge

HeartMath Institute *https://www.heartmath.org/heart-coherence/*

Heidegger, M., (1977) Basic Writings: Martin Heidegger, edited by David Farrell Krell, Routledge

Hobbes, Thomas (1949) The Citizen, Appleton Century Crofts

Hock, D., (1999) Birth of the Chaordic Age, Berrett-Koehler

Hoeller, S., (1982) The Gnostic Jung, Quest Books

Holliday, M., (2016) The Age of Thriveability, Cambrium

HRH The Prince of Wales, *et al* (2010) Harmony, Blue Door

Hutchins, G., (2012) The Nature of Business, Green Books

Hutchins, G., (2014) The Illusion of Separation, Floris Books

Hutchins, G., (2016) Future Fit, Amazon

Hutchins, G., & Storm, L., (2019) Regenerative Leadership, Wordzworth

Hutchins, G., (2022) Leading by Nature, Wordzworth

Isaacs, W., (1999) Dialogue, Doubleday

James, W., (1929) The Varieties of Religious Experience, Longmans, Green and Co

James, W., (1996) A Pluralistic Universe, University of Nebraska Press

Joiner, B., & Josephs, S., (2007) Leadership Agility, Jossey Bass

Jung, C.G., (1973) Collected Works, (ed. Gerhard Adler *et al*) Routledge

Jung, C.G., (1976) Letters 2, 1951–1961, (ed. Gerhard Adler), Princeton University Press

Jung, C.G., (1990) The Undiscovered Self, vol. 10, Princeton University Press

Kaku, M., (2005) Unifying The Universe, New Scientist, Issue 16, April 2005

Katsuki, F., & Constantinidis, C., (2014) Bottom-up & Top-down Attention, Neuroscientist, 20 (5) Pub Med *https://pubmed.ncbi.nlm.nih.gov/24362813/*

Kegan, R., & Lahey, L., (2016) An Everyone Culture, Harvard Business Review Press

Keller, C., (2008) On the Mystery, Fortress Press

King, U., (1996) Spirit Fire, The Life and Vision of Teilhard de Chardin, Orbis Books

Kingsley, P., (2003) Reality, The Golden Sufi Centre

Kiuchi, T., & Shireman, B., (2002) What we Learned in the Rainforest, Berrett-Koehler

Kotler, S., & Wheal, J., (2017) Stealing Fire, HarperCollins

Kovacs, B., (2019) Merchants of Light, Kamlak Centre

Kovel, J., (2007) The Enemy of Nature, Zed Books

Kovel, J., (1988) The Radical Spirit, Free Association

Kuhn, T., (1996) The Structure of Scientific Revolutions, University of Chicago Press

Lachman, G., (2003) A Secret History of Consciousness, Lindisfarne

Lachman, G., (2016) The Quest for Hermes Trismegistus, Floris Books

Laloux, F., (2014) Reinventing Organizations, Nelson Parker

Lancaster, B., (2006) The Essence of Kabbalah, Eagles Edition

Laszlo, C. et al (2014) Flourishing Enterprise, Stanford Business Books

Laszlo, E., (1999) The Whispering Pond, Element Books

Laszlo, E., et al (2016) What is Reality, New Paradigm Books

Lawrence, D. H., (1972) The Complete Poems of D.H. Lawrence, Sola Pinto & Roberts (eds.), Heinemann

Lear, J., (2007) Aristotle: The Desire to Understand, Cambridge University Press

Letellier, V., (2023) The Human Body, LinkedIn Pulse Blog, 26th Oct 2023

https://www.linkedin.com/pulse/human-body-journey-from-atoms-ecosystems-inspiring-letellier-rhevf

Levine, S., (1997) Poiesis, Jessica Kingsley

Lindahl, K., (2003) Practicing the Sacred Art of Listening, Skylight Paths

Lindsay, J., (1970) The Origins of Alchemy, Frederick Muller

Lipton, B., (2001) Insight into Cellular Consciousness, 2001 Vol 12(1):5 ISEEM

Lipton, B., & Bhaerman, S., (2009) Spontaneous Evolution, Hay House

Loring, P., (1999) Listening Spirituality, Vol II, Friends

Lushwala, A., (2012) The Time of the Black Jaguar, Lushwala, Ribera.

Macartney, T., (2007) Finding Earth Finding Soul, Mona Press

MacGregor Mathers, S., The Kabbalah Unveiled, Penguin

Macy, J., & Johnstone, C., (2012) Active Hope, New World Library

Malik, K., (1992) Conversations with a Painter, Temenos Number 13, Temenos Academy

Mang, P., & Haggard, B., (2016) Regenerative Development and Design, Wiley

Manjir, S-L., (2006) Punk Science, O-Books

Maslow, A., (1968) Towards a Psychology of Being, Van Nostrand

Maslow, A., (1970) Motivation and Personality, Harper & Row

May, G., (1991) The Awakened Heart, Harper Collins

Maxwell, R., (2012) Lessons from the Bees, Resurgence, Issue 272

McGilchrist, I., (2009) The Master and His Emissary, Yale University Press

McGilchrist, I., (2022) The Matter with Things, Volume I & II, Perspectiva

Merleau-Ponty, M., (1945) Phenomenology of Perception, Routledge

Michell, J., (1973) The View Over Atlantis, Abacus

Miller, L., (2021) The Awakened Brain, Penguin

Milne, J., (2008) Metaphysics and the Cosmic Order, The Temenos Academy

Milton, J.P., (2006) Sky Above Earth Below, Sentient Publications

Mitchell, S., (1999) Tao Te Ching, Lao Tzu, (translated), Frances Lincoln

Nasr, S.H., (1997) Man and Nature, ABC International

Naydler, J., (1996) Temple of the Cosmos, Inner Traditions

Naydler, J., (2005) Shamanic Wisdom in the Pyramid Texts, Inner Traditions

Naydler, J., (2009) The Future of the Ancient World, Inner Traditions

Naydler, J., (2018) In the Shadow of the Machine, Temple Lodge

Naydler, J., (2020) The Struggle for a Human Future, Temple Lodge

Neihardt, J., (2014) Black Elk Speaks, Bisson Books

Nesfield-Cookson, B., (1994) Rudolf Steiner's Vision of Love, Sophia Books

Novalis (1989) Pollen & Fragments, Phanes Press

Palmer, P.J., (2004) A Hidden Wholeness, Jossey-Bass

Palmer, P.J., (2000) Let Your Life Speak, Wiley

Parsons, T., (1995) The Open Secret, Open Secret Publishing.

Pert, C., (1998) Molecules of Emotion, Simon and Schuster Ltd

Plotkin, B., (2008) Nature and the Human Soul, New World Library

Quinn, D., (1995) Ishmael, Bantam/Turner

Rawbotham, M., (1998) The Grip of Death, Jon Carpenter

Rayner, A., (2011) NatureScope, O Books

Rayner, A,. (2013) The Fluid Boundary Logic of Fungi, Common Knowledge 19:2 Duke Uni

Romanyshyn, Robert (2002) Ways of the Heart, Trivium Publications

Rilke, R.M., (2021) Sonnets to Orpheus and Duino Elegies, Digireads Publishing

Rohr, R., (2016) The Divine Dance, Whitaker

Rooke, D., & Torbert, W., (2000) Personal & Organizational Transformations, Edgework Press

Rooke, D., & Torbert, W., (2005) Seven Transformations of Leadership, Harvard Business Review, 83

Rowland, D,. (2017) Still Moving, Wiley

Rudd, R., (2015) The Gene Keys, Watkins

Sagar, K., (2005) Literature and the Crime Against Nature, Chaucer Press

Sanford, C., (2017) Regenerative Business, Nicholas Brealey

Sardello, R., (2006) Silence, North Atlantic Books

Sardello, R., (2012) The Power of Soul, Goldenstone Press

Sardello, R., (2015) Heartfulness, Goldenstone Press

Scharmer, C O. (2016) Theory U, Second Edition Berrett Koehler

Scharmer, C O & Kaufer, K (2013) Leading from the Emerging Future, Berrett-Koehler

Schauberger, V., (2003) Hidden Nature, Floris Books

Schumacher, E.F., (1973) Small is Beautiful, Penguin Group

Schwaller De Lubicz, R.A., (1977) The Temple of Man, Inner Traditions

Schwaller De Lubicz, R.A., (1990) Nature Word, Inner Traditions

Senge, P., *et al* (2004) Presence, SoL, Cambridge

Senge, P., (2006) The Fifth Discipline, Second Edition, Random House

Senge, P., *et al*, (2008) The Necessary Revolution, Doubleday

Sennett, R., (2008) The Craftsman, Penguin Books

Sheldrake, R., (1990) The Rebirth of Nature, Park Street Press

Sheldrake, R., (2012) Presence of the Past, Park Street Press

Sheldrake, R., (2012) The Science Delusion, Coronet

Shimon Halevi, Z (1977) A Kabbalistic Universe, Rider

Siegel, D., (2010) The Mindful Therapist, Norton

Skolimowski, H., (2019) The Participatory Mind, Creative Fire Press

Smith, C., (1987) The Way of Paradox, Darton Longman Todd

Smuts, J. C., (1926) Holism and Evolution, Forgotten Books

Stacey, R., (1996) Complexity and Creativity in Organizations, Berrett-Koehler Publishers

Stacey, R., (2012) Tools and Techniques of Leadership and Management, Routledge

Stamets, P., (2005) Mycelium Running, Ten Speed Press

Steiner, R., (1994) How to Know Higher Worlds, Anthroposophic Press

Steiner, R., (2000) Nature's Open Secret, Anthroposophic Press

Stevens, A., (1994) Jung, Oxford University Press

Strauss, L., (1989) An Introduction to Political Philosophy, Wayne State University Press

Strohmeier, J., & Westbrook, P., (2012) Divine Harmony, Harmonia

Strozzi-Heckler, R (2014) The Art of Somatic Coaching, North Atlantic Books

Suzuki, D.T., (2022) Essays on Zen Buddhism, Souvenir Press

Swimme, B., (1999) The Hidden Heart of The Cosmos, Orbis Books

Tarnas, R., (2010) The Passion of the Western Mind, Pimlico

Taylor, S., (2005) The Fall, O Books

Teilhard de Chardin, P., (1977) Hymn of the Universe, William Collins, Fount Paperbacks

Temenos Academy Review (1992) Number 13, The Temenos Academy

Temenos Academy Review (2013) Number 16, The Temenos Academy

Thoreau, H.D., (1862) Walking Part II, cited *http://thoreau.eserver.org/walking2.html*.

Tomatis. A., (2005) The Ear and the Voice, Scarecrow Press

Torbert, W., et al (2004) Action Inquiry, Berrett Koehler

Tolle, E., (1999) The Power of Now, Hodder & Stoughton

Tolle, E., (2016) A New Earth, Second Edition Penguin

Tompkins, P & Brid, C., (2004) The Secret Life of Plants, Rupa

Totton, N., (2011) Wild Therapy, PCCS Books

Trungpa, C (2007) Shambhala, Shambhala

Tsao, F., & Laszlo, C., (2019) Quantum Leadership, Stanford Business Books

Tzu, L., (1988) Tao Te Ching, Translated by Mitchell, S., Frances Lincoln

Van Lysebeth, Andre (1995) Tantra, Weiser Books

Vaughan-Lee, L., (2013) Darkening of the Light, Golden Sufi Centre Publishing

Vaughan-Lee, L., (2014) Spiritual Ecology, Golden Sufi Centre Publishing

Von Franz, M-L, (1980) Alchemy, Inner City

Von Franz, M-L, (1988) Psyche & Matter, Shambala

Vossel, S., et al (2013) Dorsal & Ventral Attention Systems, Sage Journals, 20 (2) *https://journals.sagepub.com/doi/10.1177/1073858413494269*

Wahl, D., (2016) Designing Regenerative Cultures, Triarchy Press

Watson, L (1974) SuperNature, Coronet

Watson, L (1986) Earthworks, Hodder and Stoughton

Watts, M., (2011) The Philosophy of Heidegger, Acumen

West, J.A., (1993) Serpent in the Sky, Quest Books

Wheatley, M., (2016) Leadership and the New Science, ReadHowYouWant edition

Wilber, K. (2000) A Theory of Everything, Shambhala

Wilhelm, R., & Jung, C., (1972) The Secret of the Golden Flower, Routledge

Wilhelm, R., (2003) I Ching, Penguin

Wordsworth, W., (2004) Selected Poems, Penguin

Yates, F., (2002) Giordano Bruno and the Hermetic Tradition, Routledge Classics

Zimmerman, M-J., (2004) Being Nature's Mind, delvingdeeper.org/pdfs/being.pdf

Zohar, D., & Marshall, I., (2000) Spiritual Intelligence, Bloomsbury

Zohar, D., (2016) The Quantum Leader, Prometheus Books

Other Books
by Giles Hutchins

The Nature of Business

"A must-read for everyone involved in the business of the future."

—MICK BREMANS, CHAIRMAN, ECOVER

"The most positive, inspiring and practical guide I have seen."

—JONATHAN GOSLING, PROFESSOR OF LEADERSHIP STUDIES, EXETER UNIVERSITY BUSINESS SCHOOL

"Finally, a guide to take us to the next-level."

—GUNTER PAULI, FOUNDER OF THE BLUE ECONOMY

The Illusion of Separation

"An amazing tour de force... Never before, that I know of, has the choice of life, true life, or the path of degradation been put before us with such clear equanimity."

-ROBERT SARDELLO,
FOUNDER OF THE CENTER
OF SPIRITUAL PSYCHOLOGY

"Well written, well researched and full of insight!"

-STEPHAN HARDING,
HEAD OF HOLISTIC SCIENCE,
SCHUMACHER COLLEGE

"This is a wise and urgent text. With a holographic richness of resources and disciplines Giles Hutchins discloses – indeed activates – the attitude that just might provoke our needed evolution."

-CATHERINE KELLER,
PROFESSOR OF CONSTRUCTIVE
THEOLOGY, DREW UNIVERSITY

Future Fit

"This is a master-piece... It's a must-read for business people wishing for their organizations to stay relevant in the 21st century."

–MARK DREWELL, SENIOR PARTNER, THE FORESIGHT GROUP

"Future Fit is prescient and practical - drawing on a breadth of knowledge rarely seen in business books, it makes big ideas concrete by offering examples and advice."

–TIMA BANSAL, CANADA RESEARCH CHAIR IN BUSINESS SUSTAINABILITY, IVEY BUSINESS SCHOOL

"Brilliant... A must read for all leaders and entrepreneurs."

–RICHARD BARRETT, FOUNDER OF THE BARRETT VALUES CENTRE

Regenerative Leadership

"Hope is what Giles and Laura offer, exploring the wisdom, rules, and models for thinking, being, and doing that the natural world offers us. Business leaders will enjoy this mind-expanding journey."

–ANDREW WINSTON,
CO-AUTHOR OF GREEN TO GOLD

"A must-read for anyone who wants to shape a regenerative organization, the only one type which will survive."

–JEAN-CLAUDE PIERRE,
CEO OF SCOTT BADER

"This book invites leaders to lead the world into the 21st century."

–CHRISTIANA FIGUERES,
EXECUTIVE SECRETARY UNFCCC
2010-2016

Leading by Nature

"A truly exceptional and timely book – the teacher we all need!"

–SUE CHESHIRE,
FOUNDER & FORMER CEO OF THE
GLOBAL LEADERS ACADEMY

"Leading by Nature is bang on the money, a really important book."

–SIR TIM SMIT KBE,
FOUNDER OF THE EDEN PROJECT

"You know you need something different, and this is it. Giles distils wisdom from his years of experience, into practical activities. Never have we needed this work more."

–DR. JOSIE McLEAN,
CO-FOUNDER OF THE CLIMATE
COACHING ALLIANCE

"Leading by Nature is THE handbook for regenerative leadership. A must-read for every business leader who genuinely cares about the future of humanity."

–JAYN STERLAND,
CEO OF WELEDA UK

About the Author

From as early as he can recall, Giles has felt a deep sense of connection with and love for nature. Having experienced a number of out-of-body altered-state experiences, by his early twenties he made a decision to dedicate his working life to exploring how business could best contribute to life-affirming futures. Over the past thirty years, he's worked across diverse sectors, advising blue-chip corporations, successful start-ups, family businesses, public sector departments, pioneering B-Corps, and a range of international charities. Giles has occupied several senior leadership positions including Director at KPMG Consulting and Global Director at Atos International, led large multinational teams, delivered complex multi-year transformation programmes and held multi-million P&L ownership. He became one of the first wave of Global Sustainability Directors in Europe over fifteen years ago, and for the last decade has specialized in regenerative leadership, coaching leaders and practitioners across the globe. He hosts the podcast series *Leading by Nature*, is the author of six books and several leadership papers, and his coaching work has been called "life changing." Giles now lives amid the ancient woodlands of the High Weald in West Sussex, with his wife and two daughters, where he runs leadership team immersions, bespoke leadership coaching, and on-line sessions for international clients. He holds a Master of Science in Business Systems, a Diploma in Advanced

Leadership, is trained in several consciousness raising modalities, and is a certified coach and Reiki Master. For more on Giles Hutchins visit https://gileshutchins.com/

"Giles Hutchins is fast becoming one of the world's most influential and authentic guides to regenerative leadership."

–PROF. CHRIS LASZLO, AUTHOR OF *QUANTUM LEADERS* & PROFESSOR OF ORGANIZATIONAL BEHAVIOR AT WEATHERHEAD SCHOOL OF MANAGEMENT

"Giles's Springwood is not just about being in an ancient woodland – its about being with him. The energy of the forest has taken hold of him and you will get to appreciate the calm wisdom of being close to nature through his leadership programmes. A modern sage!"

–COURTNEY HOLM, VICE PRESIDENT, SUSTAINABLE FUTURES, CAP GEMINI

"Giles's work provides a treasure-trove of approaches, methods, models and living examples of ways of creating the regenerative organization of the future."

–PROF. PETER HAWKINS, AUTHOR OF *LEADERSHIP TEAM COACHING* & PROFESSOR OF LEADERSHIP AT HENLEY BUSINESS SCHOOL

"It's very clear that Giles is here at this epochal moment in human history to help leaders tap into their inner truth, courage, and wisdom; to help them cross the threshold that will allow a collective metamorphosis. With his unique way of holding space for executives, Giles enables leaders to tap into a new level of consciousness – a consciousness that we can all access, regenerative leadership consciousness."

–LAURA STORM, CO-AUTHOR OF *REGENERATIVE LEADERSHIP* & FOUNDER OF REGENERATORS

Milton Keynes UK
Ingram Content Group UK Ltd.
UKHW010158140624
444101UK00013B/346